Multicultural Behavior and Global Business Environments

INTERNATIONAL BUSINESS PRESS ®
Erdener Kaynak, PhD
Executive Editor

New, Recent, and Forthcoming Titles:

Multicultural Behavior and Global Business Environments

Kamal Dean Parhizgar, PhD

Routledge
Taylor & Francis Group

NEW YORK AND LONDON

First Published by

International Business Press®, an imprint of The Haworth Press, Inc., 10 Alice Street, Binghamton, NY 13904-1580.

Transferred to Digital Printing 2009 by Routledge
270 Madison Ave, New York NY 10016
2 Park Square, Milton Park, Abingdon, Oxon, OX14 4RN

Company and personal names mentioned in case studies have been changed to protect confidentiality.

Cover design by Jennifer M. Gaska.

Library of Congress Cataloging-in-Publication Data

Parhizgar, Kamal Dean.
    Multicultural behavior and global business environments / Kamal Dean Parhizgar.
        p. cm.
    Includes bibliographical references and index.
    ISBN 0-7890-1261-8 (alk. paper) — ISBN 0-7890-1262-6 (alk. paper)
    1. Corporate culture. 2. Multiculturalism. 3. International business enterprises—Management. 4. Intercultural communication. I. Title.
HD58.7 P376 2001
658'.049—dc21

00-050548

Publisher's Note
The publisher has gone to great lengths to ensure the quality of this reprint
but points out that some imperfections in the original may be apparent.

To my wife Ozra Mitra Esfandiari
and my children, Suzan, Robert, and Fuzhan
with whom I have a very happy life.

ABOUT THE AUTHOR

Kamal Dean Parhizgar, PhD, is Professor of Management and International Business Strategy at Texas A&M International University, Laredo. Previously in the United States, he taught at California State University campuses in Hayward, Dominguez Hills, and Los Angeles; The University of the District of Columbia; George Mason University; Georgetown University; YMCA College in Chicago; as well as at Iranian colleges and universities. Before the Iranian Islamic Revolution in 1979, he served as the Director of the Iranian Scientific Research Center for the Ministry of Sciences and Higher Education.

Professor Parhizgar obtained his undergraduate and graduate degrees from The University of Shiraz and The University of Teheran, and his PhD in 1972 from Northwestern University, Evanston, Illinois. His postdoctoral fellowship was at Northwestern University in 1983, and he spent his Hospital Administrative Residency and Internship Assignments in St. Paul Ramsey Hospital, Minnesota; NIOC Hospitals, Abadan; and Firoozgar Hospital, Iran.

Professor Parhizgar's extensive multicultural interests are illustrated by his research and teaching activities in the field of management. He has published numerous textbooks, articles in refereed journals, and proceedings research papers, and has presented papers at regional, national, and international conferences in the United States and overseas. He has been Co-Program Chair, Division Chair, Track Chair, and Reviewer for the AIB, IAoM, IMDA, SAM, ITFA, GFA, and GCA. He has served as Editor of the *Newsletter for the International Management Development Association.*

CONTENTS

Chapter 10. Multicultural Philosophies 295

Chapter 11. International Religions 321

Foreword

Multiculturalism has become a very important topic of inquiry for academicians, practitioners, and public policymakers alike around the world. From an academic perspective, our accreditation body in the USA—American Assembly of Collegiate Schools of Business Administration (AACSB)—is forcefully pushing cultural plurality into business curriculum where accredited schools of business are developing culturally focused as well as culturally enhanced courses in business. In business, we are observing increasingly diverse workforces. Consumer product manufacturers are especially encountering more and more extremely diverse consumer groups. As a result of this, the same companies are revisiting their traditional and/or established market segmentation approaches and/or strategies to meet the ever-changing needs and demands of the emerging multicultural market segments. Government departments and institutions are also paying increased attention to this emerging trend.

The book written by Kamal Dean Parhizgar is a welcome addition to this growing body of knowledge. It is mainly concerned with technical and philosophical issues of multiculturalism in the light of international/global business practices. The book discusses some of the fundamental issues of multicultural behavior and the transformation taking place in the global business environment conceptually as well as analytically. The issues and subjects discussed have greater ramifications extending over the whole area of multicultural behavior, and consequently, over all of the global business environments as well as the interactions among them.

Managing an international business corporation is an important task. In particular, assessing and forecasting changes in the macroeconomic and sociopolitical environments are key when developing global business strategies. Success of most international corporations can be traced to the ability to adapt sufficiently to the multicultural changes in the free market economies. Since the pace of development of multinational businesses is accelerating, it is essential to be well prepared to function in these areas. To this end, understanding sociocultural value systems of all nations and their economic and political doctrines in the global free market economy is a key ingredient in successful international business transactions and in investment decisions. Professor Charles W. Rudiger indicates very succinctly that "Kamal Dean Parhizgar is a consummate renaissance polymath. *Multicultural Behavior and Global Business Environments* is a timely tour de force that will serve as a road map, text, or handbook for any and all involved in or concerned with all aspects of growing global business. But it will serve especially well as a comprehensive Baedeker and frame of reference for practitioners in international trade, political science, and education." This anecdote well describes the very nature of this significant writing which addresses a major area of concern.

Multicultural Behavior and Global Business Environments speaks to a greater international concern. The content deals with theory, concepts, and lines of cultural value systems that are basic to domestic as well as international/global businesses and for that matter, to all people around the world. Multicultural behavior is provoked by numerous observations of the state of the field, chief among which is the tendency on the part of many to regard each area of global business transactions as an entity in itself, that is, as an interdependent of a general account of morality, ethics, and legality.

This book is a study of the relationship between manufacturers or providers and consumers within the international arena, focusing on cultural value systems, religious beliefs, and political doctrines. It is designed to help home and host countries improve their multicultural skills and assess the global business environments for better decision-making purposes. Chapters and cases provided in the book address various forms of cultural and political home and host country–based risks.

I firmly believe that this is a must-read for every company CEO, as well as classroom teachers and public policymakers worldwide. Professor Kamal Dean Parhizgar is to be congratulated highly for bringing this important book to its fruition.

Erdener Kaynak, PhD, DSc
Professor of Marketing/
Chair of Marketing Program
Pennsylvania State University at Harrisburg

Acknowledgments

I would like to acknowledge, with thanks, the many, many people who contributed to this book directly and indirectly. Without the help of my family, friends, and colleagues, this book could never have been completed. These people have encouraged and helped me; for this I owe them a great deal of gratitude. There are just too many people to thank, so I cannot thank everyone individually. But I do want to identify some individuals who have been especially helpful in the long and arduous process of writing this book. Several colleagues have expressed their support and contributed substantially to the final product. Particularly, I want to thank the following:

Erdener Kaynak, Professor, Pennsylvania State University, Harrisburg; Leo Sayavedra, Vice-Chancellor for Academic and Student Affairs, the Texas A&M University System; Khosrow Fatemi, Dean of the Imperial Valley Campus, San Diego State University, California; my colleagues at Texas A&M International University: President J. Charles Jennett; Provost W. Larry Boyd; Provost Ray M. Keck; Dean John P. Kohl; Faridoun Farrokh; Kamal Fatehi; Jacki Mayfield; George Kostopoulos; Ourida-Zoe Farah Kostopoulos; Michael Landeck; Michael Pisani; and Rose Rodriguez Rabin.

Special thanks to Manouchehr Mohseni Parsa, Professor of Sociology, University of Teheran, Iran; Alain Genestre, Associate Professor of Marketing, American University-Cairo, Egypt; Professor Charles W. Rudiger, Dowling College; Professor Faramarz Damanpour, James Madison University; Professor Vic Heller, College of Business, The University of Texas at San Antonio; Jacqueline Rowley Mayfield, Associate Professor and Co-Chair, Department of Management and Marketing, Texas A&M International University.

I want particularly to thank Peg Marr, Senior Production Editor, The Haworth Press Book Division. I must also acknowledge the staff at The Haworth Press, Inc. They have been especially helpful in encouraging and guiding me through the project from beginning to end. I appreciate the time and effort that they put into this project.

Finally, I owe my family a special debt of gratitude for putting up with me during the many hours that a project like this consumes. My family's support was vital to the completion of this project. More important, I appreciate the support and encouragement from my wife, Ozra Mitra Esfandiari, and three children, Suzan, Robert, and Fuzhan. Extra special thanks to my youngest daughter, Fuzhan, who has patiently tolerated my absence from home and not being with her on a regular basis.

I hope that this textbook is worthy of interest in its contribution toward understanding and comprehending the world in which we live.

Kamal Dean Parhizgar, PhD

Introduction

Multicultural behavior as an aspect of business holds special interest for employers and employees around the world. The magnitude of competitive international enterprises makes it imperative that producers and consumers develop multicultural behavioral skills to deal with today's culturally diverse global market. Cultural diversity must be viewed as a reality in international business operations. Multicultural behavior is a phenomenon associated with accelerated novelty and creating cultural synergy. It stands alone in its concern with contentious problems such as ethnicity, race, gender, color, and religious faiths. In multinational environments, the most problematic issue is the friction generated by organizational and operational functions, along with the consideration of and integration of different cultural values and perceptions into the mission of an organization.

Along with these contradictions, we find a multitude of political ideologies, socioethnic perceptions, artistic artifacts, and religious faiths, with a variety of beliefs, ideas, doctrines, and material and non-material hierarchies. Clearly, knowledge is vital for the effective managerial integration within such a complex environment.

Understanding multicultural behavior and the global environments of businesses is crucial to every manager who belongs to and leads a multinational organization. In recognition of the development and rapidly growing importance of international relations, as well as the need for educating future managers and professional experts, the American Assembly of Collegiate Schools of Business (AACSB) now requires business schools to multiculturalize their curriculum. *Multicultural Behavior and Global Business Environments* is a creative coverage of cultural differences and similarities for future use by students in both fields of domestic and international businesses; topics in this text are presented in a smooth and logical flow.

The author's intention is to establish, as powerfully as possible, a frame of reference that expresses this judgment and method of study which is appropriate to multicultural behavior. Several international business texts are available to the scholarly community. This book was written not only to be useful for practicing international management but also to be used for students majoring in other areas, such as political sciences, international relations, public administration, and educational administration.

DISTINCTIVE FEATURES

Many conceptual features ensure that this text is linked to current issues facing multicultural organizations. Multiculturalism is a highly goal-oriented effort. Its goals are not only related directly to application of business law, economics, finance, and the like, but they must also be concerned with what home and host cultures and societies value. Perhaps more specifically, in a free market economy, they are concerned with what producers and consumers want and expect. In addition, the author has become convinced that all multinational managers must travel this route for a more synergistic understanding of these environmental components.

THE PURPOSE OF THIS BOOK

In an era of highly sophisticated technology, we have found no significant evidence related to the holistically important issue of multicultural understanding among nations. We are living in an era in which we are moving from the Cold War's competitive forced technology to an exchange and sharing of technologies between East and West; from simple cultural dependency to multicultural sufficiency; from national to multinational free market economies; from representative democratic societies to participatory democracies; and from oligopolistic industries to multiple, optional conglomerate enterprises.

Multinational corporations and the World Wide Web (WWW) play a special role, not only in building cross-cultural bridges among home and host nations, but also in providing innovative multicultural understanding through their informational and practical knowledge-based resources. Multicultural expectation has brought people's thoughts, efforts, and natural resources toward more effective, efficient, and productive managerial outcomes.

Because of the rapid growth of such multinational e-commerce and the World Wide Web, people around the globe are becoming more culturally interdependent. Global interdependence is no longer a matter of belief, ideology, or choice; it is an inescapable reality. This text addresses, in a way that is both sound and thought provoking, the importance of multicultural behavior in multinational organizational management. This view, of course, is based on the fundamental focus—the managerial perspective of multicultural synergy. Multicultural synergy is a provocative effort by modern humans to create innovative thoughts and methods through application of international value systems. Multiculturalism is making possible all human efforts to create an understanding among all cultures. It is an effort to move from bureaucracy to meritocracy—a process by which intellectual innovation and creativity can meaningfully achieve synergy. Producers and consumers should not be victims of fate because of their limited resources. They should focus their concerns on the variety of choices in their physical features or intellectual ideas. People should share their efforts in making the history of humanity very successful.

It is the intent of the author not only to present a prescription for multicultural synergy but also to help develop a sense of understanding of the magnitude of multicultural synergy to minimize overall human behavioral efforts. However, in global business, managers should promote the pride of all cultures in home and host countries. Multinational corporations should provide room for the growth and development of all organizational constituencies—in sum, a human global multicultural synergy.

The author decided to examine many materials from many cultures, striving to bind the discussion of multiculturalism more closely to the theoretical and practical perspectives with which he had recently been concerned, particularly as expressed in multicultural behavior theory.

BOUNDARIES OF MULTICULTURAL BEHAVIOR AND GLOBAL BUSINESS ENVIRONMENTS

Multiculturalism is the study of concepts, knowledge, skills, and attitudes constituting multinational corporate management. It is a multidisciplinary, rather than interdisciplinary, phenomenon. The field of multicultural behavior covers an enormous territory; it is a research-oriented field and this book will be a valuable source of reference for both practitioners and academicians.

Multicultural understanding is expanding because of the diverse nature of communication and contact among nations. This is a growing discipline that will add new conceptual and scientific ideas for improving relationships among home and host countries.

The rapid demographic movements, expansion in tourism and trade industries, development in scientific resources, changing job skill specifications, and legal requirements are forcing multinational corporations to advance their organizations into the new millennium. By analyzing the behavioral philosophies, values, motives, and beliefs of an increasingly multicultural workforce, multinational managers must pay serious attention to global competitiveness in productivity as well as to the quality of their organizational performance. Therefore, multicultural behavior is a field that deals with the composition of a multinational workforce in a competitive free market economy, creating new challenges for multinational managers.

THE PLAN OF THIS BOOK

This book is deeply rooted in the variety of behavioral patterns of producers and consumers. It is not the first to seek multicultural understanding within the contextual boundaries of competitive partnership among nations, and, hopefully, it will not be the last. It is written from a multidimensional perspective to help readers gain multilateral advantages by addressing the needs of multicultural management. Achieving a multicultural behavioral synergy involves blending and capitalizing on multinational resources toward the creation of a competitive qualitative outcome.

One of the most valuable contributions of this book is its identification and clarification of the terms, meanings, and processes of multiculturalization, crossculturalization, biculturalization, enculturalization, and acculturalization. This book serves businesses as well as public administrations in understanding multinational organizations and management complexities.

This book will also help students understand the specific identity of many cultures around the globe. It will instill an appreciation of the structural operations and managerial decision-making processes and to understand new missions, strategies, and policies. It also helps multinational managers to build their cultural philosophies in order to better match their corporate fitness with their environmental conditions.

INTENDED AUDIENCES

The primary users of this book will be college students. Its secondary users will be multicultural researchers; it can be used as a reference book. Tertiary users will be academicians, who will use the book as a new multidisciplinary source for conceptualizing the further path of their research. Understanding principles of acculturalization, multiculturalization, and crossculturalization requires a very broad base of knowledge. This text provides such a base.

This book will help readers understand the specific identity of many cultures and is unique in several ways. First, it provides a view of cultural philosophies broadened to the more common interpretation of cultural economy. In the field of international business, it provides the frame of reference, for religious, governmental, and regional forces as crucial synergistic role-players in an international free market economy. Second, it has gathered information from the wave of ever-changing management literature that promotes changes in the international marketplace. Third, this text addresses the blending of ideas of multiculturalism from diverse, cultural values in order to provide a compelling call for more understanding, cooperation, and, above all, multicultural synergy. Finally, the author has cited both theoretical and practical information as well as applications of both cultural and behavioral issues, for better understanding and crystallizing the necessity of paying attention to the needs of producers and consumers.

Chapter 1

An Overview:
Multicultural Behavior
and Global Business Environments

Multiculturalism is a synergistic social chain which integrates all human synergies.

CHAPTER OBJECTIVES

When you have read this chapter you should be able to:

- develop conceptual skills to integrate all types of human behavior,
- indicate why managing people from diverse cultures is an essential task,
- understand the increased role of the level of organizational productivity through cultural synergy,
- develop a framework of analysis to enable a student to discuss how to manage multinational organizations,
- develop an understanding of the scope of multinational businesses and how they differ from domestic enterprises, and
- develop an ability to analyze and evaluate qualitative cultural value systems for multinational corporations.

INTRODUCTION

This chapter illuminates the evolutionary perspectives of multicultural management systems. It bears in mind that international management practices reflect the societies within which business organizations exist. Moreover, technological innovations, societal movements, political events, and economic forces have changed over time and are continuing to change human behavior. In today's increasingly competitive and demanding international free market economy, managers cannot succeed on their understanding of domestic culture alone. They also need good multicultural interactive skills. This text was written to help both domestic and multinational managers develop people skills in this area.

In our contemporary marketplace, multiculturalism can have a profound impact on human lives. For example, some researchers project that in ten years, ethnic minorities will make up 25 percent of the population in the United States. Copeland (1988: 52) asserts that, "Two-thirds of all global migration is into the United States, but this country is no longer a 'melting pot' where newcomers are eager to shed their own cultural heritages and become a homogenized American." In the United States in the 1990s, roughly 45 percent of all net additions to the labor force were non-European descendants (half of them were first generation immigrants, mostly from Asian and Latin countries) and almost two-thirds were female (Cox, 1993: 1). These trends go beyond the United States. For example, 5 percent of the population of the Netherlands (de Vries, 1992) and 8 to 10 percent of the population in France are ethnic minorities (Horwitz and Foreman, 1990). Moreover, the increase in representation of women in the workforce in the next decade will be greater in much of Europe—and in many of the developing nations—than it will be in the United States (Johnston, 1991: 115). Also, the workforce in many nations of the world is becoming increasingly more diverse along such dimensions as gender, race, and ethnicity (Johnson and O'Mara, 1992: 45; Fullerton, 1987: 19). For example, Miami-based Burger King Corporation recruits and hires many immigrants because newcomers to the United States often like to work in fast-food restaurants and retail operations for the following reasons:

1. flexible work hours (often around the clock) allow people to hold two jobs or go to school,
2. entry-level positions require little skill, and
3. high turnover allows individuals who have initiative and ambition to be promoted rapidly (Solomon, 1993: 58).

In a multicultural society such as the United States, businesses thrive by finding common ground across cultural and ethnic groups. But in more homogeneous cultures such as European and/or Asian countries, businesses are maintaining their local value systems. Although the concepts and principles of management in all cultures may be the same, the practice of management is different.

Hofstede (1993: 83) invited readers to take a trip around the world. He indicates that about two-thirds of German workers hold a *Facharbeiterbrief* (apprenticeship certificate), and German workers must be trained under foremen's supervision. In Germany, a higher education diploma is not sufficient for entry-level occupations. In comparison, two-thirds of the workers in Britain have no occupational qualification at all. However, these workers hold formal education certificates to some degree.

American businesses are constantly changing—their images, headquarters, products, services, and the way they do things. To Americans, change is good; change is improvement. However, European cultures and companies will not easily discard their long and proud histories. Europeans believe that patience and an established way of doing things are virtues, not weaknesses (Hill and Dulek, 1993: 51-52). Accordingly, Americans believe that businesses that try to target different demographic groups separately will be stunted by prohibitive marketing costs. Others will meet this challenge through the use of a multicultural consumer mix (Riche, 1991: 34).

From another perspective, in 1992, the European Union (EU) removed all tariffs, capital fund barriers, and people movement barriers from among its member nations. It has created a potential trading block in the industrialized world including at least 327 million people with many different cultures and languages (Fernandez, 1991: 71).

In 1997, the total monetary value of all worldwide exports was recorded in the International Financial Statistics by the International Monetary Fund (IMF) as $US5,469.5 billion (see Table 1.1). Out of that sum, the developed nations exported $US3,628.1 billion and the developing nations exported $US1,841.4 billion. In the same year (1997), the developed nations imported $US3,624.7 billion and the developing nations imported $US1,989.9 billion (see Table 1.2).

By looking at Table 1.3, we may find that the total balance of payments (BOP) of the world, developed nations and developing nations, is not consistent with the balanced trends of imports and exports. This fact indicates that most nations are more dependent on imports than exports. Consequently, they have been faced with trade deficits. The term *affordability* in the international economy refers not simply to the raw materials and components and the abilities of production capabilities of nations, but also to the solvency of the debtors paying for their debts and compounded interest. In third world countries (TWCs), *solvency* refers to the acquisition of cash or monetary resources by exploring or trading off more valuable goods. Solvency would also mean that the country is able to appreciate burdens of individual citizens' educational, health, and welfare deficiencies, nation-states' weaknesses, and national-international trade transactional deficits (Parhizgar, 1994: 109).

The North American Free Trade Agreement (NAFTA) among the United States, Canada, and Mexico has created another trading potential, some $212.5 billion annually, a base which should increase considerably (Gordon, 1993: 6). The Association of South East Asian Nations (ASEAN) is another organized intercontinental trading agreement among Brunei, Indonesia, Malaysia, the Philippines, Singapore, and Thailand that was formed to promote cooperation in many areas, including industry and trade. These and other intercontinental trade cooperatives have changed the competitive international marketplace drastically.

TABLE 1.1. Total Exports (in Billion $US)

	1970	1975	1980	1985	1990	1995	1997
World	298.4	844.0	1,921.8	1,849.4	3,377.6	5,079.1	5,469.5
Developed Nations	223.0	577.3	1,260.4	1,276.0	2,453.5	3,460.5	3,628.1
Developing Nations	75.3	266.7	661.4	573.3	924.0	1,618.5	1,841.4

Source: International Finance Statistics. International Monetary Fund (1998). LI(2), February. Washington, DC.

TABLE 1.2. Total Imports (in Billion $US)

	1970	1975	1980	1985	1990	1995	1997
World	313.7	867.3	2,000.5	1,936.4	3,466.5	5,147.2	5,614.6
Developed Nations	223.5	603.9	1,400.3	1,374.2	2,573.2	3,412.9	3,624.7
Developing Nations	81.2	263.4	600.2	562.2	893.3	1,734.3	1,989.9

Source: International Financial Statistics. International Monetary Fund (1998). LI(2), February. Washington, DC.

TABLE 1.3. Total Balance of Payments (BOP) (in Billion $US)

	1970	1975	1980	1985	1990	1995	1997
World	−15.3	−23.3	−78.7	−87.0	−88.9	−68.1	−145.1
Developed Nations	−9.4	−26.6	−139.9	−98.2	−119.6	47.6	3.4
Developing Nations	−5.8	3.3	61.2	11.2	30.6	−115.6	−148.4

Source: International Financial Statistics. International Monetary Fund (1998). LI(2), February. Washington, DC.

In the area of international business, no perceptual approach pays as much explicit attention to the conceptual bases of thoughts and normative actions as multicultural evolution. We are witnessing the emergence of multicultural alliances that rightly could be called global. This indicates that nations are closer to each other, and they need to establish a synergistic strategy to integrate the needs of all nations. As the United States manifested domestic growth, the incentive also increased for companies to move branches of operation outside the home country in the form of strategic business subsidiaries (SBS). By the mid-1990s, companies based in the United States had nearly 20,000 affiliates around the world (Jackson, Miller, and Miller, 1997: 173). In addition, today more than 37,000 companies worldwide have foreign direct investments (FDI) that encompass every type of business function—extracting raw materials from the earth, growing crops, manufacturing products or components, selling outputs, rendering various commercial services, and so on. The 1992 value of these investments was about $2 trillion. The sales from investments were about $5.5 trillion, considerably greater than the $4 trillion value of the world's exports of products and services (*World Investment Report,* 1993: 1-4). Considering the scope and magnitude of such international operations, the demand for multicultural understanding for more effective international transactions is high.

The emergence of multicultural communication began to take place as multinational corporations made a shift in their perspectives from solely domestic maximization of profitability to joint optimization of internationalization of individuals and organizational performances. Still, some political thinkers and business owners are generally prone to highlight the alienating influence of multiculturalism on their workplace. Marquardt and Engel (1993: 59) report that: "Based on the number of unsuccessful adjustments and early returns of American business expatriates, both government and private studies agree that more than 30 percent of U.S. corporate overseas assignments fail." Some corporate managers typically believe that for synergization of their corporation's wealth and maximization of their profits, it would necessitate that institutions exploit consumers and/or sacrifice workers. However, the modern philosophy of multiculturalism rejects this view of either/or reasoning and envisions that under reciprocal justness, corporate workers' and consumers' satisfaction can synergize the corporate wealth and elevate their level of profitability. This belief is anchored in multicultural assumptions about all workers and organizations that power sharing and democratic processes facilitate corporate survival toward more profitability.

There are rational reasons why multinational corporations should make an effort to synergize multiculturalism in their organizations. One of the most important views is the fact that policies concerning the workplace and marketplace affect the quality of lifestyles, the economic well-being of working populations, the social status of employees, and the synergy of technological innovations.

However, corporate managers must recognize that corporate opportunities are limited. They must also recognize that we do not live in an international meritocractic environment and that multinational corporate bureaucracies are partially political. Operating in a competitive free market economy will not allow one to escape these realities. Corporate managers and workers of the multinational corporations must truly understand and interact effectively with people from other cultures. They must understand both home and host countries' formal and informal values, rules, structures, norms, and attitudes of people and the real cultural criteria for solving social issues. For example, a multinational corporation operating in India must recognize the traditional priorities of social castes of that country in terms of appointing a manager, e.g., a person from a lower caste should not supervise employees from the higher castes.

Status-determining criteria generally have quite different meanings in regard to time, place, and conditions from culture to culture. In some gerontocratic cultures, the older persons are, the higher their status (e.g., France, Germany, Saudi Arabia, China, Russia, and many other countries). However, in a meritocratic culture, once a person reaches a certain age, the status goes downhill.

HISTORICAL TRANSITIONS
IN INTERNATIONAL BUSINESS

As Western society shifted from an agricultural to an industrial-based economy in the eighteenth century, scientists and scholars began to realize that traditional cultural philosophies were not effective enough to be useful for Western society. In 1776, Adam Smith proposed the notion of national productivity as the determinant of national wealth. Smith reasoned that nations should export those goods that they could produce at a lower cost than others (absolute advantage theory) and suggested that this labor-productivity advantage could be determined by the percentage of population at work and the "skill, dexterity, and judgment by which labor is generally applied," (Smith, 1776). In 1933, Bertil Ohlin, following the pioneer work of his teacher, Eli Heckscher (1919), provided an approach which both (a) incorporated more than one kind of input and (b) purported to account for the conditions necessary for trade (Allen, 1967: 27).

Eli Heckscher and Bertil Ohlin presented a new theory based on the work of Smith and David Ricardo. They presented the comparative advantage theory, which argues that all nations have access to the same technology but other factors determine their economic success. Natural resources, capital, land, and the quality of the labor force are among these factors. The main focus of the theory of comparative advantage is to exploit one's advantages and exchange goods with those that have different advantages. The idea that each nation should exploit what it had and trade for what it lacked made sense with the traditional theories of international trade. These theories were not congruent with a great deal of what already existed in the contemporary international marketplace. Today, there is an entirely new paradigm for multinational corporations based on global markets and invisible national borders. Multinational corporations that understand the paradigm and exploit it will succeed; the others will fail.

Today, the traditional competitive efforts for "resources exploitation" has been shifted to "resources discoveries" for finding productive labor and effective materials. This new method has resulted in the exploration of innovative knowledge and technologies. Such a synergistic integrative effort holds that technological operations need to build a mighty exporting smart machine. If we look back at the beginning of the twentieth century, some 150 years after the beginning of the industrial revolution and thirty-five years after the beginning of the industrialization of the United States, we find that businesses began to ponder more on international transactions.

Industrialization of a nation has always been viewed as a sign of economic growth and development. Multinational corporations engage in international business for three primary reasons: (1) to expand their sales, (2) to acquire resources, and (3) to diversify their sources of sales and supplies (Daniels and Radebaugh, 1994: 9). However, despite these facts, according to Porter (1990: 507-508), "Beginning in the late 1960s, broad segments of American industry began to lose competitive advantage. America's balance in merchandise trade went into deficits for the first time in the 20th century, in 1971. Trade problems widened even though the dollar fell in the late 1970s."

In the 1970s, most multinational corporations realized that a major factor in whether a corporation is profitable or not was its multicultural management strategies. Of course, not all domestic and/or multinational corporations manage multiculturalism the same way, but when these relations become well managed, these multinational corporations may have had considerable profit advantages.

The decade of 1970s is an important era in international economy. Competition in the international market caused a new battleground to emerge for multinational rivalry. In 1971, developed nations paid about $2 a barrel for petroleum produced by the thirteen-member Organization of Petroleum Exporting Countries (OPEC). By 1981, the price had jumped to an average of $35 to $36 a barrel. The increase had a dramatic impact on developed nations, which were dependent on foreign oil—both in the industrialized West and in the third world. With the transfer of wealth to the exporting oil countries, a dramatic economic shift in power occurred. Not only did the major oil-producing states control a vital resource without which all Western economies would face collapse, they also had accumulation, by the end of 1980, of some $300 billion in foreign assets (Bruzonsky, 1977).

In 1980, the trade surplus of oil-exporting nations reached $152.5 billion (compared with $82.6 billion in 1974). During that year, industrial nations and non–oil exporting developing nations suffered record deficits in their trade balances of $125.3 billion and $102 billion, respectively. Those figures represented a 50 percent increase over 1979, in both the oil-exporting countries' surpluses and the industrial nations' deficits (Wormser, 1981: 82).

In the 1980s, competitive strategic planning and organizational structural design in international business became the major concerns of top management of multinational corporations. Businesses in that decade were faced with heavy competition in efficient operational and logistical systems in order to maintain a reasonable level of sales and profits. For example, the abundant inflows of financial resources to the developing countries, such as Iran, Saudi Arabia, Kuwait, Lybia, and Iraq came to an end in 1982. The falling oil price shocked several economies that had become dependent on its continued rise, thus setting off the debt crisis. One of the consequences was the decrease in net capital flows to most developing countries. From a net creditor position of $141 billion at the beginning of 1982, the United States shifted to debtor status and by the end of 1986 owed $264 billion (U.S. Department of Commerce, 1989).

In the same decade, the corporate pretax returns on manufacturing assets averaged 12 percent in 1968 and had fallen to 7 percent (Jackson and O'Dell, 1988: 8-9). In 1960, foreign investors received only 20 percent of U.S. patents and by 1989, received nearly 50 percent (U.S. Department of Commerce, 1989). By the same token, many developing countries, burdened by internal debt, found themselves in economic difficulties and several multinational institutions became more fearful of defaults. The main source of the decrease in capital flows to the developing world came from the private sector. As a result of the debt crisis, increased private flows went primarily to meet the debt servicing needs of debtor countries and little additional capital was available for investment and sustained growth (World Bank, 1991: 25).

The persistence of the debt crisis in the early 1980s caused the debtor countries to experience a reversal in resource transfer, lower investment and growth, and higher inflation. The severely indebted middle-income economies experienced an average growth of 2.3 percent from 1973 to 1980 and 2.1 percent for the period 1980 to 1990 (World Bank, 1991: 25). The average annual percentage growth of debt of severely indebted middle-income economies declined from 25.2 percent for the period 1973 to 1980 to 16.2 percent for the period 1980 to 1990 (Parhizgar and Jesswein, 1995: 463-473).

The deep international economic recession of the late 1980s and early 1990s was coupled with high inflation and an increase in the values of hard currencies in the international market. Demand and prices for high-technology and other manufactured imports by developing nations increased sharply. Developing nations thus had to borrow heavily to finance their resultant trade deficits. These and other sociopolitical and economic factors have led to the inability of developing nations to offset their newly expanded indebtedness; however, this has also resulted in economic hardships for both lending and borrowing countries.

Today, it would be difficult to find a company that is not affected by global competitive events because most companies secure supplies and resources from foreign countries and/or sell their outputs as finished and/or refined products and/or services abroad. Almost everything that appears within the marketplace and/or market space is competitive in nature. For example, almost 80 percent of all commercial jetliners sold through 1985, in the non-Communist world, were U.S. made. By far, passenger jets had been the biggest export for the United States. In 1987 alone, the jetliner industry added $12 billion to the U.S. trade balance. To be a competitive jetliner company, a company needs a half-dozen models, and it can cost up to $5 billion just to design each one, through heavy investment in research and development (R&D).

In the late 1980s, the competitive challenge came from Europe—as a continental synergistic force. Five European nations developed a pool of resources to compete with U.S. jetliner companies. The European manufacturing consortium was dubbed Airbus Industries. Its planes have wings from Britain, cockpit sections from France, tails from Spain, edge flaps from Belgium, and bodies from Germany. By 1985, Airbus had garnered 11 percent of the world market. By 1988, its sales reached 23 percent of the international jetliner industry (Magaziner and Patinkin, 1990: 231). In the early 1990s, the Airbus Industry caused Boeing and McDonnell Douglas to merge in order to compete with European competitors.

Kolberg and Smith (1992: 17) indicate: "The New Global Commerce System (NGCS) is one in which possession of natural resources, capital, technology, and information are less important to achieving success in international trade. Consider these examples: Mitsubishi automobiles that were designed in Japan are assembled in Thailand and now being sold in the United States under the Plymouth trademark, and GE microwave ovens are sold in the United States after being designed and assembled in South Korea by Samsung."

THE CHANGING PROFILE OF GLOBAL BUSINESS BEHAVIOR

Anthropologists, sociologists, psychologists, and economists have documented the fact that people in different cultures, as well as people within a specific culture, hold divergent value systems on particular issues. Bass and colleagues (1979) studied the attitudes and behaviors of corporate executives in twelve nations and found that our world is becoming more pluralistic and interdependent. Laurent (1983: 75-96) found in his research some differences across national boundaries on the nature of the managerial role. Hofstede (1980a) corroborated and elaborated on Laurent's and others' research results in a forty-country study (see Figure 1.1), which was later expanded to include over sixty countries (Hofstede, 1980b); 160,000 employees from U.S. multinational corporations were surveyed twice. Hofstede, like Laurent, found highly significant differences in the behavior and attitudes of employees and managers from different countries who worked within multinational corporations. Also, Hofstede (1980a: 42-63) found that national culture explained more of the differences in work-related values and attitudes than did employee position within the organization, profession, age, or gender.

FIGURE 1.1. The Position of Forty Countries on Power Distance and Individualism

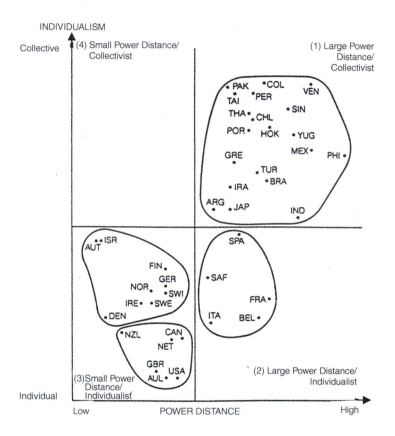

Abbreviations Used in Figure 1.1

ARG	Argentina	GBR	Great Britain	MEX	Mexico	SWE	Sweden
AUL	Australia	GER	Germany	NET	Netherlands	SWI	Switzerland
AUT	Austria		(West)	NOR	Norway	TAI	Taiwan
BEL	Belgium	GRE	Greece	NZL	New Zealand	THA	Thailand
BRA	Brazil	HOK	Hong Kong	PAK	Pakistan	TUR	Turkey
CAN	Canada	IND	India	PER	Peru	USA	United States
CHL	Chile	IRA	Iran	PHI	Philippines	VEN	Venezuela
COL	Colombia	IRE	Ireland	POR	Portugal	YUG	Yugoslavia
DEN	Denmark	ISR	Israel	SAF	South Africa		
FIN	Finland	ITA	Italy	SIN	Singapore		
FRA	France	JAP	Japan	SPA	Spain		

Source: Geert Hofstede. (1980b). "Motivation, Leadership, and Organization: Do American Theories Apply Abroad?" *Organizational Dynamics* (Summer), p. 50.

Eitman and Stonehill (1979: 1-2) state that in the world today:

> Capital raised in London in the Eurodollar market by a Belgium-based corporation may finance the acquisition of machinery by a subsidiary located in Australia. A management team from French Renault may take over an American-built automotive complex in the Argentine. Clothing for dolls, sewn in Korea on Japanese supplied sewing machines according to U.S. specifications, may be shipped to Northern Mexico (Maquiladora plants) for assembly with other components into dolls being manufactured by a U.S. firm for sale in New York and London during Christmas season. A California manufactured air bus . . . is powered by British . . . engines, while a competing air bus . . . flies on Canadian wing assemblies. A Frenchman is appointed president of the U.S. domiciled IBM World Trade Corporation, while an American establishes . . . a Swiss-based international fund.

THE NATURE OF INTERNATIONAL BUSINESS

In the late twentieth century, within the heavily competitive international free market economy, some industries reached the maturity of their markets and, in some instances, were faced with the saturation of their domestic markets. Because of this situation, product life cycles (PLC) have become shorter and technological changes are accelerating.

When a corporation reaches market saturation, business performance begins to decline. Such a move can cause international organizations to move toward conglomerate diversification. In conglomerate diversification, timing is important; early entry seems to be a key to success when established companies move into a younger industry (Smith and Cooper, 1988: 111-121).

Conglomerate diversification through acquisitions and mergers can lead established international corporations to move into attractive industries without losing their market share and/or product positions. U.S. Steel (now called USX), for example, began its slow movement into the still reasonably attractive petroleum industry with its purchase of Marathon Oil (Wheelen and Hunger, 1995: 158). However, technological change, rapid product life cycles, quality control, organizational learning, managing multicultural synergy, and innovation are primary issues for multinational organizations in the new century. Managing multicultural behavior is the key to effective management of all areas of today's international free market economy.

INTERNATIONAL BUSINESS ENVIRONMENTS

International businesses do not exist in a vacuum. They arise out of necessity for home and host countries. The host countries are in need for particular products or services and the home country is in need of market expansion, product diversification, increased sales and profits, low cost operation, and exploiting growth opportunities. As a result, international businesses must constantly be aware of the key variables in their environments. Some factors are very important in understanding the nature of the different kinds of international business entities. These factors are ownership, investment, management and controlling systems, marketing segmentation, subsidiaries' autonomy, and consumers' lifestyles. For the clarity of the terms used in this text, the following are brief definitions of international business entities (Parhizgar, 1999: 1-25).

Global Corporations

A *global corporation* is a business entity which obtains the factors of production from all countries without restriction and/or discrimination against by both home and host countries. It markets its products and/or services around the globe for the purpose of profits (e.g., The World Bank Group and The International Finance Corporation [IFC]). These organizations around the globe serve their investors, managers, employees, and consumers regardless of their sociopolitical and economic differences.

Multinational Corporations

A *multinational corporation* (MNC) is a highly developed organization with extensive worldwide involvement; it obtains the factors of production from multiple countries around the world. An MNC manufactures its products and markets them in specific international markets (e.g., Exxon in energy; General Motors in automobiles; Mitsui and Co., Ltd. in wholesale; IBM in computers; E.I. du Pont de Nemours in chemicals; and General Electric in electrical equipment).

International Corporations

An *international corporation* (IC) is a domestic entity which operates its production activities in full scale at home and markets its products and/or services beyond its national geographic and/or political borders. In return, it imports the value-added monetary incomes to its country. It engages in exporting goods, services, and management.

Foreign Corporations

A *foreign corporation* (FC) is a business entity whose assets have been invested by a group of foreigners to operate its production system and markets its products and/or services in host countries for the purpose of making profits. These corporations are controlled and managed by foreigners to the extent that they adhere to all rules and regulations of the host countries (e.g., Japanese Sanwa Bank Limited in the United States).

Transnational Corporations

A *transnational corporation* (TNC) refers to an organization whose management and ownership are divided equally among two or more nations. These corporations acquire their factors of production around the world and market them in specific countries (e.g., Royal Dutch/Shell Group whose headquarters are located in the Netherlands and United Kingdom). This term is most commonly used by European countries.

Supernational Corporations

The *supernational corporations* (SNCs) are small domestic corporations which create large market shares and product positions in the regional markets. Specifically, SNCs are emerging from e-commerce. SNCs are heavily dependent on logistics and transportation services: sea, air, and land.

Maquiladora Corporations

The *maquiladora companies* are known as the "twin plants," "production sharing," or "inbound organizations" which allow for duty-free importation of machinery, raw materials, and the components of "inbound" production. *Maquila* is derived from the Spanish verb *maquilar,* which translates as "to do work for another." The current usage describes Mexican corporations that are being paid a fee for processing materials for foreign corporations. *Maquilas* are assembly plant operations in Mexico under special customs arrangement and foreign investment regulations whereby they import duty-free materials into Mexico, on a temporary basis, and export finished goods from Mexico. These plants pay only a value-added tax on exports. The number of maquiladoras has increased significantly from 12 plants in 1965 to 2,400 in 1997, employing over 740,000 Mexican workers (Parhizgar and Landeck, 1997: 427).

THE FIELD OF MULTICULTURAL BEHAVIOR

Although multiculturalism is increasingly accepted as a focal subject of academic inquiry, many researchers conclude that multinational corporations need to pay more attention to this issue. Some corporate officers and politicians still debate whether multiculturalism should be practiced. These groups are more attuned to cultural diversity than to multiculturalism. These two terms (*muliculturalism* and *cultural diversity*) are the major issues on which this text focuses in order to clarify their meanings and applications in the field of international business.

Multiculturalism, similar to snapshots of a culture, can be taken from different angles and distances. Snapshots occur at different times within the context of multinational organizations. There is no comprehensive systemized formula to categorize human civilizations. No single multicultural picture or perspective as a multinational corporation can depict the multifaceted characteristics of human behavior, because diversified value systems differ in focus and scope of ethics, morality, and legality (Harvey and Mallard, 1995: 3).

No phenomenon has fascinated researchers in the modern globalized and free market economy more than multicultural moral and ethical value systems. In recent years, multinational management perceptions have been shaken. Much public concern has surfaced over these issues. One belief is that the value systems of humanity that made the late twentieth century's accomplishments so achievable are the result of global competitive cooperation. For example, American culture, which represents multiculturalism, emphasizes the importance of cooperation between workers and capital holders for more synergy. Some researchers concluded that there is widespread ethical commitment among U.S. workers to improve productivity (Yankelovich, 1982: 5-8). With such a breadth of American cultural perception, what causes both employers and employees to strive for productivity? Do employees view work as a necessity to continue their lives? Are people's views on work a binding contract between employee and employer? Or do U.S. workers view work as an achievement toward higher levels of profitability? The answer to all these questions indicates that the more money a corporation earns, the harder they work; the more profit they make, the higher the wages and benefits that are paid to workers.

Profitability is a social contract between workers and capital holders; it is also a legitimate agreement between society and organizations, whose mandate and limits are set by ethical, moral, and legal systems. Its limits are often moral, but they are also frequently written into law. Similar to the early days of American enterprises, the Protestant work ethic was a strong influence, providing both motivation and justification for a businessperson's activities. According to such an ethical value system, the good and hardworking people were blessed with riches; the lazy and incompetent ones suffered (De George, 1995: 14).

The work ethics in multinational corporations have different dimensions. In some cultures, for example, ethics and morality have conceptual, technological, and legal aspects, while in others, they have social, ethical, and moral implications. The conceptual dimension consists of choosing from architectural scientific alternatives in designing and planning the operational processes of a business. The technological dimension consists of developing methods of embodying the new engineering and operational systems for producing new profitable products and processes. The legal aspect consists of discipline and order to govern the rightful use of wealth and power. In such cultures, workers' perceptions are essentially rational. Even in these cultures, workers believe that Mother Nature follows the law of rational thought. Existentialists believe that thoughts and practicality coexist without overlapping. However, in other cultures, thoughts and rationality coexist in a dialectic reasoning and the results would be a synthesized conclusion in societal practicality.

However, Kirrane (1990: 53) indicates that, "The very term, 'business ethics,' tends to arouse some people's cynicism. They shake their heads and woefully recite recent scandals." Contrary to the belief that cultural and ethical value systems are merely business buzzwords, they are often the major predictors of the success or failure in either an industry or a company's strategy.

Within the globalized business environment, many people agree that some multinational corporations believe their businesses should not be concerned with international philanthropy or with corporate ethics beyond their adherence to international legal requirements. The prominent business advisor Peter Drucker (1980: 190) has written that ethics is a matter for one's "private soul." Following his reasoning, he states that management's job is to make human strength productive. Further, economist Milton Friedman (1970) argues that the doctrine of social responsibility for businesses means acceptance of the socialist view that political mechanisms, rather than market mechanisms, are appropriate ways to allocate resources to alternative uses. However, in globalization of international enterprises, altering people's cultural and ethical value systems is not the ultimate aim. Managing multicultural value systems among nations is the challenging means to achieve successful globalization.

Many multinational corporations through various statements of beliefs communicate their organizational ethical, cultural, and legal value systems. These value systems have been called credos, missions, or corporate philosophy statements. Johnson & Johnson <http://www.jni.com/who_is_jnj/cr_usa.html> addresses its corporate beliefs about principles of responsibility to: "The doctors, nurses, and patients, to parents and all others who use our products and service . . . to our employees, the men and women who work with us . . . to communities in which we live and work and to the world community as well."

A problem facing many executives, managers, and employees in globalizing corporations, is that few people within organizations comprehend all areas of organizational ethical, cultural, and legal systems in transition. An example is the company Intel, in which senior managers usually concentrated on global strategy and structure. Middle managers complained that various aspects of the corporate culture prohibited them from acting globally. Human resource people focused on building better interpersonal and cross-cultural skills (Rhinesmith, 1991: 24-27).

Understanding corporate cultural, ethical, and legal value systems in a time of conversion from domestic to global market operations, requires transition through several stages. Since members of international, multinational, and globalized organizations can enter with different cultural backgrounds and leave corporations very rapidly, managers try to leave corporate cultural and ethical value systems intact. However, along with the globalization processes of a corporation, many issues remain unresolved. For example, based on the promise that global strategy and structure can increase profits and promote growth, these concepts become the primary responsibilities of corporate managers. However, no consideration is given to cross-cultural relations between producers and consumers.

Today, some business school curricula have been designed to educate future business leaders on the basis of global *strategy* and *structure* in order to promote profit and growth. The curricula attempt to separate business operations from host countries' civic and humanitarian responsibilities. Cross-cultural experts believe that ethics is a system of beliefs that supports morality. Moral value systems involve cognitive standards of understanding by which people are judged right or wrong—especially in relationships with other people. Ethical value systems are also known as functions for making decisions that balance competitive demands.

Organizational behavior researchers have embraced the concept of cultural value systems to study such focal topics as a major commitment (Pascal, 1985), socialization (Schein, 1968), and turnover (O'Reilly, Caldwell, and Barnett, 1989). When a company changes its exporting functions to a global market, most often it establishes manufacturing, distribution channels, marketing, and sales facilities abroad. In such a transitional stage, analyzing the cultural and ethical value systems leads us to question certain commonly held beliefs about a company's culture. As Harrison and Carroll (1991: 552) indicate: "For instance, very rapid organizational growth sometimes facilitates rather than impedes cultural stability, when stability is viewed as the quickness with which the system reaches equilibrium or rebounds to it after perturbation."

When a company becomes multinational, it creates *miniatures* of itself in its host countries. These companies are staffed by other nationals and gain a wide degree of autonomy. In practice, it will often be quite difficult to classify the predominant value systems in a globalized corporation. However, it should be relatively easy to identify the sources of the value systems at home and in the host countries.

GLOBALIZATION OF INTERNATIONAL BUSINESS

In globalization of a multinational corporation, there is a fundamental requirement for definition and classification of most conceptual and practical value systems, which reflects the central elements defining the general producer and consumer rights. Since these values are central to the concepts of cultural, ethical, and legal practices of businesses, the definitions and classification of value systems should be internationally known through the international business practices. Furthermore, focusing on a unified well-defined international value system within the community of nations permits the examination of the likely effects of different types of subvalue systems on both national and corporate value cultures. Focusing on the following three value-based dimensions of cultural, ethical, and legal practices are particularly useful for legitimization of international business operations.

Corporate Paradigm Management Scale

Parhizgar (1995: 145) constructed a matrix model as a foundational philosophy for analyzing the application of the corporate paradigm management scale (CPMS) (see Table 1.4). The two-dimensional value-based matrix system helps simplify the analysis of the complex CPMS. Not surprisingly,

TABLE 1.4. Corporate Paradigm Management Scale (CPMS)

	Cultural	**Ethical**	**Legal**
Corporate Behavior and Human Relations	How do we relate ourselves with others for mutual understanding?	How are we committed to human rights globally?	How do we conduct legitimized business?
Corporate Culture and Leadership	How do we promote leadership growth successfully?	How do we perceive doing right things rightly?	How do we strive for effective cross-legal adjustments?
Corporate Strategy and Structure	How do we thrive in times of unpredictable change?	How do we allocate and align right resources?	How do we respect discipline within the workplace?
Corporate Technology and Innovations	How do we strive for problem solving through technological innovation?	How do we inspire the promotion of constructive technologies?	How do we promote cooperative and joint venturing efforts in R&D?
Corporate Politics and Diplomacy	How do we integrate various sociocultural differences?	How do we proliferate global market models with ethical integrity?	How do we legitimize corporate policies with the global legal environment?
Corporate Economics and Finance	How do we utilize sources and resources productively?	How do we adopt right systems and processes to global competitive conditions?	How do we maintain and respect global copyrights, patents, and property rights?

Source: Parhizgar, K. D. (1995). "Creating Cultural Paradigm Structures for Globalized Corporate Management Ethics." In Evans, J. R., Berman, B., and Barak, B. (Eds.), *Proceedings: 1995 Research Conference on Ethics and Social Responsibility in Marketing.* Homestead, NY: Frank G. Zarb School of Business, Hofstra University Press, p. 145.

several of these scales have been applied for analysis of corporate cultural, ethical, and legal value systems. In an international endeavor, the problem is the components of the CPMS matrix have not typically been based on global views. These components do not match with the shared values that form the core concepts of international business. Rather, they have been formulated with a broad range of variables based upon corporate national-origin cultural philosophy.

The Focus on Universal Ethical Value Systems

In a global business process, ethics can be a misleading perception because different nations perceive ethical value systems differently. Ethical perception is an individual's belief about what is right and wrong, good and bad, just and unjust, and fair and unfair. Note that ethical and moral beliefs in a culture are rules or standards governing the quality of behavior of individual members of a profession, group, or society—not a specific organization. U.S. businesses, in the 1970s and 1980s, were full of accounts of poor ethics. Big scandals, such as the Lockheed Company's bribery, Michael Milken, and Ivan Boesky, became examples of unethical and, in most cases, illegal practices of doing business in the United States and abroad (Stewart, 1991; Arenson, 1986).

For example, on September 30, 1982, seven people in the Chicago area died from cyanide introduced into their Extra-Strength Tylenol capsules. The Tylenol in question was found to have been laced with cyanide, and it was not known for several weeks whether the contamination was the result of internal or external sabotage. The Johnson & Johnson Pharmaceutical Company, the manufacturer of pain reliever, Tylenol, did not know whether the cyanide had been introduced into the Tylenol bottles during the manufacturing process or at a later time. A thorough investigation proved that the poisonings were the result of external sabotage (*Newsweek:* 1983: 32). The U.S. Food and Drug Administration (FDA) immediately issued a warning to the public not to take Tylenol. The company pulled all Tylenol from shelves in the Chicago area. That was quickly followed by a nationwide recall of all Tylenol—31 million bottles with a retail value of over more than $100 million. The loss was not covered by insurance. The company put the safety of the public first, as the company's credo says it should do (Foster, 1983: 2). The mission of the Johnson & Johnson credo, as we reported earlier in this chapter, states: "We believe our first responsibility is to the doctors, nurses, and patients, to mothers, and all others who use our products and services." Johnson & Johnson's chief executive officer (CEO), James Burke, was a marketing man who knew and understood the value of customers. Not many CEOs are comfortable with open communications in the time of a crisis, and their natural reticence can be enormously harmful to their organization when a crisis strikes (Donaldson and Werhane, 1988: 414).

By using unscrupulous means, executive managers may concede the highest value for their business operations. They need to accept corporate responsibilities by giving weight to the ethical issues concerning the well-being of operations of their companies. Nevertheless, the priority in pursuing the public safety is the highest ethical virtue of the means and ends of a corporation. The major implication in global business is that people with different beliefs will have different ethical standards. Therefore, ethical considerations are relative; they are not absolute standards of human thoughts and behaviors for all people. Ethical behavior and conduct in global business transactions depend upon the belief systems of producers and consumers. Whether the behavior of a person is ethical depends on whom the focus is upon and who is judging. There is no single best way to ensure that a corporate manager can make ethical decisions. Written codes of conduct often look great, but they may have no effect if employees do not believe or feel that top management takes the codes of ethics seriously.

Ethical considerations are just some of the multitude of factors that influence decision making in organizations. A company lives or dies by its ethical decisions and actions over a long period of time. The difficulty of understanding global business ethics is what worries people the most because they do not know what they are getting into. Are they making the right decisions? Will they get into further trouble? By understanding corporate ethical value systems, worries will be relieved because employees will know that they are making the right decisions boldly and confidently.

In the past, many portfolio investors chose to be passive instead of active stockholders. Investors are beginning to pressure corporations with tactics such as media exposure and government attention. Some have formed a class of corporate owners called *shareholder activists*. These people pressure corporate managers to boost profits and dividends. For example, in the 1990s, a number of CEOs from major multinational corporations—IBM, General Motors, Apple, and Eastman Kodak, to name a few—have been expelled by dissatisfied stockholders (Fabrikant, 1995, p. 9). Now that the markets are fluctuating, and many investors have their life savings, retirement funds, and other monies invested, people have awakened and realized that they must take an active role in their investments.

Nowadays, international stock market investors are very sensitive to the behaviors of global corporate chief executive officers (CEOs). Officers lose patience when they feel that their jobs are on the line. Therefore, they react with swift action, selling their stockholdings for minimal profit margins rather than letting them mature and then selling them for substantial profits.

The Focus on National Legal Value Systems

The rules for doing business in a global market have changed drastically. Those corporations who understand the new international rules for doing business in a free world economy will prosper; those who cannot may perish

(Mohrman and Mitroff, 1987: 37). Like people, rules and regulations have an origin. But the international regulatory process is not widely understood or practiced by nations. Usually, in industrialized societies, the government's regulatory life cycle first begins with the emergence of an acute issue. Second is the formulation of government policy. Third is the implementation of the legislation. Then, these rules and regulations will be circulated internationally.

Business operations and trade transactions are monitored and, when necessary, informal or formal corrective actions are taken. It is not easy to portray the magnitude of global business and the sheer volume of regulations to which global businesses are subject. International business rules and regulations are very complex. For example, on December 3, 1984, the Union Carbide Pesticide plant in Bhopal, India, faced a problem when a sequence of procedures and devices failed. Escaping lethal vapors crossed the plant boundaries, killing 4,037 people and caused serious injury to 60,000 more people around the plant. The lethal gas leak has been called one of the worst industrial-mass disasters ever, second only to the release of radionuclides by a Russian reactor at Chernobyl in the Ukraine in 1986. The Ukrainian authorities estimated that radiation-related deaths totaled 125,000 and elevated death rates will continue in the next decades because of latency periods for radiation-induced illnesses (Williams, 1995: A4). The catastrophes at Chernobyl, Ukraine, and Bhopal, India, were international manifestations of some fundamentally wrong actions by governments and businesses in modern times (Weir, 1987: xii). Who should and could be blamed for such catastrophes? Were the former Soviet Union and Indian governments at fault? Was the Bhopal incident the Union Carbide Company's fault? Or was it the United Nations' World Health Organization (WHO) and/or the United Nations Atomic Energy Commissioner's deficiency?

The Focus on Corporate Multicultural Value Systems

The primary focus of a global corporation is based upon cultural values concerning functions performed for and in relation to international organizations and government representatives, as well as consumers. In a cultural value system, either universal or regional, the major concern is focusing on the contexts of issues (Swierczek, 1988: 76). Managerial and organizational cultures are concerned with the particular environmental conditions or sets of problems in which skills, techniques, and approaches are applied. The key questions about managerial and organizational cultures could be raised as: "Are these applications appropriately designed considering circumstances or fixed-value systems?" and "Is the managerial and organizational framework of cultural value systems consistent with the framework of value systems in the situation in which the applications are made?" These and other questions raise several issues about the legitimacy of a national cultural value system within the context of the international environment. If management culture is universal, then the transfer of techniques will be culturally compatible. If management culture is a national phenomenon, companies must make greater efforts to transform these approaches during the globalization process regardless of their cultural heritage or origin of these cultural value systems. For example, consider a manufacturer who wishes to survive in a very intensive competitive market. He or she feels that in order to sell products a potential foreign government authority must be bribed. Is there any similar cultural and/or ethical rule in both home and host countries? In these situations, we must consider the international rule, to bribe and/or to be bribed are not universal practices. If we attempt to universalize the rule involved, we quickly perceive that it is self-contradictory: if bribery has not been made a universal rule, then bribery would not be a universal way of doing business. The main argument is that although managerial culture could be universal, organizational cultures could be different. In order for a universal management culture to be effective, there should be similarities in the organizational cultural value systems with the universal managerial value systems. Then the end result in a managerial culture becomes universal.

Global strategy and structure are important, but the heart of a global organization is its corporate culture. It is the means through which global strategies and structures are executed in order to ensure global competitiveness and profitability. A global corporate culture comprises the mission, vision, values, beliefs, expectations, and both conceptual and perceptual attitudes of its members. Most domestic firms find that their greatest weakness is their difficulty to change their corporate cultural value systems to compete in globalized markets. It is becoming clear to researchers that Japanese and European corporate cultures and management practices put much greater effort over a much longer period of time into developing global corporate cultures and human resources than do U.S. companies (Rhinesmith, 1991: 131-137). For example, the corporate cultural value systems of the Japanese are very different from those of the United States. Eccles (1991: 131-137) indicates that during the 1980s many executives saw their companies' success decline because global competitors seized their market shares.

In order to succeed as a profit-making organization, multinational corporations must move toward a task-alignment form, which means reengineering the organizational task force and employees' roles, reinventing corporate responsibilities, and reenergizing corporate relations with customers to solve specific global business problems (Beer, Eisenstat, and Spector, 1990: 158-166). Therefore, to be an effective global corporation, top management must strive toward changing the cultural, ethical, and legal attitudes of all stakeholders within their organizational context. Employees must be informed of the problems affecting the organization and dragging it into a profitless market environment. Since an organization consists of hundreds of individuals and different departments, both employees and employers are required to enforce organizational cultural, ethical, and legal value systems. In sum, the corporate management discipline system should eliminate improper occurrences of unethical and illegal conducts and promptly provide suitable alternatives in order to match their legitimized corporate mission. However, employees must recognize that in almost all cases of difficulties, they are part of the problem and a great deal of the solution. Employers and employees in a competitive global marketplace and market space must understand who they really are. Therefore, multinational corporations should strive to discover their strengths and weaknesses and then try to convert weaknesses to strengths.

MULTICULTURALISM AND CULTURAL DIVERSITY

For the clarity of the distinctive concepts and practices of cultural management, generally, there are two major sociopolitical and economic perspectives among nations which are operating in the field of international business: (1) multiculturalism and (2) cultural diversity.

Definition of Multiculturalism

Multiculturalism is a basic framework through which one views the world as a community of people. The fundamental idea behind multiculturalism is that everyone is individual and that we are more similar than we are different. This notion is based upon a civic ideology that all subcultures within a society encompass all similar values and people from all ethnicities, religious faiths, political ideologies, and traditions should be treated the same. Multiculturalism is color blind, gender blind, race blind, and bias and/or prejudice blind. Multiculturalism does not view diversity issues as hierarchical and/or class issues. Differences among individuals and classes of people are due to individual characteristics, not due to their collectivistic historical and cultural background. Multiculturalism means a healthy environment in which everyone has an appropriate place in that particular society according to his or her personal qualifications. People respect each other regardless of their differences and/or group affiliation. Therefore, multiculturalism is the means of collaborative participation among multiple cultures in one social system to share their mutual understanding for pacing the whole social system toward a meaningful achievement for all. The concepts and perceptions of multicultural management are lively and practical. These features are:

- Multiculturalism can create a sense of interdependence, interrelatedness, and above all correlated human synergies. Multicultural synergies seek an effort with combined performances that create greater efforts than the total of the sum of their parts.

- Multiculturalism is building a peaceful place for all cultural beliefs and values. It is driving international relations toward civilized synergy—no valuable human thoughts and efforts will be given up or lost.
- Multiculturalism is a potential synergy in which the major components of a firm's product-market strategy are directed toward desired characteristics of the fit between the firm and its substitute product-market entries.
- Since multicultural behavioral knowledge is a powerful managerial tool for conducting international business, it is within the described context that it has placed international business as its focal point of interest.

Definition of Cultural Diversity

Cultural diversity means the representation of majority and minority groups in a society according to their historical family wealth and political influence. It makes a distinction among ethnicity, race, color, gender, and wealth. It makes people different, with distinctly different group affiliations of cultural significance. Cultural diversity emphasizes dissimilarities among people; it emphasizes this notion that we are more different than we are similar. The difference between cultural diversity and multiculturalism is the distinction between classes of people according to their original sociopolitical and cultural ideologies. In cultural diversity, there are majority and minority groups, but in multiculturalism there is no stratification of people on the basis of race, color, ethnicity, and nationality. While multiculturalism is pluralistic societal teamwork on the basis of meritocracy, cultural diversity is based upon the original grass roots of cultural bureaucratic characteristics. This means that those majority groups who have had more power and more people deserve to enjoy more privileges. Therefore, multinational organizations should reward their employees on the basis of seniority rather than merit. We will discuss more about these issues in detail in the following chapters.

SUMMARY

The introductory chapter discussed exactly what is meant by multicultural behavior and multinational management, and outlined the general perspectives and objectives of this new field. The chapter then turned to brief historical definitions of business transactions and organizational decision-making processes. The ethical, moral, and legal implications of multicultural value systems have been analyzed. All of these observations have vast and profound implications for multinational management and the future of business enterprises. Currently, the management of multinational corporations is significantly different from what the domestic corporate management was before 1990. Everyone should be concerned about multicultural human behavior. The field of multicultural behaviorism has the goals of understanding, prediction, and assimilating individual conceptions into pluralistic ones. Multicultural management provides appropriate room for all organizational members to appreciate their value systems in congruence with other organizational members in an effort toward synergy.

CHAPTER QUESTIONS FOR DISCUSSION

1. How does the multicultural organizational management relate to, or differ from, domestic corporate management?
2. Identify and briefly summarize the major historical transitions of human civilizations.
3. In your own words, identify and summarize the many variations in multicultural management processes.
4. How does a multicultural value system synergize organizational productivity?
5. Identify and explain the viable conceptual reasoning methods in multicultural management.

LEARNING ABOUT YOURSELF EXERCISE #1

What Do You Value?

Following are sixteen items. Rate how important each one is to you on a scale of 0 (not important) to 100 (very important). Write the number 0-100 on the line to the left of each item.

Not important		Somewhat important		Very important
0	25	50	75	100

_____ 1. A high-paying job
_____ 2. Job security
_____ 3. A good working environment
_____ 4. Working with other nationalities
_____ 5. Working with other ethnicities
_____ 6. Interest in other religions
_____ 7. My religion
_____ 8. A career to work in other countries
_____ 9. Spending time with my family
_____ 10. An ethical and moral environment
_____ 11. Continuing my education
_____ 12. Working for myself
_____ 13. To be employed in a government agency
_____ 14. To work for a foreign corporation
_____ 15. A commitment to marriage cohesiveness
_____ 16. Nice cars, comfortable homes, and fashionable clothes

Turn to the next page for scoring directions and key.

SCORING DIRECTIONS AND KEY FOR EXERCISE #1

Transfer the numbers for each of the sixteen items to the appropriate column, then add up the four numbers in each column.

Financial	International	Social	Spiritual
1. _____	4. _____	3. _____	7. _____
2. _____	6. _____	5. _____	10. _____
12. _____	8. _____	9. _____	11. _____
16. _____	14. _____	13. _____	15. _____
Your Totals _____	_____	_____	_____
Total Scores 400	400	400	400

The higher the total in any dimension, the more importance you place on that set. The closer the numbers are in four dimensions, the more multiculturally oriented you are.

Make up a categorical scale of your findings on the basis of more weight for the values of each category.

For example:

 1. 400 Spiritual
 2. 375 Social
 3. 200 Financial
 4. 150 International

 Your Totals 1,025
 Total Scores 1,600

After you have tabulated your scores, compare them with others. You will find different value systems among people with diverse scores and preferred mode of perceptions.

CASE STUDY: IBM ARGENTINA

International Business Machines (IBM) is a very well-known multinational corporation. IBM headquarters is located in Armonk, just outside of New York City. IBM Argentina is one of its subsidiaries, located in Buenos Aires. IBM has two fundamental missions. First, it strives to lead in the creation, development, and manufacture of technology, including computer systems, software, networking systems, and microelectronics. Second, it translates these advanced technologies into value for its customers worldwide through its sales and professional service units.

IBM has open system centers in thirty-four countries. One of its business goals is to expand its market share and product positions through the client/server computing services. On May 20, 1997, in Buenos Aires, Argentina, the court indicted ten of IBM Argentina's managers on charges of bribery in connection with a scandal over a contract between the local subsidiary of IBM Argentina and Banco Nacion, a state-owned bank in Argentina. IBM Argentina was accused of paying $249 million in bribes to Banco Nacion's authorities in order to computerize 525 branches.

In the United States, the FBI and the Securities and Exchange Commission had also been investigating the bribery case. However, IBM's corporate headquarter manager denied any wrongdoing.

The Banco Nacion is one of the largest financial institution in Argentina with assets of $11 billion. Under the contract in question, IBM Argentina had reached an agreement with an Argentinian company, Capacitación y Computación Rural S.A., or C. C. R., to provide back-up software for a main program to connect Banco Nacion's 525 branches to a computer network. IBM Argentina paid C. C. R. $21 million before auditors from Argentina's tax agency began asking questions. What concerned the auditors was that IBM (the main office in New York) received nothing in return and that C. C. R. paid out most of $21 million to phantom subcontractors, some of which deposited the money in Swiss bank accounts.

The incidents of this case happened very quickly. Both IBM Argentina and Banco Nacion were found guilty by the Argentina court. One was guilty of offering the bribe and the other for accepting it. However, IBM sued the bank, which canceled its contract with IBM after the scandal surfaced. There are many ways that could help IBM headquarters in New York prevent this embarrassing situation in its subsidiaries around the world.

Since a corporation is a legal entity with legal rights and responsibilities, it must have high moral standards and monitor all its subsidiaries' opera-

Source: The New York Times (1997). "10 Indicted Over I.B.M. Contract." May 21, Section D, p. 12.

tions, because there are limits to what the law can do to ensure that business decisions and operations are socially and morally acceptable. All decisions and operations of a trustworthy multinational corporation require trust and confidence. IBM needs to establish realistic and workable codes of ethics for all its subsidiaries in order to prevent such an embarassing incident.

Chapter 2

Multicultural Understanding

Multicultural understanding is a just cause for coexistence.

CHAPTER OBJECTIVES

When you have read this chapter you should be able to:

- understand human nature and indicate why people behave in different ways,
- define components of our culture,
- know what the concept of culture is and how it can help us better understand other cultures, and
- understand how society at large orients human beings toward continuity in their lives.

INTRODUCTION

As discussed in the previous chapter, this text is essentially concerned with finding and analyzing the major factors that impact multinational organizational behavior. The list of those variables is long and contains some complicated concepts. Many of the concepts—conception, apperception, beliefs, values, faith, ethnicity, attitudes, motivation, expectation, adaptation, and specifically the nature of people—are hard to understand. It might be valuable, then, to begin by looking at cultural and behavioral stratifications that easily can be viewed via three modes of understanding: optimistic, moderate, and pessimistic views. This chapter is devoted to these issues.

FOUNDATION OF INDIVIDUAL BEHAVIOR

The future of the benevolent coexistence among people around the globe depends upon the right multiplicity of thoughts and acts by all nations (see Figure 2.1). The endless search for multicultural understanding among nations can affect the quality of life, happiness, and self-satisfaction. The search for improving production and consumption habits provides nations hope, help, and power.

Multicultural acceptance of international corporate missions can improve the quality of lifestyles of nations. It can manage ecological resources effectively and create some degree of conscious awareness. Multiculturalism in socioeconomic terms is the idea of corporate citizenship to reconcile the drive for profit with societal welfare. This involves *international pareto optimality,* a micro socioeconometric idea which promotes that the scarce resources of the world should be used efficiently by manufacturers. The products and services should be distributed effectively by competitive sociocultures. Consequently, it would be impossible to make any single na-

FIGURE 2.1. The Nature of Human Beings and Their Interaction with the Environment

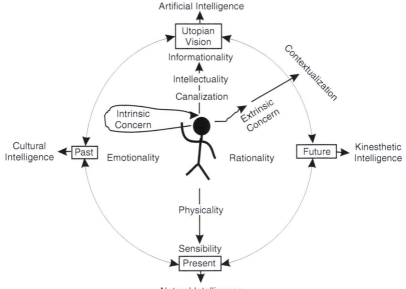

Source: Parhizgar, K. D. (1994). Conceptual and perceptual paths of cultural power-gender philosophies towards entrepreneurial management. In Yin, W. S., Kao, R., and Liang, T. W. (Eds.), *The Main Proceedings of the ENDEC World Conference on Entrepreneurship: The Pursuit of Opportunity.* July 7-9. Marina Mandarin Singapore: NTU-Entrepreneurship Development Center, Nanyang Technological University: 524-534.

tion better off at the expense of harming other nations (Hosmer, 1991, p. 36).

The increasing globalization of modern life prompts questions about the depth and persistence of people's awareness about socioeconomic growth and political and diplomatic uncertainty. It includes the potential for self-discovery both in a general sociological and in a psychological sense. In today's international market, there are many issues about producers and consumers concerning the ecology of our planet and technological competition and breakthroughs. Finkel (1994: 79) states that: "We live in a society which holds as its principal tenet, continuous growth and development, the apex of conventional economics. Actualized within the boundaries of our current mores and values, this historically based hierarchical goal has become the basis of an almost irrevocable commitment to self-indulgence and ultimately to self-deception."

Itzhak Harpaz (1990) conducted a multicultural research project to identify under what conditions the varied social, political, and religious beliefs of people in different nations influence material values. He found that people in different nations have different goals. He randomly selected people in the labor force of seven different industrialized nations (Belgium, England, West Germany, Israel, Japan, the Netherlands, and the United States). He surveyed 8,192 people from those countries. They were asked to identify their most important work goals. Specifically, they were asked to rank each of these goals from most important to least important:

- Opportunity to learn new things
- Good interpersonal relations with others
- Good opportunity for promotion
- Convenient work hours
- A great deal of variety
- Doing interesting work (work you really like)
- High amount of job security
- Good match between personal abilities and job requirements
- Good pay
- Pleasant working conditions
- Considerable autonomy (freedom to decide how to do the work)

Harpaz observed a very high correlated degree of agreement among people from the various nations surveyed (see Figure 2.2). Specifically, by a wide margin, the paramount work goal was found to be "interesting work." In fact, people in four of the seven nations perceived this as the most important goal, and people in the remaining three rated it second or third. Next in popularity were "good pay" and "good interpersonal relations with others." The lowest ranked goal, by a wide margin, was "opportunity for promotion." These findings are important in several respects. First, the results of this survey indicate that Maslow's conclusive result that "all hierarchical

FIGURE 2.2. What Motivates Workers? An International View

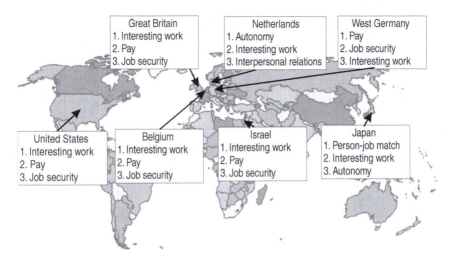

Great Britain	Netherlands	West Germany
1. Interesting work	1. Autonomy	1. Pay
2. Pay	2. Interesting work	2. Job security
3. Job security	3. Interpersonal relations	3. Interesting work

United States	Belgium	Israel	Japan
1. Interesting work	1. Interesting work	1. Interesting work	1. Person-job match
2. Pay	2. Pay	2. Pay	2. Interesting work
3. Job security	3. Job security	3. Job security	3. Autonomy

Source: Harpaz, I. (1990). "The Importance of Work Goals: An International Perspective." *Journal of International Business Studies,* Vol. 21, pp. 75-93.

needs must be satisfied before higher-level needs become activated" could be challenged. This hypothetical assumption is not valid in different cultures, specifically in most European industrialized nations. However, this survey did not include people from developing countries, especially less industrialized ones, therefore making it more difficult to reach a generalized and universal determination on such a conclusive result.

THE CONCEPT OF AN INDIVIDUAL PERSON

People have always searched beyond their ages, probing the real and the universal image of finality. The universal image helps shed light on a variety of images in order to understand their natures and the entity in which they are living, perceiving, and proceeding. Their natural and cultural identities are conceived as:

1. Physical body
2. Sensibility
3. Emotionality
4. Rationality
5. Intellectuality
6. Information

Regardless of age, gender, marital status, or ability, all people do share similar characteristics. To clarify these characteristics, brief descriptions follow.

Physical Body

A comprehensive analysis of people's lives must account for their physical nature as well as the variety of their intellectual competencies. Although the ideas of *contextualization* and *canalization* state that the physical body reflects a general materialistic trend within which one begins to develop, it also focuses on the relationship of the person to objects in the immediate environment. *Contextualization* refers to being an individual in a contemporary postindustrial society, which is not different from being an individual during the early stages of human culture on this planet (e.g., Neolithic or Homeric eras). *Canalization* refers to the tendency toward interconnectivity of any organic system (e.g., the nervous system, the digestive system, the blood system) and to follow certain developmental behavioral patterns. In other words, a component of learned behavior can be channeled or influenced by biologically based pain and/or joy reflexes. All these characteristics can be affected by physiological and psychological needs.

Needs are *deficiencies* of human beings. Needs are created whenever there is a physiological and/or psychological imbalance. Maslow's (1965) need hierarchy theory indicates five stages in human needs disposition. Primary needs are physiological and safety; secondary needs are social, esteem, and self-actualization needs.

If we think about ourselves, the majority of conscious behavior is acquired through learning and interacting with other members of our culture. Even those responses to our biological needs (e.g., eating, coughing, and defecating) are frequently influenced by our culture. In fact, the natural biological process of digestion is influenced by our behavioral perceptions. For example, every year in the city of Freer, Texas, a festival is held in which the meat of rattlesnake is eaten. The idea of eating rattlesnake meat in Texas and Korea, greyhound meat in China, and frog legs in France is repulsive to many people and this repulsion can cause people who ingest these foods to vomit. Clearly there is nothing in rattlesnake, greyhound, or frog leg meats that can cause people to vomit. Occasionally, for those who have internalized the opposite idea—that these meats should be eaten—no such digestive tract reversals occur (Ferraro, 1994: 21).

Sensibility

Behavioral scientists such as Berelson and Steiner (1964: 87) generally acknowledge that: "(1) All knowledge of the world depends on the senses and their stimulation, but (2) the facts of raw sensory data are insufficient to produce or to explain the coherent picture of the world as experienced by the normal adult." The physical senses are sight, hearing, touch, smell, and taste. There are many other so-called "sixth senses," or, as I have called them, kinesthetic senses. The intuitive sensors pay attention holistically to the synergistic *contextualization* of the five senses and to what could be rather than to what actually exists.

The five senses are constantly interactive with the numerous intrinsic and extrinsic forces of the physical body. However, the sensations chiefly deal with very elementary behavior that is determined by physiological functioning. Such a holistic deterministic bodily movement can be called *kinesthetic* sensation. For example, those involved in sucking, looking, and proceeding to behavioral acts that fall increasingly under the control of environmental variation and individual intentions would be a sign of kinesthetic sensation. In an individual's body, senses prefer to respond to the specific *canalized* needs and can become frustrated with vague instructions from the brain. It is relevant to add that a new integrated form of sensation is composed of the essence of all senses within the contextual boundary of five senses with respect to the holistic movements of the physical body. Therefore, the kinesthetic sensation is the holistic (synergized) functional motions of human senses within a dynamic and intelligent environment. In this way, people use the senses synergistically with the cognitive potential of their brains (minds) to experience color, brightness, shape, loudness, pitch, heat, odor, taste, lightness, and weight (in a kinesthetic sense).

Approximately 70 percent of people in the United States are sensors (Myers and McCaulley, 1990). For example, Americans like jobs that yield tangible results and enjoy using established skills more than learning new ones. Employees in German-speaking countries like managerial jobs that stress team objectives.

However, in other cultures, *intuitionalists* like solving new problems and become impatient with various details. They enjoy learning new ideas and skills more than actually using them. Kinesthetic senses tend to function with several things at once.

Emotionality

Emotion is the experience of an affective state of consciousness in which joy, sorrow, fear, hate, love, and sympathy, or the like are manifested in human behavior. It is distinguished from cognitive and volitional states of consciousness. In addition, emotion is viewed as the agitation of feelings caused by experiencing certain emotive conditions and usually accompanied by certain physiological changes, such as increased heartbeat, respiration, and often overt manifestations, such as crying, shaking, laughing, and crying-shouting-laughing together. Emotion also can be manifested as sadness, happiness, or a mixture of both.

Emotion is a vast magnitude of dimensions ranging from anxious, depressed, angry, insecure, and excitable at one end to calm, enthusiastic, poised, and secure at the other.

People in different cultures carry different connotations of emotion. Sociologists and psychologists have studied people on the basis of their race, ethnicity, age, and gender. For example, being status and title conscious, German managers accept promotion readily and will be aware of the responsibilities of new positions and their chances for promotion. German managers show reluctance to delegate authority and are less open than American managers. They manifest cold behavior toward their subordinates. They believe that it is not necessary for subordinates to know everything (Moran and Harris, 1982: 254).

Emotion is used to express feelings about certain objects, but not to make any assertion about them. Therefore, we can categorize people into two groups: *assertive* and *expressive. Assertion* is for the "cognitive" elements of thinking, and *expression* is reserved for the "emotive" manifestation of feelings. However, ethical terms may not only express feelings but also evoke feelings in others (Ayer, 1950: 107-108). In addition, the distinction between "expression of feeling" and "assertion of feeling" manifests two major states of group behavior: (1) *thinkers* and (2) *feelers.* The *thinker* views events in a quantified logical, objective fashion, whereas the *feeler* perceives events in a personal and value-oriented way. For example, Nelson and Quick (1994: 87) indicate that: "The general U.S. population is divided 50/50 on the thinking/feeling performance, but it is interesting that two-thirds of all males are thinkers, whereas two-thirds of all females are feelers.... Thinkers tend to analyze decisions, whereas feelers sympathize."

Rationality

Human beings exist as an end in themselves, not merely as a means to be arbitrarily used by this or that will; but all their actions, whether they concern themselves or other rational beings, always must be regarded at the same time as an end. Human beings, by their very nature, are very well organized. By the same token, they are organizers. Human beings are *rational beings.* They are called *persons,* because their very nature points them out as ends in themselves, that is something which must not be used merely as means. Human beings are *objective ends*—an end moreover for which no other can be substituted. The foundation of this principle is the rational nature of human beings.

Human beings always have placed themselves as an end in nature. Such a maxim is consciously oriented because they have involved themselves in a universal cause of existence which carries the validity for every rational being. Therefore, human beings by their very nature never conceive themselves as means, but as the supreme rational objective to achieve their survival ends.

Intellectuality

It is proper to speak about human intellectual proclivities which are part of our culture. Human beings are born into cultures that house a large number of domains such as disciplines, crafts, and other pursuits in which one can become encultured and then be assessed in terms of the level of competence one has attained. There is a relationship between domains and the intellectual abilities of human beings. More generally, nearly all domains require proficiency in a set of intellectual capabilities; and any intellectual ability can be mobilized for use in a wide array of culturally available domains.

Socialization is one of the characteristics of *acculturalization* of human beings for the acquisition of societal cultural wisdom. *Acculturalization* means conscious familiarity with other cultural values. It occurs principally between the individual and the domains of the multicultures. Intellectuality should be thought of as emerging from the interaction of three nodes: (1) the individual with his or her own profile of intellectual capabilities and competence; (2) the domains (e.g. music, art, science, and craftsmanship) available for study and mastery within a culture; and (3) the judgments rendered by the societal cultural wisdom that is deemed competent within a nation.

Human beings possess considerable intellectual potential to be creative and innovative. Where is intellectuality? The answer is that intellectuality should be thought of as inherent principally to the brain, the mind, or the personality of a single individual. Specifically, an intellectual person is one who regularly and effectively uses his or her intelligence to solve problems or fashions products in a domain and whose work is considered both novel and acceptable by the community of scholars and scientists (Gardener, 1993: xvii).

For the purpose of understanding the fifth dimension of human nature, we should identify two distinctive domains of knowledge: (1) *doxa* (what is believed to be true) and (2) *episteme* (what is known to be true). Knowledge, which is considered the main ingredient in human intellectuality, should be acquired—is more controversial. Therefore, an intellectual person is one who makes every scholarly attempt at acquiring knowledge to improve his or her scientific potential. However, some people make use of their potentials and others do not.

Information

In a sociological perspective, international information systems have provided human beings with superiority over the other five characteristics constructing human identity. It is human beings' conviction that individuals must learn how to conceive of themselves and perceive others from past and present. Human beings, through their cross-cultural understanding, have learned how to discover their real potential, but not beyond finality to conceptualize their identity. This means that individuals need to be realistic rather than idealistic. Human beings are committed to survival in order to adapt all perceptual aspects of their understanding to a meaningful conceptualized lifestyle in days to come.

Almost all things that appear in human's conceptual form of understanding—metaphysically, epistemologically, axiologically, and aesthetically—are relative and comparative in humans' minds, because our world is pluralistic. Consequently, our cultures are becoming highly integrative. Human beings are living in a physical world in which their priority objective is to understand its propensities. They can come to know these propensities well through familiarity with the real identities through *multiculturalism.* They sense an involvement with their physical world which gives them the ability to predict which objects will fall, how well-known shapes look from other angles, and how much force is required to push objects against friction. However, they lack corresponding familiarity with the forces on charged particles, forces in nonuniform dimensional forms, and the effects of non-forecasted geometric transformation of high inertia and low-friction motion.

CULTURAL ORIENTATIONS

The human mind by its very nature and structure is cross-culturally oriented. It is also interculturally oriented and has the capacity to understand and realize the different nature of causes and effects and world events effectively. Multicultural behavior in a super industrial era needs to operate effectively through the following perspectives (1) *transorganizationally*—across families, divisional, departmental, and disciplinary entities; (2) *transnationally*—across cultures, countries, national boundaries, and continents; (3) *transideologically*—across the ideological beliefs of the East, West, North, South, and developed and least and/or less developing nations (LDCs); and (4) *transcendentally*—going beyond ordinary limits, surpassing extraordinary modes of infinite beliefs, supranational abstracts, and beyond the contingent and accidental reasoning in human experience, but not beyond all human knowledge (Parhizgar, 1993).

Heenan and Perlmutter (1979) list ethnocentric, polycentric, regiocentric, and geocentric as four cultural orientations toward the subsidiaries in a multinational enterprise.

- *Ethnocentric* mentality views the international market as the extension of the domestic market. Some multinational corporations ascribe their superiority to everything from the home country and label everything foreign as inferior (Fatehi, 1996: 19).

- *Polycentric* mentality is an attitude in which some multinational corporations believe that all foreigners are different and difficult to understand. They use their home-country culture along with expatriate personnel in key positions everywhere in the world. In the absence of the expatriate managers, polycentric MNCs leave managerial positions to the local host countries. Products and services are produced for local consumption in the host market and the subsidiaries are operated by host managers.
- *Regiocentric* multinational corporations hire foreign nationals among their home countries and leave them alone as long as their subsidiaries are profitable. Regiocentric multicultural corporations hire managers from neighboring countries on the basis of their geographical and/or cultural stratification, such as Spanish managers for maquiladora plants.
- *Geocentric* multinational corporations attempt to integrate all nationalities and cultures through a global perspective in decision making and operations. In this case, priority is not given to nationality, ethnicity, religion, and gender. All groups with their meritorious capabilities can contribute to the corporation's productivity.

Multicultural management can create and recognize an understanding on the basis of similarities between two or more nationalities that makes their organizations very competitive. Such a model can create pluralistic organizations to serve all stakeholders, such as investors, managers, workers, and consumers. As a result, the rule of multicultural management is to involve identity of their key stakeholders. This examines the quality of their relations, the fair share of their efficacy, and the dynamic pluralistic synergy to greater competitiveness on the basis of partnership.

THE CONCEPTUAL DIMENSION OF CULTURE

The cultural orientation of a society reflects the complex interaction of conceptions, apperceptions, beliefs, values, faith, ideology, attitudes, motivations, expectations, adaptation, and behavioral modification displayed by its members (Adler, 1986: 9). As shown in Figure 2.3, an individual's personality is the centerpiece of a cultural orientation. Personality includes both characteristics of the person as an actor and behavior as the symbolic meaning of their behavior—culture. People's attempt to understand themselves is called the *self-concept* in personality theory and to understand their

FIGURE 2.3. Components of Culture and Ethnicity

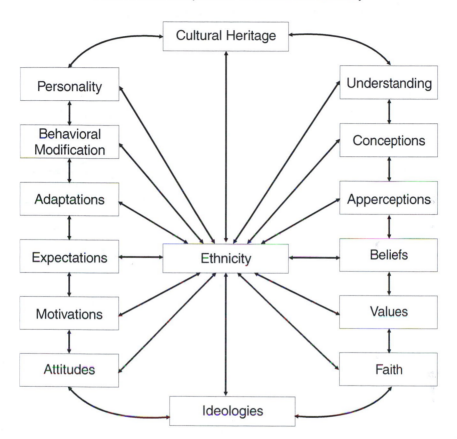

social traits is called the *dimension* of personality because they can be measured on a mathematical *continuum*. For the clarity of such a cultural continuum, we shall briefly define the components of a culture.

Conceptions

Conceptions are cognitive processes of thoughts, feelings, and emotional bindings in human nature. A concept yields a unique pictorial perception about the world. Each person may have quite a different perception from reality. There is a great deal of understanding about the relationship between sensation and conception in a physical sense. The conceptual process involves a complicated interaction of selection, organization, and interpretation of our imagination, reasoning, and judgment.

Apperceptions

Apperception is the activity of processing and fitting new perceptions into one's own culture—memories, habits, desires, interests, and beliefs. All cultural traits and patterns of behaviors are human-made instruments for stimulating certain kinds of psychometric responses in human beings. They are somewhat like fingers touching the buttons of a highly complex electronic magnetic machine, which activate far-reaching imaginative processes of historical thoughts of all generations. The stimulus can be a sequence of conceptual ideas striking the brain (the culture), and/or of dynamic movements striking the eyes (the society). Such conditioning can result from previous intense, emotional experiences, or from repetitive learning and habit, as can be found in multicultural training processes. Such a train of associated ideas will never, in itself, present a definite stopping place. It can always be prolonged as a step for further discovery. Cognition and reasoning play a varying part in it. Some apperceptions can take place with only a small amount of conscious attention, and others can get through persistent interest and motivation. There are no sharp lines between sensation, perception, and apperception, but it is a degree of eustressful (a prosperous pressure) effort in the mind and the body of a human being.

Beliefs

Beliefs are inferences made by and observed about underlying states of expectancy. Beliefs seem to form the core conceptual ideas and opinions concerning the acceptability of something or to be denominated by some faiths. Sproul (1981: 204) states: "A belief is an understanding that represents credible relationships between objects, properties, and ideas." Beliefs are imbued with powerful emotional feelings. The fervor with which people hold their religious or dogmatic ideologies is a good example. Beliefs are viewed as confidence in truth or existence of something not immediately susceptible to rigorous proof. In religious terms, beliefs are tenets to acceptance of the truthful existence of God.

Values

Values are preferred and standardized expected modes of apperception and behavior in a culture. Terpstra and David (1991:106) state: "Values are priorities for sorting out the options and, when one has the will and the resources to do so, for implementing one code of behavior rather than others. . . . Values direct society's people to selectively attend to some goals and to subordinate others." They are the ways an individual expects all people to think and behave when they face a given situation. For example, foreign students from certain Asiatic countries bow slightly and respectfully when addressing a university professor; the bow is their norm or expectation of behavior given that situation.

Values are rationally pre-set priorities for sociability, for an individual to be accepted in a society. A human being without cultural values is assumed to be a savage. Values usually manifest underlying assumptions by bringing to the surface certain behaviors of people regarding faith, beliefs, trust, and confidence in self and others. Norms are expectations of the ways people should ideally act, not anticipations of the ways people really will act. Values are expectations of proper behavior, not requirements for that behavior. There is a difference between cultural and legal values. Cultural values are not published, may not even be obeyed, and cannot be enforced—but they are expected. Legal values are published and should be enforced (Hosmer, 1987: 82).

Faith

Faith is an emotional enforcement in believing reality. It is a meaningful reliance on a strong emotional belief that can provide an individual with a psychological reinforcement for spiritual well-being. Faith helps eradicate anxieties, end self-doubt, and strengthen the belief in truthfulness, worthiness, and righteousness. Faith is the presumably factual reinforcement of the attitude that peace and revelation (the reduction of fear, misery, and inferiority feelings) are the only ends for a human being. Finally, faith is an emotional and sensational fidelity and loyalty to a phenomenon, person, promise, and/or an oath. Failure to fulfill the obligation would be breaking the belief. For example, in somewhat the same way that the pantheist (the doctrine that God is the transcendent reality of the material universe and human beings are only creatures who can perceive God everywhere) sees God in the trees and the birds and the very air, religious and or political beliefs are also ubiquitous, albeit in more concrete forms.

Ideologies

As a factual belief, human beings live within two integrated environments: (1) the natural (we can identify it as ecology), and (2) the artificial (we can identify it as culture). From the standpoint of a material view, the ecological environment provides all organic elements, including human beings, animals, and plants, with appropriate conditions to survive. However, the artificial environment—culture—provides specific human-made conditions to survive. Those conditions which are the authoritatively approved set of political ideas are ideologies; thus, the specificity of conditions could be called ideologies. Political ideology is a set of political ideas—a formalized belief system that explains and justifies a preferred political order for society. Ideologies offer a sociopolitical and cultural strategy (processes, institutional arrangements, programs, and hierarchical power) for their attainment (Mullins, 1972: 498-511). For example, Lane (1962: 3-15), in his book *Political Ideology,* undertook to discover the latent political ideology of the American urban common man through in-depth interviews with fifteen American males. He describes ideologies as "group beliefs that individuals borrow."

As Marger (1985: 16) indicates: "Ideologies comprise beliefs that, through constant articulation, become accepted as descriptions of the true state of affairs." Ideologies are worldviews which are built upon and reinforce a set of powerfully dominant beliefs and values in societal interactions. For example, the idea of progress, which has been a defining ideology in traditional Western civilization, was built on the set of beliefs of capitalism. Capitalist ideology included economic efficiency, self-interest as a major motivator, and exploitation of resources through impersonal market mechanism. Such an ideology created enormous inequalities of wealth and opportunities. On the other hand, in the modern American democracy, beliefs and practices of the ideology of democracy are a combination of popular sovereignty, political equality, and majority rule. American culture continuously seeks to reconcile these competing beliefs and values. However, Barrett (1991) has found six notions in defining ideology, explained as:

1. the opposite of material reality (illusory);
2. a sublimate of material life processes serving class interests (class-bounded);
3. an expression of the dominant material relationships (superstructure);
4. a terrain of struggle resulting from material transformations (revolution);
5. a mediation between classes as a postponement of class rule (Bonapartism); and
6. reification or mystification (fetishism of commodities).

In a multicultural analysis, in all these approaches, an ideology implies a thoughtful reality, which concludes subjectivity of the world in which we live.

Ethnicity

Kinesthetic (the sensation of movement and strain in muscles, tendons, joints, and skin) natural conditions of human beings are different in geographical and topographical nature. On the basis of this fact, ecological survival conditions shape human characteristics. Human beings are divided naturally into different skin colors and hues. However, all human beings ecologically share the same characteristics to survive, but they live in different artificial human-made conditions (cultures).

Since human beings acquire their characteristics from two major sources, genetics and kinesthetic cultures, they physically identify themselves and mentally manifest their behavior through these two characteristics. The kinesthetic natural physical traits of human beings manifest intrinsically specific mentality through their artificial conditions of intelligence, personality, culture, and education. Such natural and artificial conditions can innately differ humans' personal thinking and societal groups behavior. Therefore, the levels of human socialization, through accessibility, suitability, and profitability of both natural and environmental privileges, lead the idea of ethnicity. "Ethnicity" is an artificial perceptual classification of human beings into different groups through ideologies. Ideologies do not necessarily reflect reality; in fact, they are to a great extent mythical. Basically, ethnic groups are groups of men and women with similar cultural traits. It is very interesting that the term *ethnicity* is relatively new. Glazer and Moyniham (1975) note that the term *ethnicity* did not even appear in standard English dictionaries until the 1960s. In modern civilization, people are grouped into sociocultural groups referred to as ethnic groups, where previously they were thought of as races or nations.

Attitudes

Attitudes are contradictory beliefs, feelings, and perceptual tendencies toward other persons, things, and/or phenomena. Attitudes are expressed by values and dispose a person to act or react in certain ways toward something. Attitudes are often present in the relationship between a person and some kind of objects (physical and metaphysical). Attitudes are personal habitual reactions to certain repetitive modes of apperceptions and/or behaviors.

Motivations

All people have their own definition of motivation. To some, motivation is a basic psychological process and to others it is reinforcement for movement. Many people equate all causes of human behavior with motivation. Usually one or more of the following words are included in the definition of motivation: needs, desires, wants, wishes, objectives, goals, motives, and incentives.

Within the nature of human beings, intrinsically there are need-drive-goal motivational cycles. Sometimes, people are very energetic, pleasant, and nice; sometimes they are not. The pleasant and nice side of human psychic motives cause positive pressure in an individual's behavior to fulfill delightful objectives. Such a positive pressure is called *eustress*. Eustress is a counteractive drive that motivates people to be more active and humanized. But, on the other side of human nature, there are negative and unpleasant motives which can cause dissatisfaction. The negative motive is called "stress." Berelson and Steiner (1964: 240) define it as: "A motivation is an inner state that energizes, activates, or moves (hence 'motivation'), and that directs or channels behavior toward goals." Sanford and Wrightsman (1970: 189) described motivation as follows: "A motive is relentlessness, a lack, a yen, a force. Once in the grip of a motive, the organism does something. It most generally does something to reduce the relentlessness, to remedy the lack, to alleviate the yen, to mitigate the force." The key to understanding motivation, it appears, lies in the interactive processes and relationships between, needs, drives, and goals, and their outcomes (Luthans 1985: 183). In nondiscriminatory cultures eustressful efforts can result in high success, but in some discriminatory cultures stressful efforts can cause frustration and disappointment. However, highly eustressful efforts do not necessarily manifest high success.

Expectations

Expectations are thoughts and other cognitive intervened promises between incoming information and final behavioral responses. Cultural expectations are reciprocal prospective future orientation of good and kind behaviors which members of a society are looking forward to being exposed to and/or to be confronted with others.

Adaptations

Adaptation is a very clear concept for integrative survival. To adapt successfully, a culture must be aware of its environment—how an environment could be changed, how people could be acculturalized—and make the necessary adjustments. It may interrelate or integrate some facts, conditions, concepts, or beliefs such as goodness, truthfulness, beauty, justice, evolution, creation, gravitation, democracy, or relations among God, nature, and humans. Generally, cultural adaptation is participation of individuals in societal life based upon timeliness, attendance, and relations.

Behavioral Modification

Behavioral modification is the application of new learned cultural value reinforcements to the behavior of a person. The behavioristic teaching-training theory has certain advantages over laboratory experiment. The field trip and/or traveling to other cities, countries, and continents can provide great experiences. Such experiences stem from direct observation of events. Such experiences can manifest various behavioristic group discoveries. Learners in such a cross-cultural experiment tried to assess their own cultural knowledge and relate it to others' cultural observable outcomes. Specifically, in behavioristic modeling, trainees became familiar with relevant behaviors in other cultures.

Institutions

Institutions are those more or less formalized and acculturalized ways by which society tries to bring order and discipline. They are orderly forms, conditions, procedures, and methods of group activities. Societal institutions are systems of command, communication, cooperation, coordination, and control.

CULTURAL AND BEHAVIORAL STRATIFICATION

The perceptual relation of an individual to the culture is based upon life orientation. People place themselves and their possessions under the direction of the common cultural value systems of their societies; in return, societies protect the rights and freedom of the individuals. People as individuals, their relationship to nature and the world, their relationship to other people, and their orientation in time, place, and space are influenced by their cultural value systems. Adler (1986: 12) raises several questions regarding six dimensions of the individual: Who am I? How do I see the world? How do I relate to other people? What do I do? and How do I use space and time? Responses to these and other questions vary from culture to culture. Some cultures are more synergistic than others, some cultures are more materialistic, and others are more spiritualistic. To understand how some of these factors might influence behavior of human beings, Moran and Harris (1982: 19) adapted cultural influences on life issues from Kluckhohn and Strodtbeck (1961) as shown in Table 2.1.

In relation to the above cultural value systems, briefly we will look at the three major cultural dimensions: (1) optimistic views, (2) moderate views, and (3) pessimistic views.

Optimistic Views

How Do Optimistic People Perceive Human Nature?

Some people basically perceive themselves and others as good—as reflected in a utopian cultural value system. Some cultures perceive human beings as the best products of nature, comparing humans to other creatures. They apply good nature to human beings in order to trust one another with a great deal of reliance. In a highly respectful society, there is no secrecy about human affairs because people live in harmony with themselves and their environments. People are open-minded and individuals enjoy liberty. The judiciary philosophy of these cultures is based upon this connotation:

TABLE 2.1. Cultural Influences on Life Issues

	Optimistic	Moderate	Pessimistic
What is the character of human nature?	Man is good*	Man is a mixture of good and evil*	Man is evil*
What is the relationship of man to nature?	Man is master of nature	Man is in harmony with nature	Man is subject to nature
What is the temporal focus of life?	To the future	To the present	To the past
What is the modality of man's activities?	Activity that is motivated primarily toward measurable accomplishments	Activity that emphasizes as a goal the development of all aspects of the self	A spontaneous expression in impulse and desires
What is the relationship of man to other men?	Individual—the individual goals are most important	Collateral—group goals are primary. Well-regulated continuity of group relationships through time are not critical	Lineal—group goals are primary and an important goal is continuity through time

*This assumes that human nature is either mutable or immutable.

Source: Adapted from Kluckhohn, F. R. and Strodtbeck, F. L. (1961). *Variation Value Orientations.* Evanston, IL: Row, Peterson and Company, p. 11. In Moran, R. T. and Harris, P. R. (1982). *Managing Cultural Synergy.* Volume 2. Houston: Gulf Publishing Company, p. 19.

People are considered innocent until proven guilty. They freely share their knowledge and experiences and help each other by all means and ends. They are very sincere and friendly. In these societies, change is permissible toward betterment and progress with good faith. For example, American society is currently representing this type of cultural perception. The burden of proof is on an accuser. However, if we look at Spain's culture, we find that in such a society, people are suspicious of one another; they believe that they constantly must watch customers in their stores as shoplifting is a pattern of expected behavior in Spain.

What Is an Optimistic Individual's Relationship to His or Her Institution?

A general cultural pattern indicates how people can dominate their social institutions and overcome the nature of obstacles. People perceive no real separation between institutional and individual boundaries. Their cultural beliefs allow them to live alongside their institutions—as their institutions are growing, they are also developing their capabilities. In an optimistic culture, policies and regulations have been mandated to alter natural opportunities to the people needs. People are allowed to alter and modify the nature of their institutions in order to enhance their lifestyles. Societal institutions help, guide, and assist people in searching for better understanding. Change is possible because development, growth, and progress are the results of change.

What Are the Primary Relationships of Individuals to Others?

Human beings are not born with ready-made relationships with others. Individuals create their own contacts and relationships. However, one cannot achieve this state of existence unless he or she is free. Human beings exist to create their positions and relationships with others. This indicates the reality which human beings attribute to their value systems.

What Are the Primary Modes of Human Activities?

Cultural value systems in a society reflect the differentiated relationships among people. People are oriented with the modes of "will-er." The "will-er culture" is more oriented to prosperous practical activities. The psychological and sociological "will-er" orientations speed up the process of change and the specificity to change direction for themselves and their environment. Progressive assessment of individuals' achievements is not perceived inherently by the nature of performers. The measurement is based upon the societal standards of expected behavior. Optimistic people are more motivated to efficiency through hardworking habits.

What Is the Temporal Focus of an Optimistic Individual to the Society?

It is the human's perception that an individual should physically live in the present and metaphysically perceive the future. Future-oriented cultures are more innovative in sciences and technologies. Conservative and, as we call them, pessimistic cultures prefer to maintain their traditional value systems and people hardly believe in drastic change. They are very satisfied with the status quo. However, optimistic cultures evolve with new hopes and prosperity toward progress and development—individually and collectively.

Moderate Views

Americans traditionally see people as a mixture of good and evil, capable of choosing one over the other. They believe in the possibility of improvement through change (Adler, 1986:13). This notion brings to mind that

American culture is a balanced culture. We will examine the same connotations through the moderate views as follows.

How Do Moderate People Perceive Human Nature?

Although many people do not hold extreme positions of saying that individuals virtually "can do no wrong or no right" at all times, they believe that the individual nature of a human being is a dualistic function of mind and body. In religious connotations, at one time the soul of human beings existed in the world of pure spirit and enjoyed the highest bliss—pure contemplation. However, because of some contact with evil in a world of pure spirit, at the same time the soul of a human being had been condemned, became a part of body, and formed an organic unit to live on the earth. Since the soul of a human being has formed an organic unit with the body, it is subject to weaknesses. The end result of such a dualistic functioning does not have a heavenly existence.

Plato states that a human being's superior faculty is attributed to the soul (e.g., mind, logic, and reasoning) and inferior organic existence is attributed to the body (e.g., evil, change, corruption). People with such a cultural belief tend to categorize individuals into two major categories: (1) Those people with the highest intellectual abilities who can be considered rulers. Rulers must be intellectual authorities who should be perfectly educated; (2) Those people who have less intellectual ability and should be subordinated to the first group. If we consider the caste tradition in India, we find that Indian people conceptually make distinctive class stratifications among themselves on the basis of their cultural family heritage.

What Is a Moderate Individual's Relationship to His or Her Institution?

Some cultures strongly believe that life is the essence of conscience. Individuals should live in harmony with their organizations and be loyal to their institutions. In return, organizations should provide them lifetime employment. There should not be a separated view between employees and employers in such a society. Institutions should serve both organizational members and consumers as part and as a whole.

What Are the Primary Relationships of Individuals to Others?

Some cultures are more group oriented and strive to serve one another. In general terms, although people share their views and help one another, individuals maintain and reserve their privacy and independence. Mutual interests among professional groups facilitate harmony and helpfulness in these societies. These cultures are searching for and are proceeding toward unity through diversity. The surest paths to the truth in these societies rely upon expert authorities and scientific findings. Lateral group membership includes all people who are currently part of an institution and provides opportunities for people who desire to join one. The prime criteria for recruitment of organizational members are trustworthiness, loyalty to the group, compatibility, and comparability with other co-workers. For example, French culture is perceived to be more individualistic and less synergistic than other cultures (Moran and Harris, 1982:19).

What Are the Primary Modes of Human Activities?

Balancing organizational priorities in a moderate culture can provide each member with adequate opportunities for growth and development. Institutional authorities within the contextual boundary of a moderate culture tend to develop loyalty and normative behavior in their employees in order to better coordinate different organizational factions. Under a moderate cultural view, institutions maintain more autonomy and responsibility toward organizational stakeholders.

What Is the Temporal Focus of a Moderate Individual to the Society?

Some cultures, under the moderate view of cultural value systems, prefer to perceive the use of time within the present outcomes. These people like to live in the moment. They react to the short-term profits and make priorities to meet their short career path. In a general behavioral mode description, we call them "do-er" cultures.

Pessimistic Views

Although all human beings have distinctive cultural norms and values, it would be a mistake to judge and label them with a pessimistic value judgment. Geertz (1970: 47) indicates that: "We are, in sum, incomplete or unfinished animals who complete ourselves through culture." However, some cultures are more attached to past traditions, and others lean either to the present or future. By the same token, some cultures are more optimistically oriented and others are either more pessimistic or moderate. Pessimistic cultures start by viewing things with more emphasis on negative views and finally try to evolve with positive outcomes. By viewing different studies on this direction, we provide the following connotations regarding pessimistic views.

How Do Pessimistic People Perceive Human Nature?

Some cultures function negatively. People tend to view others as basically evil. They suspect and mistrust each other. People in daily behavioral interactions are very cautious. They maintain reservation to avoid being open with one another. People do not change voluntarily; because of their cultural orientation, they are controlled through very rigid value systems. In these cultures, interpersonal change within their personality is very difficult. In the event some mandatory change happens, the end results of changes carry some degree of personality degradation. In these cultures, the judiciary philosophy is based upon this connotation: People are considered guilty until they are proven innocent. Suspicion, resistance, and disloyalty to the cultural authorities are very popular in these cultures.

What Is a Pessimistic Individual's Relationship to His or Her Institution?

Cultural obedience is one of the distinct manifestations of normative behaviors in pessimistic cultures. In these cultures, people do not trust one another. However, they need to rely on some forms of authority. These cultures give more credit to the rulers' power and losing the sense of individual liberty. People are expected to be obedient to the rulers' wishes in order to be privileged at time of necessity. All members of a pessimistic culture are virtually dominated by elite ruling groups.

What Are the Primary Relationships of Individuals to Others?

As indicated before, under the pessimistic cultural views, human beings are considered evil. Therefore, people under such conditions misbehave. The belief is that people with selfish instincts and stereotyping relationships with others should be constantly controlled. Society should not provide maximum freedom for individuals, because if they are provided with the liberty, they will revolt against authorities. They stick with the cultural story of Adam and Eve, who revolted against God in the Garden of Eden (Dupuios, 1985: 10). Therefore, organizational members should be obedient, silent, and ordered by authority. Society should restrict freedom of individuals through rigid policies. Societal members are controlled by the high-ranked authorities. They strongly believe in collectivistic judgment. If a person of the group is suspicious toward another, other members of the group without question adhere to such a connotation. They believe that organizational members who are known by others, or vice versa, can be trusted by all others. Under the pessimistic cultures, the process of policy is less flexible because it is less time consuming.

What Are the Primary Modes of Human Activities?

Human perceptions under the pessimistic cultural view tend to be more passive. They are more attached to their past experiences. They like to minimize their activities, because they believe that they will not enjoy adequate profits out of their efforts. They tend to be motivated toward fewer hours, because they believe that generation of wealth will not provide them happiness. People believe major changes will occur at their own often slow pace. They do not need to push or to be pushed to achieve long term objectives. They believe everything and everybody is subject to the process of birth and death and that fate and destiny migrate from one authority to another sooner or later.

What Is the Temporal Focus of a Pessimistic Individual to the Society?

Under pessimistic cultural views, people perceive that future life is the extension of past experiences; we call this type of people "be-ers." Under this view, all cultural value systems should be evaluated according to past experiences, and innovations and creativity should be justified accordingly. For example, like most Asians, the Vietnamese have a more extended concept of time than that of most Americans. Americans measure time and react by the clock, Vietnamese by the monsoon. Vietnamese are suspicious of the need for urgency in making decisions or culminating a business deal. Traditional experiences in patience remain the ultimate Confucian virtue in personal life as well as in business (Smith and Pham, 1998: 174).

SUMMARY

This chapter detailed exactly what we mean by human beings and outlined the perspectives of cultural characteristics of both modern and traditional societies. The natural and cultural identity of human beings can be perceived as: physical body, sensibility, emotionality, rationality, intellectuality, and information. The physical nature of human beings reflects a general materialistic trend within which individuals live and develop. It also reflects a person's relationship to the things/objectives in the immediate environment. All knowledge of the world depends on the human's senses and their stimulation. The physiological senses are considered to be vision, hearing, touch, smell, and taste. There are many other so-called "sixth senses" which can be called kinesthetic or intuitive senses. The kinesthetic senses are constantly interactive with numerous intrinsic and extrinsic forces. Emotion is an experience of affective state of consciousness in which joy, sorrow, fear, hate, love, and sympathy are manifested in human behavior. Human beings by their very nature are very well organized. They are rational beings that exist as an end in themselves. Human beings are born into domains of a culture. They judge on the basis of their individual and cultural wisdom. Human beings inherently learn how to discover themselves and others through effective canalization of information. Conceptions are cognitive processes of thoughts, feelings, and emotional bindings in human nature. Apperception is the activity of processing and fitting new percepts into one's own culture. Beliefs are inferences made by and observed about underlying states of expectancy. Values are preferred expected modes of apperception and behavior in a culture. A faith is a positive

thought of well-being. Ideologies comprise beliefs that, through constant articulation, become accepted as descriptive signs of human socialization. Ethnicity
is an artificial categorization of human beings into different groups through
ideologies. Motivations are interactive dynamic forces within a human being.
Adaptation is assimilation of a person into a new condition and/or culture.
Behavioral modification is the application of new learned cultural value reinforcements within the behavior of a person.

CHAPTER QUESTIONS FOR DISCUSSION

- In your own words, identify and summarize the various frameworks
  for understanding human nature.
- Identify and explain the variable components of culture.
- Why is the study of human behavior important to multinational organizations?
- What is the comprehensive definition of personality? Give brief examples of each of the major elements.
- Do you agree with the opening discussion of this chapter that people
  are human information processors? Why?
- What effect can the conceptual and perceptual processes have on organizational behavior?

LEARNING ABOUT YOURSELF EXERCISE #2

How Do You Judge?

Following are fifteen items for rating how important each one is to you on a scale of 0 (not important) to 100 (very important). Write the number 0-100 on the line to the left of each item.

Not important	Somewhat important		Very important
0	25	50	75	100

It would be more important for me to:

_____ 1. Get more help from others
_____ 2. Give more help to others
_____ 3. Be balanced to give and to receive
_____ 4. Tell the truth, even to betray myself
_____ 5. Work hard to enhance my experience
_____ 6. Work hard to contribute my knowledge and experience
to the organization
_____ 7. Pay more attention to my feelings
_____ 8. Pay more attention to my rights
_____ 9. Get along with intellectual people
_____ 10. Get along with funny people
_____ 11. Judge by my heart
_____ 12. Judge by my head
_____ 13. Approach people if they approach me first
_____ 14. Analyze my behavior on the basis of my cultural background
_____ 15. Be an innovative person

Turn to the next page for scoring directions and key.

SCORING DIRECTIONS AND KEY FOR EXERCISE #2

Transfer the numbers for each of the fifteen items to the appropriate column, then add up the five numbers in each column.

Sensational	Emotional	Rational
1. _____	2. _____	3. _____
5. _____	7. _____	4. _____
8. _____	10. _____	6. _____
14. _____	11. _____	9. _____
15. _____	13. _____	12. _____
Your Totals _____	_____	_____
Total Scores 500	500	500

The higher the total in any dimension, the higher the importance you place on that set. The closer the numbers are in the three dimensions, the better sociopsychologically oriented you are.

Make up a categorical scale of your findings on the basis of more weight for the values of each category.

For example:

    1. 400 Emotional
    2. 375 Sensational
    3. 200 Rational

    Your Totals   875
    Total Scores   1,500

After you have tabulated your scores, compare them with others. You will find different value systems among people with diverse scores and preferred mode of perceptions.

CASE STUDY:
BADISCHE ANILIN & SODA FABRIK (BASF):
COMPETITION AND COOPERATION

Badische Anilin & Soda Fabrik (BASF) was incorporated in 1952 as one of three chemical successor companies to I.G. Farbenindustries. It was originally founded in 1865, with its present name adopted in 1973.

BASF is one of the world's largest chemical companies. Its headquarters are located in Ludwigshafen, Germany. The BASF's subsidiaries are located in thirty-nine different countries. Some of its major affiliates include: BASF Espanola S. A; BASF Argentina; BASF India Ltd; and BASF Australia Ltd. BASF is continuously at the forefront of expansion and product development. Currently, BASF's operational activities include health and nutrition, finishing products, chemicals, plastics, fibers, oil, and gas. These divisions provide a large array of products, such as natural gas, oil, and basic chemical products through innovative intermediates to specialities, high value-added chemical crop protection products, and pharmaceuticals. The number of employees as of December 1977 was 104,979.

In 1995, BASF acquired DuPont's 50 percent holding in a joint venture with Idemitsu Petrochemicals Ltd. (Japan), producer of 1,4 butanedoil in China and Japan. In 1958, BASF and Dow Chemical Company established Dow Badische Company as a joint venture. In 1995, BASF and IVAX corporation (United States) set up a joint venture to market genetic products in Europe. The company, BASF Generics, was a subsidiary of Knoll Norton and began business in 1995.

The BASF company is committed to strengthening its market share throughout the world. The company is still underrepresented in the Americas according to BASF president/chemist Carl A. Jennings. The naphtha JV cracker project with Fina at Port Arthur, Texas, will be the first commercial license of ABB Lummus Global's metathesis technology, which converts ethylene and C4 olefins into propylene and enables the cracker to produce more propylene than ethylene.

If BASF implements its project, it must contend with a workforce which was devastated in a chemical explosion. They must commit to restoring confidence in this workforce and ensure them that adequate measures will be taken to provide a safe working environment. They must also be committed to developing a sophisticated workforce which uses new technology in development of ethylene and C4 olefin into propylene and enables the cracker to produce more propylene than ethylene. In addition, BASF needs to compete with DuPont and Dow Chemical. These companies are its largest competitors in North America. BASF company has several joint ventures with both companies. None of these joint venture partnerships are within the North American marketplace.

Sources: Wood, A. (1998). "BASF Doubles U.S. Spending, Targets More Chemicals Expansion." *Chemical Week,* May 6: 10; *Moody's Industrial Manual,* (1999). Zottoli Jr., D. A., Publisher, New York: Moody's Investors Service, Inc. pp. 921-924.

Chapter 3

Understanding Global Environments and Cultural Value Systems

The unexamined cultural value system of a society does not serve the means and ends of civilized people.

CHAPTER OBJECTIVES

When you have read this chapter you should be able to:

- understand the concepts of a society,
- indicate why people behave in different ways,
- define culture,
- know how knowledge can help us better understand other cultures, and
- understand how society at large orients human beings toward continuity in their lives.

INTRODUCTION

The theme of this chapter concentrates on people around the world who have different grouping structures and how these structures have bearing on people's cultural orientation and behavior. More specifically, in the following pages, key components are defined that make up a community and its cultures, a dozen or more structural design forms of cultural behavior are presented, distinctive cultural components that make a society different from others are identified, and the different effects of cultural orientation on international business are considered.

THE CULTURE AND GLOBAL ENVIRONMENTS

There are holistic perceptions about periodic views on questions such as: What is human? What is life? What is the potential of people's cultural context? How can a culture enhance or retard people's social behavior? Contemplating these and other questions has caused many philosophers, artists, scientists, and technologists to revisit these phenomena through different angles.

Through culture, we have learned and practiced how to conquer nature: tame the wilderness, make war on pests and vermin, control land, make dams on the rivers, and finally, battle against the elements where only the fittest survive and where whole species of life-forms that got in our way are exterminated. In most cultures, people are taught to see nature apart from themselves as the enemy to be pushed around in a world composed of separate entities, unrelated to each other, each on its own journey to infinity (Finkel, 1994: 80).

Much that is puzzling in other cultures can be understood only when they are considered evolved as a nation. Technologists, enamored by the persistence of their own gadgetry, reassure us that a better world is within our grasp. The critical-thinking synergy of technological explorers is the result of many generations who have developed their research capabilities to relate their cultural, creative, and artistic expressions in mechanisms of combination of synergistic thoughts and actions. It is true that all people are products of natural law, but they are also creators of their own cultures. Culture is free of, or apart from, natural law only to the extent that human thoughts can be apart from natural laws (Gilford, 1960: 341).

Many unprecedented innovations are taking place in people's cultures. Innovations do not just happen. Individuals within their lifetime and the boundaries of their cultural orientation and personal curiosity make innovative ideas and methods happen. Cultural innovations are subject to people's conceptions, perceptions, imaginations, beliefs, wills, goals, and choices. Within the contextual boundaries of people's awareness and cultural synergy, people have been viewed as innovators of their own cultural times because of their capability to think abstractly and move in practice from the historical trends of technological eras (e.g., from teleolithic, eolithic, paleolithic, and neolithic technologies to electronic robotics and nano technologies). All these achievements have come from pluralistic efforts among multicultural contacts.

All societies have been changed as a result of cultural borrowing from one another. Peter Drucker (1995: 12) suggested that the greatest change in the way cultural business is conducted is the accelerating growth of relationships based not on ownership but *partnership.* In the five-year period from 1990 to 1995, the number of domestic and international knowledge-based technological alliances has grown by more than 25 percent annually (Bleek and Ernest, 1995: 97).

Cross-cultural understanding through contacts between individuals and groups is as old as recorded history. People in all generations and times have traveled to other lands to trade, teach, learn, settle, exchange ideas, convert, or conquer others. They changed their lifestyles due to economic conditions, technological developments, and sociocultural status. In the prejet age, people were much more centered in their interests and goals. Today, because of scientific advancement and technological breakthroughs in transportation and communication, scholars, explorers, travelers, adventurers, refugees, traders, missionaries, and tourists are exposed to and communicating with other cultures directly through multidimensional informational virtual reality. This is the real face of today's human civilization.

THE BASIC CONCEPTUAL MODEL OF A SOCIETY

People by their very nature are not self-sufficient. They need to cooperate with one another to fulfil their needs. If they are to survive over time, they must develop social relations and maintain social order. Socialization is a continuous process throughout life. Socialization involves the process by which people develop and acquire a set of customs and procedures for making and enforcing decisions, resolving disputes, and regulating the behavior of themselves and others. Every society must maintain pluralistic decisions on the basis of the enormously wide range of behavioral potentiality which could be open to them starting at birth through their biological, cultural, and family influences. These are customary and acceptable according to the standards of, initially, the family and, later, social groups and affiliated organizations (Mussen, 1963: 60-61).

As used in this book, the term *society* encompasses all tangible and intangible concepts and things related to a lively group of human beings. Society generally means a nation and/or a professional group of people. This concept of society includes people with ideas, beliefs, attitudes, ideologies, expectations, values, perceptions, and material things. These concepts are arranged in scales of values or performance systems. These help individuals and organizations to set and seek common ends. For example, in American society the institution of law clearly reflects and affects major civic values. I have mentioned this here because of the importance of the concept of law to our implementation of the so-called free market. When we begin discussing how different countries approach free markets, an understanding of moral, ethical, and legal behaviors will be crucial.

Society is dynamic because all individuals and organizations are constantly in motion and interacting to make changes. Therefore, the term *society* from a sociopolitical perspective means, essentially, to conceive when one speaks of a lively dynamic nation and/or civilization. Inherent to this concept are eight fundamental interrelated parts that make up the abstract of a dynamic society. These are (1) people, (2) culture, (3) institutions, (4) material objects, (5) knowledge and technology, (6) religion, (7) intellectual potency, and (8) governments (see Figure 3.1).

The People

Marger (1985: 16) defines: "Societies comprising numerous racial, religious, and cultural groups can be described simply as *multiethnic*." *People* can be defined as groups who come into contact for a purpose and are dependent on one another to achieve their societal objectives. Human beings who gather for the purpose of satisfying needs are called *people*. There are two major groups of people in a society: (1) primary groups of people and (2) secondary groups of people. Primary groups of people are composed of family members: nuclear, single parent, extended, mixed, and homogeneous families. Secondary groups of people are societal formal and informal citizens and residents of a nation who congregate and live together with political, cultural, economical, emotional, or similar objectives. Formal citizens or residents of a nation can comprise different groups of people such as task groups, command groups, work groups, professional groups, friendship groups, ethnic groups, and others. Each group of people displays a unique set of cultural subtraits

FIGURE 3.1. Component Parts of a Dynamic Society

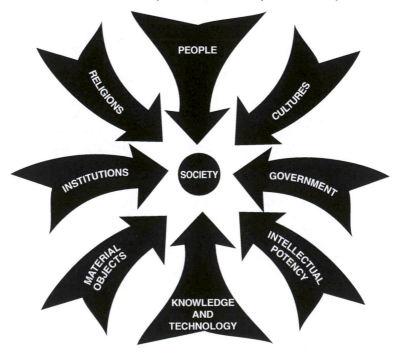

and patterns of expected behavior. People within a culture display a sense of commonality of community among themselves.

The citizens and/or residents of a nation of large groups create a sense of "peoplehood." This sense of oneness derives from an understanding of a shared ancestry, cultural heritage, and/or a common cause for their unity (Gordon, 1964). Sometimes people live together in a particular area on the basis of their ethnocentric identity, geographical territory, culturally ascribed denomination, or commonality in their religious faith and similarities in their political ideologies.

The Concept of Culture

Historically, people tried to put diverse or disparate concepts and elements together and capitalize on similarities for meeting their societal needs. The objective of such integration is to increase effectiveness by sharing perceptions, insights, aspirations, and knowledge. Thus, human culture is the way of living together, of developing and transmitting values, beliefs, and knowledge, of struggling to manage uncertainties, and of creating an artificial (versus natural) degree of social life precision.

People in a society generally develop cultural values that tell them what is important, how it got that way, and how things should be. Such perceptual concepts form the substance of a culture. More specifically, a *culture* is the integration of human group ideas, attitudes, customs, and traditions in a unified pluralistic system. In general terms, that unified system of socialization is accepted in a somewhat established standard of perceptual and behavioral modes toward an attempt to meet the people's needs. Culture copes in overt and covert ways to make group behavior unique by adapting people's perceptions to their physical and ecological surroundings.

Culture Is Defined

Culture is a means to cope with surrounding uncertainties by providing predictable ways of expressing and affirming pluralistic values, beliefs, and norms of understanding and behaving toward an end. When cultural anthropologists tried to define culture, they included all aspects of human societal life as parts of a culture. Two prominent cultural anthropologists, Kroeber and Kluckhohn (1952: 181), after cataloging more than 160 different definitions of the term culture, offered one of the most comprehensive and generally accepted definitions, which follows:

> Culture consists of patterns, explicit and implicit of and behavior acquired and transmitted by symbols, constituting the distinctive achievement of human groups, including their embodiment in artifacts; the essential core of culture consists of traditional (i.e., historically derived and selected) ideas and especially their attached values; culture

systems may, on the one hand be considered as products of action, on the other as conditioning elements of future action.

Hofstede (1994: 4) states: "Culture is the collective programming of the mind which distinguishes the members of one group or category of people from those of another." Culture, therefore, makes people's lives very smooth and allows them to get on with the necessities of living (Trice and Beyer, 1993). Brown (1976: 15), in his research in defining culture, indicates a culture is:

> (1) Something that is shared by all or almost all members of some social groups(s), (2) something that the older members of the group(s) try to pass on to the younger members, and (3) something (as in the case of morals, laws and customs) that shapes behavior, or . . . structures one's perception of the world.

Although there is no complete agreement on the underlying theories of cultural definition, cultural anthropologists agree on certain characteristics. Hofstede (1980: 25) defines culture as: "The interactive aggregate of common characteristics that influence a human group's response to its environment." Downs (1971: 35) states that: "Culture is a mental map which guides us in our relations to our surroundings and to other people." And perhaps most succinctly as "the way of life of people" (Hatch, 1985: 178).

Spradley (1979: 5) defines a culture as: "The acquired knowledge that people use to interpret experience and generate social behavior." Symington (1983: 1) defines culture as: "That complex whole which includes knowledge, beliefs, art, law, morals, customs, and any capabilities and habits acquired by a man (or woman) as a member of society."

Moran and Harris (1982: 108) define culture as: "The way of living developed and transmitted by a group of human beings, consciously or unconsciously, to subsequent generations. More precisely, ideas, habits, attitudes, customs, and traditions become accepted and somewhat standardized in a particular group as an attempt to meet continuing needs."

In sum, all scientists capture the essence of what makes a person's culture similar: it is the general agreement that a culture is collective, dynamic, learned, shared, transgenerated, symbolic, patterned, and adaptive. All attributes will be described briefly here and revisited many times throughout future discussions.

Culture Is Learned

Cultures are not genetic or biological, they are relatively perceived as permanent changes in behavior or potential behavior resulting from understanding and experiencing our life events. During the first half of the twentieth century, psychologists and other social scientists tended to explain people's behavior in terms of various instincts or genetically based propensities. Today, this instinctive interpretation of human behavior is no longer held (Ferraro, 1994: 19). However, we cannot deny the effects of biological and genetic characteristics on human socialization. For such reasons, most social scientists agree that human beings are social creatures. The most widely studied determinants of human socialization are biological, social, and cultural. Biology influences personality in a number of ways. Our genes help determine many physical characteristics, and these may in turn affect personality. Genetic factors may also directly affect personality, because we inherit some of our emotional and sensational traits from our parents and/or ancestors. It is very difficult to separate "nature" from "nurture"—social and cultural (Van Fleet, 1991: 35). The term "nature" denotes all genetic characteristics that people acquire from their parents and environments through their physical identity (e.g., color, feature, race, and ethnicity). The term "nurture" means all social behavior and psychological characteristics that people learn from their associates and surroundings (values, attitudes, motives, ideologies, ideas, beliefs, and faiths).

Culture is learning to change. People who have been accultured or encultured are changed. Although learning does not necessarily imply a positive or negative change, you may learn, for example, through your cultural orientation to be a "straight-faced liar" or a "pathological liar." The changes resulting from cultural learning are usually long lasting.

Culture is the essence of reproductive efforts of human intellectuality through learning and experiencing. However, people interact with their surroundings through their learning traits from past generations and communicate with future generations in complex ways. They interact with their social and biological traits. Therefore, cultures should be learned through understanding and experiencing.

Culture Is Pluralistic

Culture manifests pluralistic intellectual and emotional traits reflected on the social mirror of a group of people in a society. Culture is the general identity of individuals' interactions, interdependence, and interrelatedness of concepts and behaviors in terms of their collective lifestyles. Cultures are both the individual's depositories and repositories of what a society agrees about their pluralistic lifestyles. A pluralistic culture is one in which many cultural traits and institutions exist through which power is diffused. The invisible dynamic forces manifested on both individuals and groups about how to interact with and counteract constraining forces in their environments is called culture. Steiner and Steiner (1997: 60) identify several features of American culture that contribute to its pluralistic nature:

1. It is infused with democratic values.
2. It encompasses a large population spread over a wide geography and engaged in diverse occupations.

3. The Constitution creates a government that encourages pluralism.
4. A pluralistic culture functions within a free market society and imposes immediate, concrete, and close boundaries on the discretionary exercise of cultural power.

Culture Is Shared

People in a nation become bonded together by sharing views of their concepts and world events. They socially bond with one another with ethical, moral, and legal commitments. A culture is not a special manner for a single individual; it is a collective identity of a group of people who share similar characteristics. People look to other members of their culture for support and confirmation of their shared meanings and expected actions. They also expect approval and disapproval of their own and others' behaviors from other people.

People depend on one another for emotional and practical support, which facilitates cultural prosperity and synergy. They share their ideas and values and depend on other members of their culture to help them get through life's uncertainties and difficulties. Members in one culture build their cohesive ties by sharing information and piling up positive rewards and avoiding pain, which increases their cohesiveness. Terpstra and David (1991: 106) state that: "Coordinated action among humans is possible only when understandings of reality are shared and can be communicated to others." The cultural management theorist Webber (1969: 10) describes the nature of cultural sharing by making an analogy with the sea: "We are immersed in a sea. It is warm, comfortable, supportive, and protecting. Most of us float below the surface; some bob about, catching glimpses of land from time to time; a few emerge from the water entirely. The sea is our (shared) culture."

Culture Is Dynamic

Cultures are not static, they are dynamic. Cultures are collective dynamic efforts to cope with change and agents of change. No matter the speed by which cultures change, one fact is evident: no cultures remain completely static year after year. Cultures are evolved and evolving. While cultures create continuity and persistency of values between generations, they are reproductive. Snow (1959) created a stir by asserting that there are two different and sometimes conflicting cultures in human civilization: science and humanities. He cited that the most important revelation is a difference in mode of dynamic thinking. Culture is the artistic production of human beings' conception. Verbal, logical, and cause-effect thinking first takes place in the culture of the humanities, especially in the works of artists, while a dynamic combination of visual and spatial thinking is a major requirement of technology and most of the sciences. This dynamic mode of thinking offers the answer to the relationship of arts with technology and science, because art, even more than technology or sciences, depends upon spatial thinking. There is a synergistic factor that connects three modes of cultural thinking and places them within what Snow (1959) sought to call a "single culture" or what I call "dynamic and organic cultures."

Culture Is Adaptive

Each society consists of two interacting systems: a cultural system (which prescribes the structural operational patterns and the way in which people should behave) and the individual's character (which defines the personality of individuals). Hence, optimal outputs can be obtained when the two systems are joined. Evans-Pritchard (1954: 54) indicates that:

> The function of culture as a whole is to unite individual human beings into more or less stable social structure, i.e., stable systems of groups determining and regulating the relation of those individuals to one another, and providing such external adaptation to the physical environment, and such internal adaptation between the component individuals or groups, as to make possible an ordered social life.

Theories of personality are abundant. Evolutionary, dialectical, cyclical, and biological analogies of the birth and death of civilizations are among the sweeping yet often exciting interpretations of changes in human cultures and behavior. Social change is the process of dynamic movement of a social system from one relatively homeostatic structural cultural character balanced toward another. *Homeostatic* structural character denotes describing a structural organism in physiological equilibrium maintained by coordinated functioning of the brain, heart, nervous system, etc. Shifts in the structure of behavior interaction of individuals are not social changes unless they are sufficiently powerful and prolonged to cause modification in the culture and in the motivations and values of individuals.

Cultural adaptations are not to be confused with social changes of which they are a part. Shifts in individual drives, needs, and tendencies are less likely to be confused with cultural changes than are structural and functional shifts. They are nevertheless part of the total. However, cultural patterns and the adaptive tendencies and motives of individuals to cope with the sociocultural changes in a society are inevitable: Cultural changes lead to individual character changes; individual character changes lead to cultural and social changes; and finally, cultural and social changes lead to structural changes in a society. Then, the total result of all these changes is cultural adaptation to the new changes. This is definitely not to say that an individual citizen's personality and characteristics are unimportant in cultural change processes. The timing of adaptive change patterns can vary. There is no doubt that after World War II, for example, the Confucian and Shinto value systems combined in Japanese culture to support structural development. Japanese culture emphasized "familial" loyalty, obedience, frugality, and hard work to adapt their traditional rigid culture (as Samurai Culture) into a supportive and assimilative culture of modernization by elite dedicated leaders and their subordinates (Bellah, 1957: 35).

Culture Is Integrative

At one time many American anthropologists, sociologists, and social psychologists believed American culture was a "melting pot." Harvey and Allard (1995: 3) argued that there is diversity of opinion about this; there are those who argue that the "melting pot" only existed outside the organization gates while inside the white male culture dominated. Still others argue that there never was a melting pot at all. Therstrom (1982: 3) states that: "There never was a melting pot; there is not now a melting pot; . . . and if there ever was, it would be such a tasteless soup that we would have to go back and start all over."

American culture is diverse and resembles a "salad bar." All subcultures maintain their integrity but are in harmony with other subcultures, much like a beautifully colorful plate of food. Petracca and Sorapure (1995: 3) indicate that: "Although we may place ourselves in specific folk or high cultures, subcultures or countercultures, we are aware of, perhaps even immersed in, the broader popular culture simply by virtue of living in society." Such a connectivity is called multiculturalism.

Ferraro (1994: 34) indicates that: "Cultures should be thought of as integrated wholes—that is, cultures are coherent and not logical systems, the parts of which to a degree are interrelated." Harvey and Allard (1995: 3) state that: "Culture envelopes us so completely that often we do not realize that there are other ways of dealing with the world, that others may have a different outlook on life, a different logic, a different way of responding to people and situations."

Culture Is Transgenerational

The historical perspective of cultural heritage indicates that culture is cumulative in its development and is passed down from one generation to the next. Emile Durkheim (1858-1917) often stressed the need for causal analysis in addition to functional analysis, suggesting that culture is rooted in human history. Similar to philosophers August Comte (a positivist) and Herbert Spencer (an empiricist), Durkheim borrowed his methodology to study culture from the natural sciences: distinguishing between causes, functions, and structures. Durkheim (1938) noted the importance of causation, which is a manifestation of ideas from cumulative development of reasons through historical experiences that have been passed down from generation to generation.

Culture Is Symbolic

Terpstra and David (1991) indicate that the interrelation of cultural symbols and meanings is not mechanical, as in the parts of a machine; it is an interrelation of contrasts that makes a difference to persons in society. The interrelation of symbols and their meanings has consequences: a change in one element will change in relation to other elements. Each society practices its own traditional value system. For example, owning a car in American culture is a symbol of mobility, but in a third-world country, it represents a symbol of wealth and the importance of the social class of a family. Therefore, culture is symbolic, because a citizen of a developed country may not understand the meaning of poverty without understanding the meaning of wealth.

Culture Is Socialization

Social learning is part of an individual's socialization. *Cultural socialization* means getting into, breaking in, learning in, settling in, perceiving in, and practicing in a culture—whether the culture is corporate, national, regional, international, and/or global. There are three component parts in socialization: (1) learning, (2) behaving, and (3) evolving.

Learning indicates to a person what principles, facts, philosophies, and techniques have adapted in his or her behavior and how he or she has learned all the customs and traditions in a specific culture.

Behavior involves cognitive and behavioral changes that occur in a learner's performance, from learned habits and experiences.

Evolving involves the results which occurred in such areas as reduced individual frustration, deficiency, and fatigue in the modes of perceptual and behavioral reductions, in grievances, and in improvement in quality of life.

The Concept of Institutions

All social organizations are institutionalized in terms of written and unwritten rules and regulations to which people in a society must conform to maintain legitimacy in such a society. Institutions are those more or less formalized and acculturalized entities by which society tries to bring order and discipline. They are orderly forms, conditions, procedures, and methods of grouping people and their activities. Societal institutions are systems of command, communication, cooperation, coordination, and control (the five Cs). As Wheelen and Hunger (1986: 294) have indicated, all institutions and/or organizations can be grouped into four basic categories.

1. *Private for profit:* These institutions operate their activities on the basis of the market economy for generating their means of survival (profit). Examples of these institutions range from small businesses to major corporations.

2. *Private not for profit:* These institutions are created by law and given limited monopolies to provide particular goods and/or services to a population at large or a subgroup (e.g., Department of Defense, courts, and public utilities).
3. *Private nonprofit:* These organizations operate through philanthropic, humanitarian, religious, and goodwill contributions. The major sources of these institutions are provided by donations, contributions, endowments, religious levies, and other charitable organizations (e.g., The United Way, churches).
4. *Public agencies:* These organizations operate on the basis of constituted laws and authorities to collect taxes and assess penalties while providing public services for all people in a community.

If a society is desiring and willing to be prevailed upon, then institutions can provide people with the basic cultural philosophical knowledge, cultural experiences, and political ideological practices.

The Concept of Material Things

The fourth element in a society encompasses tangible material things, such as stocks of resources, capital, labor, land, minerals, and all manufactured goods and products. These resources help a nation to shape society, and they are partly products of the nation's institutions, ideas, and beliefs. Economic institutions, together with the quantity of stock of resources, determine in a large part the type and quantity of a nation's material things. As material things change, the nation's ideas and beliefs also change. In the manufacturing and service industries, three factors have traditionally been identified as major instruments: (1) *Capital,* which is subject to interest; (2) *Land,* which is subject to ownership, rent, and/or lease; and (3) *Labor,* which is subject to legal, ethical, and moral contractual bindings.

For the past 100 years in industrialized nations, both neoclassical and neo-Marxist political economies have, to a large extent, distanced themselves from classical political economy, which emphasized land, capital, and labor. Instead, they emphasized the two-factor models, which aggregate land with rent and/or lease and capital with interest. The appropriateness of neoclassical labor-capital models in a capitalistic society is denoted in those economies where land, not capital, is dominated by landowners. Such a perception has not changed. Nevertheless, the terms of rent and lease are not explicitly recognized. Recently, attempts have been made to rebuild neoclassical economics to accommodate *institutional behavior.* These initiatives are now reversing to the grassroots systems of special historic rights, but, again, without defining property rights in any way immediately useful to the interests of labor (Smiley, 1995: 290). However, it should be indicated that nowadays, the emergence of technological patents, trademarks, and copyrights have provided skillful and specialized labor privileges for obtaining some bargaining power and advantages from manufacturing and/or service operations.

Some cultures are highly materialistic, some to such an extent that the ruling class views their subordinated classes of people as soulless commodities to be bought and/or sold (e.g., communist countries, slavery, and Islamic theocracy). These cultures are usually regarded as the first formalistic believers that universal principles are necessary to constitute existing things as the presence of *matter.* Atomists view that all things are made of molecules—basically water. The Greek philosopher Anaximander believed that all things in the universe are formed from an original chaos or gas. Thus, on the basis of such a cultural belief, Anaximander foreshadowed modern nebular theories of the origin of the universe in the nineteenth century (Weber, 1960: 163).

In some cultures, material things are means and ends of the social order and competition. Having access to material things divides people from one another. Instead of all people sharing and living in harmony and peace, possession of material things divides a society into classes of people. The owners of material things are viewed as the means of production on one side and the tenants as workers on the other. For example, in communist and authoritarian countries, societies are divided in two basic classes of people: very rich and powerful and very poor and powerless. The states, laws, courts, police, schools, churches, and media are all controlled either by the political elite ruling class, by plutocrats, or by both. The end result is exploitation of human resources. Exploitation of human resources is the alienation of the lower classes of people to the full benefit of the elite ruling class. In primitive societies, classes of citizens have been categorized only by material ownership, not by intellectuality. The consequential results could be called, in a general term, exploitation and alienation of human resources through wage slavery. Materialistic cultures cannot exist without the exploitation of material things, including people.

The Concept of Knowledge and Technoculture

The fourth element in a society encompasses its scientific, artistic, and technological capabilities. An individual is a highly systemized and integrated creature. For the discovery of their environment, individuals use three tools: sciences, technologies, and arts. They take in data through their biological perceptual senses from surroundings. Then they start processing the data through experimenting and distinctive judging. Finally, they express themselves through intuitive declarations of findings. Thinking is a type of intuitive process that is based not only on individual intelligence, but on rationality as well. Experience refers to the reflective behavioral thinking of habitual order of past actions in practice and conveying these memories to the present. Sensations refer to those processes in which individuals take in information via their senses. In contrast, intuition refers to those final decision-making processes which typically absorb information by means of imagination—by viewing the whole assessment of causes and effects. Individuals are teleological purposeful creatures through their own experimental preferences. Human beings are multidimensional purposive creatures viewed as sophists, scientists, technologists, and artists: (1) A sophist views the whole reasoning of causes and effects of existence. He or she theorizes reasons for continuity of survival and finalized life. (2) A scientist applies his or her intellectual capabilities to generalize scientific theorized problem solving. (3) A technologist conveys scientific pragmatic intuitions into material things and innovates and invents software and hardware. (4) An artist creates sensational and emotional expressions through manifestation of his or her own modes of feelings and desires.

Perhaps the most important cultural implication of technology is the growing social role of knowledge. Societies are learning that people need to attend not only to the importance of science and technology alone, but also to knowledge and the institutions of knowledge in general. Acquisition of knowledge refers to those individuals' perceptual capabilities that typically take in information via scientific methodology. They are most comfortable when they are containing the details of all possible and feasible situations, and are more quantified, concrete, and understand specified facts. Technology has its own characteristics:

1. It multiplies material or physical possibilities.
2. It changes its physical features.
3. It removes some previous options.
4. It creates new opportunities.
5. It diversifies capabilities.
6. It explores human efforts.
7. It forms social changes.
8. It creates new values.
9. It has powerful means to urge itself into adoption
   and widespread use of diversified resources and tools.

Throughout history, scientists and technologists have developed new techniques and resources such as machines, computers, and data and information processing systems. All of these resources, such as software and hardware, disseminate information and the results become integral parts of societal cultures. Technological experiments brought significant changes in individuals and societal value systems. One important feature necessary for the success of all industries is ethical and moral intelligence gathering. Shani and Sena (1994: 247) state that:

> Previous research has come up with what is called a social ethical subsystem, which considers every organization to be made up of a social

subsystem and a technical subsystem to produce something valued by the environmental subsystem.

This takes into account the fact that today's cultures are becoming more automated in every aspect of discoveries. Moreover, automation and technology have become a target in those societies that are pursuing higher productivity.

The result of the integration of sciences and technologies is very fascinating. It has created a new form of multicultural knowledge. Kodama (1992: 70) states that it will have a great impact within the biological and chemical industries, which will create a fourth generation of material. He claims that: "The fourth generation will allow engineers to custom design new materials by manipulating atoms and electrons." One product that is being considered as qualifying for this category is carbon fibers, which are being used to make airframes for airplanes; the next in biotechnology is cloning.

Today, the use of videotape, teleconference, and computer media has become a vital part of our multicultures. With these technological facilities, people around the world can communicate with one another in seconds.

In the ever-changing world of technology, cultures now face increased competition. This forces some nations to open their sociopolitical doors and others to react and go with the multicultural flow. Many nations have been able to adapt to this change with flexible automation and many of these sophisticated technologies can help nations tremendously. It can save nations time and money through the use of networks, e-mail, groupware, "chat" systems, videoconferencing, and multimedia. Businesses can also reduce the cost of operations and labor. A groupware information system categorizes integrated knowledge of individuals into departments, departments into divisions, and divisions into the total organizational knowledge. Organizational groupware information systems provide both vertical and horizontal linkages to all positions. Nevertheless, there is an inherent tension between vertical and horizontal groupware information systems. Whereas vertical linkages are designed primarily for commanding and controlling the information flow, horizontal linkages are designed for coordination, cooperation, and collaboration to minimize the tension among organizational groups.

Telecommunication systems in organizations increase profits tremendously. In the education industry, for example, it saves time and effort not only for the student but for professors as well. The use of networks provides that extra edge in obtaining information from the mainframe of resources. In the medical industry, it allows doctors and nurses to look up information about a rare disease or even to see what serious side effects a medication can have on patients. As McAteer (1994: 61) states:

> New technologies provide information on demand, build banks of shared knowledge, and enable real-time, structured learning events to transcend boundaries of time and space. The technologies become tools that we use to build our solutions.

Everyday technology is becoming more advanced, giving marketers a helping hand. In the early part of the 1980s, the Corning Glass Corporation, for example, invested heavily in the research of waveguides—glass fibers created to replace traditional phone lines. Such breakthrough technology revolutionized human civilization, specifically the communication industry. It provided telecommunications by light instead of electricity, boosting information capacity hundreds of thousands of times. One hair-thin glass fiber—a waveguide—can carry 6,000 telephone calls—as much as a four-inch-thick bundle of copper wires. This new product carried more capacity in less space (Magaziner and Patinkin, 1990: 266).

The Concept of Religion

The sixth element in society is religion. What is religion? Defining religion is a tool and to some degree it is arbitrary. Religion is an abstract of beliefs. We need not undertake a history or catalog of definitions. A hundred or more can be gathered in the space of a few hours; for our purposes, as Yinger (1970: 4) states: "Three kinds of definitions will suffice. One type expresses valuation; . . . what religion 'really' or 'basically' is in terms of what, . . . (1) It 'ought' to be . . . Other definitions are (2) 'descriptive' or (3) 'substantive.' They designate certain kinds of beliefs and practices as religion but do not evaluate them. . . ." For some years, a number of writers have expressed the view that Tylor's (1924) definition of religion: "belief in Spiritual Beings," was essentially sound (Goody, 1961: 142-164; Horton, 1960: 201-226). On the other hand, some may prefer to define religion in terms of value or in terms of essence.

Religion should not be viewed as only a cultural fact; it should be viewed also as a manifestation of behavioristic character of an individual and as one aspect of a group of people. Also, religion could be defined as that with which we are concerned ultimately. Bellah (1964: 358) asserts that: "Religion is a set of symbolic forms and acts which relate men to the ultimate condition of his [or her] existence." Briefly, as Geertz (1966: 4) defines,

> A religion is: (1) a system of symbols which acts to (2) establish powerful, pervasive, and long-lasting moods and motivations in men by (3) formulating conception of a general order of existence and (4) clothing these conceptions with such an aura of actuality that (5) the moods and motivations seem uniquely realistic.

Since the above definition is highly abstract, in an adequate view, it would seem, we must recognize that an individual has potentialities both for social life and hostility as well as for the self-centered pursuit of values. How do societies manage to keep the latter at a minimum (or at least aimed in a direction not likely to injure the social order) while strengthening the potentialities for social life? One may assert that those societies that did not learn to do this were simply torn apart and disappeared.

The Concept of Intellectual Potency

The seventh element in a society is intellectual potency. Artificial potency, compared with people's intellectual potency, however, can be considered a new part of society. The instrument of this new type of potency — mental potency — is the computer. In essence, our resources are controlled by information. This dimension may be the most important part of industrialized society. Although resources have contributed to our welfare, our use of them can bring about constructive social consequences too; but misapplication of technology or information raises serious doubts and inspires fear. Our educational and academic challenge is to harness the power of mental potency to the benefit of the human race—not to the destruction of humanity.

The Concept of Government

The eighth element in society is government. The social system and the laws of public policies governing citizens' rights and duties are major considerations for the concept of government. There is today no aspect of societal operations that government cannot and will not regulate if the occasion to do sound popular or legislative support exists. There are three major philosophical foundations for the establishment of a government: utilitarian, egalitarian, and universalism.

Government is found in serving:

- The greatest good for the greatest number and the greatest misery for the smallest number (utilitarianism)
- The greatest good for the smallest advantaged or disadvantaged number, and the greatest misery for the greatest number (egalitarianism)
- A balancing of various principles of fairness for all (universalism)

McCollum (1998: A28) states that: "Jeremy Bentham, English philosopher, is often thought as the founder of *utilitarianism,* the school of philosophy that holds that the purpose of government is to foster the happiness of the individual, and that the greatest happiness of the most people should be the goal of human existence." This type of philosophy can be found in representative democracy.

Egalitarians base their philosophical views on the position that all human beings are equal in some fundamental respect. Each individual should have an equal access to a society's resources including products and services. They believe that resources should be allocated in equal portions regardless of people's individual natural and historical cultural differences. Egalitarianism holds that the maximal role of government is to maintain justice in duty and rights among individuals. Inequality is justified only if its existence causes all individuals (especially the favored advantaged or disadvantaged classes of people) to be treated equally for the benefit of the society. This type of philosophy can be found in authoritarian governments.

The third philosophy is the universalization of the role of the government, which can also be called *intuitionism.* That role of the government is not to promote happiness for either majority or minority groups of people, but for all. The role of government cannot contradict the happiness of another group of people within a nation. The government's role is commanded to do what is right for all, not for a part. Intuitionism government is perceived as the accommodation of several multiprinciples of justice, including liberty, property rights, and equal human rights for all. All people are free to choose the kinds of opportunities they want to take, or the kinds of contributions they want to make. They have a universal humanitarian responsibility to own and dispense their properties, including intellectual ones, as they choose. Human beings are considered not as means (majority or minority groups), they are considered themselves as agents to be ends in themselves, free to act according to their humane purposes. This type of philosophy can be found in participatory democracy.

Political considerations define the political ideology and legal parameters in which the social institutions must or may wish to be considered. All nations around the world, in the course of political ideology, have a general theme of political viewpoints or perspectives about themselves, their social lifestyles, and their political environments. These points of views vary in the degree to which they are visionary, conscious, and codified. In this matter, we use the term "formal doctrine" to represent complex combinations of viewpoints that are visionary.

Political ideology or a visionary theorization of other societal order could serve as well, although it tends not to emphasize the conscious and codified aspects. The political doctrine includes an elaborated system of concepts, spelling out the entire structure of political means and ends, without specified institutional arrangements. Sometimes, in analyzing the social reality of a political doctrine, it becomes clearer by stepping back from the concrete images of day-to-day activities and events and analyzing the larger historical context of a political doctrine.

In the conceptualization of a political doctrine in a nation, apart from its substantive content, several cultural dimensions seem significant. They include the degree of formalization, the degree of abstractness, the degree of consistency, and the degree of effectiveness.

- *The degree of formalization:* A formal political doctrine which could be called "a manifest function" contains the sole statement of political goals and objectives for which a nation strives. Also, it contains subgoals to be approached "on the way" toward the more general and ultimate objectives. Similarly, it contains specific means—that is, alternative actions of social structure and procedures—that holds a high probability of attaining the political goals. In effect, it is a comprehensive, integrated, and correlated political plan—a guide for all individual citizens and groups of a nation to enjoy equal protection.

- *The degree of abstractness:* Political doctrines may vary also in the degree to which they are abstract or concrete. As citizens use a doctrinal language system, it is an abstract and provides legitimate rights and duties. The problem is in variability of concrete interpretations. For instance, in the political doctrines of some nations we find "equal opportunity in education." But in implementation of this phrase we find interpretations and operational practices, which differ from their political doctrines.
- *The degree of consistency:* The degree to which the content of a formal doctrine is consistent or integrated with the national objectives seems another dimension worthy of further cultural understanding. In this analytical domain, we should find out how a doctrine is organized, with what degree of variation it has been formalized — simple as opposed to being complex or complicated—and, related to the complexity, the doctrine's pervasiveness or the scope—that is, how much of societal life of the individual citizen's is covered by that political doctrine.
- *The degree of political effectiveness:* A doctrine could be analyzed, irrespective of its content, in terms of the degree to which it does have effectiveness or emotional qualities. In this matter, we should distinguish a difference between the doctrine's goals and objectives, which necessarily committed the individuals and social organizations, to its implicit value systems. A doctrine in our judgment is ultimately acting a cultural faith in effectively endorsing certain ends in societal life and the degree to which it is phrased on irrelevant or highly tenuous grounds.

In political environmental analysis the existence and exercise of power are other matters which we should carefully review. "Power" is one of those value-laden words about whose definition there is general agreement. Nevertheless, there is a wide disagreement on its meaning in an operational setting. Fundamentally, power is the ability of an individual, group, or organization to influence or determine the behavior, expectations, and actions of other individuals, groups, or organizations to conform to one's own wishes, or in a political context, to a doctrine's objectives. Power is always related to authority and influence. Authority may be viewed as the right to exercise power. Coercion can be either a form or a component of power. Dominance or domination is a form of power. Consequently, power is a set of dynamic functional forces used to implement the desirable items of an ideology or a doctrine among people.

Sociopolitical and economic forces are forms or tools of power. Both material gains and prestige are consequential results of political power. In our society, there are some strongly held views about power, strength, right, jurisdiction, control, command, domination, and authority—often interchangeably used words. Without elaborating on their different meanings, they all project physical might, mental ability, or moral efficacy.

The modern concepts of power look more toward the functions performed by a power holder than did earlier concepts. The modern concept of political power is conceived as a force to resolve societal problems (see Figure 3.2).

In a pluralistic society there are many semiautonomous and autonomous groups or institutions through which power is diffused. No one group has overwhelming power over all others, and each has direct or indirect impact on all others. The political doctrine and constitution combine a unified set of beliefs that citizens must respect them. This combination sets up social institutions, establishes hierarchies, and allocates societal power. Legitimized

FIGURE 3.2. Societal Power Envelope

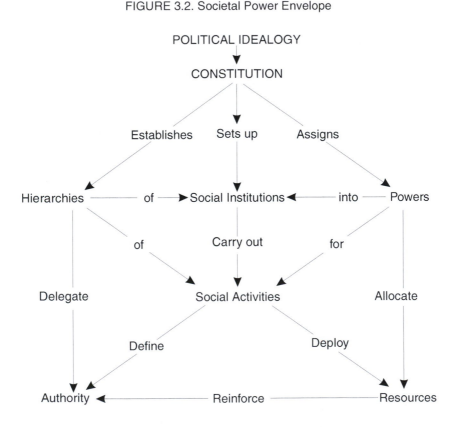

power should be implemented in organizations through hierarchical authorities in order to deploy different resources for achieving social goals and objectives.

Finally, bases of power refers to the sources which are available to power
holders as they exercise either authority or influence. Several bases of
power are available in a society. These depend on the sources and the types
of power, such as: coercive, remunerative, normative, traditional, charis-
matic, and knowledge-based power.

SUMMARY

People by their very nature are not self-sufficient. They need to work together to fulfill their needs. Socialization is a continuous process throughout
life. It involves the process by which people develop and acquire a set of
customs and procedures for making decisions, resolving disputes, and regulating their behavior. The term society encompasses all tangible and intangible concepts and things related to a lively group of human beings. It is a nation and/or a professional group of people. Inherent to this concept, there are
eight fundamental interrelated parts that make up the abstract of a dynamic
society. These are people, culture, institutions, material things, knowledge
and technology, religion, intellectual potency, and governments. All individuals who gather for the purpose of satisfying their needs are called *people*. *Culture* is a means to cope with surrounding uncertainties by providing
predictable ways of expressing and affirming values, beliefs, norms, and expectations toward an end. It is a collective programming of the minds and
behaviors of people to make their societal lives very smooth. Culture needs
to be learned, shared, and transferred. Culture is learning, behaving, and
evolving. *Institutions* provide those basic cultural philosophies and political
ideologies in which a society desires and is willing to be promoted. Material
things such as stocks of resources, capital, labor, land, minerals, and all
manufacturing goods and products are viewed as necessities of human life.
Religion is an abstract of human beliefs. Religion is believing in spiritual
being(s). It valuates what the belief ought to be. *Intellectual potency* means
mental synergy. The *government* is a social system which regulates citizens'
behavior.

CHAPTER QUESTIONS FOR DISCUSSION

1. How do you define the concept of a society?
2. How do you define people in a society?
3. How do you perceive the concept of culture?
4. How do you label a culture?

5. How do you define the concept of institution?
6. How do you perceive material cultures?
7. How do you apply the concept of knowledge and technoculture?
8. How do you perceive the concept of intellectual potency?
9. How do you define the concept of government?
10. How do you understand the concept of religion?

LEARNING ABOUT YOURSELF EXERCISE #3

How Do You Understand Your Culture?

Following are fifteen items for rating how important each one is to you on a scale of 0 (I don't believe) to 100 (I strongly believe). Write the number 0-100 on the line to the left of each item.

I don't believe		I somewhat believe		I strongly believe
0	25	50	75	100

How do you perceive the following statements about your national culture?

_____ 1. My national culture is very conservative and I like it.
_____ 2. My culture is a part of the national political ideology.
_____ 3. My culture is futuristic and promotes change.
_____ 4. My culture is rooted from denominated historical cultural groups' political-religious ideologies.
_____ 5. My national culture is resistance to change.
_____ 6. My national culture promotes civic commitments.
_____ 7. My national political leaders are ethical and moral.
_____ 8. I trust people.
_____ 9. My national culture should be universal.
_____ 10. My government is truly defending our national interest.
_____ 11. The national judiciary system of my country strives for justice.
_____ 12. Our religious leaders are very spiritual.
_____ 13. I trust mass media.
_____ 14. In my culture, most corporate managers are cheating the government and people.
_____ 15. Bribery is a popular form for doing business in my country.

Turn to next page for scoring directions and key.

SCORING DIRECTIONS AND KEY FOR EXERCISE #3

Transfer the numbers for each of the fifteen items to the appropriate column, then add up the five numbers in each column.

Idealistic	Bureaucratic	Pragmatic
1. _____	2. _____	3. _____
5. _____	4. _____	10. _____
7. _____	6. _____	12. _____
8. _____	11. _____	13. _____
9. _____	14. _____	15. _____
Your Totals _____	_____	_____
Total Scores 500	500	500

The higher the total in any dimension, the higher the importance you place on that set. The closer the numbers in the three dimensions, the more aware you are of your society.

Make up a categorical scale of your findings on the basis of more weight for the values of each category.

For example:

    1. 400 Idealistic
    2. 375 Bureaucratic
    3. 200 Pragmatic

    Your Totals   875
    Total Scores   1,500

After you have tabulated your scores, compare them with others on your team or in your class. You will find different judgmental patterns among people with diverse scores for the national cultural understanding.

CASE STUDY:
THE WHISTLE-BLOWERS:
SMITHKLINE BEECHAM PLC

Whistle-blowing can be considered a morally, ethically, and legally neutral act by an employee and/or an informant making public some wrongdoings of a firm's internal operation, practice, or policies that affect the public interest. Bribing government authorities and cheating the public are illegal in the United States and in many other countries. This case is about a "Labscam" investigation conducted by the Department of Justice in a multinational corporation in the United States.

SmithKline Beecham PLC was incorporated on January 24, 1989, under the name Goldslot PLC. On April 11, 1989, SmithKline entered an agreement for the merger of Beecham Group PLC and SmithKline Beckman Corp. excluding Allergan Inc., Beckman Instruments Inc., and their respective subsidiaries. This transaction was implemented on July 26, 1989, through an exchange of securities. In 1992, the company acquired the Corsodyl business from ICI Pharmaceuticals. During 1992, SmithKline Beecham PLC (SKBPLC) disposed of the Manetti Roberts Toiletries business in Italy, and the Personal Care Products business in North America, List Pharmaceuticals in Germany, and the Collistar cosmetics business in Italy. During 1992, SKBPLC also acquired the Clinical Trials Division of Winchester Research Laboratories and many other companies.

SKBPLC continuously produces innovative medicine and consumer health care products. The company specializes in the development and manufacture of pharmaceuticals, vaccines, over-the-counter medicines and consumer health care services. In addition, SKBPLC is better known for its clinical laboratory testing and disease management. Some of the testing services they offer include blood, urine, and tissue testing for use in screening and diagnosis. They also serve as a central laboratory testing location for clinical trials for pharmaceutical and biotechnology companies in Europe and North America. SKBPLC offers emergency twenty-four-hour toxicology tests and substance abuse testing which is certified by the U.S. Department of Health and Human Services.

SmithKline Beecham PLC has its main headquarters in New Horizons Court, Brentford, Middlesex, United Kingdom. This company has several subsidiaries all over the world, some of which are located in France, Germany, Argentina, China, India, Italy, Mexico, Japan, Austria, Panama, and many other countries. This company runs its operation with a total of 52,400 employees. It also has 119,136 stockholders.

Sometime during 1997, through a nationwide "Labscam" investigation done by the Justice Department of the United States with the help of three

Sources: The Wall Street Journal (1998). "U.S. Judge Says Whistle-Blowers to Get $42.3 Million." April 10, p. 1; *Moody's International Manual* (1998). Zoholi Jr., D. A., Publisher. New York: Moody's Investors Service, Inc., pp. 10777-10779.

whistle-blowers (Robert J. Merena, Charles W. Robinson Jr., and Glenn Grossenbacher), SmithKline Beecham Clinical Laboratories Inc., a strategic business unit (SBU) of SmithKline Beecham PLC, was found to be involved in Medicare fraud. The company was accused of paying kickbacks to doctors while billing the U.S. government for laboratory tests not performed, along with other numerous violations. Although the company has denied the allegations, stating that the violations were unintentional as a result of confusion with regulations and guidelines, through a court hearing process, it agreed to pay the U.S. government $325 million in 1997.

Another issue of such a settlement was the problem of payments for the three whistle-blowers. The Justice Department had resisted paying the three men the 15 to 25 percent share of the SKBPLC's settlement specified for the whistle-blowers by the federal False Claim Act. The Justice Department argued that most of the $325 million settlement had been obtained through its nationwide "Labscam" investigations which had nothing to do with the three men. Nonetheless, U.S. District Court Judge Donald W. VanArtsdalen ruled that the three whistle-blowers made a major contribution to the government's case and that they helped bring in nearly all the settlement.

In relation to this case, SmithKline Beecham PLC acted unethically, immorally, illegally, and inhumanely toward U.S. society and specifically to elderly American patients. They betrayed the medical profession by paying kickbacks to medical doctors. They misled the government by billing them for Medicare patients' test fees that were never performed, and provided false laboratory results for elderly patients to be kept in their medical record files.

Finally, Judge VanArtsdalen said the three whistle-blowers accounted for all but about $15 million of that total. The U.S. government agreed to pay the three whistle-blowers a minimum of $9.7 million but only if they dropped claims to a larger portion. However, the Justice Department did not prosecute SKBPLC's fraud which provided doctors and patients with false laboratory results. The Justice Department ignored its accountability to those patients who were mistreated and suffered from side effects of the consequential results of misdiagnosis and mistreatment by false laboratory results. The government's concern was only the financial side of the case. The case was closed.

Chapter 4

Contemporary Multicultural Behavior

The unexamined scientific analysis of multiculturalism can be viewed as an ignorant castle that imprisons a manager within his or her perceptions.

CHAPTER OBJECTIVES

When you have read this chapter you should be able to understand human behavior through:

- three branches of the common body of knowledge: philosophy, science, and technology,
- indication of the principle concerns of philosophical inquiries,
- indication of the scientific concerns of human behavior, and
- illustration of the technological effectiveness on human behavior.

INTRODUCTION

People's behavior can be studied through application of natural, social, and behavioral sciences, philosophy, and informational technology. In a general traditional view, the basic academic integration of anthropology, sociology, and psychology and their rigorous research approaches made excellent contributions to the emergence of a new subacademic and cross-fertilized knowledge—namely behavioral culturalogy. Such a diffusive and integrated body of knowledge can be applied for better understanding of peoples' relations and behavior in the newly global environments of international business.

This chapter will begin with a review of the required body of knowledge in the field of behavioral culturalogy. By defining the terms, functions, and approaches of culturalogy, you will be familiar with different beliefs and value systems in the field of international business. This chapter offers a very in-depth and broad scientific, behavioral, and cultural studies discussion which should establish a new look at today's multinational and multicultural organizations.

In this chapter, you will learn how to apply scientific theories for finding multicultural similarities and differences in a multinational physical environment. The definition of each branch of knowledge will allow you to understand an explanation of the relationship among scientific, technological, philosophical, and artistic understanding of cultural behavior. A discussion of the typology of a holistic knowledge illustrates how cultural behavior in home and host countries could improve a multinational corporation's operational capabilities.

THE NEW FIELD OF BEHAVIORAL CULTURALOGY

Traditional scientific management, bureaucracy, human relations, organizational behavior, system theories, and other approaches are valid theories to some extent to be applied in domestic organizational problem solving. Those theories have taken heuristic, cognitive, behavioristic, pragmatic, and humanistic approaches for modeling organizational behavioral decision making. However, none of the above management theories paid special attention to the application of behavioral culturalogy in their hypothetical theorization as a new form of problem solving.

Today, the emergence of cultural behavioral variables and their consequential effects in multinational and multicultural organizations have drastically changed managerial decision-making processes. Behavioral culturalogy within the context of the international free market economy is a new field of inquiry and needs to be applied and directed synergistically for positive outcomes.

The scientific application of behavioral culturalogy is critical to the goal achievement of multinational and multicultural organizations. Multinational managers should be familiar with cultural philosophy and medical symptomalogy of both home and host countries. The use of the behavioral culturalogical approach is an interdisciplinary *holistic* knowledge that applies philosophical, social, behavioral, and natural sciences, and technological information in international problem solving. Application of the behavioral culturalogical approach can directly help managers better understand, predict, and direct the international expected behavior of international producers and consumers (see Figure 4.1).

INTERCULTURAL CONTACT:
PROCESSES AND OUTCOMES

For more than a century, most management approaches ignored traditional beliefs and values of peoples and purely neglected the crucial effects

FIGURE 4.1. Holistic Interdisciplinary Relationships Between Academic Philosophy, Sciences, and Technology

I.   PHILOSOPHY

Metaphysics:
Cosmology, Ontology, Theology, and Causalogy

Epistemology

Axiology:
Morality, Ethics, Aesthetics: Humanities, Arts, Music, Dances, and Movies and Theatrical Drama

II.   SCIENCES

Observational Sciences:
Astronomy, Geology, Physics, Chemistry, Phenomenology (Science of Mathematics, Science of Logic, and Scientific Quantitative Methods)

Natural Sciences:
Zoology (Animals), Botany (Plants), Protistology (One-Celled Organisms), Biorheology, Biology, Physiology, Microbiology, Immunology, Ecology and Evolution, Molecular and Cellular Biology

Social Sciences:
Economics, Geography, History, Political Sciences, and Demography

Behavioral Sciences:
Anthropology (Physical Anthropology, Cultural Anthropology, Archaeology, Anthropological Linguistics, Ethnology/Ethnography), Demography, Sociology, Psychology, and Social-Psychology

III.   TECHNOLOGY

Traditional Technologies:
Eolithic, Neolithic, Monolithic, Craftsmanship, and Synthetic

Modern Technologies:
Mechanistic, Automotive, Robotics, Cybernetic, Cyberrobotics, Microtechnology, Nanotechnology, and Cyberspace Technology

Source: Part I adapted from Weber, C. O. (1960). *Basic Philosophies of Education.* New York: Holt, Rhinehart, and Winston: 12.

of humanities, philosophy, religion, and other cultural perceptions within the workplace. For such a crucial shortfall, after briefing an overview on definition and application of philosophical, natural, social, and behavioral sciences, and technology, a general approach in multinational behavioral management has been provided in this chapter.

Intercultural contact among individuals has an ancient history, and cross-cultural interchange among nations is as old as recorded history. Historically, people traveled to other lands to settle or conquer, trade, convert, teach, and learn. Cohn (1979: 18) has identified various motives for cross-cultural contacts among individuals. He has found five modes of contacts: recreational, diversionary, experiential, experimental, and existential. Indeed, probably the best accounts of both intercultural and cross-cultural contacts come from interdisciplinary social scientists, novelists, playwrights, and philosophers.

Perhaps the most important question in multinational corporations is: What is the main philosophy behind intercultural and cross-cultural contacts? The answer is fairly easy: to discover potential opportunities for the exploitation of those markets. Other reasons in conjunction have been identified partly due to a shrinking world as a result of the jetliner and silicon-chip age, but largely also due to governmental intervention. For example, American expatriate managers who move abroad and back again to the United States are simply motivated by economic rewards. However, Torbiorn (1982) found in his study of Swedish business persons that motives and behaviors were much more complex. He found both "push motives" relating to dissatisfaction and "pull motives" relating to a belief in increased satisfaction being associated with the move. "Pull motives" included a special interest in the particular host country, increased promotion prospects, wider career opportunities, or generally more favorable economic gain. "Push motives" included negative rather than positive, and lesser rather than greater, freedom in choosing the host country. Such motives were associated with lower levels of adaptation and satisfaction.

Today, the universality of behavioral culturalogical approach indicates that preferred levels and modes of need-perception in all cultures are not the same. However, the ingredients of the modes of need perceptions are similar in all cultures. For example, let us start with the appeal of nudity in international advertising. The fascinating motive is not how much sex there is in international advertising. Contrary to cultural impressions, sexual appeals in advertising may be viewed as a sinful and/or unethical and immoral act in one culture and a joyful, praising, and/or legal act in another culture. Table 4.1 identifies intercultural and cross-cultural similarities and differences in American, Australian, Asian, and Middle Eastern cultural advertising perceptions and beliefs in nudity.

Englehart and Carnally (1997: 37) indicate that:

> Cross-cultural variation does not simply reflect the changes linked with modernization and post modernization processes: . . . each society works out its history in its own unique fashion, influenced by the culture, leaders, institutions, climate, geography, situation-specific events, and other unique elements that make up its own distinctive heritage.

While there may be several ways of classifying the importance of these unique cross-cultural characteristics, each society maintains its own uniqueness.

TABLE 4.1. Nudity's Cultural Appeal in Advertising

American Culture	Australian Culture	Asian Culture	Middle Eastern Culture
Nudity is legal under appropriate licensed conditions.	Nudity is a common perception in its aesthetic cultural behavior.	Nudity is a hidden agenda in personal perception for enjoying sexual life.	Nudity is illegal, immoral, unethical, ugly, and is sinful behavior.
Nudity in advertising has the effect of reducing brand recall.*	Nudity in advertising is more effective on men than women.	Nudity in advertising is part of the popular culture.	Nudity in advertising is prohibited by all means and ends.
Nudity in advertising is viewed as a psychological stimulation for companionship.*	Nudity in advertising is viewed as a cultural appeal for attraction of more tourists.	Nudity in advertising is viewed as a sense of cultural hospitality.	Nudity in underground advertising is viewed as a motive for individuals' sexual curiosity.

*Fowles, J. (1995). "Advertising's Fifteen Basic Appeals." In Petracca, M. F. and Sorapure, M. (Eds.), *Common Culture: Reading and Writing About American Popular Culture.* Englewood Cliffs, NJ: Prentice-Hall, p. 64.

The importance of cultural orientation of people toward individuals' existence and sociocultural and psychological needs plays an important role in shaping their cultural perceptions. In cross-cultural studies, we need to identify the prioritized similar and dissimilar needs of people in both home and host countries.

In cross-cultural study one particular list of fifteen needs has proven to be especially valuable. Fowles (1995: 61) has indicated in his research these needs as:

1. The need for sex
2. The need for affiliation
3. The need to nurture
4. The need for guidance
5. The need to egress
6. The need to achieve
7. The need to dominate
8. The need for prominence
9. The need for attention
10. The need for autonomy
11. The need to escape
12. The need to feel safe
13. The need for aesthetic sensations
14. The need to satisfy curiosity
15. Physiological needs: food, drink, sleep, etc.

To understand the importance of these needs, we need to understand not only the people themselves but also their cultural orientation and environmental conditions. Except for the physiological needs, the other fourteen needs are learned through cultural orientation. To do research in cross-culturalogy we need to identify six methods of knowledge.

SIX THEORIES OF BEHAVIORAL CULTURALOGICAL KNOWLEDGE

There are six theories of understanding things: revelation, coherence, presentative, representative, pragmatic, and intuition (Weber, 1960: 13-14).

The Revelation Theory

"This view holds that the final test of the truth of assertions is their consonance with the revelations of authority" (Weber, 1960: 13).

For example, when John H. Sununu was governor of New Hampshire (1983-1987), he greatly increased his expert credibility by taking sole control of the computer system that kept track of the state's finances (Van Fleet, 1991: 185).

The Coherence Theory

"This theory says that a statement is true if it is consistent with other statements accepted as true" (Weber, 1960: 13).

For example, when Robert J. Eaton took the position of CEO replacing Chrysler's "Mr. Charisma," Lee Iacocca, he believed in quantifiable short-term profits. Such a view is also being articulated by CEOs at Apple Computer, IBM, Aetna Life and Casuality, and General Motors (Robbins, 1998: 391).

The Presentative Theory

"This view holds that reality as presented to the mind in perception is known directly and without alteration. Errors of perceptions occur, but further observation is able to detect and explain them" (Weber, 1960: 13).

For example, on April 23, 1985, Roberto C. Goizueta, chairman of Coca-Cola, made a momentous announcement: "The best has been made ever better," he proclaimed. After ninety-nine years, the Coca-Cola Company had decided to abandon its original formula in favor of a sweeter variation, presumably an improved taste, which was named "New Coke." On that date, the chairman made an intercultural strategic decision to change the taste of Coca-Cola and within twenty-four hours, 81 percent of the U.S. population knew of the change (Demott, 1985: 55). Early results looked good; 150 million people tried New Coke. The decision looked unassailable, but not for long. On July 11, 1985, the top executive appeared on the stage in front of the Coca-Cola logo to announce that two types of Coke were available: (1) for those who were drinking New Coke and enjoying it, and (2) for those who wanted the original Coke. The message was that "we heard you," and the original taste of Coke was back. Despite $4 million and two years' research, the company had made a major miscalculation and "New Coke" became Coke in 1992. The original Coke is called Coca-Cola Classic (Hartley, 1998: 160).

The Representative Theory

"This view, again favored by certain realists, holds that our perceptions of objects are not identical with them. This differs from the presentative view sketched above which states that when we perceive truly, our perception is identical with the object perceived. This implies that the object perceived literally enters the mind which perceives it—a rather startling conclusion. The representative realist tries to be more cautious on this point. What we see when we look at a tree is only its image. The tree cannot be identical with this image. The image is in one's mind, and the mind is somehow located in the brain; if the tree is fifty feet high, there is not enough room (physically) in one's brain to accommodate it" (Weber, 1960: 14).

For example, researchers have introduced the idea of *culture distance* to account for the amount of distress experienced by a student from one culture studying in another. Babiker, Cox, and Miller (1980: 109) hypothesized that the degree of alienation, estrangement, and concomitant psychological distress was a function of distance between the student's own culture and the host culture. Also, Furnham and Bochner (1982) conducted a similar study and found that the degree of difficulty experienced by sojourners in negotiating everyday encounters is directly related to the disparity (or culture distance) between the sojourners' culture and the host society.

The Pragmatic Theory

"This view holds that statements are true if they work successfully in practice. If an idea or principle is effective in organizing knowledge or in the practical affairs of life then it is true" (Weber, 1960: 14).

For a society to continue over time it is imperative that it works out systematic traditional value systems for mating, childbearing, and education. If it fails to be regulated, it will die in a very short time. Some societies permit random mating and others have rules for determining who can marry, under what conditions, and according to what traditions. All societies around the world have patterned systems of marriage (Ferraro: 1994: 25).

For example, there are three *pragmatic* different legal systems concerning marriage: "common law," in England; "code law" in France; and "Sharia law" in Middle Eastern countries. "Common law" refers to that practical part of the law that grew up without benefit of legislation and resulted from court decisions. These rulings then in their pragmatic term became the precedent for subsequent litigation (Pegrum, 1959: 21) (e.g., in the United States a couple who have been living together for many years without church and/or governmental documentation could be considered by law as married). The code law refers to the body of laws of a state or a nation regulating ordinary private matters (e.g., in France, a mandatory marriage performed and documented by a government official rather than by a member of the clergy is upheld as legal marriage). The "Sharia law" refers to the traditional religious law which is upheld by both the state and the church through Moslem scripture (e.g., in the Middle Eastern cultures, men officially can marry four women either by law and/or by the Mollah or Ayatollah. However, men can marry many women on a temporary basis by following neither the state nor the church. This type of marriage is upheld by law and by the church, because it is an agreement between two adult people).

The Intuition Theory

> "This view varies so much in its definition that it sometimes becomes identical with some of the other theories . . . At one extreme, intuition refers to a mysterious and immediate inner source of knowledge apart from both perceptual observation and reasoning. . . . At the other extreme the term intuition has been used to designate generally accredited and immediate ways of knowing, such as immediate sensation, or the immediate awareness we may have of self-evident or axiomatic truth." (Weber, 1960: 14)

The U.S. economy is a commercial-exchanging economy based on the system of free enterprise (free entry and free competition) (Cohen, 1995: 5). By his intuitive efforts, forty-five-year-old William H. Gates III became the richest man in America, and Microsoft and its leader made over $7 billion within two decades. It should be noted that William H. Gates III was a college dropout. In 1974 at age eighteen, he and his friend Paul Allen established a small company in Albuquerque, New Mexico, and developed software for the Altair, the first personal computer. Yoder (1992), in *The Wall Street Journal,* described: "The generational shift in the computer industry is unfolding. . . . As leadership slips away from the old behemoth . . . it is being picked up by two young juggernauts—Intel Corp. and Microsoft Corp.—which both were nurtured by IBM."

KNOWLEDGE-BASED INTEGRATION
OF PHILOSOPHY, SCIENCES, ARTS,
AND TECHNOLOGICAL INFORMATION

Behavioral culturalogical approach is relying on synergistic knowledge-based integration of philosophy, technology, arts, and sciences. The main reason for applying the interdisciplinary approach in multicultural behavior is based on a holistic view of the concept of peoples' culture, which includes all human-made knowledge. Among some of the special features of multicultural behaviorism that contribute to multinational organizations are: active participatory observation, the emic view on cultural values, the fundamental value orientation of cultural concession, the synergistic behavioral end results, and holistic cultural relativism.

The behavioral culturalogical approach holds that organizational behavior is essentially universal. Labor forces and customers around the globe, particularly in the United States, are becoming more diverse in terms of national origin, race, religion, gender, predominant age categories, and personal preferences.

With a fair viewing on global cultures, certain features have been initiated originally in one or several parts of the world independently and then spread through the process of diffusion to other cultures. The congruence theory of managerial knowledge holds that the crucial test of reality concerning the universal nature of human behavior in the workplace is the degree of harmony between employer-employee propositions regarded as true. Such a global mandate urges multinational corporations to strive for establishing multilingual and multicultural management systems.

The world is shrinking rapidly. Multinational corporate assignments are becoming a standard part of a well-rounded business. Cross-cultural understanding and behavioral skills are a necessity. As a result, the traditional management knowledge, which has been highly fragmented and incomplete, is not effective anymore. With an eye toward educating tomorrow's global managers, we need to think and behave globally.

Today, multinational organizations are faced with unsolved potential problems and issues based mainly on the misunderstanding of multicultural value systems. It is necessary to move from tolerance to appreciation when managing multicultural organizations. The main challenge of today's and especially tomorrow's managers is to be aware of specific multicultural changes, along with the factors contributing to the organizational synergy.

In such a domain of inquiry, the main question is: what about human behavior within multicultural environments? The answer is very complex. This complexity can provide multicultural synergy, because when values are synthesizing and emerging in a new favorable condition, the end result will be synergy. Multicultural synergy sometimes can be demonstrated by the mathematical analogy that $2 + 2 = 5$ instead of 4. If the multicultural synergy is beyond the sum of the total parts, then positive synergy has occurred

(Weber, 1960: 113; Moran and Harris: 1982: 5). However, given the various cross-cultural barriers and cultural deficiencies, the end result may be represented by the equation $2 + 2 = 3$, if the sum is below the total parts. This will illustrate that the organizational incumbents are in conflict.

Philosophy

Philosophy is the basic foundation for conceptual understanding of human life by the examination of cause and effect of existence. In traditional conception, philosophy endeavors to integrate all human knowledge. Inquiries such as the following domains of knowledge have shaped philosophy:

- Was there a beginning of time?
- Will there be an end to time?
- Is the universe infinite or does it have boundaries?
- Is the universe expanding or is it shrinking?
- Or could it be both infinite and without boundaries?

On viewing these conceptions and others, the current problems of philosophers still relate to three areas of inquiry: metaphysics, epistemology, and axiology. Thus, philosophy is the integration of all human knowledge and erects a systematic view on the nature and the place of human beings in it. In an attempt to study multicultural behavior of different groups of people, we should try to understand the three above modes of arriving at knowledge.

Metaphysics

This concerns issues on the nature of reality and humanity's place within it. What is the matter in its essence, and how does it form the vast material cosmos ordered in time and place (cosmology)? What is the essential nature of the mind and/or soul? What about the existence and the nature of a superpower—God (theologically)? What does it mean to exist? What is the criterion for existing (ontology)? (Ontology refers to knowledge of the nature of the world around us.) What are the ultimate causes of things being what they are (causalogy)?

Phenomenology

Phenomenology is a scientific manner of thinking that considers things as phenomena. It is a kind of knowledge that reveals a fact, occurrence, or circumstance observed or observable that impresses the observer as extraordinary phenomena. Phenomenology describes values of remarkable things or persons through scientific appearance or immediate intuitive objective of awareness in the human mind. Phenomenology is a qualitative conceptual awareness which can be manifested constructively by quantitative value judgments in the human mind. Rational decision-making processes in the field of business consist essentially of using certain axioms or assumptions, stated as principles of applicability of successful experiences and knowledge of the world of business experience.

Epistemology

Espistemology has to do with the problem of knowledge: We have knowledge. How is this possible? What does knowledge mean? Can all knowledge be traced to the greatest gateways of our senses—to the senses plus activity of reasoning, or to the means and ends of reasoning? Do feelings render wordless but true knowledge? Does true knowledge ever come in the form of immediate intuition? How can we identify different branches of knowledge?

Axiology

Axiology is concerned with the problems of value. There are three main traditional fields of value inquiries: (1) morality, (2) ethics, and (3) aesthetics.

Morality. The term "moral" is derived from the Latin word *Mores.* In *The Oxford English Dictionary* (1963) "moral" means "habits in life in regard to right and wrong conduct," or "Of or pertaining to character or disposition, considered as good or bad, virtuous or vicious; of or pertaining to the distinction between right and wrong, or good and evil, in relation to the actions, volitions, or character of responsible beings." In an etymological sense, it means "pertaining to the individual's manner and custom of judgments." *Morality* is the term used to manifest the individual's virtue. Morality also has to do with an individual's character and the type of behaviors that emanate from that valuable character. *Virtue* refers to the excellence of intellect and wisdom. Morality's end result, through intellectual truthfulness, righteousness, and goodness of thoughts and conducts, is happiness. *Conscience* is a base for moral acts. It is the ability to reason about self-conduct, together with a set of values, feelings, and dispositions to do or to avoid conceiving and perceiving actions. If *morality* is viewed as telling the whole truth, then *amorality* is telling a partial truth. Each individual is morally obligated to develop an objectively correct conscience; but their own usually is obligated to behave in accordance with his/her conscience. Failure to fulfill one's self moral commitment can lead not only to blame and shame, but also to remorse (De George, 1995: 119).

Ethics. The term *ethics* is derived from the Greek word *ethos.* Ethos means the genius of an institution or system. Also, it refers to the science of morals and the department of study concerned with the principles of human duty. Ethics concerns itself with human societal conduct, activity, and behavior, which are manifested through knowledge and deliberated behavior.

Ethics is the collective societal conscious awareness of a group of people. Ethic's end results, through societal conscious understanding of fairness, justness, and worthiness, can lead human beings toward social justice and peaceful behavior.

Aesthetics. Of particular interest to human concepts are the formal aspects of art, color, and form, because of the symbolic meanings they convey. Aesthetics pertains to a culture's sense of beauty and good taste and is expressed in arts, drama, music, folklore, and dance (Ball and McCulloch Jr., 1988, p. 269). It is the reflection of the human expression in humanities: arts, music, dance, movies, and theatrical drama. Of particular interest to multicultural behaviorism is the artistic combination of humanities: arts, colors, and forms specifically in exhibitor conceptions and perceptions; because each group conveys symbolic meanings and values in humanity's cultural tastes.

> *Humanities.* Humanities are those branches of knowledge concerned with human thoughts and culture. Humanities have primarily a cultural character and usually include languages, literature, and arts.
>
> *Arts.* Arts are the productions or expressions of what is beautiful, appealing, and/or of what is more than of ordinary significance. Arts are the establishment of human unity in variety, similarity, proximity, and connectivity in bounded perceptions. Arts are expository, detailed modes of creativity of novel things. Arts manifest compositions of an individual and/or a group of human beings' emotional, sensational feelings and thoughts to explain or manifest something in specific causal forms.
>
> Artists manifest the interrelations, tendencies, and/or values of human beings with their environments. Such behavioral modes represent the interpretation of cultural facts, conditions, concepts, theories, beliefs, and relationships between the individual's diametrical conception and the cultural circumferences of the human life cycle. Arts try to explain humanity's inner motivations at a particular time and place.
>
> *Music and dance.* Music is the art of sound in time that expresses ideas and emotions in significant forms through the elements of rhythm, melody, harmony, and color. Dances are the rhythmic movement of one's feet, body, or both in a pattern of steps.
>
> *Movies and theatrical drama.* Movies, or motion pictures, are a genre of art or entertainment. Movies are selling specific motion pictures of kissing, ideas, body movements, fashion, sex, history, political ideologies, sociocultural values, and industrial lifestyles. (Parhizgar, 1996: 309)

Sciences

Science deals with human understanding concerning the discovery and formulation of the real world in which inherent properties of space, matter, energy, and their interactions can be perfectly scrutinized. Science is a rational convention related to the generalization of environmental norms, expectations, and values. It is nothing more than the search for understanding the real world. In a general term, we can define science as simply the empirical process forming the generalized inquiry by which viable understanding is obtained. In the field of scientific inquiry, a scientist uses analytical scientific methodologies to discover valuable alternatives for generalized problem solving techniques. Therefore, scientific findings are reliable and validated to further problem-solving alternatives. For a scientist, mathematics is a tool for building models and theories that can describe and eventually explain the operation of the world—be it of the world of material objects (physics and chemistry), of living things (biology), of human beings (social or behavioral sciences), of the human mind (cognitive science), or of human truthfulness, justness, and fairness (cognititive science). Therefore, science is the manifestation of positivistic conception of inquiry and has provided an acceptable understanding of nature. The distinction between science (normal science) and nonscience or quasi-science (pseudoscience) is therefore blurred.

Berelson and Steiner (1964: 16-17) indicate that organizational behavioral researchers strive to attain the following hallmarks of science:

1. The procedures are public.
2. The definitions are precise.
3. The data collecting is objective.
4. The findings are replicable.
5. The approach is systematic and cumulative.
6. The purposes are explanation, understanding, and prediction.

Taxonomy of Sciences

Acquisition of knowledge refers to individual perceptual and practical capabilities which typically take in information via the senses through scientific methodology. They are most comfortable when containing the details of any feasible situation in a quantified understanding process. Sciences generally can be classified into four major categories:

1. Observational sciences
2. Natural sciences
3. Social sciences
4. Behavioral sciences

Observational Sciences

Observational sciences include astronomy, geology, physics, and chemistry. The primary aim of these sciences is to discover a cause-and-effect relationship between material things. The observational sciences offer the best possibility of accomplishing this goal simply through manipulation of independent variables, to measure their effect on or the change in the dependent variables.

Natural Sciences

Natural sciences include zoology (animals), botany (plants), protistology (one-celled organisms), biorheology (deformation and deterioration), and biology (physiology, microbiology, immunology, ecology and evolution, and molecular and cellular biology). Natural sciences identify real characteristics of causes, functions, and structures of all material things.

Biology concentrates on the study of all living things, examining such topics as the origins, structures, functions, productions, reproductions, growth, development, behavior, and evolution of different organisms. For an international manager, familiarity with both biological and ecological conditions of the workplace is a must. In most cases, both endemic and epidemic diseases are the most organizationally interruptive problems in multinational organizations. Many organizations annually lose a portion of their budget because of tardiness and absenteeism.

Social Sciences

Social sciences include economics, political sciences, demography, history, and geography. Economics is the study of production, distribution, and consumption of goods and services. Social scientists concern themselves with the areas of the labor market, capital intensity, synergistic dynamic of human resources planning and forecasting, accessibility, scarcity, and suitability of productive resources, as well as assessment of profitability concerning economic development and growth through cost-benefit analysis.

The mainstream of thought of modern civilized societies through history concerns power, politics, people, and public policy. Politics in all societies is a fact which has made our modern life very complex and has been defined in a number of ways. Politics is considered to be the fundamental concern in today's international diplomacy (Parhizgar, 1994: 110). A common theme of politics is exercising influence through exertion of power (Meyes and Allen, 1977: 672-678). Politics is the study of diplomatic behavior: decision making, conflict resolution, focusing on interest objectives of groups, coalition formation, preservation of classes of power, power distance, and rulership.

Demography is the science of biostatistics and quantitative statistics of populations, including records of births, deaths, diseases, marriages, numbers, means, percentages, all both material and nonmaterial value systems, etc.

History is a branch of scientific analytic knowledge dealing with past events. It is a continuous, systematic narrative of the chronological order of past characteristics of human civilizations as relating to a particular people, country, period, and/or person.

Geography is the science dealing with the real differentiation of the earth's surface, as shown in the character, arrangement, and interrelations over the world of such elements as climate, elevation, soil, vegetation, population density, land use, industries, or states.

Behavioral Sciences

Behavioral sciences include anthropology (physical anthropology, cultural anthropology, archaeology, anthropological linguistics, and ethnology/ethnography), sociology, and psychology.

Anthropology is the science of humankind, literally defined as the science of human generations with the interactions between generations and environments, particularly cultural environments. Cultural anthropology deals with convinced learned behavior through cultural orientation as influenced by people's cultures and vice versa. In a general form and term, cultural anthropology studies the origins and history of humanity: their evolution, development, and the structure and functioning of human cultures in every place and time. Since the definition of a total culture is usually beyond the scope of a single specialist, anthropologists have developed specialization of this science into: psychological anthropology, economic anthropology, urban anthropology, educational anthropology, medical anthropology, rural anthropology, and applied anthropology. In sum, as Harvey and Allard (1995: 11) indicate, "An anthropologist takes the role of an observer from a culture more developed than our own and describes features of our civilization in the same manner as we describe cultures we view as primitive."

Cultural anthropology studies the origins and the history of human cultures, their creation, evolution, development, structure, and their interactive functions in every place and time (Beals and Hijer, 1959: 9).

Physical anthropology is the study of the human condition from a biological perspective. Essentially, it is concerned with restructuring the evolutionary record of the human species and dealing with how and why the physical traits of contemporary human populations vary across the world.

Cultural anthropology deals with the study of specific contemporary cultures (ethnography) and with more general underlying patterns of human culture derived through cultural comparison (ethnology). Cultural anthropologists provide insights into such questions as: How have traditions, habits, orientations, and customs relating to a group of people emerged? How are marriage customs and kinship systems operated? In what ways do people believe in supernatural power? How do migration and urbanization affect each other?

Archaeology is the study of the lifestyles of people from the past through excavating and analyzing the material remains of past human life and activities. Archaeologists reconstruct the cultures of people who are no longer living. Archaeologists deal mainly with three basic components of culture: material culture, ideas, and behavior patterns.

Anthropological linguistics is the study of human speech and language. This branch of knowledge is divided into four distinctive branches: historical linguistics, sociolinguistics, descriptive linguistics, and ethnolinguistics.

Sociology is traditionally defined as the science of society, for searching for and solving social problems within the context of its dynamic processes, purposes, and goals. Sociology is the science of human groups and is characterized by rigorous methodology with an empirical emphasis and conceptual consciousness (Luthans, 1985: 36). Sociology is also the study of social systems such as families, occupational classes, and organizations. The overall focus of sociology is on social behavior in societies, institutional behavioral patterns, organizational structures, and group dynamics.

Psychology has been defined as the science of human and animal behavior. Psychologists study the behavior of human beings and their perceptions in both industrial and/or agricultural organizational ecology. Psychologists also study the behavior of people in organizational settings. There are many formative schools of thought in the field of psychology. The most widely known are structuralism, functionalism, behaviorism, gestalt psychology, and psychoanalysis.

Structuralism was founded by Wilhelm Wundt in 1879 in Germany. He had established a laboratory for studying human psychology. The theory revolved around conscious experience and attempted to build the science of mind. This theory applies to a structural breakdown of the human mind into units of mental states such as sensation, memory, imagery, and feelings.

Functionalism was developed in America by William James (1842-1910) and John Dewey (1859-1952). This theory of psychology is based upon the function of mind. Emphasis is placed mainly on a human's adaptation and adjustment to his or her ecological environment. This theory of the mind emphasizes human sensory experience such as: learning, forgetting, motivation, and adaptability to a new situation. Morgan and King (1966: 22) state that: "Functionalism had two chief characteristics; the study of the total behavior and experience of an individual, and an interest in the adaptive functions served by the things an individual does."

The foundation of the *behaviorism* theory is based upon the connectivity of the human mind toward behavior. Behaviorism was influenced by the Russian psychologist Ivan Pavlov (1849-1936). Since the structuralists were concerned only with the mind, and functionalists emphasized both mind and behavior, behaviorists focused on consequential results of such a connectivity in relations with observance, objective behavior, and the significant outcomes of human mind and body movements.

Gestalt psychology or *synergism* was founded by Max Wertheimer (1880-1943) around 1912. The term *gestalt* roughly means *form, whole, configuration, organization,* or *essence.* Gestalt psychology maintained that psychological understanding could be understood only when viewed as organized and structured phenomena as wholes and not broken down into primitive perceptual elements (by introspective analysis) (Zimbardo, 1992: 267). For example, the Muller-Lyer illusion, which follows, shows that by human perception, the two lines X and Y are of equal length. However, because of the kinesthetic perception of the human mind in relation to the total ecological environment of the surroundings, the lines are perceived to be unequal because of their relationships to the whole.

The Muller-Lyer Illusion

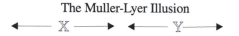

In other words, the whole is perceived differently from the way the sum of parts would be perceived. However, according to Euclidean geometry (surface geometry) both lines X and Y are equal; according to spherical geometry, X seems greater than Y, because of the illusion of human beings to which it seems the line X has occupied more space than the line Y.

Psychoanalysis psychology has come from Sigmund Freud (1856-1939). His theory is about unconscious motivation, the development and structure of personality, and his treatment techniques.

Social psychology is academically interdisciplinary. It consists of an eclectic mixture of sciences and arts (Luthans, 1985, pp. 30-38). Social psychology is generally a synthesized scientific theory of psychology and sociology. If social psychology emphasizes individual behavior, its close tie is with psychology. Also, it is equated with behavioral science. From the standpoint of emphasis on sociology, social psychology is the study of individual behavior within relation to groups (group emphasis).

Behavioral Sciences and Research Perspectives

Historically, scientific multicultural behavior emerged from the concept of human beings considering a variety of cultural value systems to enhance their living styles. Multiculturalism perceives the world as a whole and that the utility of consumerable things is the essence of cultural experiences. Nevertheless, human perception has been very egocentric and ethnocentric. Each individual and group regards the world from their own standpoint of personal values and the kinship of the individual's and/or group's interests.

In recent years, it has become commonplace for one discipline to borrow terminologies and models of research from another. Multifunctional, biological, mechanical, ecological, and cross-boundary divisional frameworks have caused the urgency to accelerate the emerging path of new scientific endeavors in all aspects of human behavioral knowledge.

The new visionary conception of an international market economy and diplomacy has been viewed to support the position that international management should rely on development of psychological and physiological characteristics of human adaptability and loyalty. The technopsychological mentality of the twenty-first century will focus on international multi-cultural behavior. This new dimension has similarly spanned across and germinated in disciplines such as the political sciences, military sciences, and ecological sciences.

In the field of management and other social sciences, new multidis-ciplinary sciences have been used long before: the models we refer to in this text are the highlights of all social sciences, humanities, philosophies, and technologies. The model of multicultural behavior is not a simple one. As Moran and Harris (1982: 5) indicate: "In multinational organizational de-velopment, they have used a list of ethnocentric, polycentric, regiocentric and geocentric as four orientations toward the organization behavior. Within the internal organizational behavior, there are too many complexities with application of these models."

As a result of international diplomacy, super-technomilitary interven-tions, multinational commercial transactions, and multicultural understand-ings all have made human behavior more difficult and more complex than ever. Consequently, international cross-culturalizational behavior could be best described as multidisciplinary, rather than interdisciplinary.

As mentioned earlier, all multicultural behavioral models discussed so far depend upon a rigorous research methodology in order to better under-stand human cultural and multicultural behavior. This search for why hu-mans behave the way they do is based upon their conceptions, perceptions, values, attitudes, beliefs, ideologies, faiths, social influences, and leader-ship. As these topics indicate, multicultural behavior can be studied inter-disciplinarily through all bodies of knowledge. In fact, the magnitude of multiculturalism is so broad that researchers, scholars, philosophers, and technologists argue that there can be no precise scientific direction for studying multicultural behavior.

Technology

Terpstra and David (1991: 136), through a broad anthropological sense, state that:

> *Technology* is a cultural system concerned with the relationships be-tween humans and their natural environment. A society is well adapted to its environment when its technological system is: (1) environmen-tally feasible in that it produces a livelihood for inhabitants without depleting the natural resources; (2) stable in that it can respond to tem-porary natural disturbances such as droughts, storms, and epidemics; (3) resilient in that it can return to a normal state of operations after a natural disturbance; and (4) open to revision when a natural distur-bance reveals its inherent shortcomings.

Behavioral Culturalogical Framework

Behavioral culturalogy is very young but has the advantage of growing very quickly. It establishes a synergized framework for human thoughts and actions. Consequently, with the "new world order," all traditional organizational behavioral approaches seem to be in a dilemma. Why? Because searching for a popular theoretical orientation has not solved human conflicts within a culture and/or among cultures.

The two fundamental differences between national and international cultures are geographic dispersion and multicultural conception in terms of assimilation and integration. National cultural boundaries delineate the sociocultural values, political-legal ideologies, and economic systems within geographic boundaries of nations. It is within and beyond these geographical and/or political cultural boundaries that multinational and multicultural organizations must operate. Multiculturalism is the normal experience of most individuals in the borderless information systems in academia, for they are perforce drawn into the microculture of administrators, teachers, physicians, and others who have power over them.

Fatehi (1996: 153) indicates that: "While a domestic firm embodies the basic attributes of its national culture, a multinational company is influenced by the multicultural nature of their global environment." Each multinational organization perceives its own culture as a system of shared meaning among members. Organizational theorists now acknowledge that cultural institutionalization is a relatively recent phenomenon. However, in a domestic organization, the origin of cultural philosophy is viewed as an independent variable affecting an employee's attitudes and behavior. It can be traced back fifty years to the notion of institutionalization (Selznick, 1948: 25). Interestingly, institutionalization of a cultural framework in an organization takes on a life of its own, apart from any of its members, and acquires immortality.

A framework of scientific-based knowledge of traditional behavioral sciences and their research methods, with a breadth of viewing on today's international behavior spectrum, is a prerequisite for comprehending a diverse modality of knowledge. A diverse behavioral modality of knowledge is what separates the traditional scientific organizational behavior approaches from the complex multi-institutional behavioral approaches such as multiculturalization, cross-culturalization, acculturalization, enculturalization, and parochialization. Although the domain of multi-institutional cultural behavior is very wide and possesses different approaches, through scientific analysis it identifies many inherent dynamic causes and effects. Therefore, those approaches will be defined to avoid many encountered difficulties in multinational organizations.

Demographic mobility, such as tourism and individual migration particularly, have been the major causes of thinking and dealing with cross-cultural and multicultural issues. The conditions of circumstances—socioeconomic, political, religious, ethical, and educational ones — can cause people to leave their motherlands and immigrate to other countries. Then, these immigrants must be institutionalized with the new cultural environments. In such a recip-rocal orientation, we can find six different processes of cultural *institutionali-zation:* (1) multiculturalization, (2) cross-culturalization, (3) parochialization, (4) enculturalization, (5) acculturalization, and (6) biculturalization. Through these forms, people must cross their national cultural boundaries and be fa-miliar with their host countries' cultures. Therefore, behavioral culturalogy identifies how people in different cultures can identify and understand their own and others' cultural similarities and differences. For example, American culture has multiple subcultures because of its great diversity and its strong emphasis on individualism, democracy, and freedom as a cherished valuable institutionalized culture. Individualism encourages development of idiosyn-cratic belief systems. However, democracy encourages like-minded individu-als to band together to express similar concerns and further their beliefs in all sectors of societal life (Trice and Beyer, 1993).

Multiculturalization

The term multiculturalization is submaximization of diversified cultures. Historically, since the 1960s, the term *multiculturalization* has been an um-brella for the inclusion of several social and intellectual cultural movements around the world. It shares inclusive ideas that most often refer to pluralism. The different ethnic groups that have changed over time include: blacks or African Americans; Native Americans or American Indians; Hispanics, La-tinos/Latinas, Chicanos/Chicanas, and Puerto Ricans; Asian Americans or American Orientals; and others. Parallel to the growth of such a notion in American culture there has been the growth of feminist or gender groups too.

In terms of multiculturalization, a controversial issue surrounds the tradi-tional arguments for the existence of a major culture in a society. It is argued that even in applicability of a specific value of a major culture within a con-textual vision of a national cultural boundary, it could not predict harmony within diversified majority and minority ethnic groups. Actually, in all cul-tures, women's cultures or feminist cultures have been perceived as minor-ity cultures. Although women are in the majority demographically, they do not have the sociopolitical position of power to enable them to stabilize their actual cultural majority of feminism. Moreover, if in all cultures women are a majority, they are a majority whose members belong to every culture and subculture. As a result, women have both areas of community and diver-gence, both of which are reflected. Also, other controversial issues are the traditional epistemological arguments that our international cultural value systems would recognize multiversities under a single general term of multiculturalism. The same holds true of traditional arguments concerning the philosophy of language, that universal and international are the immediate semantical values of predicates of meanings and thoughts. Such controversial issues and perceptions have led many philosophers and scientists to believe that the surest argument for the existence of a universal culture has come from the cognitive perception of virtual beauty in relationship to artificial and real beauties. So, even the arguments are successful when they indicate that the doctrines of all cultural professional philosophies exist independently of each culture. The major reasoning is that all universal cultural value systems are uniquely suited to carry certain kinds of modal national information and traditional perceptions in their imaginative superiority.

As a terminological modeling of thoughts and reasons, multiculturalization could be used for propositions as well as for propensities and relatedness. Such an argument applies against conditional nominalism (the doctrine that universals are reducible to names without any objective existence corresponding to them), and also against conceptualism (the doctrine that concepts enable the mind to grasp objective reality, which is midway between nominalism and realism) in terms of realism.

Multiculturalism in multinational corporations means the inclusion of all distinguishable parts of cultural values and beliefs of both home and host countries which could be labeled universal. If we believe in multicultural synergies, then the arguments of majority and minority will not be used because the emphasis is on the need for a unified intuitionism (the ethical doctrine that virtue is based on usefulness of thoughts rather than beauty of physical bodies). Recognition of universal values asserts that the statement of international beliefs is a synergistic phenomenon which can provide harmony and peace among people.

By reviewing the literature, even some of the nominalist, conceptualist, and realist scholars have tended to neglect this notion that multiculturalism should have the inclusion of all large cultural value systems within the contextual boundary of a multinational organization. By this token, multiculturalism is the inclusion of all *similar* values that are universal and uniquely suited to carry a certain kind of international value proposition. Then, the urgency within a universal conceptual vision is based upon international terms and meanings of multicultural value systems, which will be acceptable for all nations.

It is a factual assumption that through virtual beauty of multicultural value systems, multinational corporations can achieve the meaning of synergistic existence. In synergistic terms, all phenomena that exist in human cognitive perceptions are viewed as holistic realities that exist. Since human perceptions vary from person to person or culture to culture, the outcomes of their perceptions can cause them to make different value systems for perceiving the realities of those phenomena. In other words, the difference in perceiving the actual value system depends on cultural value orientations. In fact, there are two systems of cultural perceptions: actualism and possibilitism. Cultural actualism perceives the existence of phenomena as they exist. Cultural possibilitism perceives that the existence of phenomena is based on how they can possibly be perceived. Therefore, we should note that multiculturalization should not be focused on demographic numbering of the majority of people's beliefs. It should be denoted to the international values of all cultures for maximization of consequential positions—because the international value objectives are maximization in the path reaching to the ultimate intellectuality. Also, it should not be restricted by political or racial cultural boundaries. However, multiculturalization in terms of virtual intellectuality should be a nonconsequentialistic framework for valuing the universal moral and ethical doctrine.

Cross-Culturalization

Cross-culturalization is the task of optimization of diversified cultures. One of the major tasks of international managers is to identify similar cultural values and beliefs among home and host countries. These similarities have been observed from the common characteristics of all people around the world. There are several motivational theories which indicate that human needs are similar and universal. Similarity and universality of human basic needs indicate that people are responding to these needs according to their cultural orientation. It should be noted that this assumption that "one size fits all" is misleading, because people are different and consequently their levels of need-satisfaction are different too.

Traditionally, all cultures have four main functions or, more accurately, four levels of social functioning. These are: (1) mass-cultures and subcultures, (2) enhanced cultures and enriched cultures, (3) utilized cultures and facilitative cultures, and (4) refined cultures and crystallized cultures.

Mass cultures and subcultures. Mass cultures refer to information we receive through written documents. While mass culture is often denoted as the common culture, it also has to be treated as an important component of a national culture, as it is referred to, the commonality of value systems and beliefs of a nation. The term *subcultures,* on the other hand, denotes implicit or explicit special group cultures to conform to a common culture. Subcultures are specific segments of class-cultural and/or group-cultural value systems which exist outside the core of a mass culture. Subcultures occupy the most important portions of a culture—such as political, professional, occupational, and so forth. For example, American common cultural value systems resemble those of the Europeans. However, the judiciary and educational subcultures of these two continental cultures are different. Americans place a particular importance on individualism, while Europeans emphasize socialization of the basic needs (e.g., social medicine and free education). However, the Middle and Near Eastern cultures often sacrifice personal comfort and endure financial hardship for the sake of maintaining their familial brotherhood ties.

Enhanced cultures and enriched cultures. Enhanced cultures emphasize spirituality of faith and belief in daily expected behavior. These spiritual cultural values are the foundation of socially acquired needs in a rich culture. These spiritual needs have come from religious and humanitarian values, processing cultural thoughts and behaviors—such as educational, religious, ethical, moral, and so forth.

Cultural utilizers or facilitators. Cultural utilizers or facilitators utilize certain cultural traits and patterns for harmonizing thoughts and behaviors; such as liberty, freedom, democracy, and so forth.

Cultural refrainers and crystallizers. Cultural refrainers develop certain working skills for cultural reproduction—specialization in research and development in alliances through basic research, applied research, development research, accelerated research, and cross-matching research.

Utilized cultures and facilitative cultures. Utilized cultures provide certain cultural traits and patterns of values for harmonizing thoughts and behaviors. These trends and patterned value systems have come from political ideologies such as liberty, freedom, democracy, and so forth. Facilitative cultures stem from educational and technological capabilities such as research and development (R&D), the mainframe of computer systems, computer-controlled numerical systems, computer-controlled robotics systems, computer flexible manufacturing systems, computer-aided design systems, and computer-integrated manufacturing systems.

Refined cultures and crystallized cultures. Refined cultures develop certain working skills for cultural reproduction such as specialization and development in alliances through basic research, applied research, development research, accelerated research, and cross-matching research. Crystallized cultures develop highly codified sophisticated value systems for creating and maintaining a very capable and in tune know-how and technology in order to maintain cultural supremacy.

All of these functioning cultures integratively move a culture toward the future. In cross-culturalization, there are two dimensions which should be recognized:

1. Internal-dominated dimensions of a culture.
2. External acculturalization dimensions.

On one side, all native cultures utilize techniques and methods for developing a more or less culturally differentiated type of outcome. On the other hand, people cross their native cultural boundaries toward integration heterogeneously or unificationally in a homogeneously oriented environment—toward a new system of class domination or denomination.

For understanding the real means and ends of cross-culturalizational effectiveness, we must start with analysis of the following causes and effects:

1. Comparative analysis of cultural functionalization in terms of political interests, scientific acquisition, economic development, and technological innovation

2. Comparative analysis of social orientation and class-relations in terms of consequences of their behavior
3. Comparative examination of new perceptions and class-relations influence the courses of action and directions of societal changes
4. Comparative analysis to reaching down to the depth of the levels of both national and international crises and solutions

With application of these scientific tools in cross-culturalization, we may be able to realize the common elements and grounds which can be effective in cross-cultural relations. Through cross-culturalization we are able to communicate with and relate ourselves beyond the native boundaries of our mind and visualize the world in which we live. The scientific, vocational, educational, and cross-national acculturalization offers so many intercultural challenges for increasing more cultural effectiveness.

In cross-culturalization, differences do not necessarily mean barriers. They can become bridges to understanding and enriching our relations with the world of outsiders. In a cross-culturalization process, we are selecting, learning, conceptualizing, and interpreting new values and will try to adopt them in our culture or try to adapt other culture to our culture.

Parochialization

Through the history of humankind, the relationship between geographical locations and demographic movements, as well as the adaptation of people from one area to another, exist for a wide number of reasons. As a consequence of people movements, both host and home populations benefit and suffer from the strengths and weaknesses of one another. From one dimension, the cultural assimilative theory of parochialism exposes host people to culture shock, because they are not able to express and exercise their own cultural patterns and expectations.

Parochial culture means viewing the world solely through one's own eyes and mind's perception (Adler, 1986). A culture with parochial perception does not recognize another culture's different ways of thinking, perceiving, and proceeding, nor that such differences have serious consequences. A parochial culture is attached to the idea of being part of its own culture. Although all cultures to a certain extent are parochial by this definition, some cultures are more so than others. Moreover, a parochial culture is inordinately proud of its cultural ideology, myths, and utopian visions and seeks to have other countries adopt them. This egocentrism seems to convince the members that they have a unique mission in the world and that they are superior to other cultures.

Parochial cultures have problems, such as racism, group superiority, ethnocentrism, discriminating perceptions, bias, stereotyping, ambition, expansionism, and externalism. A parochial culture does not recognize cultural diversity or its impact on their population's lives. In a parochial culture, members universally believe that "their way is the only way," and "their way is the best way," to conceive, perceive, and proceed. No nation can afford to act as if it is alone in the world (parochialism) or better than other nations (ethnocentrism).

Enculturalization

Perhaps the biggest difference between past and present cultural contacts is the trend of cultural assimilation and integration. Cultural assimilation is related to enculturalization; cultural integration is related to acculturalization.

Assimilation is the term used to describe the swallowing up and digesting of one culture by another. This occurs when an enhanced cultural group and/or a capable technopolitical group gradually and/or suddenly forces the dominated groups to adopt the lifestyles and often the languages of the dominant cultural power group. Interculturally, after a few generations of assimilation, minority groups tend to lose their original cultural identity and heritage and become members of the mainstream of the dominant culture (Furnham and Bochner, 1986: 26). The best example of assimilation is the "melting pot culture."

Therstrom (1982: 12) indicates that the title of a 1909 Israel Zangwill play, *The Melting Pot,* has often been used as a metaphor to describe the phenomenon of people changing their names, learning a new language, and adapting their culture to better blend into a new cultural lifestyle.

The melting pot culture indicates that the ideal objective of a nation is to assimilate people into a unified system through public cultural trends in order to reduce the cultural and structural divisions between minority and majority groups (Zangwill, 1909: 193).

Under the melting pot model according to Abramson's (1980: 150-60) views, there are three possible forms of complete assimilation. Each involves a different path and a somewhat different objective. First, a racial or ethnic minority group is assimilated or absorbed into the wider society. For example, many Asian and Pacific ethnic groups have assimilated themselves into the Hawaiian culture over the past several centuries. Second, minority racial or ethnic groups may assimilate into the majority culture through their religious faiths. The Ethiopian Jews that immigrated to Israel are an example of this type of assimilation.

In today's international business transactions, multinational corporations cannot implement the melting pot culture because the trends of conducting businesses changed dramatically in the 1990s. Multinational businesses are moving to global multiculturalism, because managers perceive that their success is bound to globalization rather than denomination of their businesses. In addition, global corporations are learners and collaborators with host nations rather than hierarchical and controlling.

In modern societies such as the United States of America, corporations do not perceive enculturalization anymore. They are thinking and practicing accommodation and even appreciation of diversity. No longer are American corporations thinking in terms of assimilation; instead, they think and perceive of "managing" diversity.

Acculturalization

When two or more culturally disparate groups of people come into contact with one another, they will have enormous impacts on one another's social structures, institutional arrangements, socioeconomic and political processes, and value systems. The nature and the extent of these effects depend upon the conditions under which the contact occurs. Usually, cultural contact groups are emerging from travelers (e. g., tourists, students, scholars, traders, immigrants, missionaries, and, in a general term, integrators).

The term *integration* is used interchangeably with *assimilation.* However, these terms have quite different meanings and outcomes in the process of intraculturalization. *Integration* refers to the accommodation that comes about when different cultures maintain their respective core cultural identities, while at the same time merging into a superordinate group in other, equally important respects (Furnham and Bochner, 1986: 28). For instance, historically Iranian culture is an example of a successfully integrated multiracial and multireligious society which shares a common culture, while on the one hand, it is composed of Persians, Turks, Turkmen, Kurds, Luris, Baluchis, Afghanis, Azaris, Gilakis, and Arabs, and on the other hand religiously it is composed of Shiite and Sunni Moslems, Christians, Jews, Zoroastrians, Baha'is, Armenians, and Assyrians. Although the official language of Iran is Farsi and all these enthnicities speak Farsi for their formal communication, at the same time, all ethnicity and/or religious groups communicate with one another with their own dialogues and practice their own cultural traditions. It is surprising that even after the Iranian Islamic Revolution, which took place in 1979, that Iranian culture still is highly integrated and acculturalized.

Biculturalization

The most fundamental concepts of biculturalization with which I will deal are ethnicity and race. I will have two views concerning biculturalization. First, biculturalization is viewed as an objective unit that can be identified by distinct ethnic traits of a group of people. These people remain loyal to their original ethnic group while imitating and practicing the new culture (e.g., Anglo-Franco: Canada; Germano-Franco: Switzerland; Hispanic American and African American: United States). Second, biculturalization is viewed merely as the product of people's thinking of and proclaiming dual cultural value systems among both home and host countries (e.g., Mexican American, Texmex, Arab Ajam). To avoid the extreme of these views, biculturalization can be defined as both an objective and a subjective phenomenon. However, we need to identify two versions of biculturalization: in-culture and out-culture.

In-culture refers to the way of perceiving biculturalization within the "natural" boundaries of the geographical proximity of two cultures to each other (e.g., Texmex, which identifies Mexicans and Texans on the border area, such as Laredo, or Calexico on the border area of California and Mexico).

Out-culture refers to the way of perceiving biculturalization beyond the proximity of the geographical boundary of two cultures (e.g., French Canadian, English Canadian). However, it should be noted that biculturalization is a form of reciprocal social affiliation, dependency, and binding between two different cultures.

SUMMARY

An overview on the common body of knowledge concerning multiculturalism can provide a necessary foundation for the study of human behavior within multicultural organizations. Defined as a common body of knowledge, multicultural behavior is the essence of philosophical, natural, social, and behavioral sciences, and technology. Multicultural synergy can be defined as the mathematical analogy that $2 + 2 = 5$ instead 4. If multicultural synergy is beyond of the sum of the total parts of a culture, then positive synergy has occurred.

Multicultural synergy relies on synergistic knowledge-based integration of philosophy, technology, and sciences. Philosophy is the basic intellectual foundation of the human mind concerning the examination of one's own judgment. Philosophy is the integration of all knowledge to understand the cause and effect of existence. Cosmology is concerned with realizing the nature of reality and the place of human beings in the universe. Theology is essential to understanding the human mind and its relation to the nature of the superpower—God. Ontology is the idea of existence due to the relationship with nature. Causality is concerned with the ultimate causes of things being what they are in reality. Causalogy is a method of searching through pragmatic applications of scientific reasoning to identify the major elements or processes of effective forces which can manifest the original factors of a process or an accident. Epistemology has to do with the problem of knowledge. Axiology is concerned with the problems of values. Morality means the habits of right and wrong conduct, or good and bad, virtuous or vicious, and to right and wrong in relation to actions and conducts. Ethics is concerned with the human social conduct, activity, and behavior of the societal conscious awareness of a group of human beings. Aesthetics pertain to cultural senses of beauty, excellent thought, and illustrative elegant visual tastes.

Science deals with humankind's understanding concerning the detection and formulation of the real world experiences inherent to properties of space, matter, energy, and their interactions. Science is a rational convention related to the generalization of the environmental norms, expectations, and values. Observational sciences include astronomy, geology, physics, and chemistry. The primary aim of these sciences is to deliver cause and effect relationships between material things. Natural sciences identify the real characteristics of the causes, functions, and structures of all material things. All material things can be explained in terms of their natural causes and laws, without attributing moral, ethical, spiritual, or supernatural significance to them. The foundation of all natural sciences is based upon phenomenalogy of mathematics, quantitative methods, and logic. Social sciences include economics, political sciences, demography, history, and geography. Economics is the study of production, distribution, and consumption of goods and services. Politics is one of the behaviors aimed at exercising influence through exertion of power. Demography is the science of biostatistics and quantitative statistics of populations including births, deaths, diseases, marriages, numbers, means, percentages—all both material and nonmaterial value systems, etc. History is the branch of scientific analytic knowledge dealing with past events. Geography is the science dealing with the areal differentiation of the earth's surface, as shown in the character, arrangement, and interrelations over the world of such elements as climate, elevation, soil, vegetation, population density, land use, industries, or states.

Behavioral sciences include anthropology (physical anthropology, cultural anthropology, archaeology, anthropological linguistics, and ethnology/ethnography), sociology, and psychology.

Anthropology is literally defined as the science of human generations with interactions between generations and environments, particularly cultural environments. Sociology is traditionally defined as the science of society, for searching and solving social problems within the context of its dynamic processes, purposes, and goals. Psychology has been defined as the science of behavior.

CHAPTER QUESTIONS FOR DISCUSSION

1. How can the common body of knowledge facilitate better understanding of human culture?
2. How does philosophy differ from sciences?
3. How do natural sciences differ from social and behavioral sciences?
4. Why is scientific study of multicultural behavior important to multinational organizations?
5. Briefly summarize the various schools of thought in psychology.
6. Briefly summarize the various branches of anthropology.

LEARNING ABOUT YOURSELF EXERCISE #4

What Do You Need?

Following are fifteen items for rating how important each one is to you on a scale of 0 (not important) to 100 (very important). Write the number 0-100 on the line to the left of each item.

Not important	Somewhat important		Very important
0	25	50	75	100

_____ 1. The need for sex
_____ 2. The need for affiliation
_____ 3. The need to nurture
_____ 4. The need for guidance
_____ 5. The need to egress
_____ 6. The need to achieve
_____ 7. The need to dominate
_____ 8. The need for prominence
_____ 9. The need for attention
_____ 10. The need for autonomy
_____ 11. The need to escape
_____ 12. The need to feel safe
_____ 13. The need for aesthetic sensations
_____ 14. The need to satisfy curiosity
_____ 15. Physiological needs: food, drink, sleep, etc.

Turn to the next page for scoring directions and key.

SCORING DIRECTIONS AND KEY FOR EXERCISE #4

Transfer the numbers for each of the fifteen items to the appropriate column, then add up the five numbers in each column.

Quiddity Needs (Vital)	Equilibrium Needs (Sufficiency)	Essential Needs (Necessitated)
1. _____	2. _____	3. _____
5. _____	7. _____	4. _____
12. _____	8. _____	6. _____
13. _____	10. _____	9. _____
15. _____	14. _____	11. _____
Your Totals _____	_____	_____
Total Scores 500	500	500

The higher the total in any dimension, the higher the importance you place on that set of needs. The closer the numbers are in the three dimensions, the more multidimensionally balanced you are.

Make up a categorical scale of your findings on the basis of more weight for the values of each category.

For Example:

Your actual needs	Your life objectives
1. _____: EQUILIBRIUM NEEDS	= STABILITY ORIENTED
2. _____: QUIDDITY NEEDS	= SURVIVAL ORIENTED
3. _____: ESSENTIAL NEEDS	= GROWTH ORIENTED

Your Totals   _____
Total Scores   1,500

After you have tabulated your scores, compare them with others. You will find different value systems of needs among people with diverse scores and cultural need orientations.

CASE STUDY:
TUSKEGEE SYPHILIS EXPERIMENT:
DOING GOOD IN THE NATURE OF BAD?
OR DOING BAD IN THE NATURE OF GOOD?

Prior to the twentieth century, diagnostic, treatment, and prognostic procedures for the medical profession were thought to be effective on the basis of experiments. Physicians were very careful to not violate medical ethics. Nevertheless, most experimental clinical research studies were harmless, but ineffective. In the twentieth century, medical practices began to apply the scientific results of the structured random clinical trials (SRCT). The purpose of the SRCT was to validate application of research-oriented treatments by physicians. The human subjects were selected for admission to a SRCT project on the basis of diagnostic criteria formulated by prescribing as precisely as possible in order to ensure that patients all have the same illness. Implementation of the SRCT projects were based on procedural screening systems:

1. To find a group of patients who have similar diseases.
2. To divide patients into two major groups: (a) control group, (b) experimental group.
3. To identify the placebo control group from a regular control group. A placebo group is referred to as a group of patients who believe that the placebo effect can be helpful for their medical treatments. Placebo patients believe that a physician can do something that will relieve the illness and typically they have some improvement from the psychological beliefs and/or religious faith for healing their illnesses.
4. To categorize a control group into two identical groups for the purpose of eliminating doubt from the experience. This type of control group is called double-blinding.
5. Random assignment refers to alternative treatments randomly for the purpose of identification of differences attributed to the treatments.
6. Statistical significance refers to the importance in discussions of the ethical issues related to SRCTs.

Among numerous bioethical research projects is the famous Tuskegee Syphilis Study. Tuskegee was conducted in a covert project by the government of the United States from 1932 until 1972. The details of the Tuskegee research project were revealed to Peter Buxtun by a U.S. Public Health Service whistle-blower, Jean Heller, in 1972. Buxtun revealed the testing procedures to the national press in full detail. What has become clear through Jean Heller was that the Public Health Service (PHS) was interested in using Macon County, Alabama, and its inhabitants as a laboratory for studying the long-term effects of untreated syphilis; instead of in treating this deadly disease. At that time, the Tuskegee area had the highest incidence of syphilis in the nation, and more than 400 of these men had sexually transmitted diseases, for which limited treatment was then available (U.S. Congress, Office of Technology Assessment, 1993: 3).

The study has become a powerful symbol of ethical misconduct in human research. In 1932, the U.S. Public Health Service and several foundations began a study on approximately 600 male black American citizens in Tuskegee, Macon County, Alabama. All 600 subjects (399 experimentals and 201 controls) were desperate poor people. They were promised free medical treatment, food, and burials. Initially, they were given mercury and arsenic compounds—then standard therapy—when the drugs were available. Also, they endured spinal taps without anesthesia and were denied penicillin long after it became available in 1945.

They never told the syphilitic men that they might have infected their wives, or doomed their children to devastating congenital infection. The 1974 settlement included free health care for life for the surviving study participants to be provided by health care workers chosen by the patients themselves. The 1990s have been a time of reflection upon the Tuskegee Study and its troubling implications. In February 1994, the issue was addressed in a symposium titled: "Doing Bad in the Name of Good?: The Tuskegee Syphilis Study and its Legacy," at the Claude Moore Health Sciences Library. The discussion at this gathering led to creation of the Tuskegee Syphilis Study Legacy Committee which met in Tuskegee in January 1996. In its final report the following May, the committee urged President Clinton to apologize for the wrongs of the Tuskegee Study. The committee's work bore fruit on May 16, 1997. The President apologized on behalf of the United States Government to eight elderly black men, the surviving participants of the study. These men and members of the Legacy Committee were invited to the White House to witness the apology for this federally sponsored medical misconduct.

Chapter 5

Foundations of the Individual Identity: Quiddity and Kinetic Needs, Motives, and Drives

The essence of the motives of existence in human beings is the holistic reflection of the quiddity of human needs.

CHAPTER OBJECTIVES

When you have read this chapter you should be able to:

- define the concept of needs and describe the basic motivational process,
- describe several historical and contemporary perspectives of needs and motivation theories,
- discuss three important need theories, and
- discuss three important theories of motivation.

INTRODUCTION

In this chapter, I want to focus on how people are motivated effectively to work in different cultural environments. It is the objective of this chapter to link the theories to practice. In the following pages, I review a number of motivational theories that have gained varying degrees of acceptance in practice. Also, this chapter is devoted to the basic cultural motivational process and various theoretical approaches to the individual needs, motives, and drives.

Interactive cultural behavior can occur at the individual, group, and/or organizational levels. Individuals interact on the basis of their own motivational forces. All individuals have their own causes of behaviors and expectations. If they succeed at their causes, they become satisfied with themselves, and/or with others; if they do not, they blame themselves and/or others.

All people have their own definition of motivation. Usually, one or more of the following words are included in this definition: "needs," "desires," "wants," "wishes," "objectives," "goals," and "motives." Manifestation of an individual behavior does not always occur in a smooth way along with these phenomena. In addition, the need-drive-objective cycles and their fulfillment are varied according to the importance of needs disposition. Within contextual boundaries of personality of an individual, there are usually a number of competing needs and motives, a variety of ways of expressing drives and objectives, and different manifestations of behavioral roles. All these can occur in both positive and negative reinforcements attached to the individual's behavior. These competing forces complicate the behavior of individuals and their adaptability to organizational environments. Since multinational corporations hire and retain many workers from host countries, they need to realize how and why these workers view the "need to work." To clarify these issues, first, I will explain the very nature of needs, motives, and drives, and second, I will review motivational theories and their applications in the international marketplace.

THE MEANING OF NEEDS

Needs are basic deficiencies that an individual experiences at a particular point in time. The deficiencies may be physiological (e.g., a need for food), psychological (e.g., a need for self-realization), or sociological (e.g., a need for association and recognition). In a homoeostatic (describing an organism in physiological equilibrium maintained by coordinated functioning of the brain) sense, needs are sources of efficiencies which make an individual behavior become imbalanced. Needs are viewed as energizers or triggers of behavioral dynamic movements. When a person's sense of deficiency becomes strong enough, that person will search for a way to satisfy the need.

The implication is that when need deficiencies are present, an individual's behavior can be manifested either by motivational activities of the manifestly physical and/or psychological or by an epitomized rationality of their intelligence. This divorce between the "physical" and "mental" has not frequently been coupled with the notion of what individuals do with their body and mind. This sharp distinction between the "reflective" (physical and emotional) and the "active" (intellectual and rational) need is not drawn in other creatures. This fact should at least make us pause before concluding that a particular legacy of a person's needs is a universal imperative. However, it should be noted that social needs vary by culture. For example, according to Max Weber (1969), a German sociologist, the Protestant ethic in regard to the need to work was viewed as a means of revelation. Adhering to this religious belief, people preferred to transform productivity gain into additional output rather than into additional leisure in order to energize their economic needs. Moslems, through their religious principles (zakat), believe that the need to work is not a personal cause; it is a social cause. Moslems are not only obligated to accumulate wealth, they are also committed to pay 2.5 percent of their cash balance and any other liquid assets such as gold, silver, bonds, etc., per year to impoverished and unemployed people (Awadudi, 1989: 121). Shintoism views the need to work as a family obligation in order to synergize the family wealth. Japanese people consider the need to work neither an individual nor a social obligation; they consider it a family obligation. Therefore, accumulation of wealth in these cultures is bonded to certain cultural patterns of expectations from family members (see Table 5.1).

Multinational corporations should understand the sociocultural traditions and beliefs of their marketplace. Accordingly, they are obligated to respect the traditional cultural "work habits" of their environments. Workers as the main source of the organizational productivity and consumers as the main source of profitability view differently the need to work in multinational corporations. In the United States, employees view the "need to work" on the basis of their individualistic needs. For example, a startling 70 percent of Bell South's unmarried employees support at least one child. A total of 53 percent of children under five and 66 percent of children age six to seventeen have working mothers (Labich, 1991). In other studies, as Covey (1993: 42) indicates, researchers found that most women have a higher sense of the importance of a long-term relationship. The high percentage of married women shows that women do not have to live a lonely, private life (Epstein, 1991). However, when an American and/or European culturally oriented woman considers an advancement in her career, she sometimes elevates personal work over family concerns (Coser, 1975). Such a trend is not acceptable in Asian, South American, and Middle Eastern cultures. One other important issue is the relationship between job satisfaction and family satisfaction.

When a U.S. corporation is exposed to an economic hardship, layoffs may begin immediately regardless of consequences to the family and social

TABLE 5.1. The Need to Work and the Beliefs to Distribute Wealth Among Three Religions

Protestants	Shintoists	Moslems
Individualism	Famialism	Brotherhood
To accumulate wealth for the time of individual necessity.	To accumulate and distribute wealth only among family members.	To accumulate and distribute wealth among family members and society.

lives of employees. However, in some Asian and Middle Eastern countries, employers' view the "need to work" as both a social and a family need; and in some Asian countries, employers are obligated to consider the "need to work" only on the basis of the "family needs" of their employees. A Japanese corporation's reciprocal loyalty to organization and workers is based upon mutual gains. Japanese businesses, in times of economic hardship, do not lay off their workers on the basis of the cultural philosophy of famialism. In the Persian culture, married employees are provided some special incentives as salary for their unemployed spouses. This extra salary is an obligation of the domestic and multinational corporations to the cohesiveness of families, specifically to young children.

NEEDS THEORIES

The most dynamic source for human behavior is the idea that the motive to eliminate important deficiencies is rooted in human motivation. The needs theories have been viewed as the basic energizers of human movement toward productivity (see Figure 5.1). The needs theory cycles provide the basic framework for most contemporary thoughts on cultural synergy. The best traditionally well-known needs theories are Maslow's hierarchy of needs, the ERG needs theory, and the McClelland needs theory.

In a general view, the needs theories are content oriented. They search to discover what causes motivated behavior.

FIGURE 5.1. Systemic Needs Disposition Process

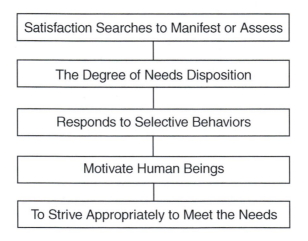

Maslow's Hierarchy of Needs

Perhaps the most popular of all needs theories was developed by Abraham Maslow (1943). He, in a classic published paper, outlined the hierarchical needs of human beings. His theory basically argues that there are two kinds of needs, *innate* needs and *acquired* needs. Drawing chiefly on his clinical observation, he believed that a person's needs can be arranged in a hierarchical manner. He then classified human needs into five major categories of needs. As Figure 5.2 shows, Maslow theorized that human beings strive to meet their needs in a specific order, that is, one set of needs must be satisfied before moving to the next needs level to further motivate behavior.

Maslow believed that most people strive to work their way up effectively through a hierarchy of needs. The hierarchy of needs are, in brief, the following:

Physiological Needs

The fundamental level in the hierarchy, the physiological needs, corresponds to the existence of being. We need air, water, and food to survive. These needs generally correspond to the unlearned primary needs. Unlearned primary needs are exhibited during a scarcity of resources. There-

FIGURE 5.2. Maslow's Hierarchy of Human Needs

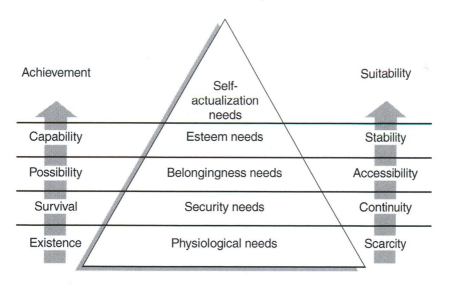

Source: Adapted from Abraham H. Maslow (1943). "A Theory of Human Motivation." *Psychosocial Review.* Vol. 50, pp. 374-396.

fore, it is the human commitment to overcome all possible barriers in order to succeed in existence. Additional mental "reflective needs" are hunger, thirst, sleep, and sex. According to this theory, once these basic needs are satisfied, they provide motivational forces for acquiring the next hierarchy of needs.

Safety Needs

A step higher on the hierarchy are security needs. This level of needs is roughly equivalent to security needs for continued survival. Maslow stressed emotional as well as physical safety. The whole physical and mental organism is a security-seeking mechanism. Needs for clothing, shelter, and health are included in the freedom from bodily harm. Maslow has viewed both existence and survival needs as the primary needs. For example, when human beings need to fulfill their sexual needs, they try to find a secure and safe place to make love—in a highly sensitive and secure environment. They do not wish to be disturbed or watched by others.

Belonging Needs

This third set, social needs, includes the need for friendship, affection, affiliation, association, and interaction and corresponds to the love and like needs. These needs are conditional to possibilities and accessibility to appropriate states of desirability.

Esteem Needs

The ego-esteem needs, which include the needs for self-respect (dignity) and self-confidence (integrity), represent the needs for power, achievement, and status. Once individuals have filled the primary needs and foundation of the secondary needs, their attention turns to the growth needs.

Needs for Self-Actualization

The highest-level needs in Maslow's hierarchy is self-actualization, which is the need to realize one's potential in its fullest sense. This level represents the culmination of all the primary and secondary needs of human beings. Self-actualization is closely related to the person's motivation to transform perception of self into synergistic reality.

Maslow argued that these needs are universal to such an extent that other researchers such as McGregor (1960) adapted this theory to another dimension of human behavior, namely Theory X and Theory Y.

Humanistic Approach of McGregor's Needs Theories

Douglas McGregor (1960) took a humanistic approach on cognitive concepts of human needs. His book *The Human Side of Enterprise* identifies two radically different management views on employees' "need to work." Theory X represents the old, authoritarian style of leadership for motivating lazy employees; Theory Y represents the enlightened, humanistic style of management. As Table 5.2 indicates, managers who subscribe to what McGregor calls Theory X have a pessimistic view of human nature and employee behavior. Some managers strongly believe that people are inherently lazy and do not have any motivational forces in their behavior to be self-motivated workers. Accordingly, they need to be controlled and forced to work. Theory X resembles the classical theory of scientific management.

Theory Y, advocated by McGregor himself as well as behavioral scientists, presents a much more optimistic view on human nature. Accordingly, Theory Y finds that human beings are progressively searching for growth and accomplishment. They are not inherently lazy; they are very active and searching for accomplishment and innovation. Work is a part of human nature and people are objectively oriented.

Alderfer's Existence, Relatedness, and Growth (ERG) Theory

Clayton Alderfer's (1972: 142-175; 1969) ERG theory extends and refines Maslow's hierarchy of needs theory in several important aspects. Sim-

TABLE 5.2. McGregor's Theory X and Theory Y

Theory X Assumptions
1. People do not like work and try to avoid it.
2. People do not like work, so managers have to control, direct, coerce, and threaten employees to get them to work toward organizational goals.
3. People prefer to be directed, to avoid responsibility, to want security; they have little ambition.

Theory Y Assumptions
1. People do not naturally dislike work; work is a natural part of their lives.
2. People are internally motivated to reach objectives to which they are committed.
3. People are committed to goals to the degree that they receive personal rewards when they reach their objectives.
4. People will both seek and accept responsibility under favorable conditions.
5. People have the capacity to be innovative in solving organizational problems.
6. People are bright, but under most organizational conditions their potentials are underutilized.

Source: Douglas McGregor (1960). *The Human Side of Enterprise* (New York: McGraw-Hill, 1960), pp. 33-34, 47-48.

ilar to Maslow, Alderfer's three basic needs categories are existence, relatedness, and growth (ERG). *Existence* needs are concerned with survival. These needs correspond roughly to the primary needs of Maslow's theory (physiological and security needs). *Relatedness* needs stress the importance of interpersonal, social possibility, and accessibility relationship needs of a person with others (belonging needs). *Growth needs* are concerned with the individual's intrinsic desire for personal development (esteem needs) and maturity in suitable achievements. Unlike Maslow, Alderfer does not draw strict lines of demarcation. Alderfer believes that a person can be motivated in more than one kind of need at any one time. Therefore, ERG theory needs are not in a strict hierarchy.

McClelland Needs Theory

McClelland (1961a) studied how basic needs, such as the need for achievement, the need for affiliation, the need for power, and the need for minimization of pain, are conditioned by early childhood experiences (see Table 5.3).

The Need for Achievement

Some people always need to look to past successful experiences to do the next job better. Creating difficult objectives and challenging risky decisions would get people to try harder in order to have a good shot at succeeding. People need to become focused—sometimes obsessed—with their work. According to this theory, which focuses basically on the need for achievement, the likelihood that a person will perform a task successfully depends on the strength of the incentive value of success.

TABLE 5.3. McClelland's Theory of Needs

Needs	Description
Need for Achievement (nAch)	The drive to reach each goal, to excel, and to succeed.
Need for Power (nPow)	The drive to control and influence others.
Need for Affiliation (nAff)	The drive to have friends and close interpersonal relations.
Need for Minimization of Pain (nMP)	The drive to understand the nature of pain. People's need can be reversed from pain to pleasure.

Source: Adapted from McClelland, D. C. (1961b). "Business Drive and National Achievement." *Harvard Business Review* (July-August): 99-112.

The Need for Affiliation

People need human association. Those people with a high need for socialization seek to be affiliated with a person or a group of people in order to get support and approval from others. These people try to win friendship. When a culture places a high value on achievement, the themes of the news and leadership become heroism, where the hero's actions lead to success.

The Need for Power

The mentality of people in terms of acquisition of power is different. Some people will do anything to get power; others will avoid power. Experts believe that people with a high need for power can be good managers if they have self-control, a genuine desire to progress, and relatively low need for affiliation.

The Need for Minimization of Pain

The need for understanding the nature of pain (sometimes defined simply as the absence of pleasure) can be viewed in increasing pleasure. According to this view, everything that people need can be reversed from pain to pleasure. Therefore, in order to get pleasure, people need to minimize pain.

Murray's Manifest Needs Theory

Murray's *manifest needs* theory was presented first in 1938. The theory identified a set of manifest needs, but at only an abstract level. The essence of this theory owes much to the work of J. W. Atkinson (1964), who translated Murray's ideas into a more concrete, operational framework.

The manifest needs theory assumes that people have a set of needs that motivates behavior. The mechanisms of manifestation of needs are very complex. In such a domain of needs, several categories of needs are important to most people and a number of needs may operate in varying degrees at the same time. In other words, multiple needs motivate behavior simultaneously rather in some precise order. In addition, some motives are manifested through very complex and hidden sets of needs. Murray did not arrange the needs in any particular order of importance. He concluded that all manifested needs are learned needs.

Murray discovered that each need has two components: *direction* and *intensity*. *Direction* refers to the individual who is expected to satisfy the need. *Intensity* represents the importance of the need (see Table 5.4).

TABLE 5.4. Murray's Manifest Needs

Needs	Characteristics
Achievement	Desires to accomplish
Affiliation	Enjoys being with others
Aggression	Enjoys challenge
Autonomy	Being unattached
Exhibition	Being the center of attention
Impulsivity	Speaks freely
Nurturance	Being sympathetic
Order	Is neat and organized
Power	Attempts control of others and environment
Understanding	Wants to understand knowledge

Source: Partially adapted from the *Personality Research Form Manual,* published by Research Psychologists Press, Inc., P.O. Box 984, Port Huron, Michigan 48060. Copyright 1967, 1974, 1984, by Douglas Jackson.

Parhizgar's Kinetic Existence Needs Theory

As we have observed all of the above "needs theories," they have mainly focused on physiological and social conditions of people on this planet. However, a human society is made up of many subordinate parts: genders, ages, groupings, professionals, economic classes, political bodies, and religious faiths. In a biological organism, the various parts are integrated into a functioning whole according to systematic innate physiological patterns that have established and maintained the very possibility of life, being, and the real existence of that organism. So far, an individual's freedom depends on the freedom of the whole society. If a society is highly fragmented, then an individual feels that there is a threat that his or her integration into the society is not possible. One way of overcoming this threat is through perception of spiritual inspiration needs (Parhizgar, 2000).

Spiritual inspiration needs is a synergistic guide to confident living through a combination of biological needs and spiritual tendencies. In such earthly living, human beings are exposed to three stages of spiritual needs: (1) positive imagery needs, (2) realistic needs, and (3) positive conclusive needs.

Although each of the various needs theories to motivation are unique, all can be integrated across several universal areas. Figure 5.3 illustrates a conceptual assessment that all primary and secondary needs are bonded with three domains of existence: universal intelligent order, global operational order, and national processional (legal) dynamic order.

The most fundamental characteristic of the existence needs theory is the notion that all human beings are the most intelligent dynamic units in nature. They have intrinsic and extrinsic desirability to meet their existence needs.

Existence needs can be perceived through three major causes: formal cause, material cause, and efficient cause. Within a matrix context of existence, there are three levels of needs:

1. *Necessity* of causes, which have been perceived as initial causes: formal needs causes, material needs causes.
2. *Sufficiency* needs, which have been perceived as evolutionary needs: spiritual needs, biological needs, and sociocultural needs.
3. *Vital* needs, which have been perceived as dynamic needs: essential needs, quiddity needs, and equilibrium needs. The *formal cause* implies the holistic dimensional multiplicity of being. It includes biological causes: physiological, sociological, spiritual, and mental beings (e.g., humanity as a concrete tangible and nontangible phenomenon).

Figure 5.3. Parhizgar's Kinetic Existence Needs Theory

Systematic Needs Order of the Universal Life

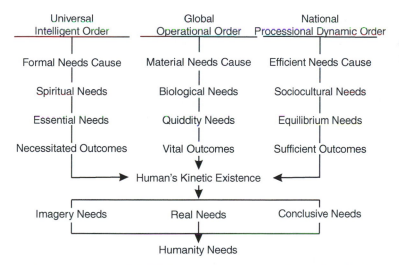

Source: Parhizgar, K. D. (2000). "Ethical Analysis of the Kinetic and Quiddity Existence Need Theory (KQUENT) in Multinational Organizations." *Journal of Transnational Management Development,* 5(3): 1-25.

The *material need cause* implies only the natural universal needs (e.g., nature as concrete tangible things).

The *efficient need cause* implies better understanding by considering the simpler cause of unity (an individual) and the multiplicity of all (all species of human beings: multiculturalism).

Spiritual needs are all intuitive knowledge and skilled performances, including a well-honed sense of understanding, where each bit of a sequence of understanding fits into the stream in an exquisitely placed and elegant way; points of repose or shift, where one phase of behavior (personal or cultural) is at an end, and some calibration is necessary before the second one comes onto the scene. A sense of intuitive need includes an objective-oriented life, a clear path and goal to which the sequence has been heading, and, finally, a point of return and/or no return toward which direction the final phase of the sequence has been activated.

The most spiritual needs of human beings have come from a person's dignity and integrity toward self and others. The results will be based upon generosity in the intellectual wisdom and manifestation of richness in the civility of behavior and in consideration of the valuable qualities of humanity, such as courteousness, coyness, shyness, calmness, and gentleness in thoughts and actions.

Quiddity needs are matters common to all concepts of the existence of a person. In Latin and Arabic cultures, *quiddity* means "what is it?" This concept in English-speaking culture is closely related to *essence,* and in Persian culture it is related to *reality (haghighat)* and *essence (zatt)* (Afnan, 1968).

Sociocultural needs are denoted as all common learned conceptual, perceptual, practical, and plural knowledge and behavior of all people.

Behavioral Kinetic Existence Needs Theory

The simplicity in understanding the *kinetic existence needs theory* exists in its surface logic which can be readily translated into practice. However, there is little research that has been conducted on such an important domain of human needs. The major conclusive domain of this theory is based upon positive thinking, perceiving, and succeeding in life. For this reason, attention has been paid to three areas of concern:

1. Positive imagery needs
2. Realistic affinity of needs
3. Positive conclusive needs

Positive Imagery Needs

People, through their rational, sensational, and emotional understanding, feel the need to deal with problems of individual tension, guilt, and anguish. Mobility, cultural contact, a changing intellectual climate, and the development of a new socioeconomic infrastructure in a society raise doubts concerning the validity and efficacy of the prevailing economic systems without spiritual faith. Even in a stable economic system, such a situation may fail to bring peaceful solutions into people's minds. Under these circumstances, spiritual faith takes on many aspects of a search for something that has been lost within a society seeking for something new—the need for peaceful living. The results of these needs will vary greatly among different members of a society, and different cultures within the international community at large. The greater the desires to be realized, the greater the expectations to be achieved. Every person has a unique combination of desirability, instrumentality, and expectancy of needs. Therefore, the greater expectancy to be fulfilled, the greater encouragement in empowerment needs to emerge.

Realistic Affinity of Needs

A great variety of spiritual needs exists within the contextual boundaries of moral needs. These needs are viewed as moral indoctrinations for various humanistic problematic solutions. These spiritual needs are rooted from theological doctrines such as dignity, integrity, and honesty. In addition, realistic affinity of needs differ from learned moral and ethical principles. Within such boundaries, people need to avoid personal degradation, reproaches, fear, inferiority, tension, misery, uncertainty, and kindred troubles in their personality. The need to free human beings from many of the modern bonds of the materialistic societal order, which have come to be felt as heavy chains of dependency, is one of the insights necessary for people's thoughts. Nevertheless, with such a feeling, people who desire to search for freedom vary from society to society, from culture to culture, and from time to time. These feelings of frustration and anguish tie an individual's materialistic needs to the spiritual power. Such a need of new relationship motivates people to establish faith in their minds and hearts for new obligations and new patterns of behavior. The higher specification of spiritual drives to be searched, the greater effort to achieve need-drive-goals to emerge.

Positive Conclusive Needs

It is well documented that both men and women go through some economic transitions. The economic transitions can be both positively and negatively experienced in adapting to new environmental opportunities and threats. People need to understand the conclusive trends of both economic development and hardship. They need to realize how to overcome spiritual and economical barriers and how to adjust to their new situations with new circumstances.

The need for world experience with knowledge is the last need for happiness. The greatest accomplishment is to overcome and realize weaknesses;

the greater empowerment within the personality of a human being will emerge.

The kinetic existence need theory emphasizes searching for reinforcement of an individual personality. The less fear, inferiority, tensions, and kindred troubles to be felt by people, the more positive achievement and rewards will succeed. The more avoidance of individual tension, guilt, and anguish to occur, the more satisfaction and happiness will emerge in life.

For understanding the kinetic existence need theory, four particular interactive dimensions of perceptual typology are of special importance. The first dimension corresponds to the breadth of biological imagination of an individual's mind, known as "intuition." These relationships are based on the kind of learned "input-data," which characteristically refers to scientific (rational thinking) phenomena of the extrinsic world of human personality. The second dimension corresponds to an individual's mechanistic (pragmatic sensations) organs. These pragmatic organs are known as somatic facilitators in decision-making processes. These pragmatic technological characteristics can integrate different kinds of technological innovativeness known as "togetherput-data." The third dimension, which corresponds to the transformation of data from the right side of an individual's brain to the left side, is philosophical (intuitive). The fourth dimension, corresponding to the transition of data, is through artistic (sensational) impressions. As a result, an individual tends to develop a preference for one mode of input in their decision-making process.

In the kinetic existence need theory, *thinking* is a type of decision making which is not only based on intelligence but rationality as well. The thoughtful imagination is a process by which a decision maker, in full awareness of all feasible alternatives, maximizes usefulness. *Experience* refers to reflective thinking of habitual orderliness of past action in practice. *Sensation* refers to those processes through which individuals take in information via their senses. In contrast, *intuition* refers to those decision-making processes which typically take in information by means of imagination—by seeing the whole. Intuitive decision makers consider a number of alternatives and options, simultaneously jumping from one step in analysis or search to another and back again. As some of the researchers perceive that the opposite rational decision maker is the intuitive decision maker. This type of decision maker prefers reflective thinking, instinct, and gut feeling. Thus, on the basis of kinetic existence need theory, a cultural understanding emerges as a "pattern in a stream of beliefs" as opposed to being "chosen."

In a sense, all human life is an integral part of intercultural and spiritual experience. It begins in our struggle between our left and right brain qualities. As Roger Sperry, Nobel Prize Winner of 1981 discovered, in most individuals, *verbal* thought is conducted primarily in the left hemisphere of the brain and *spatial* thought occurs in the right. Everyone must use both modes of thinking, perceiving, judging, and applying, but most complex problems of any sort require input from both. Moreover, both hemispheres are in instant communication and intimately integrated. Still, certain activities demand more inputs from one hemisphere than the other. This explains why an artist with extended experience in spatial thinking might be in a position to apply that thought process to work with three-dimensional mechanisms. It also confirms the fact that the heavy use of one mode of thought does not limit the development or similar capabilities of using the other mode. In a philosophical term, it could be called "spiritual synergy."

MOTIVATION AS THE STARTING POINT

The starting point of motivation is need. Motivation is a basic dynamic psychological process. It is the set of forces that causes people to behave in certain ways (Steers and Porter, 1991: 5-6). Berelson and Steiner (1964: 240) provide a comprehensive meaning and definition about motivation: "A motive is an inner state that energizes, activates, or moves, and that directs or channels behavior toward goals." Few people equate the causes of behavior with motivation. However, it must be remembered that motivation should not be thought of as the only explanation of behavior. There are many forces within individuals and their surroundings which act in conjunction with other mediating processes. Motivation cannot be seen, but it can be understood. Finally, motivation is a hypothetical construct which a researcher builds to help explain behavior.

Motivation should not be equated with behavior. By an analogy of the light from a bulb, we can trace the electricity as the major power connecting the generator to the bulb. The electricity is invisible, but the light is visible. Motivation is like the electricity. Some motives are consciously visible and some are subconsciously invisible.

Motive Stratification

People are proceeding in their lives with two set of motives: unlearned and learned. The *unlearned* motives are instinct motives. Such motives are variously called physiological, biological, psychological, or primary. They must be vital and unlearned. According to this definition, the most commonly recognized unlearned motives are hunger, thirst, sleep, thinking, suffering, enjoying, communicating, walking, laughing, loving, and hating.

The secondary motives are *learned.* These motives are curiosity, affection, competence, persuading, manipulating, competing, exploring, achieving, leading, empowering, affiliating, and others. The learned motives are closely tied to past experiences. These motives are conceptually and practically related to one another. Therefore, we can make a general distinction between primary and secondary motives by this statement: A motive must be learned through thinking and/or experiencing to be included in the secondary classification.

Theories of Motivation

Historical theories of motivation are based on the notion of need deficiency and kinetic intelligence. The intriguing point in the motivational process is a need. A need triggers a search for ways to satisfy its inner state of deficiency. A drive is a set of deficiencies with direction. Drives are action oriented and target specific motivational ends. There are six major theories of motivation:

1. The deontic theory
2. The hedonistic theory
3. The eudaemonistic theory
4. The equity theory
5. The expectancy theory
6. The two-factor theory

Deontic Theory of Motivation

The *deontic* theory of motivation maintains that motives are independent of their processing consequences. As long as individuals live within a duel motivational entity, their right or wrong motives are basic and ultimate consequences. Motivations do not depend on extrinsic good and the production of good, or the failure to produce good. Motivations are intrinsic dynamic forces of human nature. They are independent dynamic agents of extrinsic consequences. In other words, the deontic theory of motivation holds that what makes an action right is not the sum of its consequences but the fact that it conforms to the intrinsic needs of an individual.

Hedonistic Theory of Motivation

Historical views on motivation were dominated by the concept of *hedonism:* the idea that people seek pleasure and comfort and try to avoid pain and discomfort (Pinder, 1984). Hedonistic motives hold that the basic human needs are pleasure and pain (sometimes defined simply as the absence of pain). According to this theory, every need that individuals feel can be reduced in one way or another to pleasure or pain. Hence, the dynamic calculation, thought not easy, is possible because we are dealing with units of the same kind within the same contextual boundary of a specific set of needs. Therefore, human motives reinforce body and mind toward pleasure and comfort. Although this view is rational as far as it goes, there are many kinds of behavior that cannot be explained, such as why people risk their lives to rescue others. However, some motives exist in human nature that do not seek such a direction.

Eudaemonistic Motivation Theory

The *eudaemonistic* motives are based upon the challenging statement that not all intrinsic motives can emerge as the result of reducing pain and increasing pleasure. What intrinsically motivates an individual is not simply pleasure—which may differ in quality as well as quantity—but happiness. Although pleasure and pain are the result of emotional and sensational motives, happiness is a conscious awareness of succeeding the kinetic motives. Aristotle (384-322 B.C.) recognizes that the precise nature of happiness remains to be explained in a rational manner. His definition of happiness contains two vital concepts: "Activity of soul," which means the exercise of reason; and "in accordance with virtue," which describes the quality of the process of performance (Aristotle, 1980, p. 36).

Equity Theory

The *equity theory* focuses on people's desire to perceive equity and avoid inequity. J. Stacey Adams (1963) argues that motivations arise out of the simple desire to be treated fairly. The theory defines *equity* as the belief that we are being treated fairly in relation to others and *inequity* as the belief that we are being treated unfairly in relation to others (see Figure 5.4).

The equity theory is one of the several theoretical formulations derived from a social comparison process in which people evaluate their own situation by comparing it with someone else's (Goodman, 1977). According to this theory, people form their perceptions of equity and inequity by comparing what they offer an organization relative to what they get back and how this ratio compares with those of others. Adams (1963) describes the equity comparison process in terms of input/outcome ratios. *Inputs* are an individual's contributions to the organization, such as education, experience, effort, and loyalty. *Outcomes* are what that person receives in return, such as pay, recognition, social relationships, and intrinsic rewards (Greenburg, 1988).

$$\frac{\textit{Outcomes (self)}}{\text{Inputs (self)}} \quad \text{compared to} \quad \frac{\textit{Outcomes (other)}}{\text{Inputs (other)}}$$

$$\text{Inequity} \; = \; \frac{\textit{Person's outcomes}}{\text{Person's inputs}} \; > \; \frac{\textit{Other's outcomes}}{\text{Other's inputs}}$$

$$\text{Inequity} \; = \; \frac{\textit{Person's outcomes}}{\text{Person's inputs}} \; < \; \frac{\textit{Other's outcomes}}{\text{Other's inputs}}$$

$$\text{Equity} \; = \; \textit{Person's outcome} \; = \; \textit{Other's outcomes}$$

FIGURE 5.4. Alternative Responses to Equity and Inequity

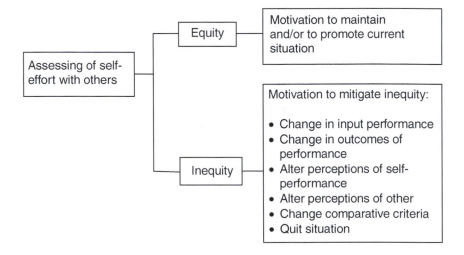

Adams (1965) has suggested six common methods for people to follow an order to reduce *inequity:*

1. *Change your inputs.* If you find out that you have been working more than you are compensated for, you might start to work less. Persons who perceive inequity, however, are motivated to increase their outcomes; the greater the inequity, the stronger the level of frustrating motivation. These people usually demand a pay raise.
2. *Change your outcomes.* If you find that you have been working less than you are being compensated for, you should start doing more work. Individuals who perceive equity, however, are motivated to increase their outcomes; the greater the equity, the stronger the level of productive motivation. These people usually find a way to improve their outcomes.
3. *Subtly alter your perception of yourself.* After all your work, you assess that it was not as good as that of your comparison-other. After perceiving an inequity, individuals may change their original assessment and thus decide that they are really contributing less but receiving more than they originally believed.
4. *You may alter your perception of the other's input/outcomes.* You should research to find out the level of contributions your competitor makes to the organization that you may not be aware of. Then you may decide to work more hours than originally intended.

5. *You may change the object of comparison.* Convincing yourself that the person you first chose is really out of your league; this person's uncle is the boss.
6. *As a last resort, quit or ask for a transfer.*

Expectancy Theory of Motivation

The *expectancy theory* concentrates on objectivity of expected outcomes that people are motivated by; how much individuals want something and how likely they perceive they are to get it. The expectancy theory is a more complex model of motivation than the equity theory.

The basic expectancy theory model of motivation emerged from the work of Kurt Lewin (1938), Edward Tolman (1932) and Victor Vroom (1964). This theory is rooted in the cognitive concepts of choice behavior and utility concepts from a classical economic theory. It tries to explain how and why people choose a particular behavior over an alternative. Victor Vroom, however, is generally credited with first applying this theory of motivation in the workplace.

According to the expectancy theory, motivation depends on how much a person desires a particular outcome and how attainable the person perceives that objective to be. The Vroom model of expectancy theory of motivation is called *valence, instrumentality, and expectancy (VIE) theory* (Figure 5.5). The basic assumption, as Vroom (1964: 14-15) states, is that: "The choices made by a person among alternative courses of action are lawfully related to psychological events occurring simultaneously with the behavior."

The word *valence* means the "quality which determines the number of atoms or groups with which any single atom or group will unite chemically" (*The Random House Dictionary of the English Language,* 1966: 1577).

By *valence,* Vroom means the strength of a person's performance for a particular outcome. Van Fleet (1991: 67) describes clearly the application of this word in motivation as: "For instance, a good grade on a test might not catch your classmate's eye, but it might earn praise from the teacher, scorn from less studious classmates, and more financial support from your parents. The positive or negative *valence* of an outcome is how attractive or unattractive that outcome seems to a particular person." Incentive monies would, in some materialistic cultures and in some socially-oriented cultures, have positive valences for most people, and distress, anger, and some scorn would have negative valences. Also, other connotations might be used in relation to cultural modes of behavior and may include cognitive perceptions, cultural values, personal attitudes, organizational incentives, and sociopolitical expected utility for motivational reinforcement.

For employees to be motivated to work hard, three motives must be recognized. First, the employees must feel that working hard for a company will improve the quality outcome of that organization: their effort-to-performance expectancy must be well above 0.0. Second, the employees' per-

FIGURE 5.5. The Expectancy Theory, or VIE, Theory of Work Motivation

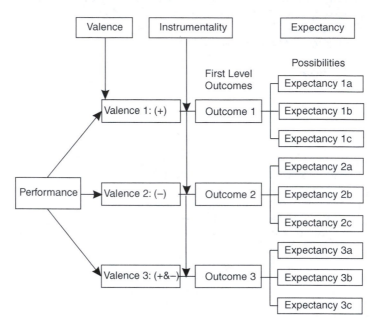

formance-to-outcome expectancy must also be high: employers must be sure that good pay will bring some value outcome. Finally, the sum of all valences of the potential outcomes must be positive. Therefore, any motivation may end up with a kind of outcome. These possible outcomes are:

1. A valence of zero occurs when the person is indifferent toward the means and ends.
2. The valence might be negative when a person is frustrated and disappointed from the expected outcome.
3. The valence might be positive when a person is very optimistic and making all efforts to achieve the expected outcomes.

Instrumentality means that individuals can achieve their expected outcome while the input of their effort into the valence level outcome facilitates in obtaining a desired second level of achievement. Assume that in an organization an employee desires to be promoted to a higher position. He or she acknowledges the need to have a very high standard of performance. As Hunt and Hill (1969: 104) state: "The first-level outcomes are then superior, average, or poor performance. His (or her) second-level outcomes is promotion. The first-level outcome of high performance thus acquires a positive valance by virtue of its expected relationship to the preferred second outcome of promotion."

Expectancy means the probability that a particular positive action or effort will lead to a set of particular positive alternative outcomes: the most desirable outcome, the most likely outcome, and the most possible outcome. In an algebraic conception, the essence of positive motivation to perform a certain assigned task will depend on the sum of the products of the valences for the outcomes (which include instrumentality: the sum of the first and second levels) times the expectancies.

In addition to valence, instrumentality, and expectancy, the expectancy theory focuses on effort, performance, and outcomes. The effort-to-performance expectancy is the person's perception of probability that the effort will lead to the expected performance, and the performance-to-outcome expectancy is the person's perception of the probability that performance will lead to certain outcomes (Moorhead and Griffin, 1992: 161-162).

Effort-to-performance expectancy. The effort-to-performance expectancy means the probability that effort will lead to performance is very strong—perhaps approaching 1.0, where 1.0 equals absolute certainty that the *optimistic* outcome will occur. However, if individuals perceive that their performance will be the same no matter how much effort is made, the *pessimistic* expectancy is very high—close to 0, where 0 equals absolutely no chance that the outcome will occur. The person who perceives that there is a correlated relationship between effort and performance has a possible outcome expectancy somewhere between 1.0 and 0.

Performance-to-outcome expectancy. The performance-to-outcome expectancy is an individual's perception of the probability that performance will lead to certain other outcomes. If a person perceives that a high level of performance is an optimistic sign to get incentives and be promoted to higher positions, this expectancy is close to 1.0. At the other extreme, no matter what the level of the performance is, pessimistically perceiving that performance has some bearing on the general levels of organizational outcomes and that organizational members do not like it, because they have initiated a very high standard of performance that other members are not able to achieve. Then the performance-to-outcome expectancy is equal to 0. Such a connotation gives the impression that this organization does not reward hard efforts.

Research results of Vroom's model and Filley, House, and Kerr (1976: 200-201) have been summarized and assessed outcomes of Vroom's model as follows:

1. In general, each variable pertinent to outcome expectancy theory has been found to have significant predictive and reliable results in some studies, but not in others.

2. The most consistently positive findings involve the expectancy that performance will result in intrinsic rewards and that intrinsic satisfaction will result from the work itself.
3. Assessing the expectancy that performance leads to rewards by the value placed on extrinsic rewards does not improve power of prediction that intrinsic self-satisfaction can be continuously maintained.
4. The theory is limited to conditions in which both managers and subordinates are subject to requisite ability, accurate role perceptions, accurate perceptions of contingent rewards, and accurate judgmental perceptions on rewards and promotions.
5. The better controlled the survey study between performance and rewards, the more support will generally be shown for the applicability and suitability of the expectancy theory.

Applicability and suitability of the expectancy model of motivation within the multinational organizations are varied. Since in a general and practical way, the philosophies of most multinational organizational operations are based on "hit and run," there is a discrepancy between employees' and employers' expectancy perceptions. Multinational corporations expect that they are able to acquire the highest profitability from the host countries to stay in those markets, and their employees expect to acquire the highest earnings from their work in a limited period of time. Consequently, both employees and employers are concentrating on monetary gains and earnings. This may raise some conceptual and methodological problems regarding the accuracy of the application of valence, instrumentality, and expectancy in these situations. Furthermore, research is needed to mandate a more careful and consistent measure of expectancy variables and test all the relevant short- and long-term variables to be considered, not just bits and pieces.

Herzberg's Two-Factor Theory of Motivation

Another theory of motivation is the two-factor theory. Frederick Herzberg's (1968) theory identifies motivation factors, which affect satisfaction, and hygiene factors, which determine dissatisfaction. Herzberg asked 200 accountants and engineers in Pittsburgh to recall times when they felt particularly dissatisfied and unmotivated with their work. And then researchers asked them to describe what caused the good and bad feelings. Surprisingly, the researchers found that two different sets of factors were associated with the two different feelings about work. In a content analysis, researchers focused on the words, phrases, and sentences used by respondents.

To his surprise, Herzberg found that the results were in contradiction to traditional theories of motivation which would have predicted that a single factor, such as pay would lead a particular worker to feel satisfied or unsatisfied. He concluded that motivational factors, such as achievement and recognition, can lead employees to feel satisfaction, but absence of these factors will not necessary lead to dissatisfaction. On the other hand, Herzberg felt that unfavorable hygiene factors, in addition to inadequate pay, security, and working conditions, could cause dissatisfaction, but that these factors are simply taken for granted if they are adequate (see Table 5.4).

Herzberg recommended that managers seeking to motivate employees to be productive should first make sure that hygiene factors are adequate and that employees are not dissatisfied with pay and security. However, Herzberg recommended that by focusing on a different set of factors to increase motivation, and by improving opportunities for achievement, recognition, advancement, and growth it will result in more productivity.

SUMMARY

Peoples' lives extend their survival through continuity of their need-dispositions. Needs are basic deficiencies that an individual experiences at a particular point in time. According to Abraham Maslow's hierarchy of needs, human needs are arranged in a hierarchy of importance, from physiological, to security, to belongingness, to esteem and, finally, to self-actualization. Alderfer's existence, relatedness, and growth (ERG) theory states that a person can be motivated by more than one kind of need at any time. Alderfer's ERG theory is a refinement of Maslow's original hierarchy that also includes sociopsychological trends, such as a frustration-regression component. Needs are not in a strict hierarchy. McClleland and Atkinson's needs theory shows that the basic needs such as the need for achievement, the need for affiliation, the need for power, and the need for minimization of pain are conditioned by early childhood experiences.

TABLE 5.4. Motivation and Hygiene Factors at Work

Motivation Factors	Hygiene Factors
Achievement	Supervision
Recognition	Working Conditions
The Work Itself	Interpersonal Relationships
Responsibility	Pay and Security
Advancement and Growth	Company Policies

Source: Adapted from *Harvard Business Review.* An exhibit from "One More Time: How Do You Motivate Employees?" by Frederick Herzberg (September/October 1987). Copyright © 1987 by the President and Fellows of Harvard College; all rights reserved.

Murray's manifested needs theory includes general aspects of socioeconomic-related needs that may operate simultaneously. Parhizgar's kinetic existence needs theory has a basic view on life through biological and spiritual inspiration needs to synergize life through existence, necessity, and vital needs.

Motivation is a basic psychological reinforcement which causes people to be active. Human beings have two sets of motives: learned and unlearned. A motive with direction is called drive. The deontic theory of motivation maintains that motives are independent of their processing consequences. What makes an action right is not the sum of its motivational consequences; it is based upon the intrinsic needs of human nature. Hedonistic motives hold that basic human needs are a mixture of pleasure and pain; every need that people realize can be reduced in one way or another to pleasure and pain. The equity theory of motivation defines being treated fairly like others. The expectancy theory of motivation holds that motivations depend on how much a person desires a particular outcome to be achieved. The valence, instrumentality, and expectancy (VIE) choices are made by a person among alternative courses of action and they are lawfully related to psychological events occurring in contemporary life along with the behavior.

CHAPTER QUESTIONS FOR DISCUSSION

1. Briefly define needs, motivations, and drives. What are some examples of each?
2. In your own words, briefly explain Maslow's theory of motivation. Relate it to work motivation and Alderfer's ERG model.
3. What are the major criticisms of the two-factor theory of Herzberg?
4. In the McClelland needs theory, how do you perceive the needs for achievement, affiliation, power, and minimization of pain?
5. How is the Murray's manifest needs theory different from Maslow's hierarchy of needs?
6. How does Alderfer's existence, relatedness, and growth theory compare with Parhizgar's existence dynamic needs theory?
7. How do you compare the deontic theory of motivation with the eudaemonistic theory?
8. How do you compare the equity theory with the expectancy theory of motivation?

LEARNING ABOUT YOURSELF EXERCISE #5

What Motivates You to Work with Others?

Following are sixteen items for rating how important each one is to you on a scale of 0 (not important) to 100 (very important). Write the number 0-100 on the line to the left of each item.

Not important		Somewhat important		Very important
0	25	50	75	100

It would be more important for me to:

_____ 1. Get along with others.
_____ 2. Work hard in order to win the competition.
_____ 3. Challenge people with reasoning.
_____ 4. Be similar to other co-workers.
_____ 5. Compete with others in order to assess my potential.
_____ 6. Work hard to influence others.
_____ 7. Enjoy my life when I am succeeding in my personal objectives.
_____ 8. Prefer to work in a difficult job with low pay but with good working conditions.
_____ 9. Resent the rigid organizational rules and policies in order to reverse them.
_____ 10. Work for myself rather than for others.
_____ 11. Set and achieve my personal objectives in the workplace.
_____ 12. Argue my personal views with my co-workers to show the merit of my intellectual reasoning.
_____ 13. Manipulate my co-workers to show my superiority.
_____ 14. Use give-and-take so that a compromise can be achieved.
_____ 15. Ignore my personal needs and respond to the organizational objectives.
_____ 16. Bring all facts to the surface in order to resolve issues with the best competitive solutions.

Turn to the next page for scoring directions and key.

SCORING DIRECTIONS AND KEY FOR EXERCISE #5

Transfer the numbers for each of the sixteen items to the appropriate column, then add up the four numbers in each column.

Competing	Achieving	Compromising	Challenging
2. _____	4. _____	1. _____	3. _____
5. _____	6. _____	8. _____	9. _____
13. _____	7. _____	14. _____	10. _____
16. _____	11. _____	15. _____	12. _____
Your Totals _____	_____	_____	_____
Total Scores 400	400	400	400

The higher the total in any dimension, the higher the importance you place on that set of needs.

Make up a categorical scale of your findings on the basis of more weight for the values of each category.

For example:

1. 375 Compromising _____
2. 300 Competing _____
3. 250 Challenging _____
4. 200 Achieving _____

Your Totals   1,175
Total Scores   1,600

After you have tabulated your scores, compare them with others in your team or class. You will find different judgmental patterns among people with diverse scores and preferred modes of self-realization.

CASE STUDY:
THE MONDRIAN HOTEL IN HOLLYWOOD, CALIFORNIA

Cultural values do not protect the short, fat, ugly, and tiny employees in the hotel and restaurant industry. In some countries such as the United States, it is illegal for a company to hire or fire employees based on gender, race, religion, national origin, age, or disability. But in a few places, the short, fat, ugly, and tiny employees are unprotected from what they say is real prejudice.

In 1996, nine bellmen were fired from the Mondrian Hotel in Hollywood because managers said they weren't "cool" enough to work at the hip venue (Beard, 2000: 20). Bellmen serve hotel guests by handling their luggage at the time of arrival and departure. Some hotel managers believe that if bellmen or bellwomen are handsome or beautiful, tall or moderate, attractive or striking, they represent a good image for the hotel and earn very good tips. The higher the tip the less salary paid by the hotel to the employees.

The Mondrian Hotel is located in the heart of Hollywood, on Sunset Boulevard, and serves both leisure and business guests. Hollywood is the capital of the entertainment industry in the world. It is a place where moviemakers view their profession as a business to sell specific images of ideas, body, fashion, sex, history, political ideologies, postmodern sociocultural values, and industrial lifestyles (Parhizgar, 1996: 309). The Mondrian Hotel rates for a double bed range between $285 to $565 per night. The Mondrian Hotel offers guests much more than just a place to stay for the night. It claims to offer a fun, exciting, and adventurous experience that lifts the spirit and touches the senses. Many movie stars, filmmakers, and directors spend leisure time in this hotel. The Mondrian offers everything within walking distance; shopping, indoor and outdoor cafes, theater, nightclubs, comedy clubs, bookstores, and coffee shops are just steps away.

In the entertainment industry ageism, sexism, and racism are hidden discriminating phenomena that in practice are exercised. Nevertheless, employers can legally be liable for appearance discrimination. But the law does not protect ugliness, shortness, fatness, and tininess of employees. Eight of the laid off bellman got $1 million from the Mondrian Hotel not because of their physical appearance, but because of ethnicity. Eight bellmen were from racial minorities and were replaced by whites, and the owner used the phrase "too ethnic" in a memo about the layoffs. The ninth bellman received proportionately the same share of the lawsuit, not because of ethnicity, but because of other reasons (Beard, 2000: 20).

Sources: Beard, A. (2000). "The Law that Doesn't Work for the Short, the Fat, and the Ugly." *Financial Times,* August 18, 2000. p. 20; Parhizgar, K. D. (1996). "Cross-Cultural Implications of the Popular Cultural Damping in the International Movie Industry." In Lemaster, J. and Islam, M. M. (Eds.), Proceedings of the 1996 Academy of International Business Southwest Regional Meeting. March 6-9, 1996, San Antonio, Texas, p. 309.

Chapter 6

Sensation, Perception, Conception, Attribution, and Attitude

When conceptual thoughts, perceptual judgments, and sensational attitudes form in our expressive behaviors, the natural instincts are at work in the same way a group of musicians plays a piece of music without a lesson.

CHAPTER OBJECTIVES

When you have read this chapter you should be able to:

- describe sensation, perception, conception, attribution, and attitude as the basic foundation for an individual's behavior,
- describe the physical and metaphysical characteristics of an individual,
- present seven major components of multiple intelligence,
- note the nature of individual differences in organizations,
- discuss basic differences among conceptual and perceptual behavior, and
- describe how managers should cope with individual differences.

INTRODUCTION

It is difficult to understand the world we first encounter at birth. The world initially is an unlabeled place, filled with an enormous number of potential events or objects whose positive and negative impacts on an individual identity are not absolute. An individual's genetics generate behavior based on senses, perceptions, conceptions, attributions, and attitudes through comprehending and learning processes of resultant categories of all events and objects.

The study of sensation, perception, conception, attribution, and attitude and their effects on individual behavior makes an important contribution for a better understanding of organizational behavior. In this chapter, I analyze both antecedents and consequences of individual behavior along with physiological, psychological, sociocultural, and econopolitical personal characteristics. In the first section, I present a scientific review on physiological senses. In the second section, I review the scientific behavioral approaches within the context of theoretical psychic analysis. Then, I focus on the sociocultural conceptions of an individual's lifestyle. Finally, I focus on econopolitical attitudes and beliefs within the context of attribution theory, which identifies the relationship between personal perception and interpersonal cognitive conception.

People become aware of and interpret their observations about the environment through sensory impressions. However, what one perceives can be different from objective reality. Why are sensations, perceptions, and conceptions important to the study of multicultural organizational behavior? Simply put, because people's behavior is based on their cultural orientation in relationship to reality. For example, some people would welcome the challenge of being employed by a multinational corporation and working in a foreign country with favorable working conditions, interesting job assignments, and excellent pay; but, as most of us know, it is very unusual to find such agreement from everybody. For others, conversely, working for a multinational corporation is not desirable due to familial hardship, cultural unfamiliarity, and physical distance from their families. Therefore, people have different perceptions about the nature of work and the environment in which they would enjoy work.

The major issue in choosing employment within a desirable environment depends on personal experience gained from one's own life and/or from the life experience of others. These perceptual positions depend on cognitive knowledge within the contextual boundary of the human lifestyle. The important question addressing this issue is: How can we relate conceptual knowledge to psychic perception in our lives? Many previous attempts to answer this question have relied on various dimensions based on the notion of information processing in an individual's brain.

ANALYSIS OF PERSONHOOD

Analysis of an individual's cognitive perception with assumption of information processing or computing in the brain is a key factor for this chapter. The brain is a highly sophisticated and selective system. It is dynamic, like a computer which is organized into cellular populations containing individually variant networks. The brain's structure and function are selected by different means during development and accelerative stages. The units of selection are collections of millions of interconnected neurons, called neural groups. Accordingly, these neural groups act as functional units to transfer environmental information to the brain. These selective and computing processes make three fundamental claims.

1. The first issue is related to the identity and manifestation of the *physiological* functioning of an individual's behavior.
2. The second issue addresses the *intellectual* potential of an individual (cognitive wisdom) and its affective role in behavior.
3. The third issue is the *phylogenic* functioning of an individual's behavior, which identifies the holistic character and behavior of a person.

Physiological Functioning

An individual is a living organism; and, in one sense, everything that an individual can ever achieve has been coded in his or her genetic material. In scientific analysis, three major areas of concern should be considered: genotype, phenotype, and phylontype (Parhizgar and Parhizgar, 2000: 185-187).

Genotype

Genotype is a physiological term that represents the composition of DNA, RNA, and their fascinating interactions. Genotype corresponds to the makeup identity of an individual determined by the genetic contributions of each parent. Because of the huge number of genes contributed by each parent and the numerable ways in which they can be combined, the notion of *variation* in genotype is equally fundamental.

Phenotype

Phenotype is an intellectual term representing an individual's observable characteristics as expressed within a given environment. An individual possesses intellectual power. He or she can put together purposeful information data and process them with a deductive mechanism in his or her brain. He or she can process information with an infinite number of meanings and uses. Equally fundamental is the notion of proclivity in phenotype. *Proclivity* manifests an individual's tendency to execute certain specifiable intellectual operations which can centrally process, while proving incapable of performing other intellectual operations. The main reason for such a discrepancy is the extent to which different portions of the nervous system are committed to carrying out particular intellectual functions, as opposed to being available for a wide range of operations. Therefore, each individual possesses certain inherent skills in practicing and using their cognitive perceptions.

Phylontype

Phylontype represents characteristics of biological diversity. The diversity of contemporary life reflects past episodes of speciation. Furthermore, when it comes to more complex human potentials, such capabilities to solve problems or to appreciate and create technology and music, individuals still are unaware of their synergistic components and phenotypical expressions. Within this boundary in searching for evolutionary relationships among diverse characteristics of organisms, individuals need to identify the functional mechanisms of their characteristics. These functional characteristics require synergistic taxonomy, identification, and classification of human behaviors.

Taken together, the synergistic powers of all genotypes, phenotypes, and phylontypes would be considered as a foundation for identification of any individual's behavior, cultural orientation, and intellectual personhood profile.

HISTORICAL SCIENTIFIC VIEWS ABOUT PERSONHOOD

Darwin's vision of the "tree of life"; Freud's notion of the "unconsciousness instincts"; Dalton's views of the atom as a tiny "solar system"; and James's views on "change and growth of personality" are the productive signs that have given rise to and enhanced the embodiment of scientific conceptions concerning individual behavior.

Historically, scientists have studied human behavior from different perspectives. These dimensions could be viewed through the physiological, psychological, and sociological sciences. For example, Charles Darwin brought biology into focus in 1859 when he published his book, *On the Origin of Species*. Darwin understood natural selection on the basis of three undeniable facts. He identified many issues about past evolutionary processes of the human race. Also, he revealed an inescapable conclusion about natural life (Campbell, 1993: 15). Darwin identified the following characteristics about an individual:

1. Individuals in a population of any species vary in many heritable traits.
2. Any population of species has the potential to produce far more offspring than the environment can possibly support with food, space, and other resources. This overproduction makes a struggle for existence among the variant members of a population inevitable.
3. Those individuals with traits best suitable to the local environment generally leave a disproportionately large number of surviving offspring. This selective reproduction increases the representation of certain heritable variations in the next generation. It is this differential reproductive success that Darwin called "natural selection," and he envisioned it as the cause of evolution.

In the early twentieth century, building upon Darwin's effort in biology, a number of psychologists, including Sigmund Freud, an Austrian psychologist, focused on application of the theory of psychoanalysis in order to understand an individual's behavior. Freud presented a comprehensive application on the *Origin and Development of Psychoanalysis*. His view on human personhood was a radical behaviorist turn based upon pessimistic European intellectual conservatism. This conservative view was based upon a historical cultural tradition which meant that people were more tuned to their past experiences than their future challenges. Freud viewed an individual's personhood as the result of a progressive development through four unconscious motivational stages: dependent, compulsive, oedipal, and nurture. These motivational stages are shaped by a variety of personality developments, each of which has sexual undertones (*Psychology Today,* 1989: 48-52). These stages, however, are not generally accepted by contemporary theorists. Freud viewed behavioral sensation as the essence of the movement through these stages as being driven largely by unconscious needs and desires (*Psychology Today,* 1989: 48-52). Also, Freud focused on the sociocultural development of the individual psyche, its battles with the individual's immediate family, the struggle for independence, and the manifold anxieties to defend the ideology of individualism. For Freud, the key factor for well-being was self-knowledge and self-actualization through confrontation with the inevitable pain and suffering for survival and continuous existence.

Erickson (1963) identified eight developmental stages in personality life cycles. In contrast to Freudian sexual dimensions, Erickson felt that relatively more attention should be paid to the social characteristics rather than the sexual adaptations of the individual. Erickson's eight developmental stages are:

1. mouth and senses,
2. eliminative organs and musculature,
3. locomotion and the genitals,
4. latency,
5. puberty and adolescence,
6. early adulthood,
7. young adulthood, and
8. mature adulthood.

For the purposes of multicultural behavior, the most relevant stages are the last three stages because multinational businesses are looking for energetic employees either to be trained for and to work in the global marketplaces.

From another point of view, American psychologist William James embraced a more positively oriented form of psychology. This dimension is less circumscribed by the biological imperatives of behavior and emphasizes more openness of manifestation of psychological motives toward the possibilities of change and growth. James stresses the important relationships of an individual with others as a means of gaining ends, offering help, effecting progress, and knowing oneself. James, in a famous phrase, commented: "A man has as many social selves as there are individuals who recognize him and carry an image around of him in their mind," (James, 1963: p. 169). James and other American social psychologists came to focus on the social origin of knowledge, and on the interpretation of interpersonal nature of an individual's sense of self (Gardner, 1983: 237-238).

Biological Bases of Personhood

Individuals make sense of the world primarily through their body reflexes, their sensory perceptions, and their physical actions upon the environment. The basic identity of an individual is based upon genetic profile. Until recently, most estimates of deciphered genetic code letters of the human genome have been estimated at between 60,000 and 100,000 but the latest research suggests that considerably more exist. Cookson (1999: 16) states that:

> It is an important milestone because, for the first time, we will be able to see how the genes are arranged along a complete functional chromosome and estimate reliably how many of them there are formed.

Scientists depicted 3 billion genetic code letters of a human genome. These research results led to the discovery of the origin of the evolutionary stages of the human race. Two main classes of cells populate the nervous system: neurons and supporting or glue cells. *Neurons* are the functional units of the nerve system and are specialized for transmitting signals from one location in the body to another. Supporting (glue) cells outnumber neurons tenfold to fiftyfold in the nervous system. They are essential for the structural functioning of neurons. Three types of neurons exist: sensory neurons, motor neurons, and interneurons. *Sensory neurons* communicate information about the external and internal environments from sensory receptors to the central nervous system. *Motor neurons* convey impulses from the central nervous system to effective cells. Sensory input and motor output of the nervous system are usually integrated by *interneurons,* which are located within the central nervous system (see Figure 6.1).

Five Prime Senses

There are five sets of sensory systems: vision, hearing and balance, taste, smell, and touch. Vision represents a relay of the light intensity information to the brain. The brain then compares the rate of nerve impulses coming from the two eye cups to the brain. When the light intensity of two eye cups becomes equal, then a sense of perception will occur. The senses of hearing and balance are located in the ears. The ear is really two separate sense organs. It

FIGURE 6.1. A Neuron Pathway Between a Receptor and an Effector

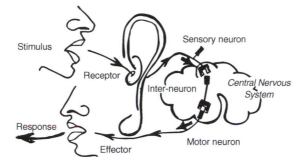

contains the organ of audition, or hearing, and that of equilibrium, or balance. Sound is detected by increases in the frequency of impulses in the auditory neurons. The auditory neurons carry the sensations to the brain through the auditory nerve. The balance apparatus is located in the inner ears.

The senses of taste (gustation) and smell (olfaction) depend on chemo-receptors that detect special chemicals in the environment. The sense of touch depends on body contact with other environmental elements in order to experience the vibrated density of material things. For example, in the United States, shaking hands symbolizes a sense of respect, friendship, and affectionate relationship through body contact. People use physical senses to experience and express taste, odor, color, temperature, brightness, shape, volume, pitch, and texture.

WHAT IS SENSATION?

Behavioral scientists generally acknowledge that: "(1) All knowledge of the world depends on senses and their stimulation, but (2) the facts of raw sensory data are insufficient to produce or to explain the coherent picture of the world as experienced by normal adults" (Berelson and Steiner, 1964: 87). The major question concerns the selective responses of neuronal groups of senses to an individual's cognitive synergy of understanding self and surroundings. It is hardly an exaggeration to claim that most parts of the body participate one way or another in the execution of synergistic motor actions. It is useful to point out that a fundamental asymmetry inherent in sensory and motor maps can function to identify the real understanding of all objects. Operationally, a sensory map is constructed by recording responses of neurons to sensory inputs. A motor map is constructed by stimulating neurons directly at the cortex and by recording responses from such neurons during an activity. The two mappings define somatotopic orders. A somatotopic order is the precision of special cells which take part in the formation of the body. These cells are becoming differentiated into the various tissues and organs.

The synergistic individual's sensory motor, such as vision, hearing, tasting, smelling, and touching, monitor the activity of these regions. These senses transmit information via the neuronal system to the brain and make adjustments in the wake of this information. The cortex serves as the "highest" center in most forms of body activity to determine movement. Therefore, all five physical senses are considered as the major sources of "regulatory sensors." The five senses are continuously bombarded by numerous stimuli from both outside and inside the body. Examples of inside stimuli include energy generated by muscles through digesting foods and glands secreting behavior-influencing hormones. Examples of outside stimuli include light waves, sound waves, mechanical energy of pressure, and chemical energy from objects that one can smell and taste. For example, the human ear is really functioning with two systems of stimuli: audition, or hearing, and equilibrium, or balance.

WHAT IS PERCEPTION?

Perception is the cognitive process of judgment resulting from attentive selectivity of some special stimuli. Perception is the consequential result of our cognitive selectivity of ideas, opinions, and tendencies concerning the relations between self and surroundings. We are constantly bombarded with many stimuli from our environment; however, we are not able to pay attention to them all. Thus perception is the refinement of judgment about special phenomena and/or objects. For example, you may look outside your window and see many objects and then select an object that attracts your interest and/or attention and ignore the others.

The difference between sensation and perception depends on the part of the brain that receives signals from the environments. Perception is much more complicated than sensation. The air vibrations we call sounds, for example, are converted by the ear into nerve impulses, which are perceived by a particular region of the cerebral cortex. These nerve impulses convey action potentials along with sensory neurons to the brain. They are called *sensation.* Once the brain is aware of the sensation, it organizes and interprets them, giving us the *perception* of sounds. Perception can be defined as a process by which individuals organize their cognitive sensory information and interpret their impressions in order to give meanings to their environments.

Basic Perceptual Processes

The perceptual process involves awareness, recognition, attention, selection, organization, interpretation, and response to information which has been transmitted by the nervous system to the brain. Although perception depends largely upon the capability of the senses in transmitting raw data to the brain, the combined cultural value systems and cognitive process may filter, modify, judge, or completely change these data. Figure 6.2 identifies the perceptual model of expressive responses to extrinsic stimuli.

Perception is influenced by the contrast, intensity, movement, repetition, novelty, attractiveness, and sharpness of the object which sets it apart from its surroundings. Also, it is dependent on the extent of the receiver's span of attention. A red dress stands out in a group of people who wear black dresses.

Attention means to attract and hold a close concentration on selective objects or events. It means noticing some things and ignoring others. Attention

FIGURE 6.2. The Perceptual Processing Model

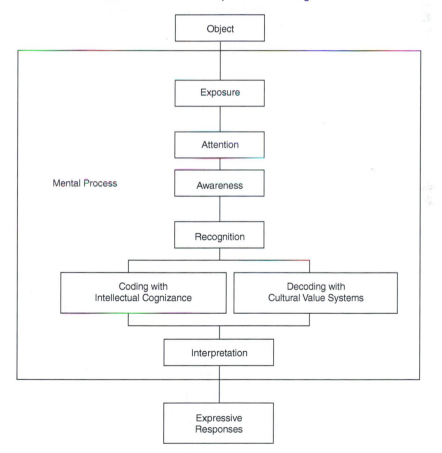

processes determine what type of selectivity is observed or deducted from an abundance of objects and events in a busy world.

Focused attention means concentrating on and holding attention on what has been selected to make it somehow more conspicuous and active than what lies without. Within a set of selected cultural values, certain parts may be emphasized more than others. Selection means to pick up certain sets of cultural values, beliefs, and patterns of behavior to focus on. Emphasis is an attentive concentration of holistic senses on a visual object or a cognitive phenomenon. Emphasis is not necessarily concentrated on a matter of rationality, rather it may be concentrated on emotional and sensational objects or phenomena.

Different people in different cultures possess different emotive powers of perception. These emotive powers vary widely from unusual compassion and gentleness to fierce aggression and hostility, from extreme friendliness to extreme remoteness, from genuine sincerity and caring to the most expedient manipulation and exploitation of others (Trice and Beyer, 1993: 182). The emotive power of perception varies considerably according to the individuals' own perceptual values, but there is also much agreement within a given culture. For example, a vital concept for understanding Korean perception is *kibun,* which is one of the most important factors influencing the conduct and behavioral relationship of an individual with others. *Kibun* means simply perceptual feelings. If one's *kibun* is good, then one functions smoothly and easily with others. If one's *kibun* is upset or bad, then things may come to a complete halt (Moran and Harris, 1982: 232).

The intensity of an object's brightness, color, and depth varies and can attract attention. For example, Hispanic-American women prefer to wear bright colored dresses such as orange, red, and green; Anglo-Americans wear white and light-colored dresses.

The following are some organizational cultural examples that point out the differences between sensation and perception:

1. A surgeon in a hospital requests new instruments for a specific surgical procedure. The hospital administrator buys those instruments that will be the best, but not the exact quality that the surgeon perceives the best.
2. A worker may be viewed by an immediate superior as a very good worker and by another superior as a very poor worker because the worker is or is not a "yes person."

In their research, de Bettignies and Evans (1977) compared European managers to American managers and examined them in specific areas of personal perception: social origins, education, career development factors, age, the climb to the top, and job mobility. They found the following differences:

1. Regarding "social origins," two conclusions evolved: first, with regard to upper-class managerial occupations, social origins did not play as major a role in the United States as in Europe; second, it appeared that top management positions in Europe are predominately of upper-class origins, whereas they are perceived as increasing middle-class concern in the United States.
2. Formal "education" with a recognized diploma is more highly emphasized in the United States than in Europe.
3. Regarding "career development factors," European companies tend to stress promotion and tenure more than American companies.
4. American executives retire early or leave for another job, while Europeans try to stay with a company longer.
5. Job "mobility" is viewed equally among European and American executives.

Factors Influencing Kinesthetic Perception

How can we justify that two individuals may look at the same object and/or view an event yet perceive them differently? A number of physiological and psychological (sensory and neural), situational (ecological), and targeting (perceptual) factors affect kinesthetic perception.

Kinesthetic perception is highly associated with bioenergetics and biopsychic energies. Kinesthetic perception is the result of integration of bioenergetic and biopsychic energies. The sharp distinction between bioenergetic and psychoenergetic perceptions results in the pattern and the types of integration of these two energies. Bioenergetic perceptions are viewed as "reflective" natural environmental energies (e.g., sunshine radiations). Biopsychic perceptions are viewed as "active" mental energies (e.g., intellectual creativity). Nevertheless, environmental natural and cultural conditions differ from culture to culture. It is worthy of note that psychologists have discerned and stressed a close linkage between the use of body energy and mental energy. Body energy is a set of mechanical movements which manifests dynamic functions. Mental energy is a cognitive power which manifests cognitive potential to understand and solve problems. The combination of both body and cognitive energy is called kinesthetic energy.

Energy is the capacity to do work—that is, physiologically, to move matter against opposing forces, such as gravity and friction. To put it another way, energy is the ability to change the way a collection of matter is arranged. Kinesthetic perception, which perceives and proceeds the activity of biogenetic and biopsychic energy, allows us to judge the timing, forcing, and extending our physical and psychological movements in order to make necessary adjustments. Kinesthetic perception calls for coordination of a dizzying variety of neural and muscular components in a highly differentiated and integrated fashion. For the clarity of this complex subject, the role of three major factors is described: (1) perceiver, (2) situation, and (3) target (see Figure 6.3).

Factors in the Perceiver

During the exposure to specific and defined targets, the physiological and psychological energetic mechanism (kinesthetic perception) plays an important role by looking at and/or thinking about a target and attempting to interpret what an individual can see, hear, and recognize. The perceiver's ability to see, hear, and recognize the target will be based upon physiological and psychological characteristics affecting perception. It is based on novelty, interest, experience, motives, attitudes, cognitive awareness, interpretation, and expectation.

Novelty means that some objects or events are attractive and easily grasp the attention of the perceiver. New objects or events in a new situation draw the attention of the perceiver unless the object is of interest to an individual. The interest of the perceiver plays an important role in the attention on an object or an event. For example, the psychological and physiological demands of an employee serving as an attention getter in the workplace causes that individual to be a perceptual target for promotion.

Experience is a great mentor and is the idea of selective continuity for or withdrawal from an action. For example, people who remain with an organization longer despite abundant opportunities in the competitive labor market are those with more pleasant experiences. The main motive to stay is based on "choice," not "force."

Motives are closely related to experiences. Unsatisfied motives stimulate individuals' kinesthetic perceptions in order to exert a strong influence on their decisions and actions. The more unsatisfied motives, the more likely the object will be perceived.

Attitudes can influence individuals' perceptions as well as their behavior. Some cultures are more attuned to the perception of past experiences, while others are either attuned to the present and/or to the future. For example,

FIGURE 6.3. The Circular Flow of Kinesthetic Perception

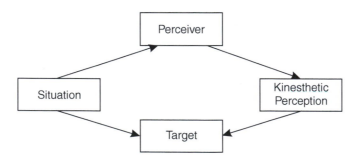

Fillol (1961) states that the attitude of Argentineans in regard to the "value-orientation profile" is one of the most important attitudes of the people of that country. It is inimical to Argentina's economic growth. Concerning such an attitude, Moran and Harris (1982: 18) state; "This 'profile,' Fillol refers to is a lack of 'cooperation-mindedness' of 'community spirit' in industrial relations." Although the community spirit is more conservatively oriented and emphasizes the past historical trends, the industrial attitude is more oriented toward the future.

Cognitive awareness is a combination of a remarkable set of characteristics, including unusual customs and behavioral patterns in detecting and revealing situations. It is not possible to separate out the purely genetic factors from those reflecting an unusual natural environment or a cultural value system. However, cognitive awareness is a differentiation of biogenetic and biopsychic capability of a group of people who live together and form a superior cultural heritage.

The way an individual interprets the meanings of facial gestures, body movements, and communicative systems depends upon the salience, deposition, and self-conceptual judgment of a perceiver. The more salient the object, the more attention the person gives it. The self-concept of an individual affects the way that a person perceives the world. People could perceive themselves on the basis of three attributions: positive, natural, and negative concepts. People who strongly feel and believe in their self-concept are likely to perceive things around them positively, whereas people who do not think and believe highly of themselves are likely to be pessimistic about themselves and others.

Perceivers' kinesthetic judgments also vary from culture to culture. For example, in some cultures promotion is based on seniority (Asians) while in others may be based on merit (United States). *Seniority* indicates that if a subordinate desires to be promoted to a higher position, the employee needs to wait and obtain sufficient years of service and longevity. However, this conceptual philosophy is different in other cultures such as the United States where promotion is based upon the merit system. In such a complex situation, superiors may perceive their own position as threatened because of a subordinate's efforts to do outstanding work. Regardless of the intention of a subordinate, the boss may perceive that others are out to "get his or her job." There are certainly differences between French and German managers. Horovitz (1979) in his research found that French managers do not perceive performance in the same way that Germans do. The French do not place as high a value on planning as do the Germans. French managers are more in favor of informal systems and centralized decision making, while Germans prefer a more formal system of producers.

The Factors in the Situation

The contextual exposure with which we pay attention to understand and define objects or to interpret events is important. Ecological factors are related to the level of comprehensive ability of a perceiver concerning the holistic situation of the surroundings. For example, the physiological ability to see and hear affects an individual's perception. The situational (ecological) factors consist of similarity, intensity, proximity, contrast, repetition, audiovisual clarity, climate, topography, and elevation (see Figure 6.4). Similarity states that external stimuli that stand out in harmony with the background are what people are orienting to in those situations that attract their attention. However, the contrast principle states that sometimes external stimuli that stand out against the mass results in attracting more attention. It must be seen or heard from surroundings which are different from it and if possible less conspicuous. Aside from differences in emphasis, variety and contrast tend to hold attention, while monotony and uniformity tend to lose it.

FIGURE 6.4. Factors That Influence Kinesthetic Perception

FACTORS IN THE PERCEIVER

- Novelty
- Interest
- Experience
- Motives
- Attitudes
- Span of Attention
- Cognitive Awareness
- Interpretation
- Expectation

FACTORS IN THE SITUATION

- Similarity
- Contrast
- Proximity
- Intensity
- Repetition
- Audiovisual Clarity
- Climate
- Topography
- Elevation

Kinesthetic Perception

FACTORS IN THE TARGET

- Attractiveness
- Persuasiveness
- Odd and Unusual
- Size
- Motion
- Stationary
- Noisy
- Challenging
- Danger

The intensity and proximity principles of attention in a situational condition state that the more intense and close the stimuli are to the individual, the more likely they are to be perceived. A bright light, a strong odor, a loud song, and thick smoke will attract the attention of a fireman faster than a dim light, a weak odor, a soft sound, or light smoke.

The repetition and audiovisual clarity of appearance of odd and novel stimuli are more attention getting than regular and familiar objects. However, repetition increases our sensitivity or alertness to stimuli (Morgan and King, 1966: 343). Ecological environmental factors such as climate and topography influence the nature of perception. For example, when we are flying in an airplane on a sunny day at a high altitude, we are relaxing and thinking about ourselves and surroundings. However, when the airplane suddenly heads into a thick cloud and descends, we cannot visualize any object outside the airplane, and our ears are reacting to the change in elevation and the sudden movements.

The Factors in the Target

In alluding to the role valued by a target in a perceiver's judgment, symbolization and canalization processes of stimuli are the major factors. For example, when an employee's behavior is getting out of order, observation of symbolization of their behavior such as facial expressions, body language, and body movements would send signals to the manager. These visual signals indicate what the impression is of the employee concerning the matter of discussion. Consequently, when a manager perceives a specific behavioral sign of action, then the manager can focus on that direction for understanding holistic behavioral characteristics of a target. This focusing system is called canalization of perception. Various internal and external factors affect perceptual selectivity. In canalization of perceiving a target's characteristics, symbolization and selectivity of the target play an important role. Symbolization means to select one or a combination of senses to be used for knowing an object. For example, selectivity means to pick out certain sets of cultural values, beliefs, and patterns of behavior to be analyzed and learned. The factors that influence the receiver's perception depend on the level of attractiveness, persuasiveness, oddness and unusualness, size, motion, stillness, noise, challenge, and danger of the target. All these factors and other attributes related to the target shape the way we see it.

Attractiveness means to absorb close attention by a perceiver to specific selective objects or events. Attention processes determine what type of selectivity is observed or deduced from the abundance of the busy world of attractiveness. If experiential training processes are to have much of a chance of attracting and holding the attention of trainees, there are several things that trainees must learn. These should be noticed in a *heterogeneous* cultural setting within a cultural environment similar to that of the host country.

Some cultural values do not demand close attention because they are similar to the trainees' cultural values.

Persuasiveness of a target implies influencing someone's thoughts or action. For example, when a capable employee is resigning from his or her job, the manager may ask "What can I say or do that will induce you to stay at your position?"

Odd and unusual objects or events motivate perceivers' curiosity to search for understanding new things or events. Closely related to intensity and proximity of the target to the perceptual vision of a perceiver, size plays an important role to understand the magnitude of the target. It says that the larger the object, the more noticeable it will be. Loud people or noisy objects are more likely to be noticed in a group than those who are quiet. The motion principle says that more attention will be paid to moving objects in the field of vision than to stationary objects.

Sociocultural Apperception

Apperception is the activity of processing and fitting new percepts into one's own culture—memories, habits, desires, interests, and beliefs. Apperception is somewhat like a finger touching the buttons of a highly complex electronic magnetic machine, which activates far-reaching imaginative processes of historical thoughts of all generations. The stimulus can be a sequence of conceptual ideas striking the brain (culture) or of dynamic movements striking the eyes (society). How does a presented cultural image set off a train of association? It acts, through sense organs, upon one's current cultural orientation—but flexible bonds in the observer's brain and nervous system. When an image has taken on many associations, some are always more familiar than others, more widely used, and more likely to come to mind when the image is presented. When the cultural interpretive phase of perception is highly developed, actively and attentively, we shall call the process *apperception*. This term is defined by Webster as "perception of meaning" or "the process of understanding" in terms of one's previous experience (Parhizgar, 1998a).

There are three major important areas of sociocultural apperception: stereotyping, halo, and similarity effects. These three factors are relevant to the understanding of organizational behavior. These are common errors among some people who exaggerate in expressing some positive or negative perceptions about others.

Stereotyping

Stereotyping was first suggested by Walter Lippmann (1922), who described it as "pictures in our heads" that we do not acquire through personal experiences. Ehrlich (1973: 21) refers to a stereotype as "a special language" which functions to "reinforce the beliefs and disbeliefs of its users, and to furnish the basis for the development and maintenance of solidarity for the prejudice."

The term *stereotype* refers to an individual's tendency to perceive sociocultural identifications about other nations, organizations, and groups as belonging to a single class or category of people. Once an individual perceives the stereotypes attached to particular groups, that individual tends to subsequently perceive other individual members according to these generalized images. For example, common stereotyped groups include women, minorities, ethnicities, race, religion, unions, accountants, and lawyers. It is an assumption that all these groups possess certain mutual emotional and sensational characteristics and traits among their members.

Stereotypes differ from rational categorization and generalization, in which the members of a group are overly simplistic and aggregated about other groups. Stereotypes are related to emotional and sensational feelings concerning others.

Although stereotypes are commonly applied in all multicultural societies, their content may change periodically and sometimes radically, depending on different economic, political, and social circumstances (Marger, 1985: 49). For example, Iranians before 1979 were labeled as rich people; after the Islamic Revolution and the American hostage crisis, Americans perceived them as terrorist-supporting people. Stereotyping consists of three steps:

1. identification of categories (race, gender, region, religion, and ethnicity),
2. labeling group attributes to these groups (Germany's cultural discipline, males' social power, Buddhist peaceful image, occupational characteristics), and
3. conclusive emotional and sensational generalization (e.g., all nurses are women, all executives are men, all lawyers are greedy).

In the 1970s, American business students were surveyed about their stereotypes concerning older workers. Researchers Rosen and Jerdee (1976) found that students tended to stereotype older workers as less creative, more resistant to change, and less interested in learning new skills.

In today's societies, the effects of mass media (television, radio, newspapers, magazines, and motion pictures) are extremely critical agents in forming social stereotypes among peoples. For example, Table 6.1 shows how Americans are stereotyped by people in several other countries.

The Halo Effect and the Similarity Effect

The Halo Effect. The halo effect leads an individual to judge and/or to perceive another person's characteristics based on the knowledge of only one characteristic. The halo effect in sociocultural perception is very similar to stereotyping. Whereas the striation is perceived on the basis of a single category and/or a single dimensional judgment, the halo effect is perceived upon the basis of one *trait*. Usually, the halo effect is a biased perception

TABLE 6.1. Stereotypes of Americans from a List of Fourteen Characteristics

Characteristics *Most* Often Associated with Americans by the Population of:					
France	**Japan**	**Germany**	**Britain**	**Brazil**	**Mexico**
Industrious	Nationalistic	Energetic	Friendly	Intelligent	Industrious
Energetic	Friendly	Inventive	Self-indulgent	Inventive	Intelligent
Inventive	Decisive	Friendly	Energetic	Energetic	Inventive
Decisive	Rude	Sophisticated	Industrious	Industrious	Decisive
Friendly	Self-indulgent	Intelligent	Nationalistic	Greedy	Greedy
Characteristics *Least* Often Associated with Americans by the Same Populations:					
Lazy	Industrious	Lazy	Lazy	Lazy	Lazy
Rude	Lazy	Sexy	Sophisticated	Self-indulgent	Honest
Honest	Honest	Greedy	Sexy	Sexy	Rude
Sophisticated	Sexy	Rude	Decisive	Sophisticated	Sexy

Source: Newsweek (1983). "What Does the World Think of America?" July 11, p. 50.

which occurs when a general impression (positive or negative) creates a halo. For example, a student's perception about a professor's grading could be perceived as a rigid one. Although that professor could be a very good professional advisor to that student, that same student may perceive that professor's behavior to be rigid.

The Similarity Effect. Another powerful perception is the similarity effect. This judgmental effect is based upon "similar/dissimilar judgment to me." Perception occurs when individuals find similarities or dissimilarities in other people like or dislike themselves, and they perceive that person to be based on their own image. A lack of similarity can be very serious in cross-cultural situations where the other person is bound to be different (Nahavandi and Malekzadeh, 1999: 161).

WHAT IS CONCEPTION?

In response to the complexity of global events today, corporate managers should conceive competition as the creation of new roles and functions of their products and/or services in the marketplace. According to this concept, successful corporate managers, employees, and individuals need to be competitive in terms of change, innovation, and novelty of ideas and concepts (Kuczmarski, 1995: 138). For example, a manager needs to take screened ideas from scientific advancement and technological development in order to convert their thoughts into a new practical path of thinking of three-dimensional description of a product. The concept or idea of a new product should describe the product features and attributes, its intended use, and its primary benefits to be conceived effectively by consumers. The manager should outline the core software and hardware technologies that will be used. The person needs to state general mechanistic feasibility of the intended products and/or services. The manager needs to state how products might be positioned against competition. Therefore, managerial conception provides an organization with organized thought to predict opportunities for understanding various situations and problems.

An individual does have the intellectual potential to categorize stimuli according to their own cognitive experiences. This ability to organize both past experience and future innovation is regarded as one of the most basic capabilities of thinking organisms (Mervis and Rosch, 1981). The conceptual categories and forms that we generate are mental representations of the kinds of related factors that are grouped in some way and are called concepts. Concepts are the building blocks of apperceptive thinking.

One common approach uses a factorial analysis of the concept. This technique breaks down general intelligence into two relatively independent components. Cattail (1963: 1-32) called them crystallized and fluid intelligence. *Crystallized intelligence* involves the knowledge a person has already acquired and the ability to access that knowledge. *Fluid intelligence* is the ability to see complex relationships and solve problems. The primary concern of innovative ideas is based on a system of knowledge to create new images for a product and/or services. In the business image, a manager emphasizes knowledge and symbols rather than habit and behavior (D'Andrade, 1984).The cognitive focus on conceptualization of an idea closely reflects the native's image of the physical environment, human nature, and society's value systems.

Conception is the intellectual ability of an individual to act or the power of forming notions, ideas, and concepts. Conception could be expressed through *tacit* knowledge and/or *explicit* knowledge. It is the holistic ability to express individual wisdom in the form of knowledge. Tacit knowledge is conceptual unsaid knowledge which contains insights of an individual's opinions and ideas. It is a talent for learning a kind of practical knowledge that can be acquired only through experience. *Explicit* knowledge is a systematic and easily communicated intellectual talent in the form of hard data or codified procedures which is known as a science (Parhizgar, 1998b: 72).

For example, a manager's conception concerning the conceptualization of a strategy is focusing on two dimensions: self and organization. The six terms from managerial self-conceptions are (1) myself, (2) stability, (3) survival, (4) my job, (5) freedom, and (6) power. The six terms of organization conceptions are (1) profitability, (2) shareholders, (3) stakeholders, (4) happiness, (5) success, and (6) harm (see Figure 6.5).

FIGURE 6.5. Vertical Icicle Plot Using Complete Linkage

```
MANAGERIAL CONCEPTIONS          ORGANIZATIONAL CONCEPTIONS

              (Down) Number of Clusters (n=10)

 1   2   3   4   5   6         1   2   3   4   5   6

 M   M   S   S   F   P         P   S   H   S   H   S
 Y   Y   T   U   R   O         R   H   A   T   A   U
 S   J   A   R   E   W         O   A   R   A   P   C
 E   O   B   V   E   E         F   R   M   K   P   C
 L   B   I   I   D   R         I   E       E   I   E
 F       L   V   O             T   H       H   N   S
         I   A   M             A   O       O   E   S
         T   L                 B   L       L   S
         Y                     I   D       L   S
                               L   E       D
                               I   R       E
                               T   S       R
                               Y           S
```

```
              MANAGERIAL                    ORGANIZATIONAL
              CONCEPTIONS                    CONCEPTIONS

        1  2   3   4   5   6   0   1   2   3   4   5   6
      XXXXXXXXXXXXXXXXXXXXXXXXXXXXXXXXXXXXXXXXXXXXXXXXXXXX
 1  *  X  X    X   X   X   X           X   X   X   X   X   X
 2  *  X  X    X   X   X       X       X   X   X   X   X   X
 3  *  X  X    X   X           X       X   X   X   X   X   X
 4  *  X  X    X               X       X   X   X   X   X   X
 5  *  X  X    X               X       X   X       X   X   X
 6  *  X  X                    X       X   X               X
 7  *  X  X                    X       X   X               X
 8  *  X  X                    X       X
 9  *  X  X                    X       X
10  *  X  X                    X       X
```

In Figure 6.6, conceptual maps that visually present managerial cognitive mapping represent how managers conceive their statutes in relation to other organizational constituencies as well as how managers conceive their business conceptions in relation with the organizational identity.

Business conception is the ability to create a meaningful organizational entity within the contextual boundary of the business environment. In a scientific analytical process, the term *conception* can be viewed as the individual's intellectual ability to expand the business opportunities and options. It is the utility of an individual's *multiple intelligences* to be applied during the developmental life of an organization, products, and employees.

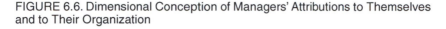

FIGURE 6.6. Dimensional Conception of Managers' Attributions to Themselves and to Their Organization

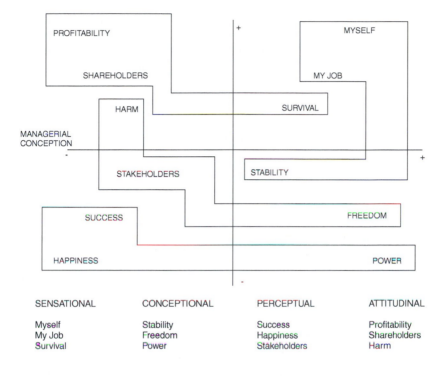

SENSATIONAL	CONCEPTIONAL	PERCEPTUAL	ATTITUDINAL
Myself	Stability	Success	Profitability
My Job	Freedom	Happiness	Shareholders
Survival	Power	Stakeholders	Harm

Multiple Natural Intelligences

In light of knowing about individual natural intelligences, it is appropriate to address certain questions, such as:

1. Should we *conceive* personal intelligence as knowledge of self?
2. Should we *perceive* it as knowledge of others?
3. Should we conceive it as being the major cognitive judgment of *self?*
4. Should we perceive it to think of knowledge of *others?*
5. Should we conceive it as being at a higher level of integrated form of intelligence as the result of the culture and historical political *ideology* to control and regulate an individual's behavior?

In responding to these questions, we need to identify natural intelligences and their attributes to the personhood of an individual. Howard Gardner (1983) cited seven major intelligences within the framework of the mind of an individual (see Table 6.2).

TABLE 6.2. Gardner's Seven Intelligences

Intelligences	Definition
1. Cognitive	Acts and processes knowing intellectual conceptions.
2. Linguistic	Addresses the meanings of thoughts and feelings.
3. Musical	Understands the special tone of speech and/or musical effects in the workplace.
4. Logical	Addresses the implicit analytical comparison among perception, sensation, attribution, and conception.
5. Spatial	Addresses the imagery and visual abilities to accurately assess the holistic pragmatic world.
6. Bodily-Kinesthetic	Addresses to create facial and gesture expressions and bodily movements.
7. Interpersonal	Addresses the interpersonal lifestyle and interpersonal information.

Source: Gardner, H. (1983). *Frame of Mind: The Theory of Multiple Intelligences,* Tenth Edition. New York: Basic Books, Harper Collins Publishers: 59-237.

Cognitive Intelligence

Cognitive intelligence acts and processes known concepts of an individual through attending, thinking, remembering, expecting, solving problems, fantasizing, and intuiting. It is an individualistic judgmental ability which takes place when an individual deals with intellectual causes and effects. In the seventeenth century, Rene Descartes declared: "I think, therefore, I am." This statement expresses a fundamental truth about the nature of human cognitive intelligence (Zimbardo: 1992: 17). People, through the cognitive intelligence, initiate mapping the processes of self-identity. Cognitive intelligence through the range or scope of causes and effects of an individual's judgments causes the choice of appropriate courses of decisions and actions. Cognitive intelligence is knowing about choices. The cognitive intelligence of managers allows them to provide awareness of the difficulty of a job to be performed. Managers, through their cognitive views, draw on their experiences and use past learning awareness as a basis for present justification of their behavior. These experiences represent presumed knowledge, or cognitive intelligence. For example, when a manager is faced with the choice of a job assignment as an expatriate manager in a foreign country, he or she will use previous experiences in deciding whether to accept or reject it.

Cognitive dissonance occurs when an individual holds conflicting beliefs and attitudes concerning decisions and actions (Festinger, 1957). Cognitive dissonance is a typical reaction after having made a difficult decision that consists of three major elements (Nahavandi and Malekzadeh, 1999):

- The decision maker considers the decision important.
- There are a number of mutually exclusive alternatives.
- All alternatives have advantages that are forgone when not selected.

Linguistic Intelligence

Linguistic intelligence addresses the meanings or connotations of words, sentences, and phrases which represent an individual's intrinsic thoughts and feelings. It arranges the imagery requirements of fundamental brain-work and its capability for discussing, debating, and arguing the individual's position in a subject matter of expression. This intelligence requires sensitivity to the various shadings around meanings, applications, and implications of collective neighboring words.

A keen linguistic memory is probably an important feature for advancement of linguistic intelligence. During oral, written, and body language communication, symbolic ordering of words and/or gestures and their infective meanings in relationship to the intuitive thoughts, feelings, opinions, and ideas play an important role in expressing self.

Musical Intelligence

A study of musical intelligence may help managers understand the special impacts of the tone of music on the workplace. For example, once I visited a retail store in downtown Los Angeles, and I found the rock music was very loud. I asked the manager about its effect on customer behavior. He said that if he turned it down, customers were not going to stay in the store and the volume of sales would immediately decrease since the majority of customers were teenagers.

Musical intelligence manages feelings, expresses knowledge about feelings, and identifies knowledge about forms of feelings. It communicates between the performers' talent and the attentive listeners. Musical management can motivate bodily intelligence to be more dynamic.

From another dimension, managers are viewed as composers who can function by the fact that they constantly have "harmony in sounds in their head." Such a harmony is the result of hearing tones, rhythms, and patterns of musical instruments. Musical intelligence begins at the moment when managers are exposed to new impressive conceptions that have come to their mind. The individual immediately crystallizes all necessary sounds to be required to form a significant impression through selectivity of melodic, rhythmic, and harmonic words. The musical tone of a manager's voice is concerned predominantly with the mechanisms of cognitive intelligence. As indicated before in linguistic intelligence, a manager's tonal expression of ideas begins with his or her cognitive memory. Once the idea emerges, the process of development and elaboration on planning and organizing as well as the accessibility of organizational structural forms appear. Therefore, musical intelligence within the mind of a manager is nothing but the endless reshaping of the organizational strategic objectives.

Logical Intelligence

Much discussion in this chapter has centered around an implicit analytical comparison among perception, sensation, attribution, and conception. Each of these domains of intelligences targets one or more dimensions of an individual identity. For example, cognitive intelligence maps the functions of understanding, learning, and judging; musical intelligence targets the management of feelings; and logical intelligence targets the management of rationality. Logical intelligence has been most closely tied to the individual's mathematical sphere of reasoning and legitimate modes of behavior. Managers need to develop their conceptual portfolio of decision-making processes on the basis of application of mathematical and statistical data. A manager applies many features of logical mathematics, such as proportions, special ratios, recurring patterns, numerical volumes, formula, and other detectable series to be used for justification of their own conceptions in decision-making processes.

Logical intelligence is a form of conception which can be traced to an individual's exposure to the world objects. It is an intrinsic assessment of thinking concerned with the exploration of meanings, utility, and efficacy of objects. Within the domain of mathematical logic, individuals order, reorder, multiply, add, divide, and subtract objects in their own minds for comprehending the representative values toward assessments of their quantities. A manager uses matrixes that identify the return on innovation and investment requirements. Innovation indices track and monitor quantitative progress.

Spatial Intelligence

Central to spatial intelligence are the imagery and visual abilities of an individual to accurately conceive and perceive both the imagery and the pragmatic world, to perform configurations, transformations, and modifications upon one's initial conception and perception, and to be able to recreate aspects of one's visual and cognitive experiences. It is the viability of an idea in the absence of relevant metaphysical stimuli. These abilities are clearly not identical. An individual may have acute visual perception, while having little ability to draw, imagine, or transform an absent world. Spatial intelligence is closely tied to, and grows most directly out of, one's observation of the visual and/or imagery intuitive world. It should be noted that both conceptual and perceptual spatial intelligences are linked to particular sensory modality of an individual's potential. For example, by designing the form and features of a product with a group of designers and engineers, spatial intelligence plays an important role.

There are significant perceptions in today's global market concerning the protection of intellectual property rights. Although intellectual property is a conceptual abstract term for an abstract concept, it is nonetheless familiar to virtually everyone. Trademarks, service marks, collective marks, copyrights, patents, techniques, procedures, and deeds of ownership are all forms of intellectual property. In the United States, laws protecting spatial intelligences of patents, trademarks, and copyrights are explicitly designed to protect and reward inventive and artistic creativity within a certain period of time. Spatial intelligence not only functions in the creativity of new products but also functions in the creation manipulation of product imitation, copying, duplicating, and piracy. Intellectual property rights infringement has been one of the greatest problems for MNCs. For example, in 1995, experts estimated that 95 percent of all software sold in Russia had been illegally duplicated (Jackson, Miller, and Miller, 1997). Such a behavior corrupts personal integrity of Russian citizens and the social order of the Russian government.

Bodily-Kinesthetic Intelligence

An individual has the potential to create objects through facial expressions and bodily actions. *Bodily-kinesthetic intelligence* manifests the ability to use one's body in highly differentiated and artistic ways, for expressive as well as objective-directed purposes. Mailer (1977: 255) indicates, "There are languages other than words, languages of symbols and languages of nature. There are languages of body. . . . Boxing is a dialogue between bodies, [it] is a rapid debate between two sets of intelligences." These characteristics sometime manifest one's identity through natural phenomena and abstracts such as good or evil and ugliness or beauty. Given these core components, I will focus upon managers who develop keen mastery over the motion of their hands, faces, and the tone of speech while they are addressing their board members and/or subordinates in meetings.

Nearly all cultural roles exploit more than one intelligence. Gardner (1983: 207) states: "Skilled use of one's body has been important in the history of the species. . . . More generally they sought a harmony between mind and body, with the mind trained to use the body properly, and the body trained to respond to the expressive powers of the mind."

Two domains of conceptions exist concerning the bodily-kinesthetic intelligence. These are *reflective* and *active* intelligences. The reflective intelligence is the direct product of our body reaction to stimuli. For example, when an object is getting too close to our eyes, immediately the bodily-kinesthetic intelligence reacts and orders our eyes to close. The active bodily-kinesthetic intelligence is the assumption of conscious awareness and deliberated bodily action on the basis of purposive objectives. Knowledge of what is coming next allows the body to perform according to the preplanned sequences of behavior. Our bodily-kinesthetic intelligences monitor all activities of movement through timing, forcing, and extending our movements and they make necessary adjustments by the time of receiving and forwarding information.

For example, when a manager is monitoring the figures of the stock market on the screen, and observes that the value of the corporation is decreasing, immediately this person shows emotional reactions through facial expressions and/or the motion of pounding the table with a fist. This action shows that the person is determined to make appropriate changes in the corporation's operation in order to reverse the values of the stock.

Interpersonal Intelligence

Interpersonal intelligence is rooted in the biological characteristics of an individual. However, it is directly related to an individual's "interpersonal lifestyle" and "interpersonal knowledge" in various "selves." Scientists, through surgical procedures, have analyzed the two halves of the brain and studied them separately. They have provided further confirmatory evidence that the left hemisphere is dominant for linguistic functioning and the right, for spatial functioning. They have concluded that an individual possesses more than a single consciousness (Sperry, 1973).

An individual possesses many "selves" in different situations and conditions. The interpersonal intelligence lifestyle of an individual is conceived in the inner realm of "selves" through manifestation of religious disciplinary faith (God fearing), consideration of ethical and moral beliefs (goodness), application of learned cultural value systems (carefulness), and compliance with civic expectation (survival). The ultimate result of interpersonal intelligence is to avoid previously learned consequences of aggressiveness and selfishness.

Interpersonal intelligence divides conception of the emotional and intellectual "selves" from each other. However, an intellectual "self" makes all efforts to stylize all these "selves" against the threat of selfishness, brutishness, tyranny, and savagery.

WHAT IS ATTRIBUTION?

As previously indicated, an individual's behavior can be attributed to specified causes and/or motives. People believe that individuals are rational and they are obligated to identify and understand the causal structure of an action or behavior. When an individual acts or observes the action and behavior of another person, the person is likely to try to understand what motivated or caused it. Since individual conceptions and perceptions tend to be so different among people, individual attributions also vary widely from person to person and from culture to culture. For example, if two managers encounter an employee who is crying and complaining about his or her co-worker, one manager may attribute the tears to the individual's emotional sensitivity, while the other may attribute the tears to be a tactic used to attract the manager's sympathy in order to influence the manager to take immediate action. Attributions are concerned with "why" questions of direct or indirect causes and motivations. Since most causes, motives, attributes, and whys are not directly observable, we evaluate them in terms of their consensus, consistency, and distinctiveness (Kelley, 1967, 1973; Kelley and Michela, 1980). *Consensus* is the extent to which people in the same situation act like one another. *Consistency* is the degree to which the same person acts in the same way at different times. *Distinctiveness* is the extent to which the same person acts in the same way in different situations.

This type of interpretation process is called *attribution theory*. Luthans (1985: 215) indicates: "Although attribution theory has its roots in all the pioneering cognitive theorists' work (for example, that of Lewin and Festinger), in de Charms's ideas on cognitive evaluation, and Bem's notion of 'self-perception,' the theory's initiator is generally recognized to be Fritz Heider." Attribution of the cause and motivational finding process of an action or behavior in the field of management is called *justification*. Causality is the art of solving difficult problems through the careful application of reasoning. Causality uses the principles and norms that have been developed and justified in consensus with cultural values and the behavior of people.

Attribution is a theory of the relationship between personal perception and interpersonal conception. It is mainly concerned with the cognitive processes by which an individual interprets behavior as being caused by (or attributed to) certain parts of the relevant environment (Kelley, 1967). We may conclude that an action motivated from within (intrinsic) or from outside (extrinsic) led the person to the behavior.

We make intrinsic attributions when we conceive the cause or the motive of an action or behavior as the result of our "inside" conception. These types of cause findings are based upon cognitive judgments. They are the result of the processes of our multiple intelligences.

We make extrinsic attributions when we perceive that causes or motives of actions or behavior are the result of our surrounding observation (perception). These types of causes are rooted in extrinsic factors that we have observed and/or felt. Extrinsic factors could be perceived as physical settings, situational circumstances, conditional agreements, task difficulty, climate, the behavior of other people, ritual cultural performances, and luck. The conclusive intrinsic motivational judgments that form a kind of idea and/or opinion are called "arbitrary decisions." The extrinsic causal judgments are called "situational and/or conditional attributions."

In the field of management, when employees are terminated from organizations, there are two phrases: *at will,* and *just cause.* Managers attribute their decisions and actions on the basis of one. In the event that the decision and action of the manager has been based upon the "at will" motive, the motivational finding is based upon personal arbitrary judgment. By using the "at will" condition, the manager does not want to reveal the real intrinsic attributions of the discharge to the public. In the situation of application of "just cause," the manager states clearly all extrinsic causes for that employment termination. In unionized organizations, managers are not allowed to use "at will" decisions and actions. Managers need to disclose "just cause," in order to provide due processes for prospective termination of employees.

ATTITUDES AND ATTITUDE FORMATION

People behave differently within the same contextual circumstances in their social interactions. An important behavioral trait of an individual is the distinction between personality types. This concept is related to moodiness, attitudinal perception, introversion/extroversion tendencies, and emotional and sensational orientations toward self, others, and surroundings. What is an attitude? How is one formed? What is a good or bad attitude? What is an attitude problem?

In addition to providing you with some insight into the above questions, I will address the analytical discussions about structural and situational views and the process involved in attitude formation. I will conclude by explaining and exploring the concepts of cognitive dissonance and attitudinal judgment about self and others.

Self-Image Theory

Although people have direct access to their own personal past experiences, we assume that our motivational conceptions, causal perceptions, and behavioral orientations are differential results of intrinsic judgment. Nevertheless, in most cases, our judgments about "self" could be deduced from other people's judgments about us. This concept is known as the "self-image theory." The self-image theory refers to an individual's tendency to search for intrinsic and extrinsic factors when asked to explain the cause-effect of his or her own tendencies. The self-image theory is a view that we assume individuals make attributions through, conceiving their motivational and causal behavior. Interestingly, when an employee perceives some organizational reputation and consequently receives monetary rewards, the employee tends to attribute these factors to be the result of hard work. Two sides exist to this idea: self-satisfaction and organizational recognition.

What Is an Attitude?

Attitudes are learned. Individual attitudes are aspects of individual differences of utmost importance in social interactions. People possess certain experiences and orientations concerning self-behavior and environmental factors. An attitude is a mental imagery tendency or behavioral orientation concerning a repetitive pattern of actions and/or expression of ideas and opinions in a preset situation; attitude is a state or quality of feelings at a particular time and place; attitude is a self-monitoring behavior that manifests sensational and emotional feelings and positions with regard to self within the contextual boundary of relationship to other people or objects. We sometimes speak of "attitude problems" or say that someone has a "good or bad attitude."

Attitude Formation

Individuals develop their attitudes on the basis of past evaluative respective causes and consequences toward objects. Many elements influence the formation of attitudes. As a result of direct experience from the past and social learning processes, people shape and reshape their attitudes. Individuals do not have any attitude of self and others unless they expose themselves to an entity or to a situation (person, object, time, and conditional circumstances) on an affective, cognitive, and behavioral basis (Allport, 1935; Gerhart, 1987). To understand the complexity of an attitude, I will analyze it through structural, situational, and conditional views.

Structural View

Traditionally, attitudes were viewed as stable dispositions to behave toward objects in a certain way as a result of experience (Allport 1935; Gerhart, 1987). According to this view, attitudes have three basic components: *affect, cognition,* and *intention.*

Attitudes are experienced as repetitive stabilized dispositions which are merged through three parts (affect, cognition, and intention) of behavioral structure (see Figure 6.7). As the result of an individual's conscious and unconscious tendencies, people are thought to behave in certain expressive manners toward certain things and situations. For clarity of subject matter, I will explain the structural foundation of attitudes.

Affect

An *affect* refers to the individual's state of expressive and dynamic emotional, sensational, and motivational feelings toward something. In many ways, affect is similar to emotion. We feel emotion unconsciously to express ourselves to others. For example, most academicians react to the content of "academic freedom, liberty, and intellectual contributions" in a manner that reflects their opinions about what these contents convey. Similarly, most people react to words such as love, liveliness, hate, sex, and integrity in a manner in which they may express their judgmental perceptions.

Within the contextual boundary of the international sociopolitical systems, in one culture, you may like the type of political ideology, dislike an-

FIGURE 6.7. The Structural View of Attitude

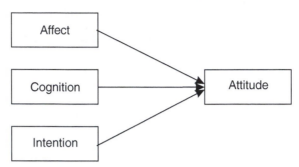

other, and be indifferent toward a third. Capitalist nations believe in "individualism," socialist nations believe in "socialism," and the communists believe in "collectivism." Although you will find different reasons for these political platforms, many attitudes are in fact based on purely affective responses. Certainly, individual rights should not be perceived as a disposal factor in any political power competition.

Cognition

Cognition is the insight knowledge through which individuals express their own judgment about conceiving an object or an event in a rational way. The cognitive, rational, or intellectual component of an attitude is what most people understand it to be: the reason for an expression of self-behavior based upon conscious awareness, knowledge, and understanding. Attitude is the matter of positive and free-will aspects of human behavior. Attitude utilizes conscious awareness such as expectancy, demand, and incentive. Since cognition is based on conceptually rational judgments, an attitude is based upon holistic feelings, thinking, and behaving. Attitude is differentiated from reality of past experiences. Cognitive information is based on truth and reality. Cognitive perception is a purposive behavior that is directed toward understanding the real nature of an objective. For example, in the international field of management, cognitive judgment concerns bribery, dishonesty, perjury, and the like, depending on conditional situations. There is a problem with "cognitive perception." Cognitive perceptions are based upon socioeconomic and cultural orientations and psychological understanding of the cause-effects of some attributions. This variation in cognitive perception is based on perceptual judgment (not conceptual judgment), and cognitive perceptions become very subjective. Therefore, the cognitive perceptual component of an attitude may be logical or illogical, rational or irrational, and relevant or irrelevant to an object. This "perceptual knowledge" may be true, partially true, or totally false. For example, shoplifting is a bad attitude among some customers. In some cultures, the attitude toward shoplifting in a monopolistic industry may be conceived as logical, because consumers believe that a business owner is ripping them off on the basis of the cost of their daily necessities. In another culture, the attitude of shoplifting is also bad because people conceive within an industry that there are many competitors with varieties of pricing systems. Therefore, the consumer-producer relationship is based on reciprocal satisfaction. People believe that it is not right for both parties to rip off and/or steal something from each other. In such an analogy, the matter of justification of perceptual attitudes is based upon "choice," versus "force." In a monopolistic market, customers are exposed to force while in a competitive market customers are dealing with choice. However, within the boundary of conceptual cognition, the actions of ripping off customers and stealing merchandise from businesses are not correct attitudes.

Cognitive Dissonance

Cognitive dissonance is a state of self-discovery in which an individual experiences a conflict between his or her attitudes (tendencies) and intellectual thoughts. It is an internal conflict or anxiety that arises from two opposing sets of knowledge or information. Cognitive dissonance occurs when an individual holds inconsistent or conflicting beliefs and attitudes along with rationalized thoughts. Cognitive dissonance leads to paradoxical decision-making processes. It escalates double standards in decisions and actions. For example, when a manager is following an organizational rule in regard to promotional procedures, they may find themselves in a conflicting decision-making process. It is a managerial responsibility to promote an employee who deserves to be promoted. Sometimes promotion is based on a very defined set of criteria and structural assessment. In the event of defined criteria, all qualities should be converted into quantities for the final comparative judgmental assessment. In this type of decision-making process, the manager's decision is based on rational and logical reasoning. Sometimes the decision is based upon the manager's arbitrary judgment. In this case, managers may make their decisions on the basis of the "heart" not the "mind." This type of conflicting and biased behavior is called *cognitive dissonance*. Therefore, cognitive dissonance is the contradictory result of rationality and emotionality.

Intention guides an individual's premeditated actions and behaviors toward an activity within the boundary of a particular direction. If you like your profession, you may develop a positive attitude toward your job. In such an event, regardless of the type of supervisory style of your organization, you are performing your job on the basis of your intentional attitudes. However, it should be noted that intentions do not always translate into behavior, because often some attitudes clash either with your rational or emotional drives. Drives are directive motivations. Some attitudes and their corresponding drives are appropriately related to the personalities of people.

The Situational and Conditional View

There is another view that challenges the structural view. The *situational view of attitudes* contends (see Table 6.3) that attitudes evolve from socially constructed realities (Salancik and Pfeffer, 1977, 1978).

Some researchers contend that research has not clearly demonstrated that attitudes are continuously proceeding with the same pattern of actions. Moorhead and Griffin (1992: 111) state, "Attitudes are stable dispositions which composed of precise components that are consistently reflected in individual responses." Instead, they argue, attitudes evolve from socially constructed realities.

The situational view of attitudes illustrates that people, through gathering information about particular situations, can help themselves to understand what kinds of attitudes and behaviors are acceptable. The situational view of attitudes has proved interesting to researchers and managers alike (Griffin, 1987). According to this view, the emerging opinion appears to be that attitudes are shaped both by objective attributes of the workplace and social information.

MANAGING SOCIOCULTURAL ATTITUDES

Sociocultural attitudes are important in all organizations. An individual's attitudes toward objects and other people are different from other individual attitudes. People differ in physical features and in mental capacities, talents, strengths, musical aptitudes, linguistic fluency, and so on. All of these inequalities are differentiated both from social learning and genetic inheritance. More important, people from different cultures have unequal access to global social rewards and ecological resources. Consequently, each cul-

TABLE 6.3. The Situational View of Attitudes

Social Context provides ⟶	information that shapes ⟶	attitudes
Example: New employee enters the work group.	Employee is exposed to current employees' attitudes about: • boss • reward system • work conditions • output norms • stress	Attitudes of employee are shaped and influenced by social context as reflected by current employees.

Source: Adapted from Moorhead, G. and Griffin, R. W. (1992). *Organizational Behavior, Third Edition.* Boston, MA: Houghton-Mifflin Company, p. 111.

ture can establish various forms of wealth, technology, power, and privileges. These differences are the result of individuals' attitudes toward their lifestyles and production-consumption expectations. However, these attitudes are of greatest consequence in accounting for who we are, who we can be, and who we ultimately may become as members of the global village.

In all nations, citizens receive different shares of resources of what are valued and scarce. These unequal attributions create different systems and classes of people. There are multidimensional models of sociocultural and econopolitical stratification that recognize several class hierarchies. Each hierarchy is based on some key social criterion: wealth, occupation, education, political power and authority, ethnicity, religion, gender, and the like. These classes of people can be based upon the political elite class system, the intellectual class system, the occupational class system, the property class system, the ethnic class system, the family class system, the labor class system, and the business class system.

Stratification of people depends upon the general cultural perceptions and attitudes of people in perceiving self and others. Through an anthropological and sociological analysis, power underlies all forms of stratification. Societal power can be viewed as a society's productive system (á la Marx) or as derivative of other criteria as well (á la Weber). Social power is essentially founded on and maintained by a differential of power holder (Marger, 1985: 26). Managing power is a matter of who is influencing whom and what attitudes evolve from these perceptions. These are the core concepts in organizational behavior.

Satisfied employees are likely to be productive, while those with a negative attitude toward the organization are likely to quit, be unproductive, or be counterproductive. There are many factors in the workplace that can cause good and bad attitudes among employees. These factors are grouped into cultural factors, organizational factors, job factors, group factors, and personal factors. All these factors are influenced by one or more sociocultural orientations such as racism, prejudice, discrimination, and bias.

Managing Racism

Racism is a social/political/cultural/historical changing concept. Omni and Winant (1986) call this "racial formation," meaning that society assigns different worths and unequal treatments to groups on the basis of its definition of race. Zin and Eitzen (1993: 110) indicate that "Racial formation touches families throughout society, not only people of color. Racism refers to systems of inequality in which some fixed group membership such as race, religion, or national origin are major criteria for ranking social positions and their differential rewards."

Racism against some homogenous ethnic group of people is a stronger group's mode of belief that their natural physiological and biological characteristics are superior to other races. Racist attitudes involve the treatment and maintenance of various members of society differently based on their historical ethnic origin. It is mainly related to the pattern of valued resources distribution among classes of people. In multicultural societies, there is no ethnic group hierarchy to rationalize and legitimize the pattern of dominance and subordination among classes of people. In multicultural organizations, employees are awarded according to their level of productivity, not for being a member of a privileged ethnic group. In these types of organizations, equality in power acquisition and privilege distribution are based upon the "merit system."

Managing Prejudice

Prejudice is defined as an extremist "faith" in favor of an ethnic, professional, and gender group, an ideology, and/or a sectarian religious faction. Prejudice is a fixed mental attitude or opinion formed beforehand or without knowledge, thought, or reason about an individual's personality. It is also a perceived opinion or feeling, either favorable or unfavorable. Prejudice is, as Berry and Tischler (1978: 235) have pointed out, "more emotion, feeling, and bias than it is judgment."

Marger (1985) identifies four major characteristics ascribed to prejudiced people: categorical, inflexible, negative, and stereotypes. It is very often that by the time of recruitment and promotion processes, some managers are prejudiced for or against a group of people. Such an attitude comes from generalized feelings and biased decisions. Individuals are judged on the basis of their group membership and affiliation, rather than on their personal attributes. Allport (1958: 9) explains, "Prejudgments become prejudice only if they are not reversible when exposed to new knowledge." Prejudice is not an emotional error in attitudes. It is a conscious awareness in favor of a group, an idea, and opinion. Prejudice is not subject to correction.

Prejudiced managers, by the time of decision-making processes, usually are so attached to their emotional feelings and beliefs that they discard the rational thoughts in the light of contrary evidence. Managers should not be prejudiced through their expressed opinions against a group of people. They should avoid any specific ascribed or negative comments targeted to groups in order not to demean them. Of course, prejudice could be positive as well as negative.

Managing Discrimination

Discrimination is a historical and cultural pattern of thought and behavior wherein the societal rights of a dominant majority group take precedence over and deny minorities their legitimate rights. The majority or dominant groups make their decisions on the basis of discriminating conscious tendencies to avert the rights of minority individuals for the benefit of the majority members. It applies to various actions against minority ethnic groups (gender, foreigners, ethnicity, race, and color) through avoidance, denial, threats, or physical attacks and mental abuse. At different repetitive times, all of these forms of coercion may be used to deny the rights of a minority group. The extremist sort of discrimination against such individuals, involving homicides of a minority group, is called "ethnic cleansing." All the above actions are collectively called discrimination.

Managing Bias

It is true that at the invisible surface of behaviorism, the nature of a human being is based upon egocentrism and selfishness. These attributions may be affected by two very common errors: the fundamental attribution error and the self-serving bias.

The tendency to make attributions to internal causes when an individual focuses on someone else's behavior is known as the fundamental attribution error (Smith, 1909). Individuals tend to make internal attributions for their own success and external attributions for their own failures (Lane and DiStefano, 1992). In other words, when we succeed, we may be biased to give ourselves all the credit, but when we fail, we blame others for our failure because we are trying to find scapegoats.

In general, we may find two types of behavior within a person: the real and the biased. The real intrinsic behavior is a natural ethical and moral judgment which is based on our conscious deliberation with the minimum effect of selfishness. This characteristic behavior is called "serving beyond self." The biased intrinsic behavior is based on selfish interest to the extent of denying reality and/or self identity. This type of bias is called "self-deception." The tendency to accept credit for success and reject blame for failures is called the self-serving bias (Miller and Ross, 1975; Tandon, Ansari, and Kapor, 1991).

Perceptual biased judgments can cause serious destructive consequences which overemphasize self-realization and self-actualization. This kind of behavior is called the *Pygmalion* effect. The *Pygmalion* effect, or self-fulfilling prophecy, refers to one's expected beliefs and influence of others' behaviors to the point that they behave as we originally expected. Maybe the best end result of the Pygmalion effect can be labeled as influencing others on the basis of our self-interests. Therefore, perceptual biases can cause serious self-destruction.

SUMMARY

Dissimilar characteristics among personalities and behaviors of people make each individual unique. All individuals are alike in general, but they are different in other specific ways.

Managers fall into two distinctive categories of decision-making processes: (1) to apply some conclusive reasons that would apply to all employees (such as equal employment opportunities, which state that all employees like to be treated with the same standards), and (2) employees are unique and they expect to be treated differently according to their unique personalities. Employees are not numbers; they are human beings. One major source of uniqueness is personality. Biological, sociocultural, econopolitical, and psychological factors all influence the formation of personality.

Sensational, perceptual, conceptual, and attitudinal characteristics of an individual are major sources of behavioral complexity. A cognitive conception of an individual manifests intellectual ability in reasoning.

CHAPTER QUESTIONS FOR DISCUSSION

1. Briefly define sensation, perception, conception, attitudes, and attributions. What are some examples of each?
2. What is attribution theory?
3. How does sensation differ from perception?
4. What does stereotyping mean? Why is it considered to be a perceptual problem?
5. What effect can the perceptual process have on individuals' behavior?

LEARNING ABOUT YOURSELF EXERCISE #6

How Do You Attribute?

Following are twelve items for rating how important each one is to you and to your organization on a scale of 0 (not important) to 100 (very important). Write the number 0-100 on the line to the left of each item.

Not important		Somewhat important		Very important
0	25	50	75	100

As a manager of an organization, it would be more important for me to:

_____ 1. Meet my own needs as the prime objective of my perception.
_____ 2. Stay in my job unless I find a better job.
_____ 3. Make decisions on the basis of common sense rather than odd behavior.
_____ 4. Satisfy the demand of shareholders.
_____ 5. Rule on the basis of my heart.
_____ 6. Show too much warmth to my organizational constituencies.
_____ 7. Maximize organizational profitability.
_____ 8. Get along with people with a reasonable amount of professionalization.
_____ 9. Implement organizational policies and regulations at the maximum degree.
_____ 10. Exercise firmly my managerial responsibilities.
_____ 11. Make sure to achieve organizational objectives by all means and ends.
_____ 12. Be patient and show tolerance to critical comments from subordinates.

Turn to the next page for scoring directions and key.

SCORING DIRECTIONS AND KEY FOR EXERCISE #6

Transfer the numbers for each of the twelve items to the appropriate column, then add up the three numbers in each column.

Sensation	Conception	Perception	Attitude
7. _____	1. _____	2. _____	5. _____
4. _____	3. _____	9. _____	10. _____
6. _____	8. _____	12. _____	11. _____
Your Totals _____	_____	_____	_____
Total Scores 300	300	300	300

The higher the total in any dimension, the higher the importance you place on that set. The closer the numbers are in four dimensions, the more sociopsychologically balanced you are.

Make up a categorical scale of your findings on the basis of more weight for the values of each category.

For example:

    1. 300 Perceptual
    2. 275 Sensational
    3. 250 Attitudinal
    4. 200 Conceptional

    Your totals   925
    Total scores   1,200

After you have tabulated your scores, compare them with others on your team or in your class. You will find different judgmental patterns among people with diverse scores and preferred modes of self-realization.

CASE STUDY:
THE GENERAL ELECTRIC MANAGERIAL PERCEPTION:
WHO WILL RUN GE?

General Electric Company is one of the largest companies in the world. The company's empire is worth a quarter of a trillion dollars. For half a century, including twenty years under the leadership of John F. "Jack" Welch, GE created $200 billion in new wealth for shareholders, which is considered the biggest financial legacy in the history of capitalism.

Since Thomas Edison started General Electric in the late 1800s, the company has steadily grown into a tremendously successful organization. In late 1879, Thomas Edison invented and produced the electric light bulb and established several light companies. Edison created the Edison Electric Light Company in 1878. In 1892, General Electric Company was founded with the merger of Edison General Electric Company and Thomson-Houston Electric Company.

As of 2000, GE offered many products and services with over 340,000 employees worldwide. Some of its services included the manufacturing of high-tech products such as aircraft engines, computer-related information services, broadcasting operations, airport navigation services, electrical appliances, and financial services. According to 2000 figures, it had 2.1 million shareholders with earnings per share about $1.27. Its net earnings were $12.7 billion. Currently, General Electric has several subsidiaries. The major subsidiaries include GE Lighting, Appliances, Medical Systems, Aircraft Engines, GE Plastics, the National Broadcasting Company, Inc. (NBC), and Transportation Systems.

The main role-player of this case is Jack Welch who retired in 2001. As the CEO of GE for twenty years, Welch ran GE efficiently, effectively, and productively. The company was looking for someone with similar managerial characteristics to take over the company. Welch said: "For the last three years it's been a rigorous process." There were six likely candidates nominated for the new CEO position at GE, all of whom lead multimillion dollar businesses. In 1998, the candidates were David L. Calhoun, 41, CEO of GE Lighting; David M. Cote, 46, Appliances; Jeffrey R. Immelt, 42, Medical Systems; W. James McNerney, 49, Aircraft Engines; Robert Nardelli, 50, Power Systems; and John G. Rice, 42, Transportation Systems. The ages ranged between forty and fifty for all these nominees.

The main issues in this case were changes in the company's culture, structure, and working environment by the time that Welch departed the company.

Sources: Stewart, Thomas A. (1999). "First: The Contest for Welch's Throne Begins: Who Will Run GE?" *Fortune.* January 11, 1999, 26-27. Colvin, G. (2001). Changing of the Guard. *Fortune.* January 8; *The GE Fact Sheet* (2001). <http://www.ge.com/factsheet.html>.

Welch's conception was the cognitive judgment about the role of new GE leadership. He believed that the headquarters of a corporation does not run its subsidiaries. Welch believed management of a corporation should focus on people. He stated that GE headquarters ran a school that taught how to run companies; it did this on the basis of talent development, which is the management's job. He spent his time focused on people. His attitude toward people was "We've got wonderful people we all like." Welch was looking for "vision" and "courage." He attributed his success to the Es: energy, edge, and execution. Energy is the ability to energize others, the edge is the ability to make tough decisions and execution is a positive attitude which brings dreams into reality. Finally, in November 2000, Jeffrey R. Immelt, 44, head of the GE medical-systems business, became the net chief executive of the world's most valuable company.

Chapter 7

Understanding and Managing Individual Personality

Personality is a completed puzzle picture of an individual behavior.

CHAPTER OBJECTIVES

After studying this chapter, you should be able to:

- realize what the major elements of "self" concept are,
- understand personality and individual patterns of behavior,
- understand various factors of the biological contribution to personality,
- understand sociocultural and ecological contributions to the formation and development of personality,
- describe the nature of individual differences in organizations,
- describe personality types and traits that affect organizations,
- analyze managerial styles on the basis of the sociocultural, psychological, and behavioral characteristics of a manager, and
- discuss how managers should cope with individual differences.

INTRODUCTION

Today, organizations are becoming borderless global institutions through the free flow of information. In-person communication is not the only way to associate with others. The association can be through e-image, e-mails, or e-commerce. Accordingly, individuals possess two types of behavior: (1) live and (2) imaginary behaviors.

Organizations can be classified according to two dimensions. First, organizations differ in the extent to which they are *domestically oriented* and culturally homogeneous. This concept is being used here to refer to the behavioral setting within a company. Theoretically, culturally homogeneous organizations are made up of personalities who are more or less working toward the same organizational identification regardless of each individual's ethnicity, race, color, religion, and so on. Second, organizations can be classified as to the extent to which they differ in being *internationally oriented* and multiculturally heterogeneous. These organizations vary according to ecological, sociocultural, psychological, and behavioral value systems. The only dilemma of organizational constituencies is individual character or personality.

Several criteria have been used to compare organizational cultural behaviors. For instance, through an anthropological view, organizational cultures have been classified according to whether they are "simple," or "complex" (Freeman and Winch, 1957: 461-466); or, through the view of marketing, organizations could be perceived through market size and product positions, global, multinational, bilateral, transnational, and international. Also, the heterogeneous view indicates that organizations can be classified into three categories: "near," "intermediate," or "far" from the core culture of the corporate's headquarter (Furnham and Bochner, 1986: 20). In addition, organizations can be classified through other dimensions such as geographic territory, political ideology, and financial ownership. They can be classified as home/host, domestic/foreign, joint ventures/alliances, and profit-making/not-for-profit organizations. All these characteristics are related to personal variable characteristics of decision makers and operators. Individuals are a combination of many factors, of which genetic, demographic, psychic, social, cultural, and behavioral dimensions emerge from their personalities. Accordingly, organizational behavior will exhibit different cultural characteristics. People possess a multitude of characteristics which function together to represent personalities. Organizational members do not function independently of their environment or the situation in which they find themselves. Situational factors and physiological characteristics can affect how organizational members respond in a variety of ways.

Today, managers are faced with the synergistic challenge to motivate and lead subordinates to achieve specific objectives. Perhaps we can define personality as the overall synergetic potential of an individual. So the more managers understand individual synergies, the better they can lead subordinates.

In this chapter, the concepts of individual differences, along with personalities, values, skills, beliefs, visions, desires, abilities, and lifestyles of people, are explored. The first section of this chapter defines and clarifies the analytical concept of personality. The next section is devoted to the development of personality along with discussion concerning some well-known theories of individual differences. The third section identifies determinants of individual personality within the framework of familial, sociocultural, and psychoanalytic aspects of ecological, situational, and conditional categories. In the fourth section, personhood will be discussed on the basis of the four major dimensions of *personalogy:* ideographic/nomothetic, types, and trait theories of personality. The final section of this chapter addresses the relationship between personality and the workplace and cultural political behavior of organizational personalities.

ANALYTICAL VIEWS ON PERSONALOGY

Personalogy is the study of personality structure, dynamics, and development in the individual (Zimbardo, 1992: 567). It is related to actual and practical biographical and past performance data. Personalogy is an analysis of the real past performance of an individual. It is based upon the data from biographies, case studies, letters, writings, and general behavioral observation. It is related to real characteristics and the end results of an individual's life events. One of the proponents of this technique is called "personalogy of neurotic managerial behavior." Finally, personalogy is the study of the type and patterns of behaviors of people.

What Is Personality?

Personality is a social manifestation of an individual's behavioral characteristics in accordance with the integration of intelligence and feelings. It is a holistic behavioral representation of "self-concept." The self-concept of an individual is similar in some ways to and in other ways different from others. The term *personality* can be traced to the Latin word *persona,* which translates as "to speak through." This Latin term was used to denote the masks worn by actors in ancient Greece and Rome. Common usage of the word emphasizes the role that the person (actor) displays to the public (Luthans, 1985: 97).

Personality represents the total characteristics of an individual. It is a critical component of individual differences. It is defined as the ecological, psychological, sociocultural, and behavioral traits and characteristics that distinguish one individual from another.

Personality is important to managers because it reflects all the behavioral characteristics of an employee's work. Numerous observers have pointed out the importance of personality in the probable outcomes of organizational performance. Personal characteristics that most often affect personality fall into four clusters: relevant ecological, psychological, sociocultural, and behavioral characteristics.

As shown in Figure 7.1, the first cluster includes variables for expressing "self." This cluster includes variables that reflect the heredity and/or genetic identity of an individual. It manifests the physiological heredity characteristics such as weight, height, hair color, eye color, body shape, gender, sensation, race, ethnicity, and appearance style.

FIGURE 7.1. Variables Influencing an Individual's Behavior

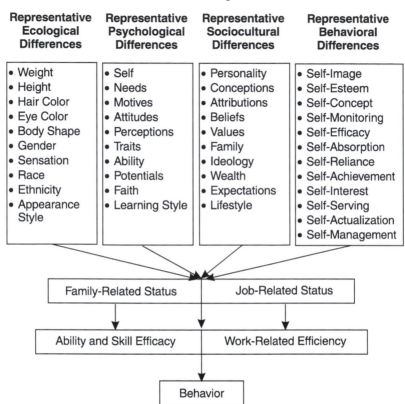

The second cluster includes psychological variables that reflect past experiences that somehow prepare the individual cognitively and emotionally for perceiving "self." This cluster concerns psychological factors such as feelings, needs, motives, attitudes, perceptions, traits, ability, potentials, faith, and learning style. Also, this cluster represents feelings of competence, trust, confidence, abilities, and intellectual potential.

The third cluster includes sociocultural variables, which are related to the level of valuable socialization and past dynamic group learning experiences. This cluster demonstrates the type of personality, conceptions, attributions, beliefs, values, family, ideology, wealth, expectations, and lifestyle.

The fourth cluster concerns behavior. This cluster identifies types of behaviors, such as self-image, self-esteem, self-concept, self-monitoring, self-efficacy, self-absorption, self-reliance, self-interest, self-serving, self-actualization, self-achievement, and self-management.

In order to understand personality, we need to analyze two major views: the common or laypeople's view and the scientific or intellectual view.

Laypeople's Views on Personality

The laypeople's or common view tends to relate personality with ecological characteristics and usually perceives it with a single dominant attribution (e.g., polite, rude, strong, weak, shy, persistent). This unique view of personality attributes some general characteristics repeatedly to the behavior of an individual. It represents the total cultural understanding of characteristics of that person. Usually, when laypeople express their opinions about the personalities of others, they perceive a general pattern of behavior across different situations and over time. Then, accordingly, they label the type of an individual's personality. For example, when a manager in all conditions shows emotion and a passionate exaggeration in praising some special people with the same degree of interest, common people perceive such a manager as having an "emotional and/or warm personality."

Scientific Views on Personality

The scientific or intellectual view, on the other hand, tends to relate personality to the holistic description of ecological, psychological, sociocultural, and behavioral synergistic factors. Although laypeople emphasize the *behavioral role,* which an individual displays to the public, scientific people emphasize the individual's intrinsic and extrinsic *traits and conditions.* Probably the most viable approach would include all characteristics.

The intellectual view focuses on specific processes that are similar in all people. These processes include neural transmission, conception, perception, conditioning, and attributions. Therefore, the heredity traits, psychological cognitive potentials, sociocultural values, and patterns of behavior are four basic determinants for understanding an individual's personality. These factors separately and collectively can influence the processes of emotional, sensational, rational, and decisional behavior of an individual.

From another point of view, it is not just that individuals behave and respond differently to the same stimulus in a common condition, there also seems to be inherent aspects that give coherence and order to behaviors. We know this core concept for each of us as our "selves." For the clarity of this complex issue, it is necessary to study the nature of "personhood."

THE MEANING OF PERSONHOOD

Kluckhohn and Strodtbeck (1961: 215) made the best statement about personhood: "To some extent, a person's personality is like other people's, like some other people's, and like no other people's." Personality manifests a holistic pattern of an individual's behavior in consistent ways in a variety of situations.

Personality is defined as the complex set of unique and consistent characteristics that influence an individual's pattern of behavior across different situations and over time. Personality represents "self" identity in relation to the extrinsic appearance and behavior, intrinsic awareness as a permanent dynamic force, and specific pattern of holistic assessment of "self." Therefore, personhood is a synergistic organization of *selves* (e.g., id, ego, and superego) that represents a general combination of sensational, emotional, rational, and intellectual characteristics to be measured and judged by "self" and others (Ruch, 1963:353).

Through a cross-cultural perspective, personality is the self-conceptualization of an individual's inherent and societal learned identity. This means that individuals represent (positively or negatively) their behavior to others and others collectively understand and judge themselves as well as their societal measurable traits in relations to others.

Determinants of Individual Differences

Ecological, psychological, behavioral, and sociocultural characteristics are the four major determinants of an individual's identity. Differences among people depend primarily upon four major groups of characteristics:

1. *Ecological and/or physical appearances:* facial features, facial gestures, ethnicity, height, weight, size, and other physical aspects
2. *Psychological traits:* intellect, extroversion, impulsiveness, flexibility, and so on
3. *Behavioral traits:* courteous, vulgar, aggressive, friendly, moral, ethical, and so on
4. *Sociocultural orientations and influences:* family-oriented, religion-oriented, educated, wealthy, poor, and so on

In addition, discovering and judging an individual's personality determinants could be based upon the essence of five different sources of data: (1) self-report judgments, (2) observer-report judgments, (3) incidental behavioral-event report judgments, (4) biographical life-event report judgments, and (5) physiological modes of appearance-report judgments. All these types of judgmental determinants can be interpreted through using two psychocultural approaches: (1) ideographic approach, and (2) nomothetic approach (Zimbardo, 1992).

The Psychocultural Ideographic Approach of Personhood

The psychocultural-ideographic approach is a holistic and synergistic approach. It is a person-centered analysis that focuses on outstanding and unique psychophysiological traits of an individual's characteristics from an integrated behavioral whole. The primary research methodologies of ideographic approach are the case study and the aggregate case study.

The Cultural Case Study

A cultural case study, used to analyze and judge the type of an individual's personality, is specifically selected from targeted incidents, manners, and traits of the biographical data of a single individual in a culture. After the careful consideration of the collected data and the discovery of a general pattern of behavior, the judgment about personality will be made. For example, Weiss (1987) discovered in a study on manufacturing, sales, and service employees that the self-esteem of recruits moderated the degree to which successful and competent supervisors served as role models in the recruits' learning of their organizations' cultures. Thus, individuals with low self-esteem tend to reduce the efficacy of their organizational goal achievement.

The Cultural Aggregated Case Study

The cultural aggregated case study is a comparison of ideographic information about an individual in different cultures by different observers. After careful consideration of the collected data from different sources, the end result of outcomes of the judgment will be made on the pattern of correlated findings in different cultures by different observers. This is a very complex and challenging method. For example, one study found that Japanese-American managers' behavior, while working in Japanese-run plants in Fremont, California, had nearly the same behavioral attitudes as Japanese managers in Japan. In addition, most American managers' attitudes in Japanese plants in Japan resembled the attitudes of American managers in the United States. These results indicate that managerial behavior is a differentiation of cultural value-oriented systems, not subject to drastic change according to new places. It takes generations to adapt behavior to new places. Other evidence indicates that cultural differences persist among immigrants despite acculturation over time to U.S. culture.

The Cultural Nomothetic Approach of Personhood

The cultural nomothetic approach is variable and relatively centered to contingent and situational cultural and behavioral conditions. People and cultures simply differ in the degree to which they inherit, change, and develop their personalities. The cultural nomothetic approach focuses on an individual's personality within the general contextual traits of a homogeneous encultured population. This approach, in determining the type of personality, is based upon assimilative methods of socialization, correlative methods of ideologies, beliefs, and religious faiths. However, this approach can be more related to the legal pattern of behavioral approach. This type of personality is centered around the civic culture. For example, when multinational managers wish to study how the civic culture of a community can change the direction of the home-host negotiations, they use the cultural nomothetic approach to understand personalities of negotiators.

FIVE CATEGORIES OF PERSONALITY

Personality is an adaptive stabilized physiological, psychological, behavioral, and sociocultural characteristic that makes an individual unique. Five major scientific categories of personality include the type theories, trait theories, psychodynamic theories, humanistic theories, and the integrative theories.

The Type Theories of Personality

The type theories presume that there are separate, discontinuous categories into which people fit. The criteria that these theories use are physiological appearance and sociocultural and/or psychological characteristics. The first element which represents a person is the physical body—outside and inside. Within the contextual boundary of the type theories of personality, we review twelve types of theories. These theories are: (1) somatotype, (2) type A, (3) type B, (4) type T, (5) extroverted type, (6) introverted type, (7) the Myers-Briggs sixteen types, (8) the five types of Parsons-Shils sociocultural, (9) the four types of Keene's pair theories, (10) the maturity type, (11) the immaturity type, and (12) the neurotic types of personalities.

The Somatotype Theories of Personality

Early researchers perceived personality to specify a concordance between a simple, highly visible, or easily determined characteristic and some invisible characteristics that can easily determine the type of personality. William Sheldon (1942), a medical doctor, through his research of interrelated physics to temperament, categorized people into three types of personalities based on their somatotype or physical body builds: (1) *endomorphic,* (2) *mesomorphic,* and (3) *ectomorphic:*

1. *Endomorphic* personalities represent those types of people who are fat, soft, and round. They are relaxed, fond of eating, and enjoy social interactions. These personalities consume their lives.
2. *Mesomorphic* personalities represent those types of people who are muscular, rectangular, and strong. They are filled with energy, courage, and expansive tendencies. These people challenge their lives.
3. *Ectomorphic* personalities represent those types of people who are thin, long, and fragile. They are brainy, artistic, and introverted. These people think through their lives.

It should be noted that Sheldon's views of body-mind personality are intriguing but do not have substantial and reliable research foundation.

Type A and Type B Theories of Personalities

Friedman and Rosenman (1974: 87) did empirical research on the use of personality type labels and their related behavior patterns in order to predict heart attacks. They introduced type A and opposing type B personalities. They defined type A personality as "an action-emotion complex that can be observed in any person who is aggressively involved in a chronic, incessant struggle to achieve more and more in less and less time, and required to do so, against the opposing efforts of other things or other persons." Type A personalities have an underlying "need for control" and strive to gain control over their environments.

In contrast, the type B personality is not concerned about time and tends to have less need for control, plus does not work as hard to gain control over events. For example, since Christian populations around the world number about 1.5 billion and Moslems number about 1.2 billion out of 6 billion, it is appropriate to compare general religious characteristics of these two faiths concerning the personalities of types A and B. Table 7.1 briefly summarizes the religious cultural value profiles of type A and type B personalities.

Rosenman and Friedman (1971) concluded in their research that type A people are more prone to the worst outcome concerning stress. Type A people experience heart attacks twice as often as type B personalities. Researchers found four type A personalities: (1) time urgency, (2) competitiveness, (3) polyphasic behavior, and (4) hostility. The four types of A characteristics are a direct result of a need to control self (Sturbe and Werner, 1985; Smith and Rhodewalt (1986).

Type T Theory of Personality

Psychologist Frank Farely (1990: 29), through his research, has defined another type of personality. He identifies a type T personality as one that lives for thrills. The type T personality is also called the hard personality. These people have a drive for life risk-taking, stimulation, and excitement seeking. Farely describes type T personalities as: "You may have not heard of this personality, but I will wager that you know some people who show the pattern of characteristics I have listed . . . I believe type T is at the basis of both the most positive and constructive forces in our nation (T plus creativity) and the most negative and destructive forces (T minus delinquency, vandalism, crime, drug and alcohol abuse, drinking and driving, etc.)." Most normal people fall between the high-risk, thrill- and stimulation-seeking types and those people who actively avoid any risk or thrill.

TABLE 7.1. Comparative Type A and Type B Personalities Through Religious Faiths

Christians: Type A	Moslems: Type B
They believe in self-efforts; free from pain, from fear, and from desire.	They believe in destiny; Islam means individuals are submissive to God's will—Ansha-Allah.
They work aggressively to achieve individual satisfaction.	They work patiently to serve God's satisfaction.
Work is viewed as a means to transform productivity gains into additional output rather than into additional leisure.	Work is viewed as a means to comfort and salvation—to serve self and others. They believe that hasty behavior is undesirable, patient behavior is Godly virtue (Koran).
Talk rapidly and briefly, point by point to get to the objectives.	Talk descriptively; assess and judge holistically.
Do many things at once.	Do things one by one.
Less emphasis on leisure time.	More emphasis on relaxation.
Make deadlines for all activities.	No deadline for living activities (God's will).
They are obsessed with statistical figures.	They are more tuned with miracles, and God's will.
They are pro-legally oriented toward life.	They are pro-naturally oriented toward life.
They are always dynamic in their minds.	They are always praying in their hearts.
They are very competitive.	They are very cooperative.
They reverse their promises on the basis of contingency situations.	They stay with their promises by all means and ends.
They play to win.	They play to have fun.
They like to work individually and gain personal benefits (capital gain).	They like to work together and share their benefits with others (zakat).
They are more multiculturally oriented.	They are more co-faith internationally oriented (brotherhood).
They are more individualistically oriented for achievement (not necessarily for making profit).	They are more family oriented toward spheres of social orientation for their happiness.
They are expressive in their feelings.	They hide and control their feelings.
First, they fall in love and then marry.	First, they marry and then fall in love.
Believe in and practice monogamy.	Believe in and practice polygamy.
Believe in having a formal spouse at one time and divorce spouses very rapidly. Men may sometimes have affairs and take mistresses.	Believe in and practice with one to four formal wives and as many temporary wives for certain period of time.
Divorced spouses or widowed women marry several times in lifetime.	Widowed women do not marry again. Widows remain single as a sign of loyalty to their late husbands.

Source: Adapted in part from Weber, Max (1969). "The Protestant Ethic and the Spirit of Capitalism," and Kember Fullerton, "Calvinism and Capitalism." Both in Webber, R. A. (Ed.), *Culture and Management.* Homewood, IL: Richard D. Irwin, pp. 91-112.

Extroverted and Introverted Personalities

Swiss psychologist Carl Jung (1971) focused his research on the assumption that people are fundamentally different, but also fundamentally alike. His classic work, *Psychological Type,* suggested that the population is made up of two basic types: extroverted and introverted personalities. Extroverted personalities have strong tendencies toward socialization and emphasize perceptual judgments. Introverted personalities have weak tendencies toward socialization and prefer to be quiet. These types of personalities are more tuned to be more imaginative and usually they are listeners.

Jung based his theory on two fundamental types of phenomena: perception (sensing and intuiting) and judgment (thinking and feeling). He greatly expanded the conception of unconsciousness. The unconsciousness concept was the essence of an individual's unique holistic life experience but was also filled with fundamental psychological truth shared by the whole human race. Jung stated that unconsiousness is responsible for our intuitive understanding of primitive myths, art forms, and symbols and to perceive the universal balancing pattern of existence.

Jung saw the healthy, integrated personality as balancing forces between perception and conception (cognitive judgment). Perception (how we gather information) and conception (how we make decisions) represent the best evidence of our holistic self—personality. For example, Jung assumed that the collective conscious personality of a family is the balance between husband and wife, or the balance between masculine aggressiveness and feminine sensitivity. This view of personality as a constellation of compensating internal forces in dynamic balance is called analytic psychology. Therefore, Jung suggested that human similarities and differences could be understood by combining preferences. It is the matter of choice that we are not exclusively one way or another; rather, we have a preference for extroversion or introversion. Also, he argued that extroverted or introverted personalities are neither different nor better than others. Differences in needs need to be analyzed, celebrated, and appreciated.

Myers-Briggs' Sixteen Types of Personalities

The Myers-Briggs type theory is based on Carl Jung's typology of personality. Myers and Briggs became fascinated with individual differences among people and developed the *Myers-Briggs type indicators* (MBTI) to put Jung's "type theory" into practical use. They assigned people into one of sixteen categories or types. They used MBTI to find "an orderly reason for personality differences" in the ways people perceive their world and make judgments about it (Myers, 1962, 1976, 1985).

Myers-Briggs type theory of personality assumes that basic differences in perception and cognitive judgment are the result of four fundamental differences in behavior. These four differences include direct sensing (S), unconscious intuition (I), judging by thinking (T), and feeling (F) (see Table 7.2).

TABLE 7.2. The Type Theory Preferences and Descriptions

Extroversion	**Introversion**
Outgoing	Quiet
Interactive	Concentrating
Speaks, then thinks	Thinks, then speaks
Sensing	**Intuiting**
Practical	General
Specific	Abstract
Concrete	Theoretical
Thinking	**Feeling**
Analytical	Subjective
Head	Heart
Justice	Mercy
Judging	**Perceiving**
Structured	Flexible
Decisive	Exploring
Organized	Spontaneous

Source: Adapted from O. Kroeger and J. Thuesen (1981). Typewatching Training Workshop. Fairfax, VA: Otto Kroeger Association. In Nelson, D. L. and Quick, J. C. (1999). *Organizational Behavior: Foundations, Realities, and Challenges.* Minneapolis-St. Paul, MN: West Publishing Company, p. 86.

Both perceptions and cognitive judgments are divided into dual ways of perceiving with two possible choices for each. The third factor added to the Myers-Briggs test was a preference for extroversion (E) or introversion (I) which focuses on either the inner or outer worlds. The combination of these preferences makes up an individual's psychological style of behavior. Sixteen types of personalities have emerged from the combination of these preferences, such as extrovert personalities who demonstrate thinking with intuition or introverts who show sensing with feeling.

The Parsons-Shils Five Sociocultural Pair Types

Talcott Parsons and Edward Shils (1951) have powerfully influenced the efficacy of sociocultural values on shaping personality by describing five different pairs of personalities. These are:

1. *Universalism/Particularism:* Am I a universalist or a specialist? Should I deal with others in terms of their particular relationships with me or on the basis of universal criteria of human rights?
2. *Performance/Quality:* Is any action to be judged by looking at how it is carried out or by whom it is carried out?

3. *Affective Neutrality/Affective:* Am I an affective neutralist or affective? Do I emphasize objectivity or affective involvement in the appropriated attitudes?
4. *Specificity/Diffuseness:* Am I a specifist or diffusionist? Are my commitments and obligations specific or are they diffuse?
5. *Self-Orientation/Collective Orientation:* Am I an individualist or collectivist? Can I appropriately pursue my own objectives and desires without fear of societal retaliation or should the objectives of the collective be governing in my society?

Fallding (1965) states that these types of sociocultural behaviors are not values in themselves, but refer to the consideration involved in electing values by different types of personalities.

Parsons emphasizes that an individual's personality possesses multiplicity of sociocultural role definitions and institutional norms. For example, there would be little disagreement in a multinational corporation with the idea that a manager-employee relationship should be universalistic, performance oriented, affective neutral, specific, and self-oriented; whereas their relationships with their children as a father/mother and son/daughter should be particular, quality oriented, infused with affective, diffuse, and collective orientations. However, in defining the type of personality through a professional perspective, some blurring of distinctions can be found not only in behavioral fact, but probably also in the sociocultural values and norms themselves. For example, a physician and/or a professor is supposed to be collectively oriented and effectively neutral but at the same time, some degree of self-orientation is expected and permitted. For a physician, a patient's bedside, or, for a professor, a student's mentoring manner that expresses some affect is expected.

Keene's Four Types of Religious and Neurotic Personalities

James Keene (1967) undertook a complicated task to study the relationships between personality and religion. Although his research's random sampling was not based on a scientific methodology, Keene was able to match fifty people from five major religions, such as Jewish, Catholic, Protestant, Baha'i, and nonaffiliated groups on the basis of age, sex, education, and socioeconomic status. Keene concluded that observed relationships are due to the religion-personality interaction and not due to uncontrolled variation in other variables. The results are too complex to report in detail. However, the main finding of Keene's observation is useful in identifying four types of personalities:

> Catholics who score low in religious participation (Irrelevant) and in beliefs in the afterlife, the soul, and God (Secular) tend to be at once Neurotic, Self-accommodating, and Ethnocentric. On the other hand,

a high rating on the Salient and Spiritual factors predicts Adaptive, Group-accommodating, and Worldminded behavior. (p. 150)

There are significant personality-religion interactions. Group means and variances are significantly different. We know something of Keene's scores on the four personality factors: (1) neurotic/adaptive, (2) spontaneous/ inhibited, (3) worldminded/ethnocentric, and (4) self-accommodating/group accommodating. More important, various interactions among the dimensions appeared. For example, participation in religion is correlated with worldmindedness in the Baha'i group and with ethnocentrism in the Jewish group (Keene, 1967) (see Table 7.3).

The Maturity and Immaturity Traits

In addition to the above types and theories of personality, there is another approach to identifying personality formation development within an organizational behavior context. Although there are some genetic physiological and psychological blueprints for identifying the type of personality, there are some cultural variations in categorization of personalities. Chris Argyris (1957) has proposed a model of the workplace personality that integrates the stage and trait approaches. His model is summarized in Figure 7.2. This model focuses appropriately on people in organizational structures and settings. Argyris applies the psychological patterns of formation and traits of personality according to the inner promotion and refinement of an individual's characteristics through experience. He believes that people at any age can have their degree of development plotted according to the seven dimensions. According to him, managers and employees develop their personalities from immaturity to maturity along seven basic dimensions. Argyris suggests that maturation refers to the process of growth in all usual organizational traits.

In order to obtain full expression of employees' personalities, the formal organization should allow for activity rather than passivity, independence, rather than dependence, long-term rather than short-term perspectives, occupation of a position higher than that of peers, and expression of deep, important abilities (Argyris, 1957: 51-53).

TABLE 7.3. Keene's Four Personality Factors

Neurotic/Adaptive	Spontaneous/ Inhibited	Worldwide/ Ethnocentric	Self-Accommodating/ Group Accommodating
Catholics	Protestant	Baha'ism	Catholics Non-Affiliates

Source: Keene, J. (1967). "Religious Behavior and Neuroticism, Spontaneity, and Worldmindedness." *Sociometry.* Vol. 30, p. 147.

FIGURE 7.2. The Immaturity and Maturity Model

Immature Characteristics	Mature Characteristics
Passive	Active
Dependent	Independent
Few Behaviors	Many Behaviors
Shallow Interests	Deep Interests
Short-Term Perspective	Long-Term Perspective
Subordinate Position	Superordinate Position
Little Self-Awareness	More Self-Awareness and Control

Source: Adapted from Argyris (1957), *Personality and Organization: The Conflict Between the System and the Individual.* New York: Harper-Collins, p. 50.

Argyris suggests that employees gain knowledge, experience, and self-confidence in their jobs. They try to move from the immature end to the mature end of each dimension.

The Neurotic Managerial Styles of Personality

Not much has been known about neurotic behavioral patterns of managers, dysfunctional organizational climates, disturbing peer interrelations, and rigidity in managerial defense mechanisms. Yet we virtually never notice these issues in modern organizational behavior textbooks. The only news we hear concerns managerial neurotic styles in the time of grievance and/or in litigations.

There are always a number of ways of conceptualizing, categorizing, and analyzing managerial neurotic behavior. Kets de Vries and Miller (1984) applied psychometric, psychodynamic, and psychoanalytic tools to study the style, the type, and the pattern of managerial neurotic behaviors. These researchers, through their findings, identified five neurotic styles that relate to the five most common types of top managers. They called these personality styles paranoid, compulsive, dramatic, depressive, and schizoid. Researchers applied seven dimensions for their deliberation. These dimensions are: (1) neurotic personality types, (2) dysfunctional group processes, (3) transferential pattern of subordinates or superiors, (4) improper modes by binding, abandoning, and proxies, (5) life-cycle-related crises during a manager's career, (6) psychodynamic defense mechanisms and resistance, and (7) disappointment and resistance caused by loss of status, security, or power (see Table 7.4).

In this chapter, we have dealt with personality types and traits. Attention has been paid to individual behavior in an organization. Furthermore, there is little attempt to explain the top managerial personalities. In this section, we are studying the type of managerial personality through psychoanalytic literature. They are used to understand, predict, and classify common managerial personalities.

TABLE 7.4. Summary of the Five Neurotic Behavioral Styles

Key Factors	Paranoid	Compulsive	Dramatic	Depressive	Schizoid
Characteristics	Suspiciousness	Perfectionism	Self-drama-tization	Feeling of guilt	Noninvolvement
Fantasy	Mistrusts everybody	Attempts to control everything	Tries to impress everybody	Feels "I am just not good enough."	Believes it is best to remain distant from others
Dangers	Distortion	Indecisiveness	Overreaction	Pessimism	Aggressiveness
Sexual disorders	Sexual dysfunction	Sexual behavioral abnormality	Deviant sexual practices	Sexual inhibition	Sadistic behavior
Organic mental disorders	Psychological abnormality	Sensible exposure	Odd behavior	Chimeric brain malfunction	Traumatic side-effects (Permanently or temporarily)
Substance-use disorders	Addiction	Aggravation	Temperate	Negligence	Abusive motives
Somatoform disorders	Hysteria	Somatic sensitivity	Somatic paralysis	Cold body	Feeling pain in limbs

Source: Adapted partially from Kets de Vries, M. F. R. and Miller, D. (1984). *The Neurotic Organization,* San Francisco, CA: Jossey-Bass Publishers, 24-25.

Trait Theories of Personalities

Trait theories of personality try to identify a holistic configuration of positive and negative characteristics of people.

An individual possesses instinct, sensation, emotion, imagination, intellect, genetics characteristics, information, knowledge, and problem-solving abilities. Therefore, we easily gain the impression that individuals are so complex in their own structure and activity that they cannot analyze as just one sort of being, distinctive and different from other living beings. Therefore, an individual is a whole and unified entity who has an extraordinary variety of behavior.

The type theories of personality presume that there are separate, discontinuous categories into which people fit. By contrast, the trait theories propose hypothetical continuous dimensions of an individual's mind-body relations. Thousands of traits have been identified over the years. Traits are generalized by the coherent relations between body-mind tendencies that people possess in various degrees. Accordingly, they combine these traits into several group forms in which an individual's personality can be recognized. Traits lend coherence to an individual's behavior in different situations and over time. For example, you may demonstrate honesty one day by a moral obligation to tell the truth to your manager while you are judging your peers, and on another day by *not* covering up deficiencies of peers who are your friends (see Figure 7.3).

Allport's Three Traits Theories

Allport (1937, 1961, and 1966) was one of the most influential personality trait theorists. He viewed traits as the building blocks of personality and the main source of individuality. He saw traits as broad, general guides that lend consistency to behavior. According to his views, traits produce coherence in behavior because they are enduring attributes and are general in scope. Allport identifies three kinds of traits: (1) *cardinal* traits, which organize an individual's life; (2) *central* traits, which represent major characteristics of an individual, such as honesty; and (3) *secondary* traits, which specify personal features that help us predict the individual's behavior, such as food, grooming, and dress preferences.

Cattell's Sixteen Bipolar Traits Theories

Cattell (1963 and 1973), another prominent trait theorist, took a different approach from that of Allport. Cattell has identified sixteen bipolar adjective combinations of traits and sources of traits. First, he determined thirty-five bipolar surface traits and then he narrowed them down into sixteen bipolar adjective combinations such as affectothymia (good-natured and trustfulness) versus sizothymia (critical and suspicious attitudes), ego strength (maturity and realism) versus emotionality and neuroticism (immaturity and evasiveness), dominance versus desurgency (depressed and subdued feelings). He finally found clusters of traits that correlated, such as affectionate-cold, sociable-seclusive, honest-dishonest, and wise-foolish. He described source traits in bipolar adjective combinations such as self-assured-apprehensive, reserved-outgoing, and submissive-dominant.

FIGURE 7.3. Dimensions of the Personality Traits

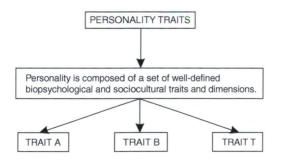

The Big Five Personality Traits

More recently, psychologists and human resource management researchers have condensed all traits into a list of five major personality traits,
known as the "Big Five" (Norman, 1963; Digman, 1990; Costa and Mc-
Crae, 1985). The five traits include extroversion/introversion, agreeable-
ness, conscientiousness, emotional stability, and openness to experience.
Description of the "Big Five" are shown in the Table 7.5. These traits are
very general and broad. They need to be tested scientifically in all cultures
in order to validate this theory.

TABLE 7.5. The "Big Five" Personality Traits

Extroversion ⟶	The person is gregarious, assertive, and sociable. Degree to which a person is talkative, active, and ambitious (rather than reserved, timid, and quiet).
Agreeable ⟶	The person is cooperative, warm, and agreeable. Degree to which person is courteous, likeable, and flexible (rather than cold, disagreeable, and antagonistic).
Conscientiousness ⟶	The person is hardworking, organized, and dependable. Degree to which a person is dependable, responsible, and forward-looking (rather than lazy, disorganized, and unreliable).
Emotional Stability ⟶	The person is calm, self-confident, and cool. Degree to which a person is anxious, eustressed, and secure (rather than indifferent, insecure, and depressed).
Openness to Experience ⟶	The person is creative, curious, and cultured. Degree to which a person is imaginative, broad-minded, curious, and seeks new experiences (rather than practical with narrow interest).

Sources: Adapted from P. T. Costa and R. R. McCrae (1985). *The NEO Personality Inventory Manual.* Odessa, FL: *Psychological Assessment Resources;* J. F. Salgado (1997). "The Five Factor Model of Personality and Job Performance in the European Community." *Journal of Applied Psychology.* Vol. 82, pp. 30-43; M. R. Barrick and M. K. Mount (1991). The Five Big Personality Dimensions and Job Performance: A Meta-Analysis." *Personnel Psychology,* 44(1), Spring, pp. 1-76; J. A. Digman (1990). "Personality Structure: Emergence of the Five-Factor Model." *Annual Review of Psychology.* Vol. 41, pp. 417-440; W. T. Norman (1963). "Toward an Adequate Taxonomy of Personality Attributes: Replicated Factor Structure in Peer Nomination Personality Ratings." *Journal of Abnormal and Social Psychology.* Vol. 66, pp. 547-583.

Psychodynamic Theory of Personality

Discussion on psychoanalytic theory of personality is traced back to the views of Sigmund Freud (1856-1939). His ideas concerning psychodynamic theory of personality involve unconscious motivation and the development and structure of personality. Freud's treatment technique is called psychoanalysis. He emphasized the unconscious determinants of behavior. Freud viewed personality as the interactional processes among three elements of personality: the id, ego, and superego. He conceived the *id* as the primitive and unconscious part of personality (the unleashed, raw, institutional drive struggling for gratification and pleasure)—the storehouse of personality. The *ego* represents reality; it rationally attempts to keep the impulsive id and the conscious of the superego in check, and represents an individual's personal view of physical and social reality (the conscious, logical portion that associates with reality). The *superego* is the storehouse of values, including moral attitudes learned from society (the conscience that provides the norms that enable the ego to determine what is right and what is wrong). There is an ongoing conflict between the id and superego. The ego serves as a compromiser creating a balance between the id and the superego. However, when id and superego pressures intensify, it becomes more difficult for the ego to work out optimal compromises.

Humanistic Theory of Personality

Humanistic or self theory of personality contends that the self-concept is the most important part of an individual's personality. Carl Rogers (1959) believed that the central motivational force in an individual is the innate need to grow and actualize one's highest potentials. The *"I"* is the personal self, the self that one believes oneself to be and strives to be. The *"me"* represents the social self. The "me" is the way a person appears to the self and the way the person thinks he or she appears to others.

This theory focuses on morality, ethics, ritual religious faith, and other distinguished traits such as philosophy, aesthetics, creativity, and innovativeness. These traits appear gradually and continually in human personality through transitory and recurrent configurations in physical objectivity and events, and in overt behavior and covert experiences. It is the natural flow of appropriate experiencing through application of self-motivated power (Parhizgar, 1995). Therefore, the humanistic theory of trait personality focuses on continuity of an individual's sociopsychological growth and improvement.

Integrative Theory of Personality

Recently, some researchers have found a correlation between personality and cultural characteristics of individuals. This view has given a broader impact to formation, growth, and development of personality. Brislin (1981) conducted intensive research among different cultures in order to discover whether a behavior found in one culture also occurs in other cultures. He applied the cross-cultural method to compare diverse sexual patterns and perceptual differences in reactions to illusions. Triandis (1990) conducted research among 100 cross-cultural studies concerning basic distinctive traits throughout the world. He addressed two basic personal characteristics: *individualistic* and *collectivistic.* He found that individualistic societies stress the individual as the most important unit; they value competition, individual achievement, and personal fulfillment. In contrast, collectivist societies place the greatest value on social group, family, community, or tribe. In general, all of the cultural characteristics influence in growth and development of peoples' personalities in all cultures. In addition, Hofstede (1980b) used the cross-cultural method to compare diverse sexual patterns and cultural factors that influence productivity. This theory has found a correlation among personality dispositions, which includes emotions, cognizance, attitudes, expectancies, and fantasies (Buda and Elsayed-Elkhouly, 1998).

PERSONALITY AND THE WORKPLACE

The psychosociological types, traits, and models of personality just discussed in this chapter are crucial factors in the field of multicultural management. They highlight the complexities of employee-employer relations as well as understanding individual behavioral differences. There are two dimensional views of the effects of personality in the workplace: (1) individual characteristics and (2) group cultural-political characteristics.

Individual Characteristics

If we consider humans as living beings, we would say their general characteristic functions are growth, metabolism, and reproduction. Also, if we consider that human beings are living beings, they possess specific features of individual characteristics such as intelligence. Intelligence makes an individual rational. To live well as a human being is to live a life of reason and the good use of reason. However, individuals possess other learned or cultural characteristics that change their behavior to other characteristics such as emotional and sensational behaviors.

The most possible direct application of the individual characteristics identifies an individual's beliefs in terms of self-behaviorism. Six of these characteristics are egocentrism, authoritarianism, Machiavellianism, racism, bureaucratism, and nepotism and favoritism.

Egocentric Behavior

Egocentrism is the extent to which a person believes only in themselves. The employee and/or employer can imagine a world from only one perspective—the egocentric point of view. This egocentric view is evident during the individual's conversations and concessions with others. Egocentrism refers to an individual's inability to take the perspective of other persons' rights and privileges into his or her judgmental perception. Egocentric employees and/or employers always try by all means and ends to get all credits and privileges for themselves.

Authoritarian Behavior

Authoritarianism is the extent to which a manager believes that power is the only tool to be used to manage other people. The question why prejudice exerts a strong influence over certain individuals but plays a relatively minor role for others is addressed by the theory of the authoritarian personality. The major factor in such a behavior is that a personality type exists that is prone to prejudicial thought. Adorno and his associates (1950) found evidence to support the notion of prejudice and extremist thoughts and behaviors in authoritarian managers. Such authoritarian managers are conformist, disciplinarian, cynical, intolerant, and preoccupied with power. The stronger the belief in power, the more prejudiced behavior the manager is said to exhibit.

Researchers found that highly authoritarian people are more likely to obey orders from someone with authority without raising any serious objections, even if they recognize potential dangers and pitfalls (*Psychology Today,* 1989: 66-70).

Machiavellian Behavior

Some managers believe that "the ends justify the means." This type of behavioral philosophy is rooted in a historical ideology by Niccolo Machiavelli, who was a sixteenth-century Italian statesman. He wrote *The Prince,* a guide for acquiring and exercising power (Bull, 1961). Machiavelli asserted how the nobility could more easily gain and use power to manipulate people. A Machiavellian personality, then, is one willing to do whatever it takes to achieve one's own objective. Researchers assert that Machiavellianism is a type of behavior that varies from person to person, time to time, and place to place. Individuals who are high on Machiavellianism personality believe and act by the notion that "it is better to be feared than loved." High Machiavellian personalities put little weight on loyalty and friendship and enjoy succeeding in their objectives by all means and ends. Low Machiavellian personalities, in contrast, value loyalty and relationship, with emphasis on self-achievement. The best expression for Machiavellian behavior is "to change the position in accordance with the wind direction to safeguard personal interests by all means and ends."

Racist Behavior

Racism is a sociocultural belief and behavior or political ideological agenda that is structured around four basic ideas (Marger, 1985):

1. People should be classified by their physical appearances.
2. Physical appearances represent intrinsic characteristics.
3. Physical characteristics such as gender, race, ethnicity, and color make some groups superior to others regardless of individual inherent characteristics.
4. The failures of a group at the bottom of the social hierarchy are assumed to be a natural outcome of genetic inheritance, rather than social disadvantage.

One of the byproducts of racism is the *narcissistic* personality. It is the development of a grandiose sense of self-importance, preoccupation with fantasies of success or power, and a need for constant attention or admiration. Narcissistic personalities often respond inappropriately to criticism or minor defeat, either by displaying an apparent indifference to criticism or by markedly overreacting (Zimbardo, 1992: 629).

Racist behavior in some societies is used as an important determinant for practicing societal privileges. In these cultures, the elite political groups classify people into majority and minority on the basis of ethnicity, race, color, and origin of birth. Ethnic groups are identified by race, gender, colors, and ethnicity to be rewarded. For example, in Kuwait, there are two groups of people: (1) Kuwaitians, whose race is traced to a tribe that practiced inbreeding, and (2) those people who are known as working-class people, whose origin of birth is not Kuwaitian, even though those people were born in Kuwait.

In contrast, in multicultural societies, there is no consideration of ethnic, racial, color, and gender classification. Accordingly, people are classified by their efforts. In multicultural organizations, recruitment, promotion, transfer, and separation will not be based upon racial appearances but by the merit system.

Bureaucratic Behavior

Organizations produce very formatted structures through continuous trial-and-error processes. Clearly, organizational structure, processes, and policies are critical determinants of the overall success of an institution. The pervasiveness of bureaucratic structure and behavioral expectations of an organization and the resiliency of Max Weber's ideal bureaucracy clearly suggest that they contain powerful effects on managers' behavior. Unfortunately, many weaknesses of bureaucratic organizations display managerial misbehavior.

Many bureaucratic managers become too rigid and inflexible, and they are not able to respond positively to the progressive trends of the changing environment. In a highly bureaucratic system, managers become obsessive about implementing rules and regulations without paying attention to the organizational causes. The end result of such an organizational philosophy is creating "impersonal behavior among organizational members." This type of behavior results in "self-alienation" and destroys cooperation between superiors and subordinates. The bureaucratic personality becomes more concerned about enforcing rules than about actually achieving intended results (Schoderbek, Cosier, and Aplin, 1991).

McFarland (1991) indicates that the spread of bureaucratic behavior in management is usually said to be part of government development—providing experience, norms, and capabilities for state structures. However, bureaucratization of people is an obstacle to democratization. Since bureaucratized managerial systems are not highly productive, innovation cannot be manifested by centralized decision-making processes. Consequently, managers trap themselves with their own rules.

Nepotism and Favoritism

Nepotism managerial behavior is a kind of family and/or friendly "patronage," which shows sympathy to relatives and friends at the time of managerial decision-making processes. Sometimes such a behavior is based upon "kickback" responses to the previous favors by patrons and alliances. This type of managerial behavior is financially oriented. A patronage system supports its patrons through controlling appointments to the public service or other political favors. When a patron receives a favor from supporters, in a traditional cultural value system, he or she should be loyal to the supporters' will and serve them by all means and ends. In addition, a patron who receives income from supporters needs to respond to the favor of those who have made his or her income possible. There are three types of people who are involved in a patronage system: (1) masters who have financial and/or sociopolitical power, (2) brokers who play the role of mediators and receive a financial and/or sociocultural percentage of favors, and (3) patrons who receive direct favors. Patrons who receive favors will be obligated and should be obedient to the will of their masters.

The practice of nepotism and favoritism depends on the cultural value system in a nation. For example, in most Arab countries and in some Hispanic communities nepotism and patronage behavior is prevalent and morally accepted; in some other cultures, such as Germany and Japan, nepotism and favoritism behavior is considered improper and illegal.

Managerial nepotism and favoritism behavior is based either upon the homogeneity group's expectations and/or "giving and receiving" deals— "tit for tat." This type of managerial behavior forces organizations to be unproductive. However, nepotism or any form of favoritism in a corporate culture that does not seem to reward via merit will negatively affect employee morale and performance. Multinational corporations whose leaders are basically tuned with productivity and innovation avoid nepotism and favoritism. They need to act on the basis of meritocracy not bureaucracy. As communities become more industrialized, the tendency toward meritocracy becomes more prevalent. In contrast, as a community or a corporation becomes more conservatively oriented with the inbreeding patronage personalities, nepotism and favoritism are more popular.

Cultural-Political Characteristics

A concept closely related to personality is politics, or political personalogy. Political behavior is the generalized objective-orientation by which people attempt to obtain and use power. A political figure is one who is more concerned with winning favor or retaining power than maintaining principles. There are two types of general skills in political cultures: (1) political skills and (2) statesman's skills. Both types of people differ particularly in their connotations. A politician's behavior is more often "derogatory." He or she suggests the schemes and devices of one who engages in politics for the benefit of the party's objectives and/or own personal advantages. A statesman's behavior is more often "eminent." He or she seeks conspicuous and noteworthy suggestions along with unselfish devotion to the interests of his or her country.

Since the primary concern of this discussion is organizational behavior, we will focus on different types of beliefs and ideologies across organizational political cultures. Nevertheless, we can note a few ideas about differences and similarities in organizational politics at the general corporate levels. Political cultures vary across organizations. Employees in companies based in the United States, Germany, India, and Egypt are likely to have different attitudes and behavioral patterns in politics. General political thinking and behavior is likely to be widespread and pervasive within a cultural cluster. However, some managers behave differently in different cultural environments.

In all organizations, there are several types of perceptual cultural-political behaviors. Figure 7.4 highlights some of the important dimensions along with organizational political behaviors, which vary. These dimensions are pluralism/collectivism, competition/cooperation, equalitarinism/inequalitarinism, high power distance/low power distance, materialism/spiritualism, and masculinity/femininity.

FIGURE 7.4. Cultural-Political Personalogy Dimensions

Pluralism _____	Collectivism
Competition _____	Cooperation
Equalitarianism _____	Inequalitarianism
Power_____	High Power/Low Power Distance
Masculinity _____	Femininity
Materialism _____	Spiritualism

Source: Adapted from Argyris (1957), *Personality and Organization: The Conflict Between the System and the Individual.* New York: Harper-Collins, p. 50.

Pluralistic/Collectivistic Behavior

A pluralistic organization is one that has many autonomous groups through which power is diffused. No one group has power over others, and each may have direct or indirect impact over others. For example, colleges, universities, and teaching hospitals are among these types of organizations. In short, behavioral relationships in these institutions are the result of a professional code of ethical conduct, moral characteristics, and conditions that encourage faculty members, student body, administrative authorities, and the community at large to maintain the boundaries of their groups independently while they are working together.

Pluralistic behavior is a type of professional value system in which individuals behave freely and autonomously within the boundaries of their own legitimate power. For example, it has been observed that Hawaii is an example of a successfully integrated multiracial society (Daws, 1968). Various ethnic groups maintain their distinct identities and cultures. Yet within a general framework of culture, U.S. civic culture binds them together. Within this cultural cluster, in principle, Hawaii maintains equal opportunities and mutual tolerance for all citizens. While each culture, with its own sphere of influence, functions in that society differently, they are sharing similarities in their civic culture.

Organizational pluralism is never an absolute separation of groups. It is an interconnectivity which binds the groups together. The role of a manager in these types of organizations is perceived to be the problem solver. For example, in societies which are characterized by corporate pluralism, ethnic groups are mainly heterogeneous, territorially concentrated, and have long historic roots in their native area (Marger, 1985: p. 81).

In contrast, collectivistic behavior emphasizes group similarities, harmony, and coalition. Collectivistic thinking and behavior is tightly integrated in social patterns with group decisions and actions (family, tribe, or community). Triandis (1990) believes that the lower economic productivity of organizational collective cultures is offset by evidence of healthier quality of life. Collectivistic behavior puts a high value on self-discipline, ac-

cepting one's employment in life, honoring organizational authorities, pre-
serving one's image, and working toward long-term objectives that benefit
the organization as whole. Unions are examples of groups in which members' unity and loyalty are paramount.

Competitive/Cooperative Behavior

A competitive organizational value system is one in which its sole objective is either rewarding efficiency and effectiveness or punishing inefficient
and ineffective constituencies. Competitive cultural value systems create
the free market economy. In addition, competitive strategies by business organizations make capitalistic ideology work. Competition in a free market
economy causes resources to be controlled and allocated with consideration
of:

1. what and how much should be produced in order to respond to the
   market demand
2. how it should be produced with what cost-benefit analysis
3. for whom it should be produced to be consumed
4. with what price commodities should it be sold to maintain the corporation's stability, survival, and profitability

Competitive experiences can provide appropriate opportunities to assess
a corporation's product marketability through trial and error. Also, successful business operational experiences maintain and stabilize the corporation's market size and product positions (see Figure 7.5).

A cooperative organizational value system is a joint intentional and behavioral combination of people for purposes of successful production toward joint benefits. Cooperative organizational behavior is a joint conscious

FIGURE 7.5. Competition versus Cooperation

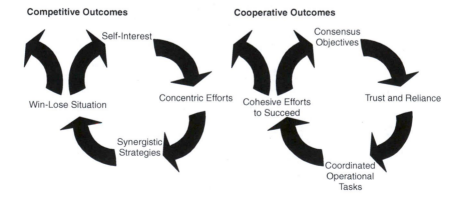

and consensus effort of employer-employee togetherness to produce a result that has a survival value for all parties. Cooperative behavior is based on trust and reliance on one another to succeed in mutual goals. It facilitates achievements in a coordinative dynamic operation to reach proper harmonious outcomes of production (see Figure 7.5).

Equalitarian/Inequalitarian Behavior

Equality is the idea that all people should have "an equal place at the starting point of their life." Equality, traditionally, meant the elimination of inequalities among organizational members with respect to opportunities for social, political, and economic access. Managers provide equal employment opportunities on the basis of ability and character of employees. Some organizations provide equal opportunities at the beginning and gradually diminish it through prejudice. In such a situation, the manager behaves at the starting line with equal opportunity processes, and further down the road it ends up with some political interests with unequal results.

Technically, in multicultural organizations, if equality exists, then there will be no dominant-minority relations among organizational members in nature. Equalitarian behavior promotes balance and cooperation among different employees within the framework of the largest set of agreed-upon principles. However, in such organizations, the competitive differences will not be diminished. This type of managerial behavior promotes a reasonable platform for higher productivity within the consensual rules of the organizational members.

In contrast, inequilitarian managerial behavior recognizes processes and outcomes of an organization on the basis of the severity of job scarcity, the employee's acute employment needs, and the political ideology of the group interest. The end result of such a managerial system is promotion of the ideological majority culture of the interest group and exploitation of minority groups. Coercive behavior, threats, and intimidation of minority employees by managers can cause high turnover and absenteeism.

High Power Distance/Low Power Distance Behavior

Cultural heterogeneity has been viewed as a power index in nations. Hofstede's (1980a) power distance index represents seven beliefs (wealth, economic growth, geographic latitude, population size, population growth, population density, and Hermes: (Greek god of commerce) in an organizational innovativeness.

Due to organizational political differences, researcher Hofstede has focused his attention to respond to this question: "Do cultures translate into differences in work-related attitudes?" He and his colleagues surveyed 160,000 managers and employees of IBM who were represented in sixty countries (Hofstede, 1980b). He used the result of his research to develop five cultural dimensions described and defined in Table 7.6. Hofstede's research is very important because it shows that national culture explains more differences in workplace attitudes than do gender, age, profession, and or positions in organizations.

Power distance refers to members of a group or culture who maintain the special group's interest among one another (Parhizgar, 1984: 110). Power distance is a tool to be used in different organizations in order to manage inequality among employees. Power distance functions in a multitude of dimensions: high, moderate, and low. Rigby (1985) indicates that power distance has been viewed in different ways: directive, paternal, and autocratic. In democratized power distance (DPD) societies, such as the United States, citizens accept the *directive power distance*. It is a principle that power functions in multitudinous institutional and organizational orientation to the societal power equalization (decentralization). In DPD organizations, power has been distributed unequally to maintain checks and balances. Managers and employees see one another as similar. The power distance is the result of legitimate authority and expertise.

In contrast, in autocratic countries the power distance scores are high, such as Iran, Mexico, Saudi Arabia, Russia, and others. The elite groups tend to ex-

TABLE 7.6. Hofstede's Five Cultural Dimensions

Power Distance	The extent to which people accept unequal distribution of power. In high power distance cultures, there is a wider gap between the powerful and the powerless.
Uncertainty Avoidance	The extent to which the culture tolerates ambiguity and uncertainty. High uncertainty avoidance leads to low tolerance for uncertainty and to a search for absolute truths.
Individualism	The extent to which individuals or closely knit social structures such as the extended family (collectivism) are the basis for social systems. Individualism leads to reliance on self and focus on individual achievement.
Masculinity	The extent to which assertiveness and independence from others is valued. High masculinity leads to high sex-role differentiation, focus on independence, ambition, and material goods.
Long-Term Orientation	The extent to which people focus on past, present, or future. Present orientation leads to a focus on short-term performance.

Sources: Hofstede, Geert (1980a). *Cultures' Consequences: International Differences in Work-Related Values.* Thousand Oaks, CA: Sage. Hofstede, Geert (1993). "Cultural Constraints in Management Theories." *Academy of Management Executive,* 7(1), pp. 81-94.

ercise power authoritatively and/or paternalistically (centralized power). In organizations with high power distance, managers are afforded excessive power simply because they are managers. Managers are protected and entitled to their privileges, and employees are considered to have very low or no power. Naturally, the distribution of political power and wealth in all of these countries depends upon the political ideological infrastructure of the cultural power distance. In the low distance power organizations, elite ruling people and experts frequently bypass the managerial hierarchical power to get work done. Denmark and Austria are among countries with a low power distance (Hofstede, 1980a).

Materialistic/Spiritualistic Behavior

Some cultural patterns of beliefs strongly value the principle of survival of the fittest at work in political and economic development. People in these cultures are striving to increase their possessions and use of material goods and services for making their financial position very strong. This "social Darwinism" value system has been a prime influence in the modern organizational cultures for productivity, efficiency, the spirit of competition, innovation, and growth. There are many countries and organizations specifically in the industrialized world that believe in pleasure. These cultures perceive that the essence of life is *pleasure*. Pleasure comes from the power of material wealth. These cultures believe that materialism perfects an individual's life. Materialism facilitates goodness when it leads at once to present pleasure and to remote pleasure. Therefore, according to the political belief of materialism, motivation to acquire more material goods and services is good, as it facilitates the desire for leisure, or for a satisfying job even though it may pay a lot more with a stressful performance and for adventures that yield a more comfortable economic life.

In materialistic cultures, the desire for pleasure is closely associated with material wealth and political power. Within the materialistic culture, there are always tendencies toward depravation, dependency, cruelty, and exploitation. For example, Japanese culture has been viewed as a materialistic culture. In October 1999, members of the Diet, the Japanese parliament, called for regulating inhumane demands by debt collection methods of the banking and loan industry. The loan default rate in Japan is extremely low. Nichiei, a Japanese consumer finance company, allegedly asked a loan guarantor to raise money by selling body parts to pay back the loan for Y5.7m. Japanese, culturally, are ashamed to admit bankruptcy. Eisuke Arai, a 25-year-old collection officer of Nichiei Company's, offered a 62-year-old debtor Y3m ($29,000) for his kidney and Y1m for his eye to help him to finance a loan he had guaranteed to a now-bankrupt company. Arai reportedly said to the debtor: "You have two, don't you? Many of our borrowers have only one kidney. . . . I want you to sell your heart as well, but if you do that you'll die. So I'll bear with you if you sell everything up to that." Traditional

Japanese banks are shrinking their loan portfolios and leaving many individuals and small businesses with nowhere else to turn. Japanese consumer finance companies enjoy huge margins, benefiting from a cost of funding of about 2.3 percent and an ability to charge interest rates of up to 40 percent for loans without collateral (Abrahams, 1999: 1).

In contrast, spirituality depends upon a deep sense of the cultural value and worth for human freedom and independence. Spiritualism views the good life is to be "happy and live happily." In these cultures, there is no literal *individual satisfaction.* These cultures believe that the happiness of individuals and the greatest happiness for all people should be the essence of the existence. Within spiritual cultures *altruism* must come before *egotism.* However, it should be noted that egotism and altruism are complementary in modern life. This means, for example, that in order to appreciate the desire to possess property, one must appreciate the property rights of others. In such a culture, individuals will wish to control their pleasure in order to provide happiness for all. For example, in Togoland, West Africa, on the Gulf of Guinea, people do not believe in physical collateral because they believe that the spirit of the borrower is present in the repossessed physical collateral properties and could come and haunt the new owner at any time. Therefore, in Togoland, bankers and lenders do not accept any physical entities such as a house or other properties as collateral for a loan because people strongly believe in spiritual power. Instead, they require that debtors have guarantors. Guarantors are people who vouch that the borrower will pay back the loan. Bankers and lenders require borrowers to provide them with legitimate guarantors to ensure that the borrower will pay them back.

Masculine/Feminine Behavior

Gender identity and role are characterized not only by different physical characteristics, but also they often are identified by cultural patterns of expected behavior in societies. Although the differences between males and females are linked to biology, many are the result of cultural socialization. Cross-gender behavioral patterns vary from culture to culture. Cross-gender behavior is linked to daily activities and the amount of tolerance by the opposite gender. There are two different sociocultural patterns of behavior: masculinity and femininity. Much of what we consider masculine or feminine is formed by our cultural perceptions.

The masculine/feminine dimensions measure the value that a culture bestows on qualities for each gender. By nature, women are communicative, intuitive, nurturing, sensitive, supportive, and pervasive (Schwartz, 1989). Researchers found that most women place a higher sense of importance on long-term relationships (Covey, 1993). Traditionally, when European and/or American women considered an advancement in their careers, they would elevate personal career over family concerns; such a trend is not acceptable in the most Asian and Middle Eastern cultures (Coser, 1975).

In contrast, men are aggressive, very competitive, risk-takers, self-reliant, and their behaviors are predictable by women (Parhizgar, 1994). Men tend to have a management mind-set, are objective oriented, and focus primarily on control and efficiency. Men exert rational power to turn people into work, while women exert their social power to respond to the needs of all organizational constituencies.

Historically, most organizations have been managed by men. In Johnson's (1976) gender congruency theory of power, he views that the gender-role stereotype influences perception of power within an organization. Masculine societies define male-female roles more rigidly than do feminine societies. Cultures that are characterized by femininity emphasize relationships with others for more socialization. For example, the Scandinavian countries, Norway, Sweden, Denmark, and Finland, are considered strongly feminine, while Japan, Austria, Saudi Arabia, and most Latin American countries are considered masculine (Hofstede, 1993).

COPING WITH INDIVIDUAL DIFFERENCES

As it was mentioned earlier in this chapter, there is general consensus that individual differences affect organizational behavior and vice versa, organizational behavior can affect an individual's lifestyle. It is important for a manager to manage subordinates first by recognizing that they are different and accordingly to act to motivate them differently too. In sum, managers should make a few assumptions about the types, traits, and characteristics of subordinates' personalities and understand them as the individuals they are.

While multicultural organizations can draw many implications from the research and theories on personality, especially important messages emerge.

An expatriate manager whose mission is to travel abroad and contact members of other cultures is facing multiple ranges of micro and macro behavioral problems. Cross-cultural relations can begin to be tackled only when a manager explicitly acknowledges that individuals and groups differ in their ecological, psychological, sociocultural, and behavioral orientations. When culturally disparate groups of employees-employers come into contact with each other, they first need to recognize that such differences exist and then act accordingly. This means that they will have an impact on one another's behavior. In general, expatriate managers, migrant workers, and both home and host authorities should simplify their relations as much as possible.

Managers should never underestimate the differences among subordinates. They should constantly analyze, monitor, and understand their behaviors and revise their assumptions, judgments, perceptions, and attributions about their associates and try to treat each individual as a unique person in a unique place and time.

SUMMARY

Although our starting point in this chapter was about the effect of personality on organizational behavior, our ultimate aim was to review different scientific theories and approaches to develop a general understanding about the nature of people. Individual differences make people unique. We are all alike in some ways, and we are different in other ways. Managers need to apply scientific tools and techniques to draw some conclusions that will apply to all organizational constituencies. However, they always need to keep in mind that individual differences and unique characteristics make managers' ability to understand people important.

One important difference among organizational members is personality. Personality is defined as the complex set of unique consistent characteristics that influences an individual's pattern of behavior across different situations and over time. Personality structure and behavioral mechanisms can be viewed from the standpoint of determinants, types, stages, traits, and analysis approaches. Finally, *management means to analyze, understand, and turn organizational members into workers.*

CHAPTER QUESTIONS FOR DISCUSSION

1. Define personality in your own words.
2. Comparatively analyze differences among personality types, traits, and approaches.
3. How does political ideology influence personality?
4. How does religion influence the formation of an individual's personality?
5. What is the scientific definition of personality?
6. Give brief examples of each of the major elements of personality.
7. What are the various factors in the ecological, sociocultural, and behavioral contributions to personality?
8. How do psychoanalytic theories differ from trait theories?
9. What are the major Freudian concepts of the "self?"
10. Why is personality important in organizational behavior?
11. Why are personality types so relevant to managerial styles?

LEARNING ABOUT YOURSELF EXERCISE #7

How Do You Judge Your Own Personality?

Before starting this exercise, you need to carefully read Machiavellian, universalist, type A, and type T personalities. The total scores for these four major characteristics are 1,600 (400 for each category). Next, give yourself a score between 25-400 for each and then add them together to find your pre-exercise scores. When you complete the following exercise, compare your judgmental scores with your exercise scores. You will find how you "feel" about your personality and how you "judge" your personality.

The Type of Personality	Score	The Range
MACHIAVELLIAN	_____	(25-400)
UNIVERSALIST	_____	(25-400)
TYPE A	_____	(25-400)
TYPE T	_____	(25-400)
YOUR PRE-EXERCISE TOTAL SCORES .	_____	(100-1,600)

The following are sixteen items for rating how important each one is to you on a scale of 0 (not important) to 100 (very important). Write one of the numbers (25-50-75-100) on the line to the left of each item.

Not important	Somewhat important		Very important
0	25	50	75	100

It would be more important for me:

_____ 1. To make a lot of money by all means and ends in my life.
_____ 2. To try to convince other people that my judgment is based on common sense.
_____ 3. To challenge people with rational thoughts, ideas, and data.
_____ 4. To challenge people with consideration for their feelings and values.
_____ 5. To work on many projects at a time and try to keep myself busy.

_____ 6. To avoid planning and just let things progress as I work on them.

_____ 7. To be objective oriented and plan ahead of time when I intend something to be achieved.

_____ 8. To deal with others in terms of their particular relationships with me.

_____ 9. To resent rigid organizational rules on the basis of universal criteria of ethics and morality.

_____ 10. To judge an action by how it is carried out.

_____ 11. To try to be indifferent if I perceive that some social activities are not either directly affecting or challenging me.

_____ 12. To be obligated to specific domains of life.

_____ 13. To judge others by whom the action is carried out.

_____ 14. To deal with other people solely upon my needs, desires, and motivational achievement.

_____ 15. To achieve my goals through hardworking efforts of others.

_____ 16. To judge other people on the basis of the predominant cultural value system of my own country.

Turn to the next page for scoring directions and key.

SCORING DIRECTIONS AND KEY FOR EXERCISE #7

Transfer the numbers for each of the sixteen items to the appropriate column, then add up the four numbers in each column.

Machiavellian	Universalism	Type A	Type T
1. _____	2. _____	3. _____	4. _____
8. _____	9. _____	5. _____	6. _____
14. _____	10. _____	7. _____	13. _____
15. _____	16. _____	12. _____	11. _____
Your Totals _____	_____	_____	_____
Total Scores 400	400	400	400

The higher the total in any dimension, the higher the importance you place on your own personality.

Make up a categorical scale of your findings on the basis of more weight for the values of each category.

For example:

1. 400 Universalist
2. 250 Type A
3. 125 Type T
4. 100 Machiavellian

Your Totals   875
Total Scores   1,600

After you have tabulated your scores, compare them with others on your team or in your class. You will find different judgmental patterns among people with diverse scores and preferred modes of self-realization.

CASE STUDY: TEXACO SEX BIAS

In 1902, The Texas Corporation was established through the exchange of all outstanding stocks from the Texas Company. The Texas Corporation was incorporated in Delaware on August 26, 1926. The following year, The Texas Company (California) was formed to acquire all assets of the Texas Company (Delaware). On November 1, 1941, The Texas Corporation merged Texas Company (Delaware) and Texas Company (California), resulting in the latter being dissolved. The Texas Corporation acquired all assets and assumed all liabilities of both companies, and thereafter, became known as the Texas Company until May 1, 1959, when the name was changed to Texaco Inc.

In 1997, Texaco had 542,139,000 stocks outstanding. These stocks were listed on the NYSE and other secondary markets. In the fifty-two weeks of its financial history, Texaco had its stock value fluctuate between $53.00 and $62.00. Texaco had a centralized management style, which was controlling 28,957 employees worldwide. Over half of Texaco employees are employed in the United States. The company has thirty-one subsidiaries throughout the world (Moodys, 1997: 6626). Texaco is a conglomerate entity that is involved in the worldwide exploration for and production, transportation, refining, and marketing of crude oil, natural gas, and petroleum products. Within the United States, Texaco is the third largest oil company. The following is an abridged list of Texaco's subsidiaries: Oil and Gas Company, Heddington Insurance Limited, MVP Production Inc., Refineria Panama, S.A., S.A. Texaco Belgium N.V., Saudi Arabian Texaco Inc., Texaco Brazil S.A.-Produtos de Petroleo, Texaco Britain Limited, Texaco California Inc., Texaco Canada Petroleum Inc., and Texaco Carribean Inc. In addition, Texaco has been practicing in six joint-venture operations (Moodys, 1997, p. 6627).

The Major Managerial Issue

The issue of guaranteeing employees' rights is not as ethically assessed as is placing value on human life, but it brings up some problems when subjected to cost-benefit analysis. It is almost always easier to place a value on the costs than to qualify the benefits. Most corporations ignore such an issue. Texaco's case of "sex bias" is one of the examples of such an issue.

Texaco is one of the big corporations that conducts business with the U.S. government. In May 1995, the Department of Labor implemented a program to audit the employment practices of companies doing business with

Sources: Stevenson, R. W. (1999). "Texaco Is Said to Set Payment Over Sex Bias." *The New York Times* (January 6), Section C, p. 1; *Moody's Industrial Manual* (1997). Zottoli Jr., D. A., Publisher. New York: Moody's Investors Service, Inc. pp. 6626-6631.

the federal government. As a result, Texaco's affirmative action programs were scrutinized for women in petroleum jobs at its White Plains headquarters and seven other offices nationwide: Dallas, Houston, Denver, New Orleans, San Antonio, Belair, Texas, and Beacon, New York. The auditors ended up finding some unfair practices of the labor law. Consequently, Texaco agreed to settle the case and to pay $3.1 million to 186 women who were found to be underpaid and undercompensated. This settlement was viewed as a relief for equalization of pay between male and female personnel.

In this case, there were three major legal, racial, and social issues. The legal and racial issues in the case addressed the effectiveness of the implementation of affirmative action programs. In regard to sociocultural issues, the case addressed gender equity.

The federal government of the United States is responsible for ensuring that companies have equitable employment packages across the industries, specially those companies with which it conducts business. Operating under the auspices of the federal government, the U.S. Department of Labor enacted a program to investigate whether these companies were complying with certain employment rules and regulations. The federal government can be equated with an entity that presupposes the laws which have been passed will protect the rights of its citizens. As a result of the Department of Labor's findings, Texaco must evaluate the salaries of its entire workforce annually while paying careful attention to the salaries of men and women at midlevel management pay grades. Although Texaco has agreed to pay a settlement for its racial and gender discriminations, the problem of discrimination among its employees is still rampant. However, Texaco has tried to right its wrong by hiring Deval L. Patrick, formerly head of the Department of Justice's civil rights division, as its general counsel and chairperson for the Texaco Equality and Fairness Task Force. This task force's purpose is to promote equality, diversity, and tolerance within Texaco.

Chapter 8

Moral and Ethical Behavior

It takes a long time to get to the top, but it takes a short time to fall.

CHAPTER OBJECTIVES

When you have read this chapter you should be able to:

- define morality and ethics,
- identify differences between ethical and moral behaviors, explain ultimate objectives of moral and ethical conduct,
- identify components of moral thoughts and behaviors,
- identify components of ethical conduct,
- describe moral idealism, realism, hedonism, and eudaemonism theories, and
- describe ethical teleological and deontological theories.

INTRODUCTION

Life is not worth living without periodically questioning what excellence is. Intellectual questioning is the structural processing of an individual's analytical mind to reach specific cognitive points of values concerning the means and ends of virtuous and passionate behavior. Since the behavior of an individual is concerned with means and ends, some people prefer to focus only on the means or ends, while others can concentrate on both. It is almost a truism to say that people act according to their emotional, sensational, and intellectual powers. Nevertheless, some people conceive their behavioral power according to the right and appropriate reasons because they believe that right reasons are suitable to their intellectual natures. This intellectual state of an individual's mind reveals that no individual can avoid either pleasure or pain and/or happiness and misery as a possible end result of behavior. Therefore, learning through intellectual questioning is an efficient method not only of bringing moral virtue into existence, but also of maintaining it as well.

To live with *virtue* and/or with *passion* is a fact for individuals. Individuals are not taught to be virtuous, but they have been told to behave properly. Virtue, as concerned with rational activity and passion, is a strong and extravagant attachment to feelings and emotions such as hope, fear, joy, grief, anger, love, and desire. The meaning of virtue depends upon the individual exhibiting the virtue.

To perceive positively the end result of organizational life, an individual should strive for the accomplishment of self-desires. This means to strive for reaching and maintaining the highest well-being. In seeking to establish and maintain the well-being of life objectives, we need to strive in order to achieve moral and ethical excellence. We must apply a mode of scientific dynamic effort, obligation, prudence, and legal compliance in our daily lives in order to complete our will. An individual can relate these holistic modes of behavior to the reasoning of what must be the ultimate objectives in life. An individual's desires as a member of an organization and/or for all people as members of a community need to establish such a state of well-being. We need to examine the means and end result objectives of our emotional, sensational, and rational achievements and failures.

In the fields of politics and business, sometimes powerful and wealthy people begin to decline and fall very quickly because of unethical, immoral, and/or illegal behavior. For example, in politics, the Watergate scandal (1972-1974) forced Richard Nixon, then President of the United States, to resign from his job. The president's unethical behavior caused the public's view of the federal government to change; they no longer considered it an instrument of high morality and pure motives (Jackson, Miller, and Miller, 1997: 259). Similarly, in the field of business, in January 1986, Ivan Boesky, an arbitrager for Ivan Boesky Corporation in New York, reported receiving a call from Michael Milken, who was the head of high-yield securities for the financial firm of Drexel, Burnham, Lambert, Inc. in Beverly Hills, California (Stewart, 1992: B1). Milken represented Occidental Petroleum Corporation through his firm for merger. Milken told Boesky that he had learned of a merger between Occidental Petroleum Corporation and Diamond Shamrock. According to the terms of the merger, Diamond Shamrock's stock would go up in price and Occidental's would fall. The merger agreement terms showed that the end result of such a deal was to split profits evenly. The ethical, moral, and legal questions rose for such a business agreement between two companies, insiders, and stockholders. After Milken's call, Boesky immediately rushed to buy as much Diamond Shamrock stock as he could. However, unexpectedly, the Diamond Shamrock board of directors turned down the merger and both Boesky and Milken lost $10 million. Considering this one case, you can imagine how the two had worked together in other deals to make an unethical, immoral, and illegal fortune. Both Ivan Boesky and Michael Milken worked together and earned more than a billion dollars. A few months later, Ivan Boesky's financial empire quickly fell as he formally pled guilty in federal court to a felony charge of stock manipulation. Five years later, both men completed their prison terms and paid fines of a million dollars.

Knowledge of wealth, such as patents, copyrights, trade secrets, inventions, formulas, trademarks, and the like, are vital aspects of businesses. Accordingly, keeping a corporation's trade secrets, inside information, and managerial decisions private are other aspects of organizational behavior. It should be noted that knowing secret organizational information may offer a business an advantage over another. We should analyze many of these issues as follows:

- From a sociopolitical and legal point of view, who owns what is in your head as an organization member?
- From a legal point of view, are you the sole owner of that knowledge or information?
- From an ethical point of view, what may be kept secret and what must be considered public information?
- From an organizational point of view, when and where should or shouldn't information be disclosed to the public?
- From a business point of view, who should have access to business decisions or who should show the corporation's information to the public?
- From a moral point of view, how should businesses value individuals' knowledge and their contributions to organizational effectiveness, efficiency, and productivity?
- In a broad sense, what are the moral, ethical, and legal responsibilities of organization members concerning knowledge, information, and secret decisions in a corporation?

These and other issues are the main focal points for further discussion in this chapter.

COMPLEXITY OF GLOBAL BUSINESS BEHAVIOR

New York City-based Windham International, which conducted a survey on expatriate employees, predicted the number of expatriate women would reach 20 percent (of all U.S. expatriates) by the year 2000. In addition, the U.S. workforce is ethnically and culturally more diverse than ever before and it is expected this trend will continue (Hardman and Heidelberg, 1998: 202). The gender gap between men and women, the cross-cultural value differences between domestic and international employees, and the specific moral and ethical principles as well as legal customs and laws that differ from culture to culture, and the severity of behavioral issues all become more crucial for managerial decision-making processes in multicultural organizations.

These and other similar issues raise many problems. For example, in multicultural organizations, what is acceptable in one culture may be disrespectful and insulting in another; what U.S. citizens may construe as sexually provocative or offensive may be acceptable in other cultures. Before 1977, for example, U.S. companies that were operating internationally had a history of paying off foreign officials for business favors (i.e., bribery). Such acts were declared illegal in the Foreign Corrupt Practices Act (FCPA) of 1977, which the U.S. Congress passed in the wake of the discovery that nearly 400 American companies made such payments over the years, amounting to payouts of about $300 million. Egregious within this sordid pattern of international bribery was Lockheed Aircraft Corporation's $22 million in secret payoffs to foreign politicians to get aircraft contracts (Shaw, 1996: 284). These and other examples raise questions concerning how a company decides which behaviors are moral and ethical in both home and host countries. Should an organization operate in a host country where there are different religious faiths and cultural value systems? Should multinational corporations conduct their businesses either on the basis of cultural beliefs, expectations, customs, and traditions of the host or home countries? Should all behavioral patterns of expatriate employees be measured according to the home-country standards or to the host-country value and legal systems? If men and women have interacted in certain ways for many years in a culture, who will judge that a type of behavior is right or wrong within a company and within the sociogeographical location of a company? To anayze these issues in the following paragraphs, I define moral, ethical, and legal ordinations and their implications in both domestic and global markets.

MORAL, ETHICAL, AND LEGAL ORDINANCES

The primary focus of this chapter is to study moral, ethical, and legal influences on individual and group behavior in organizations. These are three major behavioral "ordinances" of reasons for people who strive for achieving a common good. Ordinances of reason signify the establishment of cognitive and behavioral orders in a search for proper ends through good means. Not all ordinances establish practical patterns of expected excellent behavior. One kind of ordinance gives you "idea," another kind gives you "content," and the third binds you with "perceptual" commitments. All these ordinances are rooted in such variations in generalization, understanding, and defining fundamental principles and distinctive outcomes of these three phenomena. Ethical, moral, and legal ordinances should be understood by managers. These three ordinances are covered in the full expositions in multicultural organizations.

The various ordinances for an individual's behavior—ethical, moral, and legal means and ends—are the three major topics in this section. In addition, the notions of sensational and emotional pleasure respond to an individual's enjoyment and pleasure. The rational decisions and actions provide long-term happiness. Sometimes the means justify the ends or vice versa. Nevertheless, I will analyze both success and failure for an individual and for an organization.

Historically, conservative cultures are driven to seek a firmer "foundation" than motives to legitimize actions and behavior. In contrast, modern cultures are driven to seek practical "motives" based on objectively oriented data gathering to value peoples' competitive actions and behaviors. Consequently, one thing seems certain, and it is that in advanced industrialized, developed, developing, and decaying societies, ethics, morality, and legality play important roles in peoples' daily behaviors. For the clarity of the two types of conservative and views of the modern world, Table 8.1 illustrates the major comparisons. There are two major captions: (1) the conservative cultural worldviews, and (2) the views of the modern industrial cultural world.

As you are looking through the changes in the history of the industrialized world, you will observe how science and technology played important

TABLE 8.1. The Views of the Conservative and the Modern Cultural Worlds

The Views of the Conservative Cultural World	The Views of the Modern Industrial Cultural World
Religious Principles: Faith	Econopolitical Ideologies: Beliefs
Eternal Spiritual Life	Worldwide Material Life
End Result Orientations	Mean-Result Orientations
Theoretical Life	Practical Life
Intuitive Behavior	Rationalized Behavior
Destiny by God's Will	Human-Made Decisions and Actions
Religious Obedience	Legal Compliance
Mystery-to-Be-Accepted	Mystery-to-Be-Discovered
Community Sense of Value	Individual's Sense of Value
Services Beyond Self: Charity	Service for Self-Interest: Egoism
Compassion	Survival-of-the-Fittest
Equality	Justice
Individual's Natural Rights	Individual's Legal Privileges
Absolutism Ethics	Relativism Ethics
Stabilized Economy	Dynamic Economy
Exploitation	Exploration
Fixed Price	Market Price
Cooperation	Competition
Imitation	Innovation

roles in all societies. Table 8.1 illustrates comparative changes in all dimensions of people's lives.

Historically, both conservative and modern cultural views have articulated positions on specific political, educational, economic, cultural, social, and medical issues in all societies, which have shaped expected patterns of behaviors between homogeneous faiths and beliefs. For example, Roman Catholicism has a rich tradition of formally applying its core values to the moral aspects of industrial relations (Shaw, 1996: 12) or, as Sklare and Greenblum (1967: 322) note, Judaism does not demand social isolation or adoption of a unique style of life. Jews provide alternatives when a need is felt.

In the first instance, through modern industrialized views, the free market mechanism sought to make energized and hardworking people richer. Note that sociocultural, econopolitical, and religious doctrines partially and to some extent holistically play important roles in influencing an individual's daily behavior. People have learned from both religious faith and political ideologies how to appreciate moral thoughts and ethical principles. Different religions have given their followers moral, ethical, and legal ordinances. For example:

- "Good thoughts, good words, and good deeds," Gatta, Zoroastrianism.
- "What you do not want done to yourself do not do to others," Analects, 15:23, Confucianism.
- "Good people proceed while considering that what is best for others is best for themselves," Hitopadesa, Hinduism.
- "Hurt not others with that which pains yourself," Udanavarga, 5:18, Buddhism.
- "Thou shalt love thy neighbor as thyself," Leviticus, 19:18 KJV, Judaism, Christianity.
- "Therefore, all things whatsoever ye would that men should do to you, do ye even so to them," Matthew, 7:12, KJV, Christianity.
- (70)   "O ye who believed!
         Fear God (Allah), and
         Make your utterance
         Straight forward.
  (71)   That He may make
         Your conduct whole and sound
         And forgive you your sin:
         He that obeys God (Allah)
         And His Messenger, has already
         Attained the great victory."
         Koran, Sourah Ahzzab, Ayah 70 and 72: 1268

Moral behavior deals with an individual's ultimate state of psychosocial doctrines and religious faith. These manners are related to the individual's behavioral "ends." Ethical behavior deals with pluralistic "means" in actions. Ethical pluralistic beliefs can create a qualitative ordination to facilitate an ultimate sociocultural "ends." Legal behavior deals with the econopolitical ordinance of reason to be enforced for the "common good" (see Table 8.2).

While morality is based on individuals' "conceptual" commitments toward the end result of excellence, ethics is based on "pragmatic" collective known values by intellectual reasoning. Ethics deals with human social acts in order to direct people to a meaningful end. The laws and regulations are

TABLE 8.2. Analytical Comparative Description of Moral, Ethical, and Legal Perceptions

Morality	Ethics	Legality
Psychosocial concern for excellence	Sociocultural concern for goodness	Econopolitical concern for peace and harmony
Morality is the matter of an individual's choice	Ethics is the matter of culturally valuable norms	Legality is the sociopolitical mandated enforcement
Spiritual concern for happiness	Passionate concern for social satisfaction	Prudential concern for a secured life
Conscientious concern for self-enhancement	Conscious concern for self-refinement	Citizen concern for social development and growth
Religious concern for revelation	Humanitarian concern for community welfare	Obligatory concern for community ordination
Fear of God and shameful self-blame	Fear of social group condemnation	Fear of court's punishment and fines
Conceptual faith for mental synergy	Societal beliefs for behavioral energy	Legal expectation for profitable prodigy
Universal concern for intellectual power	Natural concern for appetitive power	Legal concern for legitimized power
Searching for the ends of self-excellence	Searching for the means of self-confidence	Searching for the minimal means and ends of goodness
Building individual dignity and loyalty toward truthfulness	Building collective integrity and loyalty toward worthiness	Building personal records of decriminalization
Developing and maintaining emotional virtues	Developing and maintaining intellectual values	Developing and maintaining the notion of common interests
Humanitarian sensibility for goodness	Humanitarian concern with intrinsic fairness	Citizenship concern for extrinsic concern of common justness
Qualitative assessment of self-behavior with heavenly rewarded expectation	Quantified assessment of self and others' behaviors with respect to human dignity	Quantified assessment of an individual's right with human integrity

based upon ideological, econopolitical, and social doctrines to establish happiness consisting primarily of peace and order. The in-depth views in research of these subject areas may be answered by the following questions:

- What are the fundamental definitions, classifications, and generalizations of moral, ethical, and legal conceptions in perceiving and operating businesses in different cultures?
- What conditions make the discussion of business ethics and moral conducts possible today?
- What does the current discussion of both domestic and international businesses mean in terms of the way people from different cultures think about the morality of global business obligations and commitments?

In order to understand the holistic means and ends of our organizational behavior, we need to define morality, ethics, legality, and their applications in human relations.

SEPARATION OF MORAL AND ETHICAL BEHAVIOR

We can understand no human thought and activity very well without defining their theoretical and practical boundaries. This is true about ethics and morality. Whatever advantages are, a shared meaning does two things. First, definition allows us to ensure that all meanings and attributes carry the same weight when discussants and practitioners use a term or refer to an idea. Second, and we closely ally this with the first, that discussants and practitioners can go after carefully defining the terms. Therefore many philosophers and social scientists spend their efforts analyzing and defining ethics, morality, and legality. These phenomena address what is true and false, good and bad, right and wrong, just and unjust, honest and dishonest, responsible and irresponsible, fair and unfair, worthy and unworthy, and the like.

The distinction between conscientious objectives marks the prevailing virtue of the intellect and wisdom of human beings of the mind and the conscious behavior of the body. Both make morals and ethics different. In making a distinction between morality and ethics, we will discover that the challenge of morality consists of intellectual generalization in universal reasoning, and that the challenge of ethics rests in the stimulation of its question rather than in the finality of its answer. Moral absolutism, which assumes that all moral issues can be measured by one universal standard regardless of cultural, religious, and political differences, has been offered as an alternative view to ethical relativism.

Etymologically, religious faiths, political ideologies, and cultural values are the three foundations of moral and ethical views among people. They have different meanings and perceptions concerning what is "common good" for individuals and groups. Most writers have stated that the term *moral* is essentially equivalent to the term *ethical*. Albert, Denise, and Peterfreund (1984: 6) state that:

> Etymologically, these terms are identical, the former (moral) being derived from the Latin word *mores,* the latter (ethics) from the Greek word *ethos,* both words are referring to customary behavior. Both terms may be used with two different antonyms. Ordinarily, the opposite of moral is taken to be immoral, so that what we mean by a moral person one who is good and does what is right, and by an immoral person, we mean one who is bad and does what is wrong. However, moral may also be used in a wider sense to refer simultaneously to right and wrong thoughts and actions. Then, morals' antonym is amoral. In this usage, people are moral in the sense that certain of their actions are subject to judgments of right and wrong . . . The same analysis may consist of the term ethically: Its antonym may be either unethical, that is, it may refer to what is wrong, or it may have as an antonym nonethical, in which case it would apply to objectives that are not subject to moral or ethical evaluation.

In some cultures, like the American business culture, people believe in "amoral" behavior. An amoral behavior is to rely on a partial truth while it conceals a good deal of the whole truth. Some American businesspeople perceive their moral obligation to show a partial truth primarily to be able to make profit. To them, to earn a profit, means individually and/or as a business entity they need to produce goods and/or provide services in buying and selling them for making profits. According to this philosophy people and/or businesses are not explicitly concerned with ethics. They do not consider themselves unethical or immoral; rather they are "amoral" as far as they feel that ethical considerations are inappropriate in businesses (De George, 1995: 5)

There is still another sense of understanding that the words of ethics and morals are used differently in other cultures. For example, in Persian culture, the term *akhlagh* used for ethics and *khooy* for morality have been perceived separately through the philosophy of *eshragh*—illuminationism. Illuminationism means that intellectual enlightenment seekers should search truthful scriptures for revelation. This behavior is based upon the divine inspiration for truth and the observation of rational and logical reasoning for blessing in earthly life and revelation in eternal life after death. Therefore, discovering the intellectual truth and acting on the whole truth can provide sound behavior.

The Buddhist cultural value system involves attention to be paid to reach mundane (such as earthly refinement) and individual problems (such as health), to salvation and morality. There are many facets related to such ethical and moral goodness. Seen from this perspective, the dominant view in the Asian culture is *monistic. Monism* is a doctrine in which moral and ethical behaviors are considered as ultimately one unit of reality. Therefore, in such a cultural perception, there is no separation between morality and ethics (Yinger, 1970: 45).

Shaw (1996: 4) states that: "In everyday parlance, we interchange 'ethical' and 'moral' to describe people we consider good and actions we consider right. And we interchange 'unethical' and 'immoral' to describe what we consider bad people and wrong action." French and Granrose (1995: 9) state that: "We use these terms (ethics and morality) interchangeably between the words ethics and morals is that the first is derived from a Greek word, the second from a Latin one. Both words originally referred to the customs or habits of a society or an individual."

As we have understood, no agreement exists among philosophers and scholars in regard to a unified and generalized definition concerning the phenomena of morals and ethics. Some people object to the term ethics and prefer to characterize ethical problems as religious problems. For example, in American culture, the subject of business ethics refers to legal market liability, business and external environment, and corporate responsibility. The Germans prefer to call it *Wirtschaftsethik,* which literally translated means the ethics of relationship between economics and society.

On the other hand, some philosophers and scholars make a distinction between morality and ethics. They define *morality* as the human conduct and values and "ethics" refer to the study of those areas. Walton (1977: 6) defines ethics as a critical analysis of human acts to decide their rightness or wrongness in terms of two major criteria: truth and justice. De George (1995: 19) perceives that "Morality is a term used to cover those practices and activities considered importantly right and wrong; the rules that govern those activities; and the values that are embedded, fostered, or pursued by those activities and practices. . . . Ethics is a systematic attempt to make sense of our individual and social moral experience, in such a way as to determine the rules that ought to govern human conduct, the values worth pursuing, and the character traits deserving development in life." Oesterle (1957: 5) defines "Ethics as the science which deals with those acts that proceed from the deliberative will of man, especially as they are ordered to the end of man." Since ethics is formally practical knowledge, morality is the meaningful knowledge of what constitutes good or bad actions.

Through a spiritually aesthetic view, morality is the very delightful, intelligible, and beautiful conscious awareness. It is an individual's knowledge. Many people feel that morality is personal and that no one should force such views on others. According to this position, each person is entitled to their own moral understanding and judgment. In contrast, many people hold another position with respect to different countries and cultures and believe that all members of a society must abide by the same cultural values. This view is another popular form of ethical relativism. They deserve careful consideration in defining and applying these terms. We need to clarify morals as a matter of individual "choice" and ethics as a matter of cultural valuable "force" which determines what action is right or wrong. Furthermore, are morals and ethics culturally determined by an individual and/or by a group? Is there a universal morality, applicable to all people in different places and times? To clarify these positions, we need to define both terms carefully: morals and ethics.

WHAT IS MORALITY?

Before we consider specifically what makes an action good or bad in a moral sense, we should have a precise picture of the notion of morality itself. The term *morality* primarily signifies a certain relation of an individual's acts that have some ends, to a standard or principle of action. Morality, therefore, is an abstract signifying the moral order of an individual's acts. Newton and Schmidt (1996: 3) have defined morals or morality as, "The rules that govern our behavior as persons toward other persons; also, duties."

As indicated before, the term "moral" is derived from the Latin word *mores. Mores* means the embodiment of the fundamental social group values. There are two main traditional fields of value inquiry: morals, which is concerned with the problems of truthfulness and falsehood, worthiness and worthlessness, and goodness and badness and their bearing on moral conduct; and ethics, which is concerned with the problems of justice and injustice, fairness and unfairness, and right and wrong and their bearing on ethical decisions and actions.

"Morality" means conformity to the rules of universal right conduct. For example, the term "honesty" is a universal phenomenon. In all cultures, honesty means to be truthful. An honest individual has been praised by all cultures. Therefore, there are some values among all people around the globe which are universal and these universal values are considered as foundational principles of humanity. In addition, if we are judging "bribery" through a moral term, we arrive at the same conclusion: that bribery corrupts the individual's character and defects the group's cultural value systems, and it is wrong. However, if bribery is the common practice in a given culture, then, is it proper to engage in bribery in that country? This raises questions concerning the distinction between ethics and morality.

Morality is a term used to manifest humanity's universal virtues. Virtues refer to excellence of intellect and wisdom needed to perceive a happy life. An individual's moral obligation is directly related to the disposition of cognizance of mind to perform its proper function effectively. Moral virtues concern habitual choices of rational thoughts in accordance with universal logical principles. The contemplation of absolute truthfulness and the discovery of the rational principles, which ought to control everyday actions, have given rise to intellectual virtues. Moral considerations deal with distinctions between good and bad, truth and falsehood, and worthiness and unworthiness. For example, a moral person may consider goodness if they habitually think, value, and act in accordance with their own intellectual conscience.

Sincerity in continuity with moral thoughts and acts is the keynote for morality. In other words, the meaning of moral is one to which a moral individual aspires (De George, 1995). Thus, morality denotes the total characteristics of intellect and wisdom of a human being. The maxim of the intellect and wisdom is careful calculation of virtues in the mind or description of the essential features of righteousness, truthfulness, and goodness of the character of a human being. Thus, when we speak of morality, we refer to a human's personal virtue through their intellectual choices. As human beings, we can make a distinction between true and false, and right and wrong. Therefore, we can make a distinction between the end results of morality and ethics. Morality's end result through intellectual truthfulness, righteousness, and goodness of thoughts and actions is revelation and happiness.

Wisdom and intellectual ability of the mind and passionate activities of the body which can be considered right and wrong are the main contextual domain of morality. The rules that govern an individual's thoughts and the values that are embedded in intellectual and rational virtues are the subject of morality. Therefore, morality is a universal, general, and intellectual characteristic of humanity. Distinct from both the real (natural) order of existing things and the logical (intellectual) order formed by human reason is the moral order. Both orders are caused by reason. It is within this context that the term morality is introduced as understanding formally an orderly thought which wisdom has established as rational reason in human acts. However, an individual's tendencies toward pleasure can change such rationalized thought and behavior and divert them into passionate desire.

An individual's passion depends on a variety of circumstances and conclusive end results. *Passion* is a motivational principle and tendentious operational factor in an individual's daily behavior. We act because of joy or sorrow, love or hatred, and success or failure. It is obvious that an individual's behavioral consequences are accompanied by either pleasure or pain, joy or sorrow, happiness or unhappiness, and courage or fear. All of these consequential motives are related to our intentional and tendentious attainment of personal objectives.

For ethical and moral behavior, individuals need to strive for excellence in behavior. Excellence in behavior is a virtue. Virtue is a positive derivative power of the mind toward happiness. Virtue is neither a passion nor a power. It is an extreme of excellence, rising above the excess and effect. Virtue regulates behavioral pleasure. It is the disposition of the intention toward good actions in a regular manner. For example, when we avoid good behavior the pain follows, or when we strive for happiness, a satisfactory end-result follows.

COMPONENT PARTS OF MORALITY

Morality contains several component virtuous parts and attributions, such as virtue, dignity, integrity, intellect, excellence in character, goodwill,

fortitude, magnificence, patience, magnanimity, prudence, and perseverance. Possession and application of these virtues enhances moral, ethical,
and legal behavior of a manager.

Virtue

Virtue regulates pleasure and pain, happiness and misery, courage and
fear, worthiness and worthlessness, and, finally, integrity and dishonesty.
Virtue is a spiritual logical habit inclining an individual to choose the relative mean between extremes of excess and defect. It is a habit consisting of
an "effective choice." Through virtue we manage anger, selfishness, pleasure, sin, and greed. Virtue is the ultimate state of excellence in intellectual
thinking and moral behavior. It includes both what is rational by nature; the
operation of reason itself and the operation of participating in a rational behavior. In other words, virtue is: What we may rationally think and how we
may rationally act.

There are two major kinds of virtues: one is a perfection of the power of
reason itself called "intellectual virtue." The other kind is development and
maintenance of the appetitive power which is rationally participating in the
behavioral virtue called "moral virtue."

What Is Intellectual Virtue?

Intellectual virtue is the intentional goodness in the essence of mind.
Good intention is therefore the immediate purpose of intellectual virtue. It is
by which we generate or initiate a sense of reasoning in order to lead us to
good thinking through useful application of wisdom. Wisdom is considered
as an order to arrive in knowledge; for we need to think well in order to acquire knowledge. Everyone must acquire knowledge by discovering self-
wisdom and intellect.

Intellectual virtue is concerned about the "effective" cause of thinking
(Oesterle, 1957: 59). The effective cause of thinking means to apply the
"right" reasoning at the right time during a thoughtful deliberation. Intellectual virtue is the essence of thinking in order to acquire knowledge. Indeed,
everyone must acquire knowledge through discovering the truth. It is through
intellectual virtues by which we achieve our good and clean thoughts and
behavior.

What Is Moral Virtue?

Since intellectual virtue has been considered as the essence of wisdom,
moral virtue is the virtue in action and behavior toward goodness. It is
viewed as conformity with common sense of rational intention and action.
Moral virtue consists of the process of an action. For the process is the measure of goodness of virtuous actions. Moral virtue is concerned with the
goodwill and intention of an individual. The rule of reason derives from an

individual's goodness. Good action, therefore, is the immediate purpose of moral virtue. Nevertheless, moral virtue is acquired by practice and application of principles of good faith.

Both intellectual and moral virtues can be taught by rigorous principles of wisdom. Since intellectual virtue is a matter of knowledge, moral virtue is application of knowledge and located in the appetitive power of an individual in which there are inclinations, tendencies, and drives toward something to be desirable.

Excellence in Character

Excellence in character refers to acquisition, development, and possession of superior and admirable knowledge in an individual's personality. It manifests knowledge and superior intention and action of an individual or a group of people. There are at least two reliable signs of excellence in an individual's character and behavior: (1) a valid universal apprehension and clear cognitive judgment which should be based on the honest and right judgment (intuition), and (2) a true universal decision to be made in perfect harmony or congruence with other universals known to be true. To be excellent in thinking and action is an ultimate objective of morality. For example, a manager needs to search for discovering the best and most suitable information on behalf of the corporation's stakeholders and then make a decision on the basis of reliable information.

Good Intellect

Good intellect is considered as perfection of human moral power, which is to say, they attain whatever is the good of a power. Good intellect differs from the power of willingness and from the sense of desiring. Both of these powers are appetitive powers, whereas the intellectual power is a cognitive power. Good intellectual power consists of grasping things in a rational and reasonable mode of thinking. To know something is good because it is good is to know something as true. For example, in an assembly line, a production manager's decision to "rework" a defective product may be considered a moral decision concerning how well a customer should be treated. It also makes workers conscious of doing what is right.

Goodwill

Choice and deliberation are two major component parts of "will." We need to understand the nature of moral obligations (goodwill) for an individual to make the right choice. An individual can make a choice on the basis of either emotional or intellectual reasoning. Emotional choices can end up with pleasure (appropriate sensational and emotional enjoyment) or pain (excessive sensational and emotional deprivation). In contrast, intellectual choices can end up with happiness (appropriate usage of intellect) and avoidance of misery (inappropriate and/or no usage of wisdom). Simple emotional acts of desire are not choices of an individual's will. Emotional desires are acts of tendencies for pleasure.

An individual's will is an intellectual satisfactory intention of reasoning. Intellectual choices are not necessarily connected with pleasure or pain. They are connected with happiness and satisfaction. Also, intellectual choices are associated with "self-volition." That is, an individual needs to be very intent on getting what they seek. Therefore, managers need to act on the basis of their will. This type of will is called "goodwill."

MORAL REASONING CONCERNING RESULTS

Intellectual Choices	Emotional Choices
1. *Apprehension* of the result	2. *Prediction* of the result
3. *Cognitive judgment* about the result	4. *Perception* of the result

MORAL REASONING CONCERNING THE MEANS

5. *Deliberation* about the means	6. *Consent* to the means
7. *Pragmatic judgment* of choices to be made for means	8. *Hypothesizing* about choices to be made for means

MORAL REASONING CONCERNING ACTIONS

9. *Uses* of rational power to execute choices	10. *Uses* of sensational power to execute choices
11. *Happiness* for achievement	12. *Pleasure* for participation

Deliberation is a pragmatic and possible individual intellectual workout for expressing reasons. We consider and evaluate reasons for or against doing something. We still need to understand the nature of choice itself because the act of choice may cause misunderstanding. Morally, a right choice should be based on goodwill. It should follow the intellectual reasoning for specifying the right means and ends. A manager without intellectual deliberation and good choices cannot be an effective manager. A good manager morally needs to apply sufficient goodwills, useful knowledge, and reliable information in order to make good choices and to take good actions.

Fortitude

Fortitude is blending the emotional endurance of fear and boldness into a mode of decision and action. People possess different levels of fortitude. These levels are the potential strength in their minds that enable them to endure adversity with courage. For example, a brave manager is one with the virtue of fortitude. Fortitude is clearly an admirable intellectual virtue that an individual may have which includes high quality in thinking, strong positioning power in choices, and positive attitudes in behavior. A manager needs to have the best known intelligible attitudes toward successful means and ends of self-conduct because of the leadership role.

Fortitude is not equivalent to courage. Fortitude brings out more accomplishment in intellectual deliberations, whereas courage is sometimes applied to an emotional action without assurance of the final possibility of positive consequences.

Magnanimity

Magnanimity means being generous in mind. The word magnanimity is made up of two Latin words: "magna," signifying "great" and "anima," signifying the "soul." Therefore, the nominal meaning of this virtue is to be generous in mind. For a manager, magnanimity means to deliberate good reasoning by demonstration of great efforts regardless of cost and benefit analysis of an important qualitative decision and action. Magnanimity is the breath of qualitative intention and action toward building and maintaining conformity in character.

Patience

Patience is a virtue that moderates frustration arising from various hasty decisions and actions. Patience promotes and develops cheerfulness and a principally tranquil state of the generous mind despite great injuries and other subversive actions. It is closely related to the extent of endurance and tolerance. Patience in the time of miserable situations prevents breakdown of morale. It ordinates grief and sorrow. Managers need to be patient because they are behaving as thoughtful leaders who have the responsibility of leading their subordinates. In contrast, impatience often promotes selfishness, hastiness, greediness, anguish, fear, frustration, and anger.

Perseverance

Perseverance is another moral virtue that occurs when an individual is persistent in achieving specific objectives regardless of obstacles and annoyances. For example, a manager perseveres in the virtuous sense, if he or she persists reasonably in achieving a difficult action, even though the length of time in that action is long and laborious. Another example: strategists need to develop the virtue of perseverance in their thoughts and behaviors because they must wait to achieve their strategic objectives through a long period of time and continual efforts.

Prudence

Prudence is an intellectual manner of careful consideration used when an individual is facing problems and issues and acting or reacting with other people. Prudence is a careful moral obligation toward particular decisions and actions for achieving a good end through good means. A manager needs to carefully assess circumstances of a decision or an action in order to understand what should be done and/or should not be done. In addition, they need to make sure that a decision or an action should have an assent to suitable means and ends. Managers need to avoid inconsistency in their intentions and negligence in actions.

MORAL THEORIES

Socrates, the first great moral philosopher, stated the creed of reflective individuals and set the milestone of the task of moral theories. Then most philosophers and writers examined human thoughts and behaviors in relation to morality and ethics. Some philosophers, whose views are oriented toward theological doctrines, appear to conceive that human beings are situated in the kingdom of God and they must be obedient to Him and follow orders from the Lord in order to have "revelation." On the other hand, nontheological philosophers, such as existentialist, materialist, and naturalist theorists, conceive that human beings are situated within the general realm of nature with their own "free choices and volitions." They believe that if human beings want comfort and peace they should not disturb or violate the rules of nature. The latter philosophers believe that human beings possess absolute control over their minds and actions and that is why they are determined solely by their volitions. In such a path of life, existentialist philosophers believe that human beings, through their decisive virtues, can discover the worthy things concerning the right way of life.

Both groups of philosophers agree that, in the kingdom of God or in the realm of the nature, human beings, through their emotional fickleness and sensational infirmities, are exposed to the mysterious flaws of greediness, bemoaning, derision, revenge, fear, anger, and discrimination. However, both theoretical ethics and morality focus their views on the nature of human beings who possess both dual efforts to overcome emotional and sensational unpleasant desires. These philosophers believe that human beings must eradicate their sensational weaknesses, emotional absurdity, and dreadful desires. In Table 8.3, you will find comparative characteristics of different moral theories.

In viewing and applying moral, intellectual, and necessitated virtues, many philosophers and researchers expressed their views through different reasoning. There are different schools of thought concerning morals, such as idealism, realism, hedonism, and eudaemonism theories of morality.

TABLE 8.3. Comparative Analysis of Moral Theories

Theorist	Causality	Deeds	Means	Ends
Idealistic Theologist	Ritual life and beyond life	Spiritual virtues	Good intention	Revelation and happiness
Realistic Naturalist	Stabilized life	Intellectual virtues	Good choices and volitions	Mental and physiological comfort
Hedonistic Materialist	Comfortable material life	Self-Interest decisions	Good short-term actions	Appetitive plea-sure and enjoy-ment through accumulated wealth and power
Eudaemonistic Existentialist	Continuity of a happy life	Necessitated virtues	Good long-term decisions	Personal happi-ness through enrichment of a meaningful life

Idealistic Moral Theory

Idealistic moral theory includes all views which hold that there is an independent world that is mental or spiritual in nature. This world is full of goodness. Avoidance of such a good state of existence may cause sinful intentions and dreadful actions. Human beings should try to stay in such a good kingdom. Nevertheless, having separation of the human mind from the godly ideal of goodness is considered in terms of good intention and actions. It is the fear of bad intentions which tempts human beings to separate themselves from goodness and join badness. They need to solve this problem by "copying, following, or imitating" knowledge. Like the installment plan of buying, copying, following, or imitating knowledge can solve problems.

We may distinguish three basic meanings from the term of moral idealism:

1. There is an ideal in the sense of excellent behavior which can be realized, as when we speak of "ideal friendship" or of "ideal weather." It is an idiom which states that: "A friend in need is a friend indeed." This is the surest state of human mind which should pursue heavenly life without corruption and defectiveness. People need to live in harmony with nature and with peace in their intellectual reasoning.

2. To search for goodness and beauty of our character not as attainable goals, but as "direction" of our endeavor toward goodness. This direction can orient human's mind toward goodness. This means that we need not only think and talk about goodness, but also to attend to goodness. Through mental goodness we will be able to reach the gate

of mental and moral health and to be motivated for applying spiritual virtues in our deeds.

3. Finally, there is the ideal in the derisive sense of something holistically visionary to pursue goodness as happiness. Moral idealists believe in happiness through attending the process of goodness.

There is no doubt, other than "gifts of nature" (e.g., intelligence), fortitude, courage, and perseverance are desirable. They may be pernicious if the will directs them that they are not good. For example, "loyalty" in an organization is not impressive as a virtue when we examine the loyalty of an auditor to an embezzler. Courage may further evil as well as good ends, as the case of the intrepid consumer abuser shows.

Goodwill is not good merely because it may not achieve desirable consequences. The value of goodwill is based upon good means and good ends. Goodwill is reverence for duty and duty is founded on reason. Reasoning seeks universal principles for being ideally, physically, mentally, and socially good.

Realistic Moral Theory

How an individual's decision and behavior become good or bad depends on a question of morality in a real pragmatic sense. Realism is old as naturalism. The term moral realism has to do with what actually exists—"seeing is believing." Immanuel Kant (1724-1804) has called this empirical knowledge "science." Kant believes in empirical moral knowledge—application of idealistic patterns of goodness and happiness in daily human life. He believes science is based on observation and direct exposure to knowledge. Such knowledge always comes after the evidence. In contrast to moral idealism, which believes in goodwill and intentions as the moral judgment, moral realists believe that good intentions are not sufficient to reach the ultimate point of goodness. Goodwill should result in good deeds. In addition, application of moral realism principles in human mind and behavior can result in a stabilized life.

Within this breadth of real endeavor, we are examining Kant's moral philosophy which is based on "good will as the means and ends of unconditionally good deeds." Kant concludes that the only thing in the world which is good without limitation is the goodwill to do one's intellectual duty (Rand, 1901: 539).

A moralist needs to be experienced with the universal principles of goodness. Experience is the touchstone of what is real. There are different perceptions in morality. These perceptions raise fundamental questions such as: What is the common sense of existence? What is an intellectual individual's sense of existence? Is morality subject to a universal sense of understanding?

Thomas Reid (1710-1796) stated that the universal conviction of human beings is dependable on moral truths. We have an immediate awareness, not only of external objects, but also of the causal and other relations between them. There are at least two main ways of conceiving universal moralism: (1) We may regard universal moral laws as separated principles which govern "forms." Forms follow the natural ordination. These forms are "mental" in their empirical nature. (2) The moral laws of nature do not govern natural processes, but they only describe such processes. These laws are the essence of common sense. Kant called it "science."

Scientific empirical knowledge is based upon good choices and volitions in human mind and actions. This is the surest moral decision and action. We can call an employer a "real moralist," because we mean that he or she never loses sight of the bitter taste of "economic hardship." Realistic moral managers usually manage a corporation to achieve their moral objectives despite "adverse" circumstances. These types of managers believe that if there are realities which cannot be altered, then realist managers should alter themselves to suit them. For example, T. J. Watson Jr. (1963: 15), former chairman of the board of IBM, states that: "The decision in 1914 led to the IBM policy on job security which has meant a great deal to our employees. From it has come our policy to build from within. We go to great lengths to develop our people, to retain people when job requirements change, and to give them another chance if we find them experiencing difficulties in the jobs they are in. . . . But policies like these, we have found, help us to win the goodwill of most of our people." It should be noted that IBM continued to practice such a tradition until 1990. Since then, IBM began to lay off 50,000 excessive employees for "right sizing" the human resources management policy.

With the same pattern of perceptions, managers in the Japanese culture believe that in times of economic recession corporations should not lay off their excessive employees because such an action will destroy laid off workers' normal lives. Japanese corporations do not retrench their operations; rather, they accelerate their operational processes to produce more goods with lower costs in order to sell them with the lowest prices after the economic recession is over. Within this managerial culture, the Japanese believe that they have served both employees and consumers, because employees will be able to continue their normal employment lives with a lower pay and consumers will be able to appreciate their purchase power with lower prices. Therefore, Japanese business culture is based on a philosophy that indicates if everything is in their favor, they enjoy it; and if not, they adapt themselves to the reality of economic life. They believe that all people should enjoy and/or endure on the basis of the reality of life. Therefore, the realistic moral temper appears in all areas of realistic national culture. In sum, moral realists seek to describe the common sense of characters and events as they really are without idealization or sentimentality.

Hedonistic Moral Theory

There are two other moral theories whose principles we can apply as means and ends in examining our good behavior. First is that all self-centric good behaviors endorse hedonism, the view that "pleasure" is the only intrinsic goodness in life worth pursuing. Second is that all egoists believe that both intrinsic and extrinsic values are not simply pleasurable—which may differ in quality as well as quantity—but instill happiness. This second view is called eudaemonistic morality, since the basic value in terms of which the assessment is made is happiness, not pleasure. For clarity of meaning, we describe pleasure through hedonism moral theory and happiness through eudaemonism moral theory as means and ends of morality.

The view that associates morality with self-interest decisions and actions is referred to as a belief that goodness as an intrinsic power can manifest in a pleasurable and enjoyable life. The theory of morality that advocates pleasurable life is considered as means and ends of goodness and is known as hedonism, a name taken from the Greek meaning "pleasure." One question that surfaces with hedonistic moral objectives is: Is there some least common denominator in terms of which we can assess our perceptual goodness? The answer is yes, through application of the moral theory of hedonism.

Hedonistic moral theory holds that basic human values should be oriented toward promotion of pleasure and avoidance of pain. According to this view, everything that people desire, want, or need can be reduced in one way or another to pleasure or pain. Pleasure means the absence of pain.

Pleasure, in its strict meaning, is the immediate accomplishment of enjoyable sensational, emotional, and physical ends. Pleasure is the powerful dynamic motive that urges individuals to respond positively to their good need dispositions. The immediacy and intensity of sensational and emotional delight would probably be the main reason for stability of human life and survival of human species. Therefore, all people need to enjoy their lives.

Pleasure is avoidance of experiencing depravation from need dispositions. Pleasure is a search for gratification to be experienced with fulfillment of physical, sensational, and emotional consequences. Depravation is a kind of momentary suffering from the state of deficiencies. Also, depravation is culturally assumed to be an aversive state that may involve withholding desired psychological tendencies. For example, in Jewish and Moslem faiths, fasting—and in Buddhism and Hinduism, meditation—is considered conscious deprivation from eating and drinking to motivate people to appreciate fulfillment. It does have something to do with the end result of self-confidence and self-realization.

There is an idiom which states "no pain, no gain." To have pleasure can be considered in two different ways: (1) to experience it as the end result of an action, or (2) to imagine it at the beginning of an action by "intention." By analyzing these two processes, interpretation of pleasure is different culture to culture. Some cultures conceive that the meaning of pleasure is striving for achieving the end result of an action. Specifically, utilitarian cultures consider that the good and bad end result of an action is based on the last thing to happen, because it is true that an end result is the last in execution of that action. But in other cultures, the end is the first, not in the order of execution, but in the order of intention. For example, some people believe in financial depravation by putting aside some income as savings for the necessity of future needs, while in other cultures people perceive pleasure on the basis of immediate intended action in spending their income for fulfilling of the end desires. This is the result of complexity of human nature. There is no doubt that both types of cultures are striving for "goodness,"—one conceives pleasure in a long period of time, while the other perceives it in a short period of time. In fact, the sense of pleasure is a trajectory state of excessive sensational and emotional enjoyment which turns an individual's behavior up from depravation and suffering to the climax of enjoyment and fulfillment and then gradually turns it back to the original state of depravation and deficiency again. This is considered as a momentum for survival of human race.

Eudaemonistic Moral Theory

The most serious difficulty for pleasure is that pleasure does not satisfy the whole ego of an individual person, nor even the best part of that person. People can share their pleasures with others through sensational and emotional enjoyments. Pleasure does not seem to provide the sort of happiness suitable to all people. Since pleasure does not satisfy long-range satisfaction for an individual—and even the best intellectual values, as Aristotle calls it, the "moral virtue"—it would not seem to provide happiness suitable to an "intellectual virtue" because it is short lived. It may be intense, but it never lasts. The magnitude of pleasure is derived from its own restriction and, at best, it is limited to certain levels of goodness. This suggests that a certain type of moral egoism is typical of those who are concerned with avoiding harm to the self rather than gaining benefits for the self (remember that eudaemonistic egoism is a doctrine that maintains that we should seek only our own happiness through intellectual virtues). Egoism contends that an action is morally right if and only if it best promotes the individual's long-term goodness.

Eudaemonistic theorists believe that people use their best long-term advantages as the standard for measuring an action's rightness. If an action produces or is intended to produce for an individual a greater ratio of good to evil in the long run than any other alternative, then that action is the right one to perform, and the individual should take that course of moral action.

Moral philosophers distinguish two kinds of egoism: personal and impersonal. Personal egoism holds that individuals should pursue their own best long-term goodness, but they do not say what others should do. Impersonal egoism holds that everyone should follow their best long-term goodness choice as a cultural value system. Egoism requires us to do whatever will best further our own interests and doing this sometimes requires us to advance the interests of others.

Several misconceptions haunt both versions of egoism. One criticism indicates that pleasurists do only what they like, that they believe in "eat, drink, and be merry." Another misconception is that self-interest endorses hedonism, the view that only pleasure is of intrinsic value; the only good in life worth pursuing is for self-enjoyment and pleasure. This will promote selfishness. Selfishness corrupts human morality and turns people into savages. Therefore, by this reason, eudaemonistic moral philosophers believe in happiness, not in pleasure, because they believe that happiness includes both intrinsic and extrinsic satisfaction.

Jeremy Bentham (1838), an eudaemonist moral philosopher, believed that morality was based on the principle that the objective of an individual's life is the promotion of the greatest "happiness" for the greatest number of people. Eudaemonistic theory holds that the basic values in terms of moral behavior are calculations of goodness and badness in terms of moral judgment. Some maintain that "happiness" is the essence of the right kind of thoughts, habits, or behaviors. Happiness is more a means than an end. One acquires wealth and power not really for one's own sake but as a means of achieving something else. However, it should be noted that if wealth and power have been accumulated for the sake of wealth and power, then the concentration of wealth and exertion of excessive power can produce either pleasure or misery. Because accumulation of wealth and power can be used for good or evil, it is perceived that happiness is an ultimate end when satisfaction and fulfillment of all intellectual desires are met. In attempting to determine objectively the moral nature of an individual's life, happiness is primarily what Aristotle calls an intellectual virtue. Manifestation of intellectually virtuous behavior makes an individual's life come into accordance with the goodness of holistic healthy body and mind.

There are two different ways to seek pleasure and happiness. First, one is searching for feelings and experiencing practical values; the second is to seek speculative cognitive knowledge in order to understand either for the sake of simply knowing or for the sake of making decisions for actions. The opinion that the state of existence consists both of pleasure and happiness deserves specific attention to be made by choices: (1) What implicitly do individuals perceive and believe about goodness in relation to pleasure and happiness? (2) What can individuals learn from scientific values, which are the end results of scientific deliberated solutions? By completing goodness, we mean an individual may seek satisfaction and happiness as the ultimate end.

WHAT IS ETHICS?

Thus far we have defined morality in terms of individual pursuit of self-interest and/or searching for self-egoism of goodness, but we have not seen what goodness is in terms of collective sociocultural value systems. Ethics involves critical analysis of cultural values to determine the validity of their rightness or wrongness in terms of two major criteria: truth and justice. Ethics examines the relationship of an individual to society, to nature, and/or to God. How individuals make ethical decisions is influenced by how they perceive themselves in relation to goodness.

In this section, we define ethics as a purely theoretical treatment of moral virtues in terms of speculative and practical collective cultural value systems. In speculative and practical knowledge of goodness, righteousness, and worthiness, we are concerned with cultural value systems, which are operable, either with intending to do something or actually doing something in the realm of goodness. Now, through these two alternatives, it might seem to define what ethical life should be, a manner of reflection in which it will indicate that it is not the kind of intending or knowing goodness, but it is the complete practical execution of goodness through collective behavior of a group of people.

Ethics is concerned with psychosocial actions and it can also deal with good deeds in a society. Philosophers have identified ethics with one or the other of these extremes. Some have understood ethics to be speculative and deliberative of good thoughts and behavior (deontological) and others have tended to identify ethics completely with practical good end results (teleological).

In homogenous European and U.S. cultures, the meaning of ethics is related to "The Love of God," and to "The Love of Wisdom" (Weber, 1960). In the Greek tradition, ethics was conceived as relating to "social niceties." Social niceties could be considered as custom, convention, and courtesy. In Chinese culture, the term *ethics* has been used to signify etiquette, *li,* which originally meant "to sacrifice," which refers to the fact that Chinese people should follow legally sanctioned etiquette, not to mention knowledge of hundreds of correct forms of behavior. The Chinese eventually came to believe that their behavior was the only correct etiquette in the universe—that all who did not follow the same meticulous rules of conduct were uncivilized barbarians (De Mente, 1989: 27-28).

Later on, a very different orientation was introduced by Judeo-Christian ethics. In this tradition, the ideals of righteousness before God and the love of God and neighbor, not the happy or pleasant life, constitute the substance of ethical behavior.

The term "ethics" is derived from the Greek word *ethos.* In the *Oxford English Dictionary* (1963) ethos means the genius of an institution or system. Also, it defines ethics as the science of morals and the department of study concerned with the principles of human duty. Ethics concerns itself with human societal conduct, activity, and behavior of people. Ethical behavior is considered a deliberate and conscious social awareness concerning good behavior. People need to knowingly and to a large extent deliberately have good thoughts and behaviors. Ethics is concerned with construction of a societal rational system through application of moral principles (virtues) by a group of people in a society.

As far as the term morality is related to the deliberation of individuals' intellectual characteristics through their conscientious awareness, ethics is the collective social conscious awareness of a group of people. Thus, morality is related to individual virtues, and ethics is related to society's fairness, justness, and worthiness—excellence. Hence, morality is the foundation of an ethical society, it also relates to the existence of moral people who make the collective distinction of right judgments from wrong and good behavior from bad. Ethics generally mandates people to behave in accordance with valuable norms and standards in excellence that they accept and to which they and the rest of society hold others.

Ethics, then, can be defined as a systematic collective attempt toward social well-being in a society in order to make sense of our individual security and social peace in such a way as to determine the rules that ought to govern human social conduct, the values worth pursuing, and the character traits deserving development in life. In other words, human beings cannot adopt ethical principles of social actions unless they can do it with consistency, and it has to be adopted by everyone else. Without an accepted universal morality—virtues—there would be no stabilized ethical society to keep the world in peace and security. Beliefs and faiths are important ingredients in ethical behavior. Different beliefs and faiths about moral and intellectual virtues can lead us to differences in what is described as ethical relativism. This is the main reason that each individual, or a group of people, perceive good differently.

ETHICAL RELATIVISM

Ethical relativism claims that when any two individuals or two cultures hold different ethical views of a sociocultural value system, both can be right. Different ethical views are products of religious faiths and/or political ideological beliefs. Thus, a mode or trend of behavior can be right for a person or one society, and the same action, taken in the same way, may be wrong for another person or society, yet the two persons or societies are equally correct. For example, some members of our society believe that abortion is immoral and unethical because it has been viewed as murder and it is a sinful action. Others who are pro-choice believe that abortion is morally and ethically permissible because it is purely related to a woman's choice to have or not to have a child. The differences are rooted in religious faiths, econopolitical ideological beliefs, and sociocultural value systems. These differences are examples of transcultural, multicultural, and intracultural relativism. Another example, in a culture with a religious profamily value system, like Moslem nations, economically advantaged men and disadvantaged women will probably seek monogamy. The main reason for monogamy is to prevent women from having illegitimate children. In the Moslem faith, to have an illegitimate child is not only considered a grant sin but it is also prohibited for men to have sex with women without religious marriage. Other nations with equal economic opportunities for both men and women, with approximately equal numbers of men and women, perceive marriage as ethical behavior. However, in many Western nations it is considered a legitimate affair when men and women have sex outside of marriage. In Moslem nations, according to the Koran, adultery is considered a "grant sin," while in other cultures it is forgivable. Adultery destroys family cohesiveness.

Many people dispute some judgments on the basis of their rationality. In some cultures, an action or judgment may be right for one person or society, and the same action or judgment, taken in the same manner, may be wrong for another person or society. What exactly is meant by these claims? For such reasoning, we divide ethical theories into teleological and deontological categories.

THE ULTIMATE MEANS AND ENDS OF ETHICAL BEHAVIOR

In arriving at a final conclusion in daily moral organizational life, employees must analyze their activities within the end result of "goodness." Goodness means the conscious deliberation of employers and employees toward the tendency to treat each party with dignity. Employers should prevent exploitation of employees, and employees should respect their duties. Employees should attract their tendencies or desires positively to be efficient and effective. They need to use their energy toward organizational productivity. Since the moral principle of morality is the realization of the self-evidence of goodness, all moral desires need to be good. The goodness that we strive for is the way that we perceive it. We perceive ourselves as the good agent of goodness. There is no doubt that people interpret desires either with pleasures and/or with happiness in their life. The problem is what constitutes pleasure and happiness as two major components of goodness. People are considered at the center of goodness and badness. Making profit and having money may be considered a legitimate moral goodness. The question arises: Is there any intrinsically valuable goodness in a piece of paper which is called money? The answer is no. What is the value of that piece of paper? The answer is: The intrinsic and extrinsic money power of that piece of paper, which can be considered "clean or dirty money" that we can use to buy the goods that we desire. Dirty money has been viewed as conducting business through unethical, immoral, and, in some cases, illegal activities such as selling and buying drugs, prostitution, pornographic films and paraphernalia, gambling, and the like. Clean money is considered as to be earned through legitimate business transactions and hard work. Therefore, the extrinsic value of money carries valuable ends, while the intrinsic value carries valuable means. The more profit that we generate, the more goods (extrinsically) we can buy (intrinsically).

Money can be used either as means or as an end. It depends on how we appreciate its value. There are two concepts concerning money. One is that people like money because they believe in "eat, drink, and be merry," as stated previously. Fulfilling our needs through these behavioral activities can result in either pleasure and enjoyment or happiness and satisfaction. Since Milton Friedman's notorious claim in 1970—that the only ethical responsibility of a corporation is to maximize profits for its shareholders— many ethicists often have criticized him. Indeed, corporations do have social responsibilities that must be met in order to be considered ethical entities. Most of Friedman's critics found his philosophical view on social corporation's responsibilities marginal. Friedman (1983: 81-83) asserts that a company has only one responsibility to society: to use its resources and engage in activities designed to increase its profits so long as it stays within "the rules of the game," which is to say, engages in open and free competition without deception or fraud. Furthermore, Friedman believes that the marketplace will punish those corporations that do not stay within "the rules of the game," and any corporate funds used toward social ends come from the pocket of shareholders and are, as such, antithetical to the corporation's purpose.

There is a lack of moral and ethical commitment in the field of international business today. The often-neglected point in modern society is the abusive knowledge wealth power, dissemination information power, material wealth power, technological synergistic power, and religious power. Virtues are defined as the state of excellence in thinking, behaving, and interacting with self and others. Virtues refer to the excellence of intellect and wisdom and to the disposition of cognizance of mind to effectively perform its proper function. Moral virtues are the core values of humanity. Moral virtues concern the habitual choices of rational thoughts in accordance with universal logical principles. However, through some ethical and legal perceptions, "real" knowledge is not objective or socially independent, but it is a subjective system of ordered procedures for the production, regulation, distribution, circulation, and operation of information contents—what we call copyrights, patents, trademarks, formulas, and the like. Thus, the "real" knowledge, through ethical and legal endeavor, is based on the socioeconomic and political value systems of each nation. The major discrepancy between universal moral value systems (virtue) and the national ethical and legal normative systems is based upon the origin of the perception of humans about life. However, convictions born of moral insight hold greater sway against buffering temptations and tendencies toward luxury and need.

COMPONENTS OF ETHICAL BEHAVIOR

Everyone is familiar to some extent with ethical behavior in relation to justice, fairness, and righteousness in decision-making processes. Since ethical decisions and judgments are based on cultural value systems, there are certain ambiguities concealed within the boundaries of these cultural value systems. For example, in the field of business we speak of a just cause, fair price, right wage, and while all these meanings are closely related to one another, they are nevertheless not wholly the same. Let us begin, therefore, with the broadest meaning of ethics as a cultural value system. It involves justness, fairness, and righteousness.

Justness

The proper object of justness is right, that which is just. The proper Latin word for "right" is *jus,* hence "right" is only another name for the just. Through an ethical point of view, justness does have three clarifications: The first is that the source of justness is natural law. Natural law is a generalized principle for individuals' actions inclining their feelings toward what is goodness in nature. The second point is related to extrinsic cultural reasoning, which is related to econopolitical and sociocultural value systems. These value systems are called "rights" in relation to and consequent upon end results of goodness. The third point is related to an individual's intrinsic cognitive conception concerning human rights. Individuals are concerned about themselves regardless of consequences to the common good. It is based upon individual liberty as the means and ends of a justified decision and action. Individual liberty is the moral order. Therefore, in a moral sense, we can say we are free to do what we have a "right" to do. In the field of international management, a manager needs to consider all these "rights" during times of ethical decision-making processes.

Fairness

We divide our ethical fairness concerning holistic sensational, emotional, and rational judgments into three domains of prudence:

1. Prudence is a careful unbiased consideration that comes from special relations between duties and obligations—impartiality.
2. Prudence is viewed as those obligations that come from particular causes for right or wrong actions—straightforwardness.
3. Prudence is viewed as those obligations that come from the particular means of actions—legitimacy.

A manager needs to make a fair judgment on the basis of impartiality, straightforwardness, and legitimacy.

Righteousness

Righteousness refers to an individual's rational judgment, which is suitable to what is supposed to occur, or what judgment should be suitable to what is in conformity with real fact, reason, standards of moral virtues, or ethical principles. From an ethical point of view, any decision or judgment could stray from the right course of action by "too little" or "too much." An obvious instance is found in our daily attachment to special habits, tendencies, extravagancies such as workism, alcoholism, sexism, and others. A manager needs to reason correctly at the time of expressing causes of judgments and decisions according to speculative order of knowledge. The right reason is true knowledge of ethical principles.

Truthfulness

Truthfulness means conformity with fact or reality. Facts are those fundamental principles that are apart from and transcend perceived experiences (e. g., the basic truth of life). The truthful ethical decisions and actions in a corporation depend on how a manager complies with the ethics of knowledge. Is it true that the concept of scientific thoughts and statements and those of ethics and values belong to different worlds? Is it true that the world of scientific thoughts and actions are subject to tests? Is it true that the world of what is is subject to tests and the world of what ought to be is subject to no tests? Is it true that the power of intellect differs from the power of will as well as from the power of sense desire? To know something well through reason is to know something as true. Truthfulness, therefore, is the reason of intellect with which to perceive facts or reality.

THEORIES OF ETHICS

There are two core assumptions of ethical perceptions: the atomistic universal of moral laws (intellect, wisdom, and knowledge) and cultural value systems. Through our intellectual cognizance of value systems, the most fundamental agent is the universal self. All people are subject to a universal equality—regardless of the separation of contextual value systems in which they exist. Philosopher Thomas Hobbes (1588-1679) (1839: 110), the most influential exponent of the egoistic theory in the seventeenth century, believed that: "Nature hath made men so equal, in the faculties of the body and mind; as that though there be found one man sometimes manifestly stronger in body or of quicker mind than another, yet when all is reckoned together, the difference between man and man is not so considerable, as that one man can thereupon claim to himself any benefit, to which another may not pretend as well as he." Perhaps the most significant reasoning for such a declaration in ethics is the isomorphic nature of human beings. Human beings are not different in nature; however, their characteristics and behaviors are different—personal and universal. The second core assumption is attributed to the atomistic self. Personal behavior is rooted in personal traits and value judgments. It is the starting point of our intellect and wisdom and it is part of our ontological makeup as human beings. In the realm of our ethical reasoning and moral actions, there is no consultation with other agents—we consult nothing outside of ourselves. Thus, manifestation of ethical intellect and wisdom is the deliberation of extracted thoughts and actions from our immediate intellectual cultural context.

In spite of the implication and chained value systems of both morality and ethics, there are two major approaches in the realm of value systems:

1. Either *objective* moral values are the universal beliefs of humanity, or
2. *Subjective* ethical values are the products of societally valued cultures in the form of cultural choices.

When we speak of ethics, we refer to our cultural value systems concerning the collective judgment of right and wrong and good and bad behavior. However, in multinational cultures there are different perceptions concerning what is right or wrong and good or bad. This variation has come from personal gains and the convenient lifestyle of individuals.

The vocabulary of ethics is rich and can be applied to a variety of reasoning. Social scientists and philosophers have documented the fact that people in different cultures, as well as people within a given culture, hold divergent ethical views on particular issues. Some cultures emphasize the causes of ends (teleological) while others emphasize the ends (deontological).

Teleological Ethical Theory

Telos in Greek means goals or results. Teleological ethical theory is reasoning on the basis of the consequences of decisions and actions. Rules must be followed not because of acknowledged obligations but because of the fear of punishment for breaking those rules. This theory is concerned with avoiding harm to the self rather than gaining benefits for the self. Followers of this theory believe that since cultural values vary from culture to culture, it is relevant to judge an ethical value system based on outcomes compatible with cultural and religious standards.

So the origin of an ethical action—its efficiency, not its final cause—is choice, and that choice is a desire with a view to a rationalized end. The primary ethical act of goodwill is devotion. Devotion is promptness in doing whatever pertains to manifest goodness. An act of devotion is the most important end of the behavior of intellectual virtue. This is why good and right choices cannot exist without wisdom and intellect or without a purified emotional state of harmony between mind and body. Good decisions and actions cannot exist without a combination of intellect and character. Intellect and wisdom themselves, however, move nothing. The intellect and wisdom must be motivated by virtue, because virtue always implies a perfection of human power. This power must be dynamic and operable by an individual's will. How the intellect differs from the power of willing and from the power of sense desiring is the subject of cognitive power. Intellectual knowing and sense knowing are cognitive power. They need to be objectively oriented through a synergistic combination of personal and social embodiment of cultural value systems.

Teleological ethical theorists reject absolute universal ethical commitments because they believe that there are exceptional circumstances which can reverse a good action to bad or vice versa. For example, in the field of business, shoplifting is not moral, ethical, or legal. However, some people believe that if a hungry person really does not have any income to buy basic foods, such as fruit and bread, in special circumstances in a grocery store, the hungry person may consume food without paying, though such an action may not viewed as shoplifting. It is viewed as sampling the taste of foods for deciding whether to buy. In addition, teleologicalists believe that in all circumstances means cannot justify ends. Therefore, ethical judgments should be focused on the end results. As deontologicalists are pro-absolutism, teleologicalists are prorelativism.

Deontological Ethical Theory

Deontos in Greek means obligations or duties. The foundation of deontological ethical theory is reasoning based on duties or obligations to self and others. Deontologicalists reject moral choices with mixed outcomes. They insist that an individual must always avoid harming self and others, whereas teleologicalists assume that harm will sometimes be necessary to achieve goodness.

Deontological views of ethics are concerned about causal reasoning for the truthfulness, righteousness, and goodness of decisions and judgments. They are not concerned about applicability of circumstances or situational factors in judging right or wrong actions. These people focus their attention on the right causes regardless of consequences. For example, shoplifting is viewed as unethical, immoral, and illegal by all means and ends. It is a wrong action, regardless of the motive or circumstances of the shoplifter.

Deontologicalists believe in three characteristics that are considered to be usually associated with good judgments. First, ethical judgments about the rightness or wrongness of an action is held to be universally applicable. Parhizgar and Jesswein (1998: 141), in regard to economic affordability of the borrowers and the right of lenders, state:

Both multinational and international lenders must, at a minimum, respect the international ethical rights of lenders and debtors. For the purported rights, there are at least three conditions that must be considered: (1) the rights must protect something of great mutual importance to both lenders and debtors; (2) the rights must be subject to substantial and recurrent opportunities and threats; and (3) the obligations or burdens imposed by the mutual rights must satisfy a fairness-affordability test for both lenders and debtors.

Within this domain of mutual ethical agreement, through the conscious intellectual cognizance of a party if an action is right for that party, it is also right for another one. If it is wrong for anyone, it is also wrong for others in similar occasions.

In the field of international business, the universal ethical rule says that it is wrong to bribe or to promote bribery for gaining an illegitimate interest. It is universal because it corrupts the dignity and integrity of humanity and it applies to everyone. Therefore, there are some universal dimensions that are central parts of moral marketing. De George (1995: 256) states that this universal truthfulness of ethical principles in advertising is: "The immorality of untruthful, misleading, or deceptive advertising, the immorality of manipulation and coercion through advertising, the immorality of preventing some kinds of advertising, and the allocation and distribution of moral responsibility with respect to advertising."

Second, ethics is a cultural value judgment and overrides other considerations. We are ethically bound to do what sometimes we may not want to do. Third, ethical judgments should properly direct an individual's behavior concerning morally right actions, and moral blame can properly accompany acting immorally. Therefore, while morality is considered to be a personal goodness of an individual, ethics is the collective intellectual virtues of a cultural value system of a group of people.

WHAT IS LEGALITY?

Since ethics is a behavioral ordinance to harmonize conflicting psychosocial interests between an individual and other people, law is another practical econopolitical attempt to resolve the disputable issues between people. Therefore, law is not formally an act of will; it is a practical reason that determines means in relation to some given ends. Oesterle (1957: 201) defines law as a "certain ordination of reason for the common good, promulgated by one who has care of the community." Two major concerns, however, may be added to this definition. The first is that, by designation, the common good is the necessary end of every law, thus we may distinguish a true law from so-called law laid down by a tyrant. Although a tyrant is in control of a state and enacts laws for the political common good, in reality, such ordinances are directed to maintain personal power in order to rule the state; they are not true laws and do not properly carry an obligation to be obeyed by all the people, including the tyrants themselves. Second, while the common good is the necessary end of every law, the common good needs to be directly effective for the benefits of the community as a whole.

Law formalizes the sociocultural and econopolitical contract under which the community limits the harm that members can do the social fabric (Ember and Hogan, 1991). As we see, law resembles ethics in that both are social institutions that aim to improve human relations in various ways. Law is an exterior principle of action in the sense that it establishes, in a universal and objective fashion, an order of action to be followed by people seeking a common end. Law, however, presents certain mandatory minimal standards of "intellectual" conduct. Legal standards regulate people's social actions with respect to what to do or what not to do. Therefore, law is an ordinance pertaining to reason. It is the expression of what is reasonable to do under special circumstances and situations.

SUMMARY

Although much has been written about philosophical approaches to ethical and moral generalized behavior, much less is known about etymological differences and genealogical distinctions between these phenomena. In the pre–Industrial Revolution era, economic relations among nations tended to be imbedded in the socioreligious sphere; in postindustrialized societies, social relations tend to be embedded in the econopolitical sphere. The one method of understanding the emergent meanings of morality and ethics is that, because of the advancement of science and development of technology, science and technology have dramatically changed cultural value systems in all nations. This is particularly true in developed societies. One way to identify different meanings, perceptions, conceptions, and applications of the terms *morality* and *ethics* is to study the evolution of human civilization through history. As far as the new world order goes, it has emerged through new necessities of human life and changed the domestic market economy toward the international market economy. Many cultural, legal, and ethical values and norms have been altered because of the new world order as well.

The business of multinational business is business. What kind of business is related to moral, ethical, and legal conceptions and perceptions of producers and consumers in both home and host countries? The problem in the international business transactions is sometimes related to some issues in which there are similarities between home and host countries' laws and ethics, and in other cases in which there are differences. Little has been written or said about the ethical and moral problems and issues for international corporate commitments and responsibilities. Every nation seems to be concerned with these issues. This may be in part because multinational corporations are proportionately powerful and influential in mapping international econopolitical diplomacy. They provide employment opportunities, produce needed products and services, and earn profits for their shareholders. Also, they create problems such as polluting the air and water and in some cases ignore human rights. International business law faces a number of problems that stem directly from the simple fact that sourcing carries a suspicious motive to be justifiable for a pluralistic gain. It carries a partisan message of distrust among customers, distributors, and suppliers. Such a lack of confidence in its inherent ability gives little reason to provide international support by all involved parties. Within the global environment of business, the business of intentional business is not charity or social welfare, nor is it robbing, abusing, misusing, or exploiting one another. What constitutes business is truthfulness, righteousness, and worthiness; the relations between employers and employees, government and businesses, home and host countries; the quality and quantity of products and services; cost and fairness; justness, and worthiness of cost-benefit analysis.

CHAPTER QUESTIONS FOR DISCUSSION

1. Explain the distinction between morality and ethics.
2. Explain the distinction between speculative knowledge and practical knowledge.
3. State and explain the definitions of morality and ethics.
4. What is moral theology?
5. What is the first principle of morality and how do we arrive at it?
6. Explain how good, as an end, is a cause of moral and ethical action.
7. What is the distinction between "all people seek pleasure" and "all people seek happiness?"
8. Through what sense do some people seek pleasure or happiness?
9. Give arguments for and against the identification of wealth and power with pleasure and happiness.
10. What are the meanings of ignorance and negligence in morality and ethics?
11. How does a desirable moral decision compare with an ethical decision of choice?
12. Explain the act of deliberation.
13. What is conscience and how it is related to consciousness?
14. What is the definition of fortitude?
15. What is magnanimity?

LEARNING ABOUT YOURSELF EXERCISE #8

How Do You Perceive Your Moral, Ethical, and Legal Behavior?

Following are sixteen items for rating how important each one is to you and to your organization on a scale of 0 (not important) to 100 (very important). Write the number 0-100 on the line to the left of each item.

Not important		Somewhat important		Very important
0	25	50	75	100

It would be more important for me as a manager of an organization to:

_____ 1. Perceive my role to satisfy my subordinates' desires and to enjoy working conditions in my department.

_____ 2. Give a hard time to employees for more productivity in order to achieve organizational objectives.

_____ 3. Make decisions on the basis of organizational policies and procedures regardless of my personal value system.

_____ 4. Satisfy the demand of stakeholders by the virtue of either too much or too little profits for all.

_____ 5. Make decisions on the basis of my heart to satisfy my moral obligations.

_____ 6. Show much prudence in traveling the road of the organization by keeping away from the ditches on either side.

_____ 7. Understand what we really mean by goodness through maximization of organizational profitability.

_____ 8. Get along with people with a reasonable amount of pleasurable behavior as a habitual manner of my personality.

_____ 9. Make decisions and actions based on my personal religious faith even though it may cause me to lose my job.

_____ 10. Work in an organization, to talk to my friends, watch television, or listen to a radio station, and even sleep in my workplace when I feel tired.

_____ 11. Make sure that all decisions that I make will be related to the right actions as outlined by the organizational mission by all means and ends.

_____ 12. Be patient and show tolerance and endurance to freely be criticized by my superiors, subordinates, and peers. I love to be criticized all the time.

_____ 13. Sell my products without consideration of the efficacy of consequences for customers. I believe it is moral if I find that the good is reasonably proportionate to the evil act.

_____ 14. Lay off excessive employees, especially very young and very old ones because I am looking for energetic employees with very high mental and physical health.

_____ 15. Convert organizational environment from a friendly relationship with all employees for giving birthday parties and serving foods and beverages during work hours to a formal environment.

_____ 16. To achieve organizational objectives through boldness and accept risky decisions and actions for profitability without fear.

Turn to the next page for scoring directions and key.

SCORING DIRECTIONS AND KEY FOR EXERCISE #8

Transfer the numbers for each of the sixteen items to the appropriate column, then add up the four numbers in each column.

Idealistic	**Realistic**	**Hedonistic**	**Eudaemonistic**
4. _____	2. _____	1. _____	7. _____
5. _____	3. _____	8. _____	13. _____
9. _____	6. _____	10. _____	15. _____
12. _____	11. _____	14. _____	16. _____
Your Totals _____	_____	_____	_____
Total Scores 400	400	400	400

The higher the total in any dimension, the higher the importance you place on that set. The closer the numbers are in the four dimensions, the more psychosocially and econopolitically balanced you are.

Make up a categorical scale of your findings on the basis of more weight for the values of each category.

For example:

1. 300 Realistic
2. 275 Eudaemonistic
3. 250 Idealistic
4. 200 Hedonistic

Your Totals   925
Total Scores   1,600

After you have tabulated your scores, compare them with others on your team or in your class. You will find different ethical and moral patterns among people with diverse scores and preferred modes of self-realization.

CASE STUDY: HILLSDALE COLLEGE

The daughter-in-law of the president of Hillsdale College committed suicide on campus after it was alleged that she had been having an affair with him. Such an incident resulted in the president resigning his position because of immoral, unethical, and illegal behavior.

Hillsdale College is a liberal arts college two hours west of Detroit. The president took office in 1971 and served for twenty-eight years. The president was very successful in fund-raising from the private sector of businesses, including receiving federal aid and financial assistance for students. He appealed to the rapidly growing conservative ethical, moral, and cultural values and asked people to help and preserve the college's independence. The president, during his twenty-eight-year tenure, raised $325 million for Hillsdale. He managed to convince the board of trustees to pay him an annual salary of $448,000.

This is the irony: While conservative cultural values are based upon ethical and moral behaviors, and despite the belief that people ought to be held accountable for their conduct, the board of trustees evidently did not wish to hold the president responsible for his misconduct for many years. Of course, conservatives sometimes avoid exposing their own immoral and unethical behaviors because they fear public condemnation. Conservatives are not the only ones who sometimes find themselves living in opposition to their cultural and religious value systems.

The alleged misconduct of the president came, therefore, as a shock when two conservative magazines, *The National Review* and *The Weekly Standard* reported an allegation that the cause of the suicide of the president's daughter-in-law was directly related to his sexual misconduct. The magazines alleged that the president had carried on a long sexual affair with his son's wife, the mother of his grandchild. Not only that, they said, he had also had affairs with other women (Wolfe, 1999). The president's daughter-in-law was managing *Imprimis,* a monthly conservative newsletter of nearly one million readers published by the college, as well as the Hillsdale College Press.

The Chronicle of Higher Education, under the Michigan Freedom of Information Act, obtained some documents indicating that the president's daughter-in-law had resigned from her job on September 8, 1999. She gave few details as to why she was leaving, as follows: "You know me, I hate to be the object of attention. I have been such an object in the college community for many years now. I just want this to be as private as possible and, most of all, I don't want to have to answer any questions." Her resignation came just days after the president announced that he planned to remarry. He

---

Sources: Wolfe, Alan (1999). "The Hillsdale Tragedy Holds Lessons for Colleges Everywhere." *The Chronicle of Higher Education,* XLVI(15), December 3, p. A72; Van Der Werf, Martin (1999). "Police Rule Death at Hillsdale College a Suicide." *The Chronicle of Higher Education,* XLVI(16), December 10, p. A42.

had divorced his first wife, who had cancer, five months earlier (Van Der Werf, 1999).

When the president's immoral, unethical, and illegal behavior surfaced, he resigned from his position and requested that the board honor him with early retirement. The board of trustees announced that the president's request for early retirement had been granted. In addition, only after widespread publicity did college officials say they would investigate the allegations.

How, then, should people respond to such an important issue? Is it fair to question the moralists and ethicists, who preach moral virtues, family values, and sexual restraint, yet act irresponsibly by ignoring moral principles?

According to critics, the president consistently acted as if he were above restraint—including ethical and moral restraints—and he seemed to have had as much respect for his son as he did for dissenting faculty members, students, and the community at large. According to some dissident faculty members, the president was an autocrat whose leadership style was authoritarian in the extreme. The president allegedly treated faculty members (at least those who dared to challenge him) as nonpersons. According to the American Association of University Professors, since 1988, after dismissing a history professor (the AAUP report criticized the college for not protecting faculty members from the improper exercise of administrative power), the president had utilized such a leadership style and the trustees were aware of these facts (Wolfe, 1999: A72).

Chapter 9

Multicultural Paradigm Management Systems and Cultural Diversity Models

Without multiple sources of knowledge, there will be no power to shed light on our minds.

CHAPTER OBJECTIVES

When you have read this chapter you should be able to:

- develop conceptual skills to understand different philosophies and practices of cultural diversity models and multicultural paradigm management systems,
- identify the three groups of cultural diversity models,
- indicate the principal concerns of multicultural paradigm management systems, and
- describe how multiculturalism can enhance multinational organizational operations.

INTRODUCTION

Radical political changes and the free flow of information characterized the early 1990s on the socioeconomic maps of the world. Many nations found themselves in a new international condition, which has been called the "new world order." Consequently, businesses concerned with international implications for their operations faced new challenges and opportunities, as well as new threats. The new world order caused many nations to come freely from every corner of the globe to break down most political barriers. For example, Hanebury, Smith, and Gratchev, (1996: 54) state that: "Russia is rapidly moving to a free economy. Nearly 40 percent of its economy was privatized by the end of 1993. U.S. exports of manufactured goods to the newly independent States reached an annual rate of $108 billion in 1993, a five-fold increase compared with 1992." In addition, many multinational corporations have experienced successful expansion ventures into Eastern European countries. Therefore, the globe becomes a small place, but friendly only to those who are prepared to understand it and to change their traditional views from cultural diversity to multiculturalism to work within it.

The difference between cultural diversity and multiculturalism cannot be explained with a single analytic tool or with two general models. It is necessary to understand that the nature of scientific research makes such a difficult job an almost foregone conclusion. Researchers found no absolute distinctive explanations or theories to identify exactly the final outcomes of their efforts; any theories pose more questions than they answer.

In this chapter, therefore, we will find no scientific explanations that have been tested and/or retested about cultural diversity and/or multicultural theories. However, we should not ignore the basic philosophical approaches when building cultural models for multinational organizations.

In viewing differences between cultural diversity models and multicultural paradigm systems, we can focus our attention on the relations among different groups who are living together within a specific geographical boundary. Since multinational corporations must establish an integrated global philosophy in which they can encompass both domestic and international operations, they need to realize that their mission is bounded with global sourcing, operations, marketing, and sales strategies. They must identify how to synergize their corporations through multicultural philosophy in order to be competitive in the international markets. For these and other reasons, they must be prepared to accept the frustration that often accompanies new ideas about potential cultural problems that may be confronted in different markets.

Although multinational corporations with their global operations often are classified as either global or multiregional corporations, most multinational corporations are mixed. They handle some of their operations with considerable global integration while conducting their internal organizational operations on the basis of their home country's multidomestic strategies. Any corporate operation, internationally, must make trade-offs between the advantage of practices of global multiculturalism and those of the multitude of cultural diversity practices in home countries.

A COMPREHENSIVE APPROACH
TOWARD MULTICULTURALISM

The study of cultural relations in home and host countries is concerned generally with the ways in which the various groups of multiethnic, multicolor, multireligious, and genders come together and interact over an extended period of time. As we proceed in our investigation, we will be looking specifically at two major models of culture: (1) multiculturalism and (2) cultural diversity. For clarity in our study, we pose three key questions:

1. What are the basic fundamental beliefs and practices concerning intercultural relations in the global market? As we will find out, intercultural relations commonly take the form of both competitive alliances and conflicts. Alliances synergize their competitive potential through partnership, and conflicts result in hostile takeover of an industry or a corporation. Just as we will be concerned with understanding why conflict and competition are so common among multinational corporations, it will also be our concern to analyze harmonious conditions of cooperation and coordination among home and host countries.

2. How do dominant giant multinational corporations in the global market maintain their positions at the top of the international market hierarchy, and what attempts should be made to synergize their positions? Dominant multinational corporations employ a number of direct and indirect strategies to protect their financial power and operational opportunities in their home and host countries. Subordinated cultures do attempt to change this arrangement from time to time. In fact, if multinational corporations do not attempt to integrate the general host's cultural value systems into their corporate cultures, it may result in organized movements against multinational corporations. Therefore, one of the chief concerns will be the ways in which multinational corporations learn how to diffuse the host's econopolitical hostility into their corporate strategies.

3. What are the long-range effective outcomes of the multicultural paradigm model in the global market? When a multinational corporation builds up its corporate culture through multicultural philosophy and practices, then multicultural value systems can exist side by side in the same market for a long period of time. They either move toward some form of economic partnership, integration, and unification, or they maintain and even intensify their differences. Again, our concern is not only these outcomes, but it is also with analyzing the sociocultural and econopolitical forces that favor both producers and consumers.

ANALYTIC STUDY OF MULTICULTURAL AND CULTURAL DIVERSITY MODELS

As we have analyzed the corporate cultural value systems of some multinational organizations, we have discovered that great differences exist between their theoretical perspectives and practical operations. This is understandable because free flow of international information and workforce diversity is emerging as a new field without a commonly accepted theoretical basis. However, building a multinational corporate cultural model is as important as managerial structures and business strategies.

Gorry (1971: 1-15), in his research, indicates that general characteristics for building a model include the following:

1. Good models are hard to build. Convincing models that include managerial role variables containing direct implications for actions are relatively difficult to build.
2. Good parametric assessment is even harder than the selection of the right models. Measurement and data assessment should be processed in such a way that they are effectively relevant to the objective outcomes. This requires high quality work at the design stage and is often very expensive to be carried out.
3. Models should be understood by the users. Usually, people tend to reject models when they perceive too much complexity by application of that model in action.
4. A model must capture the basic dynamic behavior of multinational organizational incumbents in order to explain all tangible and intangible forces within the system.

For these purposes, the selection of a multicultural paradigm model in this text will serve as a beginning point in processing multicultural interactions within multinational organizations. Although the model applied in this text is useful to study multicultural behavior, the model has not been objective as to which assumptions are warranted and whether one yields more satisfactory outcomes than other assumptions.

Societies are complex systems. Criteria of either cultural homogeneity or heterogeneity can be applied to any and/or all of their valuable facets. These criteria could be assumed as their class structure, power distance, language barriers, ecological features, topographical conditions, and so on. The present interest in this text focuses on the extent to which a society can be regarded as culturally homogeneous, heterogeneous, and/or a mixed culture.

The concept of cultural homogeneity or heterogeneity refers to the ethnic and/or cultural identity of an individual (De Vos, 1980: 101). Theoretically, culturally homogeneous societies are made up of citizens and/or residents who all possess more or less the same ethnic identification. It has been argued that a country such as Japan comes close to that condition. At the other end of the continuum is a nation such as the United States, which has always been regarded as culturally diverse. The salience of cultural diversity is the extent to which it matters whether one individual does or does not belong to a particular group.

MULTICULTURAL MANAGEMENT PARADIGM SYSTEM

A paradigm is a basic framework through which we conceive and perceive the world, giving shape and meaning to all our knowledge, experiences, providing a basis for interpreting and organizing our both conceptions and perceptions (Palmer, 1989: 15). A paradigm is more than a theory because it is the synthesized essence of our mind and actions within the historical events of our culture. A paradigm is a fundamental asserted belief that sometimes is not even articulated until brought into question by someone else's new competing paradigm. Since multinational corporations have operated in the various international markets with application of different international theories, in reality, they are faced with serious competitive challenges and/or personal attacks by some host countries. For this and other reasons, multinational corporations must find new solutions for survival and continuity of their operations in the various international markets. One of the solutions is to establish a new path of conceptual and perceptual views concerning their operations on the basis of multicultural paradigm model.

A MODEL OF THE IMPACT OF MULTICULTURALISM

With the increasing volume of foreign investments and international trade operations a deep understanding of forces within the marketplace and market space and skills to manage different forces will be the keys for successfully managing multinational corporations. Hofstede (1993: 81) found that international application of management theories are different in home and host countries. He indicates: "Management as the word is presently used is an American invention. In other parts of the world not only the practices but the entire concept of management may differ, and the theories needed to understand it may deviate considerably from what is considered normal and desirable in the USA." He found that in a global perspective, U.S. management theories and practices contain a number of idiosyncracies not easily shared by management elsewhere. Three such idiosyncracies are:

1. a stress on market processes,
2. a stress on the individual, and
3. a focus on managers rather than on workers.

By taking a systematic approach to design and implement the kinds of changes required by the diverse cultural workforce in multinational corporations, a new organizational structure must also be designed to manage a multinational corporation's operations.

In recent years, it has become commonplace for one discipline to borrow terminology and models from another. Conceptual, biological, mechanical, and ecological frameworks have cross-fertilized scientific endeavors in most social sciences. The concept of multicultural models, now well established in the field of international business, has similarly spanned across such disciplines as political sciences, organizational theory, military sciences, and cultural diversity. Researchers were using cultural diversity models long before the term "model" became a key word in international management vocabulary. However, in the age of free flow of information around the globe, the matter of developing models for multiculturalism is not a simple one. There are too many complex processes in building such models.

Table 9.1 presents the multinational management model of multiculturalism (M^4), which in this text has been developed on the basis of learning from research of the relevant literature, consulting, and teaching experience over the past four decades. There are three major dimensions within the boundaries of thirteen features of a model that this text applied as somewhat distinctive.

First, this is a holistic model designed to explicate effects of multicultural versatility for many multinational organizations with consideration of characteristics of both home and host countries. Since multinational corporations operate within various international markets, they need to consider three major cultural interest group objectives: (1) home cultures of joint venturing partnership, (2) host cultures of subsidies, and (3) corporate organizational culture.

A second point of distinction concerning the M^4 is that it treats holistically organizational constituencies in a more cohesive manner than the traditional management systems. Since the practical decision-making processes of traditional international management systems are based upon focusing on race, ethnicity, national origin, gender identification, and physical identification, the M^4 views certain similar effects of multiculturalism on home and host countries, along with the multinational organizational outcomes. For example, in the United States, organizational employees have typically been classified as blacks, whites, Hispanics, and others. In the Arabian nations, employ-

TABLE 9.1. A Multinational Management Model of Multiculturalism (M^4)

Home Countries' Cultures	Host Countries' Cultures	Multinational Organizational Culture
Individual-Level Factors	Group/Intergroup Factors	Achievement Outcomes
• Individualized identity	• Patriotic sensitivity	• Productivity
• Stereotyping	• Suspicion	• Compromising
• Prejudice	• Bias	• Harmony
• Individualistic	• Collectivistic	• Pluralistic
• Suitability	• Accessibility	• Profitability
• Segregation	• Assimilation	• Integration
• Innovation	• Imitation	• Acceleration
• Exploitation	• Resentment and sabotage	• Normalization
• Profit maximization	• Profit reduction	• Profit adjustment
• Compensation	• Appreciation	• Collaboration
• Vertical promotion	• Horizontal mobility	• Synergistic promotion
• Dynamic mobility	• Survival stability	• Outcome quality
• Enculturalization	• Acculturalization	• Cross-culturalization

ees are classified as Arab and Ajam (non-Arab). In Australia, people are identified as Aborigines and Europeans. In all of these categorical stratifications, the evidence of discrimination contains ethnicity and racial identity and puts emphasis on physiological features, color of skins, and cultural differences among people. The end result is segregation of minority groups from majority. If multinational corporations use racial and/or ethnicity as the basic criteria for recruitment and promotion, they are depriving themselves of multinational synergistic efforts.

THREE MODES OF THE MULTICULTURAL PARADIGM SCALE

Usually multicultural paradigm models possess their own characteristics and objectives that should be completely comprehensive to users. Multinational corporations and domestic businesses are facing the challenge of more multicultural workforces. Grant (1996: 123) has observed that successful and large-scale intervention efforts of cultural diversity management models proceed through six definable and predictable stages: confrontation; dialogue; experiential learning; challenge, support, and coaching; action-taking; and organization and culture change.

The model of multicultural behavior in this text is concerned with the key elements of organizational stimuli within the behavioral context and the consequential managerial facilitator's outcomes. This model can either mitigate the tension between employees and employers and/or energize observable and nonobservable problem-solving consequences.

The twelve stages of the intervention cycle of the multicultural paradigm model of this text are:

1. confrontation,
2. dialogue,
3. experiential learning,
4. challenge and competition,
5. coaching,
6. action-taking,
7. organization and culture change,
8. creating new organizational structure,
9. free labor movement,
10. meritorious equal employment opportunities,
11. sociopolitical cultural diversity, and
12. cultural adjustment.

Table 9.2 illustrates each stage with possible counteractions of these forces by the facilitator management system.

TABLE 9.2. Multicultural Behavioral Paradigm Model of Facilitator Management

Circumstance	Situational Behavior	Oppressor's Behavior	Facilitator Management
1. Confrontation	Accused Frustrated Abused Discriminated Terrorized Exploitation Utilitarianism	Conspiracy Angry Selfishness Ethnocentrism Aggression Justification Egalitarianism	Diffusion Reconciliation Prevention Avoidance Patience Prevention Intuitionism
2. Dialogue	Angry Guilty Sympathetic	Blamed Repressing Stereotyping	Mitigation End it Advising
3. Experiential Learning	Orientation Training Empathic	Misinformation Unsuitable info. Ignoring	Accommodation Empowerment Recognition
4. Challenge and Competition	Eustressful Efforts	Jealousy	Praising
5. Coaching	Rewarding	Discouraging	Supporting
6. Action-Taking	Succeeding Angry Frustrating Losing opportunity	Ridiculing Heat it up Disappointment Happiness	Encouragement Cool it down Hopefulness Reconciliation
7. Organization and Culture Change	Advocacy Self-worth Value change	Offensive Reproaching Resistance	Listening to Respecting Persuading
8. Creating New Organization Structure	Reengineering Synergizing	Not giving up Sabotaging	Take it Energizing
9. Free Labor Movement	Competition	Bureaucratic Barriers	Deregulation
10. Equal Employment Opportunities	Patriotic Sensitivity	Prejudice	Avoiding
11. Sociopolitical Cultural Diversity	Discrimination in Hiring and Firing	Racial and Ethnic Homogeneous promotion	Multiracial and Multiethnic Heterogeneous promotion
12. Cultural Adjustment	Cultural Adaptation	Class-cultural Stratification	Facilitator and Equalizer

Source: Parhizgar, K. D. (1999) "Comparative Analysis of Multicultural Paradigm Management System and Cultural Diversity Models in Multicultural Corporations." *Journal of Global Business* 10(18), Spring, p. 52.

Table 9.2 provides an in-depth view on multinational organizational management systems. It can be applied to regional economic integrations and free trade agreements among neighboring nations. The model identifies the major variables in multinational organizational management systems and also provides solutions for multicultural managerial synergy. Unlike the most behavioristic cultural diversity models, which have emphasized the need to identify observable signs of sociopolitical and economic contingencies for the prediction and control of behavior of organizational incumbents, the expanded multicultural model of this text recognizes the reciprocal interactive natures of home and host cultural value systems, the persons' cognition, and the behavioral outcomes in decision-making processes and actions.

THREE MAJOR MODELS OF CULTURAL DIVERSITY

Harvey and Allard (1995: 3) have clustered cultural-diversity models into three major groups:

1. Those groups that focus on the individual (Table 9.3),
2. Those groups that emphasize the development of sensitivity (Table 9.4), and
3. Those groups that center on the organizations (Table 9.5).

MODELS OF INDIVIDUAL CULTURAL DIVERSITY

There are three submodels of individual cultural diversity:

1. Primary and secondary dimensions of diversity
2. Panoramic photography of pulls of diverse family generations and nonfamilial environments
3. Incompatible cultural values

Primary and Secondary Dimensions of Diversity

Loden and Rosener (1991: 20) distinguish between primary and secondary dimensions of diversity, which identify characteristics of people that do not change, and secondary dimensions of characteristics which can be changed. Figure 9.1 displays the relationship between central or primary characteristics and those that are secondary in nature. Loden and Rosener claimed that women are more likely than men to manage in an interactive style—encouraging participation, sharing power and information, and enhancing the self-

TABLE 9.3. Diversity Models Centering on the Individual

Type	Focus	Theorists
Static	Individuals: dimensions on which they differ from each other	Loden and Rosener
Static	Individuals: major group memberships	Szapocznik and Kurtines
Static	Individuals: incompatible cultural values	Rivera

Source: Harvey, C. and Allard, J. A. (1995). *Understanding Diversity: Readings, Cases, and Exercises.* New York: Harper Collins College Publishers, p. 4.

TABLE 9.4. Diversity Models Centering on Sensitivity

Type	Focus	Theorists
Static	Sensitivity: elements in development (individual) of cultural sensitivity	Locke
Static/ Dynamic	Sensitivity: stages in sensitivity learning	Hoopes, Bennett

Source: Harvey, C. and Allard, J. A. (1995). *Understanding Diversity: Readings, Cases, and Exercises.* New York: Harper Collins College Publishers, p. 5.

TABLE 9.5. Diversity Models Centering on Organizations

Type	Focus	Theorists
Static	Organization: Individual, intergroup, and organizational factors	Cox
Dynamic	Organization: Action plan for changing organization climate	Thomas
Dynamic	Organization: Organizational factors matched to individual needs	Jamieson and O'Mara
Dynamic	Organization: Corporate approaches to managing diversity	Palmer
Dynamic	Organization: Melting Pot Model Cultural Pluralism Model Civic Culture Model	Zangwill Kallen, and Steinberg Fuchs

Source: Harvey, C. and Allard, J. A. (1995). *Understanding Diversity: Readings, Cases, and Exercises.* New York: Harper Collins College Publishers, p. 6.

FIGURE 9.1. Primary and Secondary Dimensions of Diversity

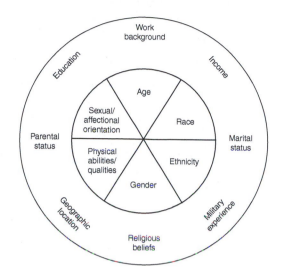

Source: Loden, M. and Rosener, J. (1991). *Workforce America! Managing Employee Diversity As a Vital Resource.* Homewood, IL: Irwin, p. 20.

worth of others. Rosener claimed that women tend to use "transformational" leadership, motivating others by transforming their self-interest into goals of the organization, while men use "transactional" leadership, rewarding subordinates for good work and punishing for bad.

Panoramic Photography of Pulls of Diverse Family Generations and Nonfamilial Environments

Szapocznik and Kurtines (1993: 400-407) also built their model on the basis of focusing on the individual, but from a broader perspective. Their model is a panoramic photography that illustrates the individual within the family, embedded within an environment compromised of diverse cultures. This model identifies that the individual faces the pulls of diverse generations as well as the pulls of a diverse nonfamilial environment.

Incompatible Cultural Values Model

Rivera's (1991) model of cultural diversity (see Figure 9.2) is based upon how managers view the world and how they learn to succeed in it. Although individual cultural values, background, talents, and training contribute to

FIGURE 9.2. Incompatible Individual Cultural Values Model

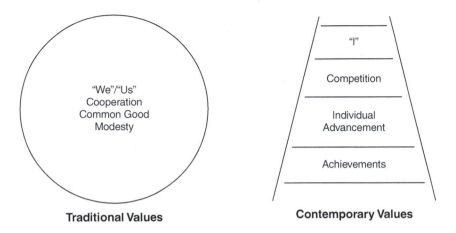

"We"/"Us"
Cooperation
Common Good
Modesty

Traditional Values

"I"

Competition

Individual
Advancement

Achievements

Contemporary Values

Source: Rivera, M. (1991). *The Minority Career Book.* Holbrook, MA: Bob Adams, Inc. Publishers, p. 15.

each individual's unique experiences, this model provides a base from which you can begin to understand the differences—subtle and striking—that minority people face.

Figure 9.2 illustrates a comparison between a set of "traditional" cultural values and a set of "contemporary" cultural values, and/or a historical domestic values and a set of modern international values.

MODELS OF SENSITIVITY DEVELOPMENT

There are three models of sensitivity learning diversity:

1. Cultural assimilation
2. External/internal diversity awareness training model
3. Dynamic approach in intercultural sensitivity learning

Cultural Assimilation

Locke (1993: 1-13) has built his model of cultural diversity on the basis of sensitivity learning in order to increase emotional and sensational binding toward other cultures. This model places individuals in a series of widening contexts (family, community, cultural, and global) that influence sensitivity, and then the model describes elements to explore for a better understanding of other cultures. For example, individual sensitivity learning in Japan is emphasized through cultural pragmatic experiences. Rohlen reports five major sensitivity learning programs for a Japanese employees' bank. The philosophy for such training programs is based on an assumption that employees should focus on loyalty in order to fulfill their roles. Loyal employees are identified by their moral obligation to work hard for their company (Rohlen, 1973: 1543). This model contains five stages in its training program.

Stage 1: Zen Meditation

The trainees should visit a famous Zen temple and spend a few days there. The Zen monks teach them how to embrace a very austere regime with equanimity. They believe such training will reduce anxiety. Trainees should learn concentration with thoughtful meditation, along with controlled breathing. Then the Zen monks will ask trainees to concentrate on their serious problem. They show how, by meditation, they can overcome their problems. In Japanese culture, the workplace is assumed to be a family environment. Therefore, the result of this type of training will stimulate their mind to reduce selfishness and enable them to work with other organizational members in harmony, cooperation, and sharing.

Stage 2: Military Training

Japanese people should visit military bases in order to develop behavioral discipline and material order within a group. Military training teaches soldiers the spirit of determination, devotion, and fulfillment of their mission. A part of this training is the lecture on "mission in life." This lecture is inspired by the kamikaze pilots (suicide squads) of World War II. Trainees are inspired by kamikaze volunteers who knew that Japan would lose the war and that their suicidal missions meant certain death. They were committed to proceed with it because they were soldiers and because of their willingness to serve their country rather than to pursue individual pleasure.

The author of this text experienced such a behavioral mentality during the Iran and Iraq War, in the 1980s. The Khomeini regime used to apply such a technique for young soldiers to defuse mines in the battle zone through spiritual suicide actions. It should be indicated that in the cases of both Japanese and Iranian cultures the age similarity between the suicide war heroes and the trainees proved to be a striking point.

Stage 3: Rotoo

Rotoo is voluntarily working for strangers without pay. This is a tradition in Japanese culture that promotes a sense of brotherhood among Japanese people. This tradition clarifies the meaning of work in which the enjoyment of succeeding depends on the person's attitude toward it. Also, it shakes the trainees out of social lethargy by using self-volunteer perception. They must ask acceptance of strangers without social crutches, such as rank or family. The bottom line of this type of training program is to stimulate the spirit of Japanese youth toward self-esteem. It forces trainees to ask themselves: "Who are we?" Self-realization is the major objective of this type of training program for satisfactory achievement in a strange environment.

Stage 4: A Weekend Among Farmers

Working in an agricultural community can establish a sense of harmony with the natural environment. This exercise provides appreciation of social interdependence and social services as well as for the more self-aware and self-reliant nature of farm people and a fostering of the ingenuity of the simplicity in the farm living. This type of training program is stimulated to appreciate the hardworking people in the Japanese community, and to establish a sense of "searching for the last grain in the lunch box."

Stage 5: An Endurance Walk

The final capstone is physical exercise that requires trainees to walk twenty-five miles: nine miles as a group, nine miles in smaller squads, and the last seven miles alone, in silence. The objective is to create a feeling of endurance and tolerance for walking a long distance. Competition is not the point; all they must do is finish the course. Of the last seven miles, Rohlen (1973: 1555) reminisces: "I could see that I was spiritually weak, easily tempted and inclined to quit."

Terpstra and David (1991: 51) indicate that: "Overall, the training program stressed: (1) the importance of teamwork, (2) the close relationship between physical condition and mental well-being, and (3) the importance of dogged persistence in accomplishing almost any task."

External/Internal Diversity Awareness Training Model

Johnson and O'Mara (1992: 45-52), in their experimental research for 27,000 employees at Pacific Gas and Electric (PG&E), have applied four key behaviors for measuring the effectiveness of diversity awareness. They are:

1. self-knowledge,
2. leadership,
3. subject matter understanding and expertise, and
4. facilitation skills.

They found that managing diversity training programs improves the corporation's competitive advantage in recruiting and retraining both line and staff employees. The end result is to improve productivity, quality, creativity, and morale.

Dynamic Approach in Intercultural Sensitivity Learning

Bennett (1986: 182) has developed a pragmatic intercultural photograph of intercultural sensitivity learning. This model is based on a learning continuum: at one end is ethnocentrism and on the other is ethnorelativism. This continuum identifies three stages for each end: denial, defense, and minimization for ethnocentrism; and acceptance, adaptation, and integration for ethnorelativism (see Figure 9.3).

MODELS OF ORGANIZATIONAL CULTURAL DIVERSITY

Organizational cultural diversity has been perceived as a situation in which several cultures coexist within the same organization or the same society (Higgins, 1994: 427). In a broad context, it means people from several cultures working together. Although the focus is on the ethnic origin of both majorities and minorities, in a broader context the term includes women and older workers, as well as people from different nationalities, working together in an organization. Five major models of cultural diversity have been established. They are:

1. The conceptual model of diversity
2. The flex-management mind-set model
3. The intermediary organizational roles model
4. The three paradigms of cultural diversity models
5. The melting pot, cultural pluralism, and the civic culture models

FIGURE 9.3. Stages of Development in Experience Differences

Development of Dynamic Approach of Intercultural Sensitivity

Denial	Defense	Minimization	Acceptance	Adaptation	Integration
Ethnocentric Stages			Ethnorelative Stages		

Source: Bennett, M. (1986). "A Developmental Approach to Training for Intercultural Sensitivity." *International Journal of Intercultural Relations, 10*(2), p. 182.

However, it should be noted that in all of these models the utilitarian philosophy of distribution of wealth and power has prevailed. Utilitarianism philosophy views that justness is the greatest good for the greatest number of majority cultural groups.

The Conceptual Model of Diversity

Cox's (1993: 1) conceptual model of cultural diversity is based upon a social system that is characterized by majority and minority groups. The majority group is the largest group, while a minority group indicates a group with fewer members represented in the social system compared with the majority group. On the basis of sociopolitical ideology of the cultural diversity model of Cox, the majority group signifies that members have historically held advantages in sociopolitical power and economic resources compared with minority group members. Cox (1993: 6) indicates: "In the United States, organizational examples are found in industries such as insurance and banking, in which the work force is typically 60-70 percent female but the management ranks typically have more men than women."

Usually, the cultural diversity model identifies both larger quantitative number of people from one culture to maintain greater power and economic advantages to other minority groups. As Cox (1993: 6) indicates: "In most large corporations in the United States, White American men of full physical capacity represent the largest, most powerful, and most economically successful group."

The Flex-Management Mind-Set Model

Jamieson and O'Mara's (1991) flex-management model is a new mind-set model which is different from other models (see Figure 9.4). Flex-management philosophy is based on a set of core cultural values that provides specific conceptual thoughts as frameworks for decisions and actions. The flex-management philosophy is the antithesis of a "one size fits all." It requires management to tune in to people and their needs in order to create options that give people choices and balance diverse individual needs with the needs of the organization.

The structure of this model is based upon three principles:

1. systems,
2. policies, and
3. practices

All three of these components can serve diversified cultures.

FIGURE 9.4. The Flex-Management Mind-Set Model

Source: Jamieson, David and O'Mara, Julie (1991). *Managing Workforce 2000: Gaining the Diversity Advantage.* San Francisco: Jossey-Bass Publishers, p. 37.

The flex-management model is based on four principles:

- A deep appreciation of individual differences and understanding that equality does not mean sameness
- People are viewed as assets to be valued, developed, and maintained
- Management is based on the value of greater self-management, which leads to provide more options that people select themselves
- Management-flex is the mind-set of flexibility not rigidity

The Intermediary Organizational Role Models of Cultural Diversity

For multinational business operations within cultural diversity, companies must play three roles in order to succeed:

1. organizer,
2. interpreter, and
3. multicultural mediator

These three roles should be kept separate and should be assigned to different departments in order to avoid conflict of interest (Heskin and Heffner, 1987: 525).

Three Paradigms of Cultural Diversity Models

Palmer's (1989: 15-18) three different paradigm models of cultural diversity models have created different opportunities for different cultures. These paradigms are:

1. The golden rule
2. Right the wrongs
3. Value the differences

The Golden Rule Paradigm of the Cultural Diversity Model

The fundamental imagery of the golden rule paradigm is that we should treat everyone the same. People should judge themselves and others on the basis of equality and avoid biased judgments. The golden rule paradigm model conceptualizes oppression as coming from only a few "bad' or "prejudiced" people in isolated incidents. Differences among people are due to individual characteristics.

The Right-the-Wrongs Paradigm of Cultural Diversity Model

The fundamental imagery of the right-the-wrongs paradigm model is that specific groups in an organization, as well as in a large society, have been systematically disadvantaged. It is not the wish of managers to treat employees differently and continue these injustices, but the system has been designed that way. Managers want to change the system. The main objective of cultural diversity under this model means the establishment of justice for specific targeted groups. Once justice has been established, the same principles would be applied to other disadvantaged groups. The class-cultural struggle can emerge under this paradigm management system. Therefore, the targeted group's strategy is based upon the belief that "no one gives up power—you have to take it."

The Value-the-Differences Paradigm of Cultural Diversity

The fundamental imagery of the value-the-differences model is that differences among individuals in an organization are appreciated because differences can cause synergy. So the effectiveness of cultural diversity is greater than the sum of all of its parts. Under this paradigm, treating and grouping everyone the same is rejected. The synergistic result of differences among employees and treating them differently can energize the organization by using and rewarding the talents of all types in the organization. A phrase for this paradigm management system is "value all differences."

THE MELTING POT, THE SALAD BAR, AND THE CIVIC CULTURAL MODELS OF PLURALISM

In the past decade, several researchers published articles and books dealing with cultural diversity in the United States. Schlesinger Jr. (1992: 137-138) calls for an appreciation of cultural diversity while cautioning that the foundation of American culture is adapted Europeanism and that repudiation of that heritage would "invite the fragmentation of the national community into a quarrelsome spatter of enclaves, ghettos, tribes." Culture wars are derived from different and opposing bases of moral authorities, ethical beliefs, and religious faiths within worldviews (Hunter, 1991: 43).

Gates Jr. (1992: 176) asserts that by common sense "we are all ethnic, and the challenge of transcending ethnic chauvinism is one we all face." Therefore, these and other advocates of cultural diversity believe that the prospects for understanding multiculturalism seem bleak. However, cultural diversity occurs in our daily life at all levels of society and we cannot ignore it.

Today, many organizations are beginning to implement new approaches to cultural diversity and are responding to a range of new issues. Among new cultural diversity models, the three models of Carnival and Stone (1995: 13) are of great interest. They indicate that it is a debate concerning culture wars that has raged since the founding of the United States, taking different expressions with each generation. Whatever the case, diversity issues have deep roots in America's history. Three models of cultural diversity are:

1. The melting pot
2. Cultural pluralism
3. The civic culture

Melting Pot Organizational Culture (MPOC)

The title of Israel Zangwill's play (1909) *The Melting Pot* has often been used as a metaphor to describe the phenomenon of people changing their names, learning a new language, and adapting their cultural values to blend into other cultural lifestyles, which all occur when people immigrate to a new country. The MPOC indicates that the ideal objective of a nation is to assimilate people into a unified system through public cultural trends in order to reduce the cultural and structural divisions between minority and majority groups (Zangwill, 1909: 198-199). In *The Melting Pot,* Zangwill invoked the "Great Alchemist" who "melts and fuses" America's varied immigrant population "with his purging flames." Although today the validity of such a metaphor is often questionable in terms of adapting to lifestyles outside of organizational work, in the workplace certain norms, values, and beliefs usually are based upon certain ethnic experiences that dominate the whole society (Harvey and Allard, 1995: 40). However, those immigrants who believe in keeping their motherland's cultural identity never blend in; even if they have an option, they feel they should maintain their cultures. These groups of people believe that if they assimilate themselves into a new culture, they are in the denial of their own cultural identity. This can result in a further denial of the way in which they believe.

According to Abramson's (1980: 150-160) views, under the MPOC model there are three possible forms of complete assimilation. Each involves a different path and a somewhat different objective. First, minority cultures may assimilate into the dominant majority groups. Second, minority cultures may assimilate into an entirely majority culture. This is the popular notion of the "melting pot," in which all minority cultures surrender their ethnic heritage but in reality they create a hybrid society. In an international view, Israel is a modern melting pot on such a course. Third, minority cultures may assimilate into another nondominant cultural background.

In a corporate cultural perception, the traditional metaphor of the melting pot organizational culture is based upon the "management" value system which mandates their beliefs along with conformity, conservatism, and obedience to the rules, willingness for team playing, and loyalty in all aspects of an organization. This type of organizational culture is similar to the "mechanistic" one, which indicates that assimilation of a "stranger" into the cultural streamline of a host country would probably have survival for a cause. It also indicates how new employees tolerate ethnic prejudice, biased comments, and jokes. Usually, those blue-collar workers assimilate themselves very easily into the new organizational culture. This has been viewed as the sole cause to continue working: in order to guarantee the breadwinner responsibility for his or her family.

In a MPOC, usually employee turnover rates escalate when people think that they are valued for their differences, not similarities. Harvey and Allard (1995: 41) indicate that: "When diverse employees are subject to sexual harassment, ethnic jokes, homophobic attitudes, organizational policies and practices that do not support them, they either leave, sue, or stay but contribute less to the organization."

The mechanistic organizational culture emphasizes quality improvement and cost reduction (Schoderbeck, Cosier, and Alpin, 1991). This approach motivates corporate managers to believe that most jobs should be highly structured with minimum pay. Consequently, the corporate culture forces employees to ignore their own personal values and assimilate themselves into the corporate melting pot culture. The corporate managerial value systems in MPOC emphasizes efficiency—"doing things right," instead of perceiving and maintaining "doing the right things."

In today's international business transactions, multinational corporations cannot implement the MPOC because the trends of conducting businesses changed dramatically in the 1990s. Multinational businesses are moving toward global multiculturalism because managers perceive that their success is bounded to globalization, rather than domestication, of their businesses. Today, global corporations are learners and collaborators with host nations rather than being hierarchical and controlling toward them.

The MPOC value systems perceive that to do what the corporate culture has been doing is a matter of strategic fact. However, it should be noted that in today's international free market economy, nearly 40 percent of U.S. corporate profits result from overseas investments (Toak and Beeman, 1991: 4). By the year 2000 it is estimated that one-half of the world's investments will be controlled by multinational corporations (Feltes, Robinson, and Fink, 1992: 18-21).

The philosophy of the MPOC is based upon the creed of "doing business better." However, this belief in efficiency changed dramatically due to the new world order—from "doing business better" to "doing the right business." The new world order has changed the course of business transactions. Competition in the contemporary marketplace in most developed countries becomes intense to such an extent that all corporations face very unstable environments. In an intense competitive marketplace, change and change agents are destabilizing the environment. Consequently, multinational corporations are exposed to very shaky environments both at home and in host countries (Harvey and Allard, 1995: 3).

In modern societies such as the United States, corporations do not perceive enculturalization anymore. They are thinking of and practicing accommodating and even appreciation of diversity. No longer do U.S. corporation managers think in terms of assimilation; instead, they think and perceive of "managing" diversity.

Salad Bar Organizational Cultural Diversity (SBOCD)

In most developed nations, there is no longer a melting pot corporate cultural philosophy in businesses. Organizations are exposed to cultural diversity forces. Cultural diversity increases—with cross-functional, cross-discipline, and cross-national work teams—the frequency of international sociable contacts. What was taken for granted as international interactions in professional work organizations are now viewed as the maintenance of multiculturalism.

In a mechanistic and/or melting pot corporate cultural environment in the 1960s and 1970s, according to Alpin and Cosier (1980: 59), an efficiency-oriented maintenance structure was beneficial for an organization in a relatively stable environment. Gradually, in the late 1980s, this pattern of corporate culture was changed to the organic culture and/or salad bar organizational cultural diversity. The SBOCD promotes diversity instead of homogeneous work identity. Heterogeneity in the professional workforce involves a high tolerance for cultural diversity. Heterogeneity in corporate cultures manifests a new value system with few rules and regulations, open confrontation of conflicts, risk-taking behaviors, tolerance of whistle-blowers, and more respect for employees' personal moral and ethical beliefs and expectations.

The SBOCD emphasizes "effectiveness" to give careful consideration to shaping, reinforcing, and channeling the corporate culture toward high quality and productivity in the corporation. Such a drastic shift causes corporate managers to depart from "mechanistic" and/or melting pot cultural mentality to "meritocratic" and/or fragmented culture. For example, historically, due to the changes in technologies and diversity of population, the U.S. government deregulated many industries in the 1980s. There is some evidence that many multinational corporations, such as AT&T, have moved from a melting pot and/or mechanistic culture to a salad bar of "organic" culture. Tichy (1983: 254) supports this fact with the following excerpt on strategic change:

> A major concern will be changing the cultural system. This will entail much strategic cultural change as represented by AT&T's shift to support innovation, market competitiveness, and profit or by cultural changes which reflect new values regarding people, productivity, and quality of work life, as is also reflected in Westinghouse's productivity efforts. The loss of world competitiveness by major U.S. firms is increasingly attributed to managerial failure, especially with regard to people management and the culture of the organization. Japanese management has paid careful attention to the shaping, reinforcing and channeling of their organizational cultures to support high quality and productivity.

Multicultural Organizational Civic Culture (MOCC)

Unlike the MPOC, the MOCC model entails several dimensions and forms. Multicultural pluralistic civic culture means that a society is composed of many different cultural groups through which the values, beliefs, and expectations are synthesized. At the same time that these groups are practicing their cultural value systems within the boundary of their cultures, they are valuing a general consensus cultural rule which governs equally over their society. Multicultural civic culture lays down certain expected behavioral rules as the "rule of the game." These rules apply to all members regardless of their cultural group affiliation. Dealing with multicultural environments often raises problems, and often these conflicts are disruptive pressures over the whole society. The only trend that can bring together different groups is one in which radical group power is diffused. Then, in such a situation, no group has overwhelming power over all others, and each may have direct or indirect impact on others.

Multicultural pluralistic ideology cannot be found in all societies because it may be most effective in an environment which encourages pluralism. Multicultural civic culture is a new trend which is antiautocratic, antitheocratic, antiaristocratic, and antibureaucratic. It is based on natural rights and equalitarian ideals.

In the late 1990s, the shift toward multicultural organizational culture re-flected the turbulence in many multinational corporate environments. Changes in consumer preferences, regional economic integration, relax-ation in governmental trade policies, and economic conditions have caused nations to attempt to lessen segregation in various spheres (e.g., housing, schools, work, and politics) and to equalize access to power and privileges (e.g., affirmative action programs, voting rights) in many countries. How-ever, the form and ultimate objectives of the global civic culture may vary in the minds of majority groups of policymakers as well as members of both dominant-majority and dominated-minority groups in different nations.

The MOCC model can be called an equalitarian harmonizer system by law. It is characterized by intercultural relations among diversified cultural groups designed by the law of a nation. Fuchs (1990) holds that civic culture is the unifying characteristic of American society and protects individual rights, including the right to diversity. He believes that the American experi-ence is one in which diversity is recognized and protected by civic culture, and that the civic culture provides equal opportunity as a commonality. For example, in the United States there are four major laws: constitutional, statutory, common, and administrative (Mills, 1989: 97).

- *Constitutional law* is a written document that is the highest form of law. All other laws must conform to its provisions.
- *Statutory law* is the enactment of "laws" or "statutes" which Con-gress, state legislatures, and other representative bodies may enact.
- *Common law* is the action of courts and the customs of the people constituting a body of law. Common law rests primarily on decisions of courts and upon the willingness of one court to follow what an-other has done (i.e., to follow "precedent").
- *Administrative law* is the regulations and decisions issued by govern-mental agencies for particular statutes.

Generally the civic cultural diversity model views diversified cultures as retaining their traditions for the most part, while participating freely and equally within common legal regulations. All diversified groups have given allegiance to a common cause, participate in a common economic system, and understand a common set of broad legal value systems.

The civic cultural diversity model can unify characteristics of American society and it is there to protect individual rights, including the right to di-versity. According to Fuchs (1990: xv), "Since the Second World War the national unity of Americans has been tied increasingly to a strong civic cul-ture that permits and protects expressions of ethnic and religious diversity based on individual rights and that also inhibits and ameliorates conflicts among religious, ethnic, and racial groups. It is the civic culture that unites Americans and protects their freedom—including their right to be ethnic." In addition, Carnival and Stone (1995: 16) assert that the American experience is one in which cultural diversity is recognized and protected by the civic culture. In sum, within the boundaries of this model, there are two forms of cultural diversity: first, different cultural groups maintain their cultural and structural autonomy but remain relatively equal in justice bureaucracies. Second, the dominant majority cultural groups spell out the formal cultural values of society regardless of the characteristics of the dominated cultural minority groups. However, it is a fact that the dominant majority groups rule over minority groups on the basis of their historical legal terms. The best expression for this model is "the law of the land."

Pluralism Cultural Diversity Model

Like the melting pot model, the pluralism cultural diversity model entails several dimensions and forms. Kallen (1915/1979) expounded an alternative model, cultural pluralism. According to his model, ethnic groups in the United States should retain their own identities while remaining loyal to the country and participating fully in national life. He believed that people should be respected for their contribution to the whole, not judged on the degree to which they are assimilable (Mann, 1979: 136-148).

Pluralism is the opposite of the melting pot model because pluralism is simply the condition that produces sustained cultural differences and continues heterogeneity (Abramson, 1980: 150). Marger (1985: 79) indicates that: "Pluralism is a set of social processes and conditions that encourages group diversity and the maintenance of group boundaries. Pluralism is never perceived as an absolute separation of minorities and majorities. However, through social processes, majority groups continue to maintain power and distribution of wealth with their historical traditions." In sum, the pluralized cultural diversity model at some points is based upon this expression, that all diversified cultures are navigating their ships simultaneously in the ocean, and they may sink or swim together in that society.

In viewing differences among these modes of cultural perceptions, the focus should be attuned to the whys and wherefores of relations among different value systems of groups who are working together within a specific geographical boundary in contemporary international marketplaces. Since multinational corporations must establish an integrated global philosophy in which they encompass both domestic and international operations, they need to realize that their mission is bound with global sourcing, operations, marketing, and sales strategies. They need to identify how to synergize their corporations through multicultural philosophy to be competitive in the international market (see Table 9.6).

The previously discussed multicultural behavioral approaches have provided an in-depth view of multinational organizational management systems. They can be applied to regional economic integrations and free trade

TABLE 9.6. Comparative Characteristics of Three Models

	Melting Pot Organizational Culture (MPOC)	Salad Bar Organizational Culture Diversity (SBOCD)	Multicultural Organizational Civic Culture (MOCC)
Respect for individuality	Little respect for employees' cultural identity	Maximum respect for employees' individual identity	Equitable respect for both employees and organizational multicultural identities
Values	Little tolerance for employees' ethical and moral values	Maximum tolerance for employees' ethical and moral values	Professional tolerance between organizational, legal, and employees' ethical value systems
Beliefs	Beliefs in centering the organizational culture as the main agenda	Beliefs in focusing on individuality as the main agenda	Beliefs in balancing value judgment between employees' individual values and organizational mission values
Expectations	Employees' fear about what happens if they do not assimilate themselves into the organizational culture	Organization is expecting employees to express their honest ideas and opinions without fear of retaliation	Respect for individual identity and organizational retribution
Rites	Consolidation of various forms of cultural expressions into one event	Organizational development for employees recognition as a source of individual cultural identity	Organizational formalized and standardized criteria for each meriting event
Loyalty	Loyalty to the organization by all means and ends	Loyalty to the individual's moral, ethical, and legal truthfulness	Contingency loyalty due to legal bindings
Efficiency	Values on product timeliness as an appropriate priority for term efforts	Values on product timeliness as a matter of employees' merited contribution to performance	Values on product timeliness as a matter of employees' expected performances
Effectiveness	Preferential values for management's quantitative concern for organizational profitability	Preferential values for employees contribution toward organizational efficacy	Preferential values for organizational quality productivity

agreements among neighboring nations. These models identify the major variables in multinational organizational management systems and also provide solutions for multicultural managerial synergy. Unlike most behavioristic cultural diversity models, which have emphasized the need to identify observable signs of sociopolitical and economic contingencies for the prediction and control of behavior of organizational incumbents, the expanded multicultural civic model noted here recognizes the reciprocal interactive natures of home and host cultural value systems, individual cognition, and the behavioral outcomes in decision-making processes and actions.

For multinational business operations within multicultural organizational civic cultures, multinational corporations must play three roles to succeed: (1) organizer, (2) interpreter, and (3) multicultural mediator.

These roles should be kept separate and should be assigned to different departments to avoid conflicts of interest (Heskin and Heffner, 1987: 525). The managing multicultural organizational civic cultural model is a conceptual theory and researchers have found no logic in the valuing diversity argument to explicitly support their assumptions.

Managing Cultural Diversity Model

Cox and Blake (1991) have addressed a new theory for managing cultural diversity. The basic argument of this model focuses on how managing diversity can create a competitive advantage for a corporation (see Table 9.7). Cox and Blake viewed cultural diversity management on the basis of the social responsibility goals of organizations, which is only one area that benefits from the management of diversity. In addition, this model has focused on seven other areas in which sound management can create a competitive advantage:

1. education programs,
2. cultural differences,
3. mind-set about diversity,
4. organizational culture,
5. human resources management systems (bias free),
6. higher career resource acquisition, (involvement of women),
7. heterogeneity in race/ethnicity/nationality.

Figure 9.5 briefly explains their relationship to diversity management.

The managing cultural diversity model is a conceptual theory, and researchers have found no logic from the valuing diversity argument explicitly to support their assumptions. Researchers are aware of no research article that reviews actual data supporting the linkage of managing diversity and organizational competitiveness.

In sum, if we revisit all of these models of cultural diversity with flexibility kept in mind, we may find some models more oriented toward monopoly on applicability of their ideological beliefs. Each model has a degree of validity—sometimes more than others. However, it should be indicated that they are all cultural diversity models which are always applicable to a portion of the population.

TABLE 9.7. How Managing Cultural Diversity Can Provide Competitive Advantage

1. Cost argument	As organizations become more diverse, the cost of a poor job in integrating workers will increase. Those who handle this well will thus create cost advantages over those who do not.
2. Resource-acquisition argument	Companies develop reputations on favorability as prospective employers of women and ethnic minorities. Those with the best reputations for managing diversity will win the competition for the best personnel. As the labor pool shrinks and changes composition, this edge will become increasingly important.
3. Marketing argument	For multinational organizations, the insight and cultural sensitivity that members with roots in other countries bring to the marketing effort should improve these efforts in important ways. The same rationale applies to marketing to subpopulations within domestic operations.
4. Creativity argument	Diversity of perspectives and less emphasis on conformity to norms of the past (which characterize the modern approach to management of diversity) should improve the level of creativity.
5. Problem-solving argument	Heterogeneity in decision-making and problem-solving groups potentially produces better decisions through a wider range of perspectives and more thorough critical analysis of issues.
6. System flexibility argument	An implication of the multicultural model for managing diversity is that the system will become less determinant, less standardized, and therefore more fluid. The increased fluidity should create greater flexibility to react to environmental changes (i.e., reactions should be faster and at less cost).

Source: Cox, T. H. and Blake, S. (1991). "Managing Cultural Diversity: Implications for Organizational Competitiveness." *Academy of Management Executives, 5*(3).

SUMMARY

The main aspects of multinational organizational cultural relations between home and host countries are (1) the nature of behavior among different groups of people who are dealing with each other; (2) the organizational structure and the societal ethnic, race, gender, and religious relations in the international marketplace; (3) the manner in which the multinational corporation dominates or is dominated by special interest groups and/or how subordination among ethnicity of partner groups is maintained; and (4) the

FIGURE 9.5. Spheres of Activity in the Management of Cultural Diversity

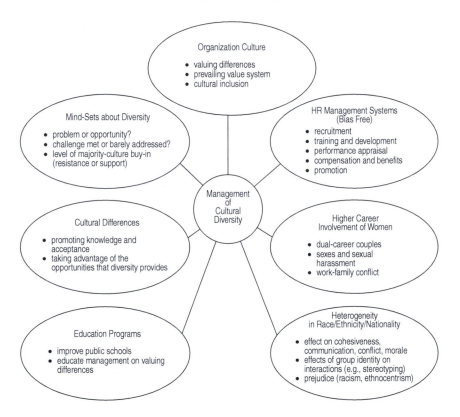

Source: Cox, T. H. and Blake, S. (1991). "Managing Cultural Diversity: Implications for Organizational Competitiveness." *Academy of Management Executives, 5*(3).

long-range synergistic outcomes of multicultural relations, that is, either emerging greater integration or increasing separation and segregation in partnership.

CHAPTER QUESTIONS FOR DISCUSSION

1. What is cultural diversity?
2. What is multiculturalism?
3. State the difference between cultural diversity and multiculturalism.
4. What is a melting pot culture?

5. What is a salad bar culture?
6. What is a civic culture?
7. With which set of cultural values, ethical and moral virtues, are we raised?
8. Discuss what is meant by cultural synergy?
9. Do you think all organizations have identical cultural characteristics?
10. How does cultural diversity affect majority and minority groups?
11. Which set of values, cultural diversity models, and multicultural paradigm management systems have been viewed? Describe philosophical and practical foundations of each model.
12. There is a trend today toward multicultural cooperation in multinational organizations. Discuss what this means in terms of the multidomestic, multiregional, and multinational value outcomes.
13. There is also an international trend in today's multinational corporations concerning innovation toward synergistic organizational management. Discuss how this might affect someone from a domestic cultural value system.
14. Do you think all multinational organizations have identical missions and cultures? What does it mean for the stakeholders and stockholders?

LEARNING ABOUT YOURSELF EXERCISE #9

How Do You Judge Yourself and Your Cultural Orientation?

Following are fifteen items for rating how important each one is to you on a scale of 0 (not important) to 100 (very important). Write the number 0-100 on the line to the left of each item.

Not important		Somewhat important		Very important
0	25	50	75	100

It would be more important for me to:

_____ 1. Be proud of my ethnicity and/or race.
_____ 2. Recognize that freedom is the most important part of my culture.
_____ 3. Believe in individualistic ideology.
_____ 4. View other people as evil.
_____ 5. Believe that I am living in a discriminatory society.
_____ 6. Believe that our justice system is impartial.
_____ 7. View that I am living in an environment in which even wolves eat wolves.
_____ 8. Welcome other people to criticize my cultural values.
_____ 9. Communicate with other people from other cultures to learn new values.
_____ 10. Travel abroad in order to be familiar with other nationalities.
_____ 11. Prefer usually to talk in my own language while I am living in other countries.
_____ 12. To beat my competitors with all means and ends.
_____ 13. Get along with the majority of people and ignore my personal values.
_____ 14. Prefer to marry a person from my own ethnicity and/or race.
_____ 15. Prefer to get help from other people in order to be able to give help to others.

Turn to the next page for scoring directions and key.

SCORING DIRECTIONS AND KEY FOR EXERCISE #9

Transfer the numbers for each of the fifteen items to the appropriate column, then add up the four numbers in each column.

Internationally Oriented	Ethnocentrically Oriented	Individualistically Oriented
6. _____	1. _____	2. _____
8. _____	5. _____	3. _____
9. _____	11. _____	4. _____
10. _____	13. _____	7. _____
15. _____	14. _____	12. _____
Your Totals _____	_____	_____
Total Scores 500	500	500

The higher the total in any dimension, the higher the importance you place on that set of needs. The closer the numbers are in the three dimensions, the more well sociopsychologically oriented you are.

Make up a categorical scale of your findings on the basis of more weight for the values of each category.

For example:

1. 400 individualistically oriented
2. 375 internationally oriented
3. 200 ethnocentrically oriented

Your Totals   975
Total Scores   1,500

After you have tabulated your scores, compare them with others on your team or in your class. You will find different value systems of needs among people with diverse scores and preferred modes of self-realization.

CASE STUDY:
THE BLIND AMBITION OF THE BAUSCH AND LOMB
COMPANY'S CULTURAL MIRRORS IN HONG KONG

Bausch and Lomb Optical Inc. (B&L) was incorporated on March 20, 1908, in New York. Today, it is a leading international company that develops, manufactures, and markets products and services for the optical and health care fields. The vision care segment includes contact lenses and lens care products. Pharmaceuticals manufactures and sells generic and proprietary pharmaceutical prescriptions. The health care division of the company provides biomedical products and services, hearing aids, and skin care products. The fourth segment of the company is eyewear, comprised of premium-priced sunglasses and optical thin film coating services.

Between 1994 and 1995, the business financial results of B&L Inc. were favorable. Net sales for 1994 were $1,892.7 million, growing in 1995 up to $1,932.9. But in 1996, the net sales took a slump, down to $1,926.8 million. Operating earnings were also favorable between 1994 and 1995, going from $119.8 million to $210.6 million. Dropping by 1996 to $190.8 showed a 9 percent change from 1995. The net earnings were $31.1, $112.0, and $83.1 million, respectively, exhibiting a 26 percent change from 1995 to 1996. The company's inventories for 1995 were 304,300 and by 1996 they totaled 339,800. Total liabilities equalled $1,620,800 in 1995; by 1996 the liabilities had increased to $1,721,500.

During the 1980s and early 1990s, Hong Kong was the star of B&L's international division, often racking up an annual growth of 255 percent as it rocketed to about $100 million in revenues by 1993. The B&L in Hong Kong appeared to be a great investment for the stockholders.

Trouble appeared in recent years: some of the reported sales were faked, and the goods were not shipped. In the Cantonese language, the words *ba dan* mean "white sheet." But for employees at B&L Inc.'s Hong Kong operation, they had another meaning: *Ba dan* signified a white invoice with a phony sales record on it. These secret *ba dan* invoices, which B&L headquarters never saw, would instruct staffers to send goods to an outside warehouse in Hong Kong. The headquarters soon found out the real reason for their great sales. Due to heavy pressure to maintain high sales, B&L Hong Kong pretended to book big sales of Ray-Ban sunglasses to distributors in Southeast Asia. In reality, the goods were not sent to the distributors but to the warehouses, and the unit would create secret *ba dan* invoices. Later, some of B&L's sales managers tried to persuade distributors to buy the excess. Some of the glasses may also have been funneled into the black market. A buyer could profit by shipping them to Europe or the Middle East, where wholesale prices were higher.

Source: Maremont, M. (1995). "Blind Ambition: How the Pursuit of Results Got Out of Hand at Bausch and Lomb." *Business Week,* October 23, pp. 78-92.

By 1994, the international division of B&L was having trouble keeping up with the schemes and was showing falling revenues and climbing receivables due to the fake invoices that no one was paying off. The B&L headquarters in the United States sent a team of auditors to the division in Hong Kong. The auditors questioned Mr. Chan, the head manager of the B&L Hong Kong division, who claimed that tough pressures from top management to keep up with double digits allegedly forced them to fabricate the *ba dan* invoices. The company also suspected Mr. Chan of selling sunglasses to the black market to boost sales.

A *Business Week* investigation showed that this was not an isolated case. The executives claimed that Daniel E. Gill, chairman and chief executive officer of B&L, drove demand for achieving a double-digit annual profit growth. The managers funneled glasses into the black market, were promised to give long-term payments to customers, and even threatened the distributors to take on big quantities of unwanted products or they would cut them off as their distributors. Other divisions sent goods to the customers before they ordered them and booked the shipments as sales.

One of the former managers, according to *Business Week,* claimed that the signals sent from the top led to cutting corners. The company's compensation plan was also a menace to the employees. Finally, the problems appeared internally and forced the company and its executives to produce profits for them from the managers of the divisions. It was not the customers who wanted more products, it was the executives in charge who were looking out only for themselves and their profits. The managers did not care what problems their "cut corners" would create; they only wanted to keep their jobs and would do anything to ensure profits.

Chapter 10

Multicultural Philosophies

The unexamined philosophical understanding who we were, who we are, and who we will be is not worth thinking.

CHAPTER OBJECTIVES

When you have read this chapter you should be able to:

- understand fundamental principles of multicultural philosophies,
- describe what is meant by a cultural philosophy of a human's image,
- identify the mainstream of key thoughts in perceptual paths of cultural philosophies,
- conceptualize the multicultural civilization,
- discuss the cultural resources fitness of a culture,
- describe the knowledge-based wealth of a civilization, and
- identify structural dimensions of cultural philosophy.

INTRODUCTION

Cultural philosophy has been given only cursory treatment in the majority of comparative academic circles that have appeared. If one reviews the research of Hoeble (1960), one finds that culture was defined as the integrated sum total of learned behavioral traits that are manifested and shared by members of a society. Cultural philosophy is an elusive concept, a fuzzy, difficult to define construct (Triandis et al., 1986). Multicultural philosophies can be defined as communicable thoughts, intellectual knowledge, and causal distinctive patterns of human minds which separate accultured from noncultured human beings.

One area of philosophical dispute involves whether culture is inherited or learned. The majority view is summed up by many researchers who believe any given culture or way of life is learned behavior which depends upon the environment and not on heredity. However, human groups lack the genetic programming to survive. Other animals have to ensure they behave in predictable patterns of behaviors that promote their collective survival. Instead, human groups possess an open and conscious perception that permits them to behave in a survival and growth condition. As Hillman and Sonnenberg indicate in *Psychology Today* (1989: 48), "Sigmund Freud first perceived that problems of human behavior were often subject to cause-and-effect relationships that people were not consciously aware of." From this view, Freud concluded that unconscious mental processes motivate much of human behavior. He called these processes the *id* (the unleashed, raw, instinctual drive struggling for gratification and pleasure), the *ego* (the conscious, logical portion that associates with reality), and the *superego* (the conscience that provides the norms that enable the ego to determine what is right and what is wrong) (Luthans, 1988). However, Geertz (1963) indicates that we are, in sum, incomplete—and not through culture in general, all human activities are integral parts of our cultural philosophies. Cultural philosophies, like other conscious and deliberate thoughts, seek to create civility of intellectuality.

CULTURAL PHILOSOPHY OF THE HUMAN IMAGE

Isolating the influence of cultural philosophies on the development of managerial value systems is a perplexing problem for comparative international management researchers (Kelley, Whatley, and Worthley, 1987; Kelley and Worthley, 1981). Differences in viewing the world we live in, the divine we believe in, and the way to proceed it, could be attributable to cultural philosophical meanings. For example, within the boundary of international consumption, the most powerful challenge comes from the "rational" choice. Multinational corporate managers occasionally believe that the importance of cultural differences should be the focal point in decision-making processes and operations. However, they ignore this fact, because implicitly they assume that, in a given consumerable situation, all people make the same "rational" choices regardless of their cultural orientations. In addition, as Inglehart and Carballo (1997: 34) indicate, modernization philosophy focuses on the differences between "traditional" and "modern" societies, each of which is characterized by distinctive economic, political, social, and cultural situations.

The framework in transitional stages of business philosophy to the new evolutionary, regionalized, and multinationalized trade zones (e.g., EU, NAFTA, MERCOSUR, and ASEAN) is based upon the new visions and images of human nature. The new image is viewed as just that—human nature—as if it is something that has always been the same. Such imagery was understood prior to the twentieth century. Within such a traditional image, people used to perceive that conditions of "existence" were much the same

with people functioning accordingly. Traditionally, philosophical perceptions of human beings for their existence were focused on how to survive.
Analytically, if we were to pick one word which could be descriptive to the
conditions of "existence" to the "traditional pattern of perception," that
word would be "harsh." Under harsh conditions, human beings' primary objective was simple. It was "proocupation" with survival. However, the dramatic changes brought about by human civilizations have changed such an
image. The "harsh" conditions have become "favorable" instead. And human proocupation with survival has become a "preoccupation" with fulfillment and achievement, which can be understood as "growth."

From the standpoint of faith, the major philosophical view of the religious human idea about existence shifted from a traditional philosophy of
"God and Universe" (double natures) to "God, Universe, and Human" (triple natures). From the standpoint of the existentialist, beliefs shifted from
"Nature and Universe" (double natures) to "Nature, Life, and Human" (triple natures). Contemporary scientists have found that space has three dimensions: width, depth, and height; accordingly, a human being also possesses these dimensions (Vazsony, 1980). Still, existence and survival are
the whole.

Historically, traditional philosophers ignored the potency of human culture, which possesses permanent superiority over two other dimensions,
namely existence and survival (Parhizgar, 1988). The most generic image of
human culture comes from philosophical information. Information is culturally learned knowledge for the purpose of taking effective actions. Both
cultural existence and survival possess their own synergistic potency which
cannot be philosophically changed into quantitative reasoning for an assessment. However, both qualitative and quantitative assessments could be mis-
conceived, when they are taken to be antitheoretical and/or even alternative.

For example, most Asian cultural philosophies from Eastern to Western
Asian countries—from mainland China to India—do not have differentiated values between the "human" and the "divine." On one hand, in Asian
cultural philosophies, the way of life has been regarded as the way of
Dharma, Karma, Samskaras, Nirvana, Kami, Zen, Theravada, and *Mahayana*— the spirit of Heaven extended into the material universe, and no
other way is considered to exist (Mason, 1967). On the other hand, cultural
philosophies in the European and American countries have perceived that
the universe originated from God as the first and sole cause, the creation of
man was the final and most important step in creation, and God created the
cosmos out of "waste" or "void," which existed with God before creation
(Weber, 1960). The Illuminationist *(Eshragh)* Persian philosopher, Suhrewardi
(1186) asserts that reality is divided into four phenomena: (1) pure light
(Nur-e-Mojarrad), (2) substantial (Zaroorat), (3) accidental (Hadeseh), and
(4) darkness (Zolmat). The first phenomenon is the origin of God. The pure
unity of the nature of the highest reality is the Light of Lights, God. It is
purely immaterial and immortal. From this One Light, another light emanates which is called *existence.* That is the substantial light, which is im-

material light and is prior to others. The third of these lights emanates both other lights and darkness which is called the *universe*. The universe has both accidental darkness in lights and substantial darkness—the "dark barriers." These lights differ in intensity and in accidents. The fourth light, through very complex interactions among lights on different levels, emanates both a vertical order of lights—the intellects corresponding to the spheres of planets—and a horizontal order—lights of equal intensity differing by their accidents. This horizontal order of lights is what in Greek philosophy Plato refers to as the Forms and what then in Persian philosophy is called angeles. It is through their solicitude that the earthly kinds of life and species are maintained (Suhrewardi, 1186).

Although all nations possess distinctive cultural philosophies and valuable patterns of ideologies, it would be a mistake to think that any particular nation has a single binding culture. Social scientists have observed that all human groups have multiple cultural perceptions in different societies at different times. For example, do coherent cultural values and patterns of behavior exist among these people? Converse (1963) illustrated that the belief systems of mass publics do not show much constraint: mass attitudes toward various issues are only weakly related to each other. Knowing a given individual's belief in one way of life does not enable us to predict their position on other issues. However, in the field of international business, cultural philosophy makes huge differences between the basic universal values of peoples in different cultural groups. I find that this is true because producers' and consumers' perceptions in a given economic and technological environment tend to go together. They do so because they are mutually supporting the notion of development and growth.

Human beings are social creatures that progress through heredity, environment, maturation, and learning. Mischel (1971: 227) states that: "Socialization is not a haphazard accumulation of bits of behavior but entails, instead, some orderly development. That is true at least to the degree that some complex social behavior patterns are sequential."

The human mind is by nature and structure cross-cultural. It is the mind that has the capacity to understand other people, comprehends the world in a more meaningful way, and even more, copes with its own internal dialectics. Thus, we can claim that all peoples are accultured. There is no human being without culture, and all peoples can be managed.

THE COMPONENT OF CULTURE

Over the past century, anthropologists have formulated a number of definitions of the concept of culture. Kroeber and Kluckhohn (1952) cited over 160 different definitions of human cultures. If we accept that all peoples are living in an integrated environment, then we can draw a distinctive line between the natural and artificial world. The natural life is an evolutionary phenomenon in which all creatures are subrogated. The artificial world is the cultural life of all human beings who have made their cultures. Therefore, culture is the product of the human mind. According to Taylor (1871: 1), culture refers to: "That complex whole which includes knowledge, beliefs, art, morals, law, custom, and any other capabilities and habits acquired by man (or a woman) as a member of society." We will define the concept of culture as everything that human beings think, do and have as members of a society. Thus, all cultures comprise (1) philosophies, (2) sciences, (3) arts, (4) information, (5) political ideologies, (6) technologies, (7) behavioral patterns, and (8) religious dogmas.

PERCEPTUAL PATHS OF CULTURAL PHILOSOPHIES

Today, many people in different cultures perceive the reality of their lives based upon traditional philosophies and beliefs about the old view of the cosmos and human nature. Most East Asian cultural philosophies perceive that "the present and tangible of the broad daylight and plainly visible is the real life" (Mason, 1967: 30). Such a conception of the cause of existence is more oriented toward the earthward imagery movement. Although cultural images of European and American nations examine the present and future, they exhibit individualism, humanism, and pervasive optimism. The traditional Oriental cultural view has been marked by institutionalism, materialism, and technological utopianism (technological utopianism is true in today's Occidental cultures too). They also have made distinctive characteristics between genders in both cultures.

In reviewing the international cultural dimensions of Asian, American, European, Middle Eastern, and some African cultures, we find three imagery philosophies in the evolution of these cultures. The three perceptual timelines—past, present, and future—illustrate a transition from early optimistic views of a better society to the more recent challenges about the future. This means that as much as a society is more advanced in regard to technological innovativeness, the more it becomes a futuristic oriented society. Although cultural images of most American, European, and Near Eastern nations deal with the present and future, they exhibit individualism, humanism, and pervasive optimism in regard of the future.

The traditional solipsist Far Eastern cultural philosophies—from India through China, Hong Kong, Thailand, Korea, Japan, and others—have not made a differentiation between the human and the divine. Etymologically, the word cultural-philosophy in most Western cultures means "the love of God," and the "love of Wisdom." However, in most Eastern Asian cultures, cultural philosophies perceive that the path of life has been regarded as originally the way of the spirits of Heaven extended into the material universe, and no other way is considered to exist (Mason, 1967). The solipsist East Asian cultural theory indicates that the self is the only object of verifiable knowledge. It is that nothing but the self exists. These two controversial beliefs are differential milestones in both East Asian and Western cultural philosophies. In the literature dealing with cultural images of both East Asian and Western cultures, there are three key concepts which are frequently used interchangeably: cultural ideology, cultural myth, and cultural utopia (Vlachos, 1978). It is necessary to distinguish among both East Asian and Western cultural aspiration of the meanings and ends of these three key word concepts.

Cultural Ideology

Cultural ideology is relatively a recent concept of the early twentieth century which has been defined as all systems of thoughts that aim at justification and preservation of the status quo (Mannheim, 1946). Cavanagh (1990: 2) defines status quo as: "An ideology is a worldview which is built upon and reinforces a set of beliefs and values." For example, the idea of progress, which has been a defining ideology in Western civilization, was built on a set of beliefs that arose with industrialism. There is an argument called social Darwinism on competition in human culture. Herbert Spencer (1888) was a European philosopher who popularized the doctrine called social Darwinism. Spencer's philosophy offered a moral basis for the accumulation of large wealth through economic competitive operations. Spencer believed that life is a continuing process of adaptation to harsh external environments. Consequently, according to this philosophy, businesses are engaged in competitive struggle for survival in which the fittest will survive. Darwin (1842) confined his principles of evolution to plants and animals, but Spencer found his own laws of development and decay everywhere—in biology, psychology, sociology—even in the evolution of planetary systems. The social Darwinism ideology stands on competition in the business world; it weeded out the unfit and drove humanity in upward motion toward betterment. There are three main philosophical cultural phases of evolutionary sequences in the business world.

At first, there is a phenomenon of concentration as in the formation of clouds, the contraction of nebulae (as resembling plutocrats: concentration of wealth), the accumulation of elements leading to the formation of elementary living cells. Some historians cite that the Revolutionary War of 1775-1783 in America was fought to free plutocratic colonial business interests from smothering British mercantile policies (Ver Steeg, 1957). The prominent historian Charles Beard (1913) argued that the U.S. Constitution was an "economic document" drawn up and ratified by propertied interests for their own benefits. His thesis was and remains controversial, in part because it trivializes the importance of the American philosophical, social, and cultural forces in the policies of constitutional adoption. In those days, the economy was 90 percent agricultural, so farmers and planters were major elements of the American political elite. In this setting, two fundamentally different sociocultural and political ideologies clashed, and one was victorious. These two cultures were *industrialism* and *agrarianism*. The ideology of industrialism derived from the basic tenets of capitalism and equated progress with economic growth and capital accumulation. The ideology of agrarianism extolled the virtues of a rural nation of landowners (Steiner and Steiner, 1997: 328-329).

Second, there will be a gradual differentiation or specialization of structures that are so impressive in the evolution of organisms (innovative shifting from property wealth to knowledge wealth or vice versa). Hamiltonian sociocultural philosophy was opposed by agrarian interests. Thomas Jefferson and his followers developed the ideology of agrarianism. He trusted in a rule by commoners. He also believed that heavy industrial development had undesirable consequences. He believed that government became a plutocracy (Steiner and Steiner, 1997).

Third, determination will occur: what Herbert Spencer means by this is that the appearance of factors that maintain integration and unity sustain the wholeness that is threatened by differentiation (the World Wide Web information superhighway with integration of all human knowledge: e.g., Microsoft). When these processes reach a certain point, a climax is reached. Differentiation becomes too complex and declines.

Nevertheless, the widespread acceptance of Spencer's doctrine made predatory behavior seem acceptable. In the following quotation, John D. Rockefeller, speaking in a Sunday school address, made the following comment. His remark was quoted in the article by Hofstadter (1970: 37):

> The growth of a large business is simply a survival of the fittest. . . . The American Beauty rose can be produced in the splendor and fragrance which bring cheer to its beholder only by sacrificing the early buds which grow up around it. This is not an evil tendency in business. It is merely the working out of law of nature and a law of God.

Evolutionary ideology in the field of international business reinforces values such as optimism, thrift, competitiveness, and freedom from elite interest group interference (Steiner and Steiner, 1997: 22). However, tensions frequently arise between cultural ideologies. For example, the heavy concentration of great wealth, which is justified by Marxism in centralized socialistic governments, can be translated into social power, which, in reality, will conflict with the tenets of democracy that offer mass population the right to check ruling elite classes in the exercise of power.

In the twentieth century, among many revolutions, two major revolutions stood out. First, in the former Soviet Union and, second, in Iran. The populace accepted autocratic ideologies, such as czarism in Russia prior to the Bolshevik Revolution (1917) and monarchism in Iran prior to the Islamic Revolution (1979). This could be perceived as the price of having ruling powers capable of manipulating national wealth. The consequences of such ideological conflicts caused tensions between rival ideologies, ignited political movements to topple both monarchies, and led the Russian and Iranian people to be exposed to other types of authoritarian power.

Cultural Myth

Cultural myth and millennial visions, on the other hand, are characterized by what may be called traditional consciousness. Here, the emphasis is on the past and on the scarce and timeless understanding of life. Some philosophers have emphasized the similarities between myth and ideology; others have stressed the differences. This disagreement stems in part from the tendency to describe the numerous connections between myth and ideology in actual social and political systems, on the one hand, and the tendency, on the other hand, to define them in analytically separate terms. To present philosophers, it seems necessary to do both of these things: in the first place, to define myth and ideology separately, then to describe their relationship in concrete social systems—the sociopolitical complexes of various societies. Perhaps this point can be illustrated by an analogy. If a chemist were so impressed by the frequency of the hydrogen-oxygen complex that they failed to define the two elements independently, then the chemist would be unable to deal with them when they occurred separately in their pure forms, or, more commonly, when they appeared in compound with other elements. To define culturally both oxygen and hydrogen separately, however, would in no sense be a denial of the phenomenon which is water. It is, to be sure, quite unusual for myth or ideology to appear in "pure" form; but it is very common for them to be found in "compound" with other systems. Myth and religion, for example, and ideology and politics are frequently interrelated in complex societies.

De George (1990: 5) states: "The Myth of Amoral Business expresses a popular, widespread view of American business. Like most myths, it has several variations. Many people believe the myth, or somewhat believe it. It expresses a partial truth at the same time that it conceals a good deal of reality." For example, the Rockefeller myth is one of the events which has attracted much attention. When John D. Rockefeller was at the zenith of his power as the founder of Standard Oil Company, he handed out dimes to rows of eager children who lined the street. Rockefeller was advised by a group of public relations experts who believed the dime campaign would counteract his widespread reputation as a monopolist who had ruthlessly eliminated his competitors in the oil industry. Rockefeller believed that he was fulfilling some sort of humanitarian responsibility by passing out dimes to hungry children. However, the dime campaign myth was not a complete success. Standard Oil was broken up under the Sherman Antitrust Act of 1890 (Kreitner, 1998: 131).

Cultural Utopia

Cultural utopia, in its classical sense, is similar to myth in that it often conceptualizes time as recurrent and not historical. However, utopia also includes a vision of things and phenomena hoped for, the substance of things not seen. Utopias are characterized by visionary consciousness with emphasis on the future. Human beings have always had a yearning for utopian paradise and for a society better than their own. In the utopian vision of their hopes and efforts, they quest for a better individual lifestyle and a collective achievement to fulfill their moral and societal obligations. In trying to describe utopian mentality, men and women realized that their visions have been the constant companion of their societal life (Parhizgar, 1996). However, the human mind, by its imitative nature, does not bring changes in cultures, because people in ascribed cultures are trapped in the swamp cultures of values that do not exist. For example, some authorities believe that free trade among nations is an idealistic way to do business around the world. This ideal, however, takes different forms. One form it takes for Milton Friedman (1962) is that people should be able to engage in economic transactions free from governmental interference or other types of human coercion. The rationale for this utopian vision of freedom is based upon the idea that "no exchange will take place unless both parties benefit from it." If the parties benefit from the trade transaction, and it does not harm anyone, then, the transaction has been culturally valuable. So people around the world with freedom of choice and exchange will, in doing what is in their own best interests, generally be doing what is culturally valuable as well (Shaw and Barry, 1998). However, it is impossible for corporations to be able today or in the near future to reach such utopian ideas. In addition, free choice and free exchange promote the "invisible hand toward coercive power" to manipulate freedom.

Primitive Cultures

Our approach to studying multiculturalism is systematic, not historical or biographical. Some attention to the history of theories, however, may help us reach a systematic statement. A fundamental feature of multicultural theory is that it is a comparative one. Perhaps this can be done effectively by stating that some of the features of the origin of cultures can look at both conceptual and perceptual behavior in the widest possible context, ranging from the most technologically simple for aging societies at one end of the continuum to the most highly sophisticated and complex societies at the other. It seems that the phenomenon of culture reaches back tens of thousands of years in the history of human beings. It seems that the story of the origins of human culture has been built out of the flimsiest of archaeological, philological, and anthropological evidence, then filled out with psychological and sociological guesses. The observations of the early scientific studies of culturalogy were based largely on data drawn from living pre-literate societies. Therefore, those illiterate societies with simple technologies, art, and creativity, once referred to as "primitive," are described by contemporary cultural anthropologists by other terms such as "preliterate," "small-scale," "egalitarian," or "technologically simple." Maybe it is not fair to call our ancestral culture "primitive," because if they could express their ethical and moral judgment about today's culture, they may call us "primitive." Because they are closer to the origin of simplified humanity. Owing to the misleading implication that something "primitive" is both inferior and earlier in a chronological sense, the term *primitive* will be avoided if possible in this text. Ferraro (1995) has used the term "small-scale" cultures and refers to those societies as those that:

1. have relatively small populations,
2. are technologically simple,
3. are usually preliterate,
4. have little labor specialization, and
5. are unstratified.

Swamp Cultures

People in swamp cultures may think that they are independent and start going off in other directions. But political ideologies and/or religious dogmas switch these deviated subcultures right back into their mythical modes (Covey, 1993). Swamp cultures are cold societies in which citizens work without any privileges such as educational and training opportunities, without equitable distribution of income and wealth, and without human rights. They just follow the political idealogies and/or religious dogmas. How can a swamp culture be turned into an attractive oasis? In order to transform a swamp culture into an oasis, people should be mentally multiculturalized. The transformation process requires patience, time, work, and tolerance.

Human beings, through their historical cultural synergy, have extended their multicultural ability to process information generation by generation. They have communicated the results of their findings through the development of artificial, computer-based information systems.

Oasis Cultures

Oasis cultures prosper from long-term commitment to the utopian cognitivism of ethical and moral transformation of individuals, as parts of society as a whole, to comply with the universal truthfulness, righteousness, goodness, fairness, justness, trustworthiness, empowerment, and alignment. The result can be called human *civilization.* Oasis cultures value teamwork, spirit, courage, earnestness, perserverance, and heroism. In sum, in an oasis culture, people envision the world in which the chief values are truth, beauty, and love. Are human cultures moving in such metaethical directions?

The growing intercontinental integration of the world economy (e.g., the North American Free Trade Agreement—NAFTA; the European Union—EU; Southern Cone Common Market—Mercosur) pushes human societies into a multicultural borderless future. In the era of multiculturalism of the business of trade and free flow of information, knowledge first, then capital, goods, and finally services are flowing to places where they earn the best returns, not necessarily where governments would like them to go. The development of international knowledge-based information superhighways can create an appreciation for multinational organizations in order to globalize their operations. Hill Jr. and Scott (1992: 6) state that: "One of the major consequences of these changes is increased emphasis on meaning cultural diversity, a situation in which several cultures coexist within the same organization or the same society." In a broader context, it can mean people from several countries working together to achieve their shared goals.

Gender Cultures

Men and women can speak the same language universally. However, men assume that, similarly, men and women should be able to perceive and understand each other equally. If the latter proposition is true, then in an Oriental or Occidental organization, do women exert the same managerial power within their workplace as men do? Ferraro (1995: 222) indicates that: "One need not be a particularly keen observer of humanity to recognize that men and women differ physically in a number of important ways. Men on average are taller and have considerably greater body mass than women. . . . Men have greater physical strength. Men and women differ genetically. . . . Humans are sexually dimorphic." From another angle: in the nature-nurture debate, do men and women behave differently because of their genetic predisposition or because of their culture? The definition of femaleness and maleness varies widely from culture to culture. Owing to this cultural variability in behavior and attitude between genders, most anthropologists now prefer to speak of *gender* differences rather than *sex* differences (Ferraro, 1995).

It is sufficient to say that most languages around the world are culturally *sexist*. In both Oriental and Occidental languages, we can find clearly that the pronouns and verbs for male and females vary. The Persian language, Farsi, is not a sexist language, because there are no different pronouns and verbs for male and female and/or for the third person. For example in the English language we use: "he" for a man and "she" for a woman. But in the Persian language there is only one pronoun for the third person which is "Oo;" it does not make any difference whether it is a man or a woman. Maybe this is one of the reasons that Persian immigrants, when they speak English, do not add "s" after the verbs for the third person. In addition, in most cultures, when women marry men they lose their last names and change them to the husband's name. In the Persian culture, a married woman keeps her own identity and maiden name through her married life.

In general terms, the classical study of gender research indicates that women are communicative, intuitive, nurturing, sensitive, supportive, and persuasive (Schwartz, 1989). Researchers found that most women have a higher sense of the importance of long-term relationships (Covey, 1993).

Women's and men's social roles are not the same throughout the world. Every culture has established certain expected behavioral trends and values about women's and men's family and societal roles. For example, in describing gender differences in American families and institutions, Zinn and Eitzen (1993: 128) state: "We distinguish between a perspective that treats role differences as learned and useful ways of maintaining order in family and society and a structural approach. . . . Of course, gender is learned by individuals and produces differences in the personalities, behaviors, and motivations of women and men. . . ." In addition, traditional gender roles in the United States concerning differences between men and women have been established through their socioeconomic characteristic roles as breadwinner and housewife. Ferraro (1995: 233) states: "Males who are frequently characterized as logical, competitive, goal-oriented, and unemotional were responsible for the economic support and protection of the family. Females, with their warm, caring, and sensitive natures were expected to restrict themselves to child rearing and domestic activities." In supporting the men's and women's behaviors that are different, Goldberg (1983: 11) states: "The feminine woman is sensual, not sexual. . . . A woman learns as a little girl that sex is nasty—sometimes men manipulate women to get something women grant as a gift and use as a source of power to control men. . . . The masculine man, on the other hand, is sexual but not sensual. He wants sexual relief but is uncomfortable with non-goal directed holding and caressing. Consequently, he approaches sex mechanically. . . ." This is why a man can very easily marry a woman, but a woman cannot easily marry a man. It is a gender characteristic that men work primarily so well in positions of power and influence and like to take advantage of these positions in a risky manner (Parhizgar, 1994: 524).

CONCEPTUALIZATION
OF MULTICULTURAL CIVILIZATION

Cultural diversity includes differences among minority and majority groups in language, religion, race, culture, and politics; ethnic heterogeneity characterizes societies on every continent. Social scientists maintained for many years that industrialization and the forces of modernization would diminish the significance of race, ethnicity, and religiosity in heterogeneous societies (Deutsche, 1967). However, in our contemporary societies, the free flow of information through networking navigation has broken down particularistic social units. Nations are not isolated through rigid political doctrines. If citizens of a radical nation physically are prohibited to travel around the world easily, they have found a way to travel freely around the globe mentally and communicate with others through the World Wide Web.

The emergence of large multinational corporations and alliances has caused particularistic nations' loyalty and identity to be directed primarily to the free flow of commodities in the international market. These corporations brought many ethnicities and races together to synergize their production systems.

Analysis of multiple cultures is complicated by variations in culture within an organization, which often reflects variations within the society in which it operates. As previously indicated, in human organizations, there is usually a widely shared or mainstream culture and a set of subcultures (e.g., popular culture, hip-hop culture, elite culture, folk culture, counter culture, common culture, national culture, international culture, business culture, high culture, Hollywood culture, Hispanic culture, Anglo culture, Afro culture, and religious culture). In addition, there are often varying degrees of acceptance or rejection of the key values of each culture (Duncan, 1989; Gregory, 1983).

Multiple cultures exist in today's highly industrialized nations for several reasons, the most obvious of which is that industrialized nations such as the United States of America have found that the key success for innovative competitiveness is *multiversity*. A group of people with different races, ethnicities, nationalities, gender, colors, ages, religions, and political ideologies is known as cultural multiversity. Within such a multiverse society, a multiplicity of cultural value systems may also exist as the result of the merging of all these subcultures into a holistic culture (Higgins, 1994: 472).

In a traditional form of strategic cultural analysis, cultural resources, which could be defined as tangible and intangible resources, include everything that might be perceived as the strengths or weaknesses for both human civilization at large and a given culture. Several researchers have attempted to derive categorization of human civilization.

Cultural Resources Fitness

There are a number of ways in which cultural resourse-based fitness can be further developed. Barney (1991) suggested that resources could be grouped into physical, human, and capital categories. Grant (1991) added to these financial, technological, and reputable resources. Wheelen and Hunger (1995) viewed resources on a continuum basis to the extent which they can be duplicated by others (i.e., transparent, transferable, and replicable). At one extreme are slow-cycle cultural resources, which are durable and enduring beliefs, ideas, values, and practices. These are shielded by conceptual philosophy, theoretical scientific findings, technological processes, and, in extreme cases, by dogmatic religious faith. At the other extreme, there are fast product life cycles (PLCs) of international cultural resources available to people to imitate them. These cultural PLCs of value systems, such as fashions, enforce tremendous pressures on people to imitate new modes of behaviors. Although all categorical classification of cultural resources are very useful in strategic decision making, these categories bear no direct relationship to Barney's (1991) initial criteria for utility, namely, value, rarity, difficulty in imitation and copying, and unavailability of substitutes.

This view is based on categorization of all cultural sources and resources into tangible and intangible resources, namely property-based resources, and knowledge-based resources with the utility values of potentiality, availability, causality, accessibility, durability, and profitability.

Knowledge-Wealth Civilization

Some cultural artifacts—either physical-based or knowledge-based resources—cannot be imitated because they are protected by property rights, contracts, deeds of ownership, or by special national interest prohibitions. Other resources are protected by knowledge barriers; by the fact that competitors do not know how to imitate a cultural artifact's process or operation (Miller and Shamsie, 1996). In reality, they cannot be imitated by other cultures because the resources are subtle and hard to understand. They involve talents and specific technological devices which are elusive and whose connection with results is difficult to discern (Lippman and Rumelt, 1982). In addition, some knowledge-based cultural civilizations often take special scientific procedures and procedural skills: technical, integrative, synthetic, creative, and collaborative (Fiol, 1991; Hall, 1993; Itami, 1987; Lado and Wilson, 1994).

The increasing globalization of knowledge-wealth, scientific intellectual property copyrights, technological patents, informational integrated discoveries, accumulation of innovative manufacturing techniques and innovative services of both infopreneurial and entrepreneurial cultures prompt questions about contextual knowledge spillover at both domestic and international cultural niche. Rahmatian (1996: 147) states: "*Infopreneur* is a term coined by Skip Weitzen in 1985 to denote a person who gathers, organizes, processes, and sells information as value-added business ventures. A decade ago, the concept of infopreneurship, its value-added nature, and its supporting technologies were all valid as evidence by a multitude of real-world success stories." The national knowledge-based fitness offers a nation an appropriate international niche in order to adapt their ideas and ideologies very effectively and to deal with cultural competitors efficiently. Such knowledge-based cultural resources may have what Lippman and Rumelt (1982) called "uncertain immutability."

Research and development (R&D), historically, used to perceive its role as upholder of leading quality and standards of innovative knowledge and innovative manufacturing systems. Within the domain of manifestation of new trends in production and consumption systems, the "fragmented domestic market segmentation" of the business world has been converted into holistic international market economic philosophy. By specifying the distinctive advantages of holistic philosophy of a market niche, it may be possible to add comprehensive precision to the research. According to the traditional modes of market niche of Miles and Snow (1978), competing domestic firms within a single industry can be categorized on the basis of their general strategic orientation as one of four types: defenders, prospectors, analyzers, and reactors. Such formulated strategies are contingent upon external environmental forces. Organizations strive for a fit among internal organizational culture, strategy, and external environmental forces. Nevertheless, rivalry cannot avoid the high cost of resources and low pricing systems for consumers.

Today, on the basis of free flow information through the World Wide Web (WWW) and with spillover information, multinational industry leaders and international academic world experts view their mission in justification of their cooperative international alliances in terms of this "philosophy." That is in the "absolutist terms" of this philosophy, what costs less is necessarily better, and quality finds reflection in the "lower cost" of the knowledge, science, and information "products" not in the properties inherent in them. In addition, to complement an industry and/or a firm's internal fitness of resources, it needs to delineate the external environmental forces in which different kinds of resources would be most suitable and profitable. Thus, the result of this philosophy is an "optimum cost" analysis in the international market economy.

From another dimension, within the domain of infopreneurial "research sourcing," there are different distributive channels for innovative competitiveness. These channels could be found through knowledge exploration, scientific discoveries, informational acceleration, and technological development. However, within the boundaries of international infopreneurial market economy knowledge-based product life cycles (PLCs), all are not moving along the same venturing path of truth-finding of the value-added outcomes. Of course, a major philosophical problem in the infopreneurial marketplace is based upon the questions: How do we have the assurance that we know something is suitable? How do we really know that we know the truthful applicability of our knowledge in problem finding and solutions? Why do we know what we must know? Why do we do things in this way? Why do we not do it another way (Jordan, 1996)?

Responding to these and other questions requires an illustrative aggregated dichotomy of rationalization which identifies object from subject and being from not being, through application of both tacit knowledge and explicit knowledge. Tacit knowledge is a talent for learning a kind of practical knowledge that can only be acquired through *experience.* Explicit knowledge is a systematic and easily communicated form of *hard* data or *codified* procedure. However, the astonishing diffusion of tacit knowledge and explicit knowledge is *kinesthetic* knowledge, which shows that everything that is organizing is organized, and everything that is organized is organizing. That thing is recognized as *intelligence.*

In reenergizing a cultural knowledge-based fitness for more economic meaningfulness of all human activities, there is a need to conceptualize a critical question. That question is: Why should we not apply the right knowledge correctly in order to energize our civilization sufficiently? In re-inventing the knowledge enterprise, there is a fundamental cause that is carefully realized by its foundational philosophies. That cause is: Why do we apply a specific right knowledge? Is there any other right knowledge? If yes: Why should we not rightly acquire it?

Knowledge-wealth acquisition is assumed to be acquired either through "direct sourcing" in innovation and exploration of the scientific research methodology or through spillover of innovation of imitated information and technological systems. In addition to the main objectives of this chapter, we are trying to analyze three fundamental philosophical knowledge-based cultural dimensions. These are epistemological, ontological, and axiological value-added cultural products of knowledge within the boundaries of info-preneurial and entrepreneurial civilization in the international free market economy.

Epistemological Knowledge-Based Civilization

As we mentioned in the previous chapter, epistemology refers to the problem of knowledge: in particular, how is knowledge acquired? How is it possible? What does knowledge mean? Can all knowledge be traced to the great gateway of the senses, to the senses plus the activity of reason, or to reason alone? Do feelings render wordless but true knowledge? Does true knowledge ever come in the form of immediate intuition? In responding to these questions, there are two basic points which need to be addressed: (1) What is knowledge? and (2) How do we obtain knowledge? Knowledge has long been an integral part of human life (Weber, 1960). The Greeks chose to classify knowledge into two types: *doxa* (that which is *believed* to be true) and *episteme* (that which is *known* to be true). The problem is a straightforward one: since human beings cannot transcend their cultural system, they therefore cannot obtain any absolute viewpoints. The solution is to define knowledge in an alternative fashion, one where knowledge is only "asserted." Knowledge is therefore not infallible but conditional; it is a societal convention and is relative to both time and place (Hirschheim, 1985).

The set of knowledge conventions is not arbitrary. They are well thought of, having the produced knowledge which has withstood the test of time. Knowledge could be acquired through meditation, consultation, and/or an oracle. This form of knowledge acquisition might be considered "unscientific" because it does not match the conception of science, but since knowledge is simply the process by which an understanding is obtained, philosophically it cannot necessarily dismiss these attempts. Spinosa (1898) states:

It has now been made clear that the passage from the state of bondage to the state of freedom requires the assiduous application of reason. Not only the emotions, but also the whole order of the Nature must be studied, and the continuous study of the causal order of Nature leads ultimately to the highest kind of knowledge. At this level, the mind no longer views things merely as finite and temporal, but rather, it grasps their essential characteristics under the aspect of eternity.

Therefore, knowledge is a particular set of assertions of philosophical understanding.

Historical conception embedded in our civilization shows that knowledge is a holistic dominance of positivitism. Knowledge is an understandable attempt to know what the alternatives are. The search for knowledge is a search for the real, and the knowledge gained is absolute, universal, and objective. Spinosa (1898) believed in three kinds of knowledge: "Knowledge of the first is mere belief or imagination; knowledge of the second kind is scientific knowledge or knowledge of cause and effects; and knowledge of the third kind is 'intuition,' in which individual things are understood through a comprehension of God." Epicures (1926) states that our understanding can be realized through philosophy, because philosophy is the quest for knowledge. Thus, in the world today all scientific, intuitive, imaginative, and innovative understanding of self and the whole universe are bounded with a holistic knowledge.

Ontological Knowledge-Based Civilization

Ontology reveals: What does it mean to exist? What is the criterion of existing? What are the ultimate causes of things being generalized as to what they are (causality) (Weber, 1960)? The Persian philosopher Avicenna (1380/1960) examined the human civilized culture on the basis of *existence* and *accidents, matter* and *form, unity* and *multiplicity,* and *wisdom* and *sensation.* Ontological concepts can be used to analyze many micro topics. Philosophy is an active quest for true knowledge and a way of looking at the knowledge that we have. It is helpful to consider at least two ways of thinking about philosophy: (1) philosophy as a process, and (2) philosophy as a content. In philosophy as a process, philosophers actively engage in the "doing" of philosophy. They not only answer very specific questions, but they also question answers. Philosophy as a content finds philosophers passively observing philosophy as it is (or was) practiced by others. Whether technical or casual, one's philosophy of life is important. Philosophy is important because it reflects human feelings and attitudes as well as conscious wisdom and conventional intelligence (Weber, 1960: 5). Many cultural beliefs, if not most ideas, are powerful agents of wisdom and intelligence in humanity. If cultural beliefs and ideas have any bearing on action, they tend, as it were, to leave the head and enter the hands, then human knowledge can be viewed as a universal truth.

Axiological Knowledge-Based Civilization

Axiology is concerned with the problems of value systems. The most viable traditional field of inquiry in information systems is ethics. It is concerned with the problems of good and bad, right and wrong, and truthfulness and false information. Ethical genealogy insists that knowledge and information power are implicated in each other. Ethics shows how knowledge not only is a product of information power but also can be a nonneutral form of abusive power. The genealogical moral, ethical, and legal approaches to the dissemination and disclosure of information are interdisciplinary issues. Genealogy, as Nietzsche argued, is a *prima facie* means of de-essentializing phenomena (Kaufman and Hollingdale, 1967).

The veridical knowledge-based information systems often are successful precisely when they deny (or they are denied) their power to intervene. Ethical, moral, and legal genealogy not only investigate obscured continuities of traditional cultural beliefs and political ideologies through a networking access, such as the knowledge-based and information-system connections, they also can be regarded as the social history of discontinuations and current knowledge as lacking their traditionally asserted intellectual unity. In such a domain, there are two major issues to be addressed. First, knowledge-based information systems are highly disciplinized within the field of computer science; however, they may not be highly disciplined within the fields of social sciences—the way in which scientific and technological order is imposed on disunified information systems. Discipline in its ethical and moral terms is the infrastructure of truthful embodiment of information which should be extended to the behavior and conduct of both informants and information users. Second, attention to the use of knowledge-based information systems is not merely about organizational social commitments, it is above all the concern about integrity of human identity (Parhizgar and Lunce, 1994). Therefore, in the new infopreneurial market, knowledge-based information systems should be institutionalized.

STRUCTURAL DIMENSIONS OF CULTURAL PHILOSOPHY

In conceptualization of the cultural philosophy of a nation, apart from its substantive content, several structural dimensions seem significant. They include the degree of formalization, the degree of abstractness, and the degree of affectivity.

Degree of Formalization

A prevailing cultural philosophy of a nation, which could be called a manifest functional structure, contains the sole statement of ideological, mythical, and utopian beliefs which a nation perceives. Also, it contains so-cietal doctrines and religious dogmas to be perceived "on the way" toward the more general and ultimate objectives. Similarly, it contains specification of means—that is, alternative faiths and expectations in the social structure, and procedures that contain high probability of attaining the cultural goals.

Degree of Abstractness

Cultural philosophies may vary also in the degree to which they are ab-stract or concrete. As citizens use a cultural doctrine philosophy, it is an ab-stract. But it provides legitimate rights and duties through their ethical and moral commitments. The problem is in variability of concrete interpreta-tions. For instance, in some cultural doctrines of a few nations we find "equal opportunity in education." But in implementation of this phrase we will find divergent interpretations and operational practices, which differ from their cultural doctrines.

Degree of Consistency

The degree to which the content of a cultural doctrine is consistent or in-tegrated to the national sociopolitical objectives seems another dimension worthy of further cultural understanding. In this analytical domain, we should find out how a cultural doctrine is organized. With what degree of variation has it been formalized—simple as opposed to being complex or complicated? Related to the complexity, is the doctrine's pervasiveness or scope very broad, and how much of societal life of the individual citizen is covered by that cultural doctrine?

Degree of Sociocultural Efficacy

A cultural philosophy could be analyzed, irrespective of its content, in terms of the degree to which it has effective or emotional qualities. In this matter, we should distinguish between the conceptual and perceptual value systems which necessarily commit the individuals and social organizations to its implicit value systems. A cultural philosophy, in our judgment, is ultimately acting as cultural faith in effectively endorsing certain ends in societal life and the degree to which it is phrased on irrelevant or highly tenuous grounds.

SUMMARY

Multicultural philosophies can be defined as communicable thoughts, in-tellectual knowledge, and causal distinctive patterns in the human mind which separate acculturated from noncultured human beings. Differences in viewing the world we live in and the divine we believe in could be attributable to multicultural philosophical meanings. Most Asian cultural philosophies do not have differentiated values between the human and the divine. On the other hand, cultural philosophies in the European and American countries have perceived that the universe originated from God as the first and sole cause, the creation of man was the final and most important step in creation, and God created the cosmos out of "waste" or "void" which existed with God before creation.

A cultural ideology is a worldview which is built upon and reinforces a set of beliefs and values. Cultural myth and the millennial visions are characterized by what may be called traditional consciousness. Some philosophers have emphasized the similarities between the myth and ideology; others have stressed the differences. To present philosophers, it seems necessary to do both of these things: in the first place, to define myth and ideology separately, and then to describe their relationship in concrete social systems—the sociopolitical complexes of various societies. Myth and religion, for example, and ideology and politics are frequently interrelated in complex societies. Cultural utopia, in its classical sense, is similar to myth in that it often conceptualizes time as recurrent and not historical.

Swamp cultures are cold societies in which citizens work without any privileges, such as educational and training opportunities, with inequitable distribution of income and wealth, and without human rights. Oasis cultures prosper through long-term commitment to the utopian cognitivism of ethical and moral transformation of individuals as parts and society at large to comply with the universal truthfulness, righteousness, goodness, fairness, justness, trustworthiness, empowerment, and alignment.

CHAPTER QUESTIONS FOR DISCUSSION

1. How does gender dominate over males and females in all societies?
2. How similar are gender roles throughout the world?
3. Do males and females in the same culture perceive things differently?
4. How do you explain cultural philosophies of different nations?
5. How can cultural knowledge contribute to the style and function of cultural perception?
6. What is cultural philosophy?
7. What does cultural philosophy do?
8. Define the branches of philosophy below:
   - Epistemology
   - Axiology
   - Ontology

LEARNING ABOUT YOURSELF EXERCISE #10

How Do You Believe or Not Believe in Your Own Cultural Philosophies?

Following are sixteen items for rating how important each one is to you and to your cultural value system on a scale of 0 (not important) to 100 (very important). Write the number 0-100 on the line to the left of each item.

Not important		Somewhat important		Very important
0	25	50	75	100

As a philosopher, I strongly believe that:

_____ 1. The universe is originated from God as the first and sole cause of existence.

_____ 2. God was real before the universe existed as an orderly cosmos. The nature of God is included the cosmos.

_____ 3. The creation of human beings was made in God's image, i.e., as spiritual beings.

_____ 4. The cosmos has emerged as a necessity of material order.

_____ 5. The creation of the cosmos is viewed as out of "waste."

_____ 6. Cultural philosophies are viewed as "social contracts." Human beings raised themselves from a state of nature in which there were no rights, but only the rule of strength.

_____ 7. Only reason or intellect is the end or complete development of the natural things.

_____ 8. Life is like the egg which might develop into a chicken, but which might also, among other things, become an egg sandwich.

_____ 9. Human beings are not unique among the animal kingdom because they are rational. They are the technological and tool-making animals.

_____ 10. Intellectual people merely develop their abilities to think critically, to read others' writings, to write their own ideas, and to speak without fear.

_____ 11. Human beings believe that the "mind's eye" or introspection are the only realities that they can know directly and incontrovertibly.

_____ 12. The scientific conception of material things is something mental. It is a conceptual construct.

_____ 13. The extent to which we can understand the reality of life must be in an expression of mind.

_____ 14. Reality of our life and knowledge are one and the same thing. When we die, our knowledge of self and the universe will die.

_____ 15. We are living in a dog-eat-dog environment for survival. "Power" (e.g., political, financial, knowledgeable, and sexual) is the source of survival.

_____ 16. The laws of nature are thoughts, but they occur on an unconscious level.

Turn to the next page for scoring directions and key.

SCORING DIRECTIONS AND KEY FOR EXERCISE #10

Transfer the numbers for each of the sixteen items to the appropriate column, then add up the four numbers in each column.

Idealistic	Realistic	Hedonistic	Eudaemonistic
1. _____	5. _____	4. _____	2. _____
3. _____	11. _____	6. _____	8. _____
14. _____	12. _____	7. _____	9. _____
15. _____	13. _____	16. _____	10. _____
Your Totals _____	_____	_____	_____
Total Scores 400	400	400	400

The higher the total in any dimension, the higher the importance you place on that set.

Make up a categorical scale of your findings on the basis of more weight for the values of each category.

For example:

1. 400 Essentialism
2. 350 Existentialism
3. 200 Realism
4. 150 Idealism

Your Totals   1,100
Total Scores   1,600

After you have tabulated your scores, compare them with others on your team or in your class. You will find different judgmental patterns among people with diverse scores and preferred modes of self-realization.

CASE STUDY: THE LA-Z-BOY COMPANY

Management may at any time determine that the managerial philosophy of a corporation should be changed in order for the company to be able to survive. Whatever the intent, it is clear that management philosophy does affect organizational structural hierarchy and manufacturing operations. The resulting structural or restructural designs reflect the new vision, image, goals, and objectives of a company. Indeed, the historical cultural philosophies of many organizations reflect the personalities of their top managers. The La-Z-Boy Incorporated's new multicultural managerial philosophy supports the evidence that managerial philosophy can enhance or retard an organization's operation.

The Floral City Furniture Co. was founded in 1929, which later on, on May 1, 1941, became La-Z-Boy, Inc. in Michigan. The company was founded by Edward and Edwin Shoemaker and was family run until 1998. The present name was adopted on July 30, 1996. In 1976, La-Z-Boy Inc. sold 50 percent interest to La-Z-Boy International Pty. Ltd in Australia. In February 1979, Deluxe Upholstery Ltd. of Canada was acquired with net assets of $3,048,266. In January 1986, the capital stock of Rose Johnson, Inc. was acquired. In January 1988, all of the capital stock of Kincaid Furniture Company, Incorporated, was acquired for $53,000,000 in cash which included $26,500,000 in goodwill. On April 1995, England/Crasair was acquired for $2,600,000 in cash, $10,000,000 in notes, and $18,000,000 in common stock. During the fiscal year of 1997, the company acquired 75 percent of Centurion Furniture shares from England. In February 1998, the company entered an agreement to acquire Sam Moore Furniture Industries Inc. The company is planning to buy 100 percent of Moore's outstanding shares if the offer prevails.

Everyone in the United States has probably owned or sat on a La-Z-Boy recliner. La-Z-Boy is well known for manufacturing recliners, but that is not all they manufacture. The company manufactures upholstered furniture throughout the United States for business, produces office seating, desks, and cabinets. Also, the company manufactures patient care seating for clinics, hospitals, and homes. The company's headquarters are located in Monroe, Michigan. In the United States, twenty-nine manufacturing plants are operated, most with warehousing capacity. It has an automated fabric processing center and has divisional and corporate offices.

When Charles Knabusch died at fifty-seven, a family dynasty ended. Edwin Shoemaker, age ninety, died soon after Charles, and when Charles' wife, June, asked for a seat on the board, she was turned down because since 1997 she owned only 2 percent of the $52.7 million shares. Problems could have arisen from this radical change, but they were not serious enough to

Sources: Barron, K. (1999). "Does Reclining Mean Decline? La-Z-Boy Hopes Not: Company at a Crossroads." *Forbes,* January 25: 60; Raburn, V. P. and Kiedaish, H. D. G. (2000). *Moody's Industrial Manual.* New York: FIS, A Mergent Company: 5903-5904.

bring La-Z-Boy down. Chairman Patrick Norton's decision could be considered as unfriendly, and disloyal to the founding family, in economical, sociological, psychological, and professional terms. First, Norton's decision could be considered as unethical because after he had steadily worked as vice-president for the company for several years under the family-oriented structure, once both Knabusch and Shoemaker died, Norton decided to change the company's cultural value system and image. Such a drastic change destroyed the family structural image of the company. Second, Norton's decision was economical because the change brought in more revenue and broadened the company's La-Z-Boy stores. Third, Norton's decision also had psychological impact on both La-Z-Boy's shareholders and employees who had associated with one another for many years. Finally, Gerald Kiser, an operational executive of La-Z-Boy was promoted to president; he raised the sales to $1.2 billion (revenues). Managers as well as factory employees are now happy with their jobs, consumers are satisfied with the good quality of the products that La-Z-Boy has brought to the market, and shareholders are very happy with their increased earnings.

Chapter 11

International Religions

The issue of religion is inherent in who knows what is meant, if not what it means.

CHAPTER OBJECTIVES

After studying this chapter, you should be able to:

- realize the major conceptions of international religious faiths and beliefs,
- understand the general means and ends of a religion,
- understand the various monotheistic and nonmonotheistic religious beliefs of international religions,
- understand the psychosocial effect of religious faith on human behavior,
- describe the nature of individual moral and ethical beliefs in supernatural power(s),
- analyze managerial styles on the basis of sociocultural, psychological, and behavioral characteristics of a dominated religion in a host country,
- discuss how managers should cope with home and host countries religious beliefs, and
- describe religious types and traits of different people that affect international business.

INTRODUCTION

This chapter is concerned with the impact of religion on human behavior. It also analyzes the impact of religious faith and behavior on political economy and policy implications for international business management. Ever since political and scientific ideologies began drifting away from the ancient wisdom of religions, each has dreamed of subsuming the other. No one can doubt that religions have survived between these extreme struggles and many generations who have been scientists, politicians, and religious people are confused whether a bridge can ever span the divide. Politicians and scientists speak of explaining away all the mysteries by empirical inquiry, leaving no need for spiritual discoveries. In contrast, religious people fervently believe in unmeasurable forces as miracles. Since scientists and politicians focus their attention on the smallest material things and on the utility of the profit-making power, religious people focus on a holistic happy life without misery and unwanted incidents.

Every few decades, this hope for reconciliation and integration of all experiences becomes a dilemma. For example, in the late 1910s, Marxist and communist ideologies eradicated religious faith from Russian, Chinese, Cuban, and Eastern European cultures. Barry and Barner-Barry (1987: 32) indicate that: "A longstanding tenet that is traceable to Marx, atheism remains a principle fully supported by the (former) Soviet leadership. The degree of toleration and harassment of believers and religious organizations has varied over time, but the basic opposition remains. No overt believer would be allowed to occupy a position of political responsibility in the country." However, in the late 1980s, such an econopolitical ideology lost its ground during the disintegration of the former Soviet Union into the fifteen independent states and again religious faith was revived in these countries. In contrast to the former Soviet Union, in the 1970s, some nations tried to merge politics with religion. These attempts, such as the Iranian Islamic Revolution in 1979, tried to integrate religious faith with political ideologies. At the beginning of the revolution, they promised to integrate religious faith and ethical and moral doctrines with politics. Here, the effort was not to make politics spiritual but to make religion political.

Life is full of joy and sadness, of natural and historical goodness and evils. So when people become upset and disappointed by scientists and politicians, they turn to religious faith to transcend incoherence, incongruities, and the ills of life. Religious faith is such a psychosocial transmutation (Niebuhr, 1968: 1).

We must not ignore the efficacy of religious faith on individual behavior and organizational culture. Nor must we make too little of effective religion in the field of international business. It is well known that many religions restrict the consumption of some items. For example, no beef for Hindus, no pork for Moslems and Orthodox Jews, no red meat on Fridays during Lent for Roman Catholics, and no alcoholic drinks for Baha'is.

WHAT IS RELIGION?

We need not undertake a history or a catalog of definitions. A hundred or more can be gathered. However, we need to identify this mysterious phenomenon that most people accept without empirical proof of its existence. Geertz (1966: 4) defines religion as: "(1) A system of symbols which acts to (2) establish powerful, pervasive, and long-lasting moods and motivations in men by (3) formulating conceptions of general order of existence and (4) clothing these conceptions with such an aura of factuality that (5) the moods and motivations seem uniquely realistic."

One of the most expressive types of religious definition is related to its valuation, which indicates what ought to be the truthful universal beliefs in eternal existence. Through this dimension, religion is believing in Maxim of Excellence of Spiritual Being(s)—God(s). It refers to heavenly perceptual value systems, such as doctrines, rites, sacred texts, typical spiritual group structures, and the like. However, all religions deal with certain phenomena: (1) the issues for definitions and meanings and (2) the issues for inspirations and intuitions.

ISSUES FOR DEFINITIONS
AND MEANINGS OF RELIGION

Some people perceive religion in terms of moral virtues (the system of norms and usages of designating right behavior—believing in the Godly intentions and actions) or in terms of essence (organized holistic spiritual tendencies toward excellence—having faith in God's excellence of existence). Religion deals with individual mental forces, cultural value systems, and sociopolitical structural establishments. For example, among Hindus, people dip their bodies in the Ganges River on auspicious days which is believed to purify the soul and release it from the bondage of reincarnation days. In India, a holy man sits as he has sat for many years in unmoving contemplation of the Nameless Reality that is his own self. In China, a nobleman meditates on the manner of the universe and seeks to conform his own being to its rhythms. In Israel, a rabbi meditates on the "laws" of Yahweh (God). In the United States, a congregational television evangelist gathers Christians on Easter morning to reaffirm the resurrection of the Lord (God). The wealthy, qualified Islamic pilgrims fulfill a vow by making their way to the "House of Allah—God" in Mecca (Comstock, 1972: 3). In all of these psychosocial efforts, people strive for and desire ritual experiences to escape from sinful, unfair, unjustified, and cruel behaviors of self and others, wishing eternal salvation and revelation. We can refer to all of the above religious experiences as ascetic, mystical, prophetic, intentional, and tendencious thoughts and actions.

Therefore, religion has direct relevance to individual spiritual wisdom. It manifests the spiritual power of a person through a symbolic form of activity, such as meditation, contemplation, praying, dancing, chanting, singing, whirling, and the like.

Religion is a socially shared set of beliefs, ideas, and actions that relates an individual's insight to a reality that cannot be verified empirically, yet is believed to affect the course of natural and human events (Terpstra and David, 1991: 3). Religion can refer to substantive mental experiences, like feelings of sacred places such as the existence of churches, synagogues, mosques, temples, and the like. Religion can be viewed as mystical visions through physical movements such as symbolic systems that include behavioral forms of communication. Religion could be manifested through body movements such as making the sign of the cross (Catholics), lifting hands over the head and crying (Fundamentalist Protestants), bowing or kneeling on the ground and praying (Moslems), whirling around self and objects while chanting and singing (Sufi Moslems in Turkey).

Religious ritual ceremony may include body movement, such as moving back and forth while a person reads religious scriptures on front of the Wailing Wall (Jews in Jerusalem, Israel). Religion can include mystical visions and ritual acts like a sacred dance with gospel songs in a church in Harlem or beating on the chest and head repeatedly and the performance of an ablutionary rite (Shiites in Mashhad, Iran).

Through a philosophical methodology, religion can be defined as an empirical order of existence. Everything in the universe is subject to the order of nature. Nature is evolving (evolution), or as a *super-empirical* order of existence. It is subject to the will of creator(s)—God(s), creation. Religion can be defined as the sacred and holy belief in God's words and actions. The experience of sacred or holy phenomena can be conceived in the sense of *tremendous*, which refers to a feeling of *majestas*, that overpowering sense of urgency, and *mysterium*, which refers to the uncanniness and mysteriousness that pervades the spiritual experience (Otto, 1965).

ISSUES FOR INSPIRATION AND INTUITION

The question is: What criteria are we going to use to determine whether a person is religious? How is an individual a religious person? What concerns a person most fundamentally? How widely do people share their faiths and beliefs with others? What types of groups form a religion? Are we perceiving religious people by their thoughts or actions? Is the best indicator of a religious person one who regularly attends services in worship places?

These are the main issues for labeling people who are or are not religious that can help to define spiritually what religion is and who is a religiously oriented person. The meaning of religious faith is not only attending mass (Catholics), service (Protestants), *Jama'at* (Moslems), and gatherings (Baha'is), it is also a cognitive behavioral measurement to be used as a criterion for the acceptance of religious cultural and ritual traditional forms of beliefs and practices. Much religious inspirational faith remains invisible because we are trained to look only for the traditional behavioral manifestations, not for the invisible and intuitive thoughts and inspirations (Luckmann, 1967).

RELIGION AND POLITICS

For thousands of years interrelated political and religious movements have caused many events: Christian Crusades, Islamic Conquests, Ireland's Catholic and Protestant bloody struggles, and the like.

It is not surprising that the relationship between religion and politics has been the subject of a great deal of discussion and disagreement, for these relationships are complex and highly variant. It is obvious that spreading misconceptions through rumors can mislead people and using the radical and biased mass media's propaganda against a faith is a very destructive tactic. In addition, religious sensitivity in promoting other religious doctrines and symbols can create controversial issues among multinational businesses, governments, and religious circles. For example, a soft drink company marketed a brand of nonalcoholic drink called Three Stars in Libya. The logo of that company had three six-pointed stars on the label and bottle cap. Because of the visual similarity of the logo with the Israeli Star of David, this soft drink was banned in Libya, a Moslem country (Terpstra and David, 1991: 102). Another example is the case of McDonald's in Israel. On June 10, 1998, a conservative Jewish religious group wrecked the outdoor tables of a McDonald's restaurant near Netania, north of Tel Aviv, Israel. They said they did it because that fast food restaurant sold pork and did not observe the Jewish Sabbath. The Sabbath is a day of religious observance among Jews. The group left a note on cardboard and identified themselves as "Commando *Habbad*." *Habbad* is an ultraorthodox group that engages in Jewish missionary activities. The McDonald's owner in Israel denied selling pork, which Jews and Moslems consider offensive. The manager said the meat they served was kosher because most Israelis want to conform to Jewish dietary laws (*Meat Industry Insights,* 1998). Kosher means a meat is ritually slaughtered in accordance with the law of Moses. *Halal* is an equivalent religious word for kosher in the dietary laws of the Islamic faith.

Political ideologies frequently have been designated to establish Godly coercive power. It can be used by tyrants to enforce their personal power under the guise of religious faith. Religious uprising can have dangerous consequences. When people appeal to their religious faiths to destroy their enemies, they establish a solid unified dynamic movement in order to exert their synergistic power. Such a monolithic power can destroy all barriers, because people feel that they are obligated to the heavenly cause of their faith either to destroy the enemy or to be destroyed. They perceive it as a Godly inspiration to go forward to a Godly destiny. A political movement becomes very crucial when the cause of uprising integrates the divinely justified causes in such a movement. For example, in 1979, the mandate of the Jurist's Trusteeship of the Ayatollah Khomeini led people to depose the Shah and caused the establishment of the Islamic fundamentalism cleric regime in Iran.

It is very evident that sometimes political ideologies cannot solve problems of order in some societies, because politically elite power groups cannot guarantee the approved means for achieving equitable resource distribution among people. The main reason for such crucial issues is the politically elite groups themselves—those who have currently established right to use coercive power—may violate the approved means to their own advantage.

Prevailing sociocultural values and econopolitical privileges, such as power, prestige, income, and the like, become scarce to common people. Subsequently, religious faith can help people set and enforce the limits of these scarce resources by coercive self-mandated power for the benefit of those who legitimately earned them. In religiously oriented societies, emphasizing common values through belief in God's decision reduces the sharpness of the tensions that result from the econopolitical inequality.

Religious faith is often empirically mixed. From an analytical view, we can see vividly how religion consistently can be in conflict with opposing political ideologies. Appeal to forcing a political ideology may ultimately lose the original heavenly cause of the religious faith and convert it into a political instrument, which can destroy itself and other political ideologies.

The relationship of religion to politics varies widely, from person to person, and from people to politicians. It depends on the religious tradition and/or socioeconomic situation in which it is found. The question is: Can we draw a distinctive line between religion and politics in a systematic way? The answer for individual behavior is no, for a political system, yes. A religious faith is a belief in spiritual goodness. Religious faith is a manifestation of human psychosocial and spiritual character. Religion is one aspect of an individual's life—the relationship between psychological anxiety and concern for the individual's eternal salvation and sociological concern for a happy life. In contrast, political ideologies, by and large, are the social phenomena of an ongoing class ordering among people in a society. It is a sociocultural phenomenon to establish justice, while avoiding error, injustice, and suffering. These are indeed the critical orientations of human earthly life. Political ideologies promise to establish justice through laws and cultural values through ethics and morality. But religion searches to purify psychosocial misconducts through Godly behavior. However, the combination of both, as Parsons (1951) indicates, is a political-religious effort toward manifestation of a mobilized effort by the masses for purifying ideas, values, and desires. Expressed in terms of his vocabulary of motivation, these are cognitive and valuative oriented behaviors.

RELIGION AND SCIENCE

There are different thoughts concerning the relationship between science and religion. Some people believe that science deals with ideas that are falsifiable. In contrast, scientific religion deals with matters of truthful faith. Faith is not omnipotent, nor it is always benign. Religious faith is arguably the most successful psychological therapy ever invented, but it has also fomented ignorance and intolerance. The benefit of scientific knowledge must outweigh the benefits of faith. Otherwise, why practice science at all (Horgan, 1999: A72)? However, some people believe that it is of vital importance for the fields of both science and religion to stick to their separate turfs (Krauss, 1999: A88). In the United States, there is a trend that separates church from state. People such as Sir John Templeton believe that a path of cooperation between the sciences and all religions can lead humanity to a deeper understanding of the universe (Johnson, 1998: B12). This group of people believes that science has discovered absolutely nothing in the past century of remarkable activity that has any spiritual implications (Krauss, 1999: A88).

The debate between science and religion is about selection of paths of discovery. Scientists believe in observation and empirical experiments starting from the smallest matter, such as an atom, then they generalize some conclusive facts; religious authorities believe in holistic theoretical methods in exploration of whole facts in relation to life. Religious philosophers search for objective truth in order to explore the "evidence of universal purpose of the cosmos." Also, religious authorities believe that consciousness, the very hallmark of humanity, could be directed to an extrinsic part of the universe and is related to the perceptual nature of God. All religions scientifically explain the source of some perceptions that we posit the existence of outside reality—a god or gods.

The problem between these groups is: Why should it not be something instead of nothing for such debate? How is it that animated matter can organize and contemplate self without ignoring the source of existence? Religion is an unknown spiritual science. Science, like religion, is ultimately built on a platform of beliefs and assumptions. No one can prove that the mystery of the existence of the cosmos is bounded only with science, because the laws of the outer hemisphere could be different from the laws of the inter hemisphere. Scientific religion is concerned about the universal laws of both the inner hemisphere and outer hemisphere. If scientists do not have empirical access to the whole cosmic truth, then it is not fair to deny the content and causes of the existence of religion. Religion covers causes, processes, and conclusions of the existence. Scientific religion is the discovery of the "undiscovered mind." It is related to the holistic spiritual end result of neuroscience, psychology, psychiatry, behavioral genetics, sociology, kinesthetic intelligence, cosmology, and the like.

CATEGORIES OF RELIGIOUS BEHAVIOR

Although the range of religious behavior is wide, it can be classified. Wallace (1966: 518) categorizes thirteen minimal behaviors. He believes these types of behaviors are found in all religions. Yinger (1970: 16) has made some modifications and has outlined fifteen types of religious behavior:

1. *Prayer and exorcism:* addressing the supernatural power
2. *Performing religious arts and playing music:* dancing, singing, chanting, playing musical instruments, and whirling around self and objects
3. *Psychophysiological exercises:* physical manipulation of psychological states through deprivation (e.g., fasting)
4. *Exhortation:* addressing others as representatives of divinity
5. *Reciting the code:* use of the sacred written and oral scriptures, and literatures, which contain statements regarding the pantheon, cosmology, myths, and moral injunctions
6. *Simulation:* imitating things for purposes of control
7. *Mana:* touching things possessed of sacred power. *Mana* refers to a kind of power that could produce extraordinary occurrences in nature and also enable man to perform acts beyond his normal capacity (Comstock, 1972: 8). Marett (1909) argued that the belief in mana probably preceded the belief in specific souls that operated at the animistic stage.
8. *Taboo:* avoiding things to prevent the activation of unwanted power or undesired events
9. *Feasts:* sacred meals
10. *Sacrifices:* immolation, offerings, and fees
11. *Congregation:* processions, meetings, and convocations
12. *Inspiration:* pursuit of revelation, conversion, possession, mystical ecstasy
13. *Symbolism:* manufacture and use of symbolic objects

All of the above religious behaviors are isolated systems and, therefore, according to Yinger (1970: 17), can be extended in two directions:

14. *Extending and modifying the code:* in connection with number 5
15. *Applying religious values to nonreligious contexts:* the consequential dimension

There are three types of behaviors in religious ceremonies: (1) ritual performances, (2) praying and (3) begging to God. All of the above ceremonies involve asking God to provide human beings with earthly comfortable life, repenting of wrong actions, and asking God to forgive sinful and cruel intentions, decisions, and actions. In addition, for some religions that believe in doomsday, they ask God for eternal graceful attention, blessing, and salvation.

DESCRIPTIVE INTERNATIONAL
DIFFERENCES IN RELIGION

Emergence of religious faith is as old as human history. Religion is the first spiritual cultural foundation of basic norms, models, insights, and visions which have influenced and shaped human faith. Gradually, through the evolutionary trends from original to advanced cultures, the spiritual foundations of humanity in the forms of believing in magic, miracles, inspiration, ethics, morality, and prophetic foundations were laid in China, India, Persia, Palestine, Arabia, and Greece. The world has a unique religious profile (see Table 11.1).

In Table 11.2, Jaspers (1953: 1) has enlarged boundaries to include the following religious and philosophical figures.

Through historical research, Toynbee (1954: 83) found that religion is one of the cultural forms through which a given civilization could be studied. Later on, he found that "historic religions catch a new vision of the spiritual presence, higher than man, in which these presences are no longer seen through the medium of human economic and political needs and activities but are seen as direct powers that are not implicated ex-officio in their local

TABLE 11.1. Adherents in Millions and As a Percentage of the World Population (1999)

Religions	Population	Percentage
Atheism	146,615,000	2.53
Bahaism	7,666,000	0.14
Buddhism	353,141,000	6.09
Chinese Folk Religions	363,334,000	6.27
Christianity	1,929,987,000	33.28
Confucianism	6,112,000	0.11
Hinduism	746,797,000	12.88
Jainism	4,016,000	0.07
Judaism	14,890,000	0.26
Islam	1,147,494,000	19.79
Shintoism	2,672,000	0.05
Sikhism	22,518,000	0.39
Zoroastrianism	272,000	0.01
Other Religions	1,045,000,000	18.02
Total Population (Estimate)	5,855,699,000	

Source: Famighetti, R. (1999). *The 1999 World Almanac and Book of Facts.* World Almanac Books, A Primedia Company, p. 687.

TABLE 11.2. The Axial Period

Unknown authors of the *Vedas* (Hinduism)	Before 1000 B.C.E.
Moses (Judaism)	1250 B.C.E.*
Confucius (Confucianism)	551-479 B.C.E.*
Zoroaster	c. 660 B.C.E.*
Lao-Tzu (Taoism)	c. 604-517 B.C.E.
Jina (Mahavira: Jainism)	599-527 B.C.E.
Gautama Buddha	560-480 B.C.E.
Jesus (Christianity)	4 B.C.E.-29 C.E.
Mohammed (Islam)	570-632 C.E.
Nanak (Sikhism)	1469 C.E.
Mohammed Ali Bab (Babism)	1819-1850 C.E.*
Baha' ullah (Bahaism)	1817-1892 C.E.**

* *The Baha'i World: The Bab* (1819-1850). http://www.bahai.org/bworld/main.cfm.
** *The Baha'i World: The Baha'i World.* http://www.bahai.org/bworld/main.cfm.

Source: Jaspers, K. (1953). *The Origin and Goal of History.* London: Routledge, p. 1.

worshipers' human concerns." However, it should be indicated that today, religion has some direct impact on a community's econopolitical performance. For example, Islam restricts Moslems from taking or giving predetermined interest, irrespective of the purpose of the loans or rate of interest charges. Accordingly, on Thursday, December 23, 1999, Pakistan's Supreme Court ruled for the country's financial system to be free of interest. The court ordered all people, banks, and institutions in Pakistan to obey Islamic law. The ruling was driven by the view that interest amounts to *riba,* or usury, under the Islamic system of running an economy, and therefore is considered forbidden (Bokhari, 1999: 4).

Smith (1965) has specified a number of Asian countries, such as Burma, Thailand, and Ceylon, that values of polity influence directly the relationship of religion and politics:

1. *Theory of history.* The course of history tends to increase a religion's involvement in politics.
2. *Attitude toward other religions.* Attitudes of intolerance reinforce the tendency to use the political process for communal advantage.
3. *Capacity for ecclesiastical organization.* The more highly organized the religion, the greater its involvement in politics.
4. *Political and religious functions.* Fusion of politics and religion tends to change spiritual faith into political beliefs.
5. *Tendency to regulate society.* The more religious influence on daily sociopolitical values, the more tension between state and religious authorities.

The focus of this section is descriptive for the following major religions: Jainism, Zoroastrianism, Taoism, Shintoism, Buddhism, Zen, Confucianism, Hinduism, and Sikhism as major religions in Asia; and Judaism, Christianity, Islam, Babism, and Bahaism in the Near and Middle East, North Africa, Europe, Australia, and North and South America.

Zoroastrianism

Zoroastrianism is an animated and humanized religion. It was born in Iran in 660 B.C.E. Zoroastrian faith in its final shape was evolved as "the Thoughts, Words, and Deeds of Goodness," by a single personality, the prophet Zarathushtra or Zoroaster (Yasna 30 verse 3). The Zoroastrian holy scripture is called *Avesta.* It is divided into five holy books: (1) *Yasna,* (2) *Yashtha,* (3) *Vaspered,* (4) *Vandidad,* and (5) *Khordeh Avesta.* The Zoroastrian population around the world is estimated at 272,000 by one account, who live mainly in Iran, India, North America, Europe, and Australia (*World Almanac and Book of Facts,* 1999: 687).

Elements of the Zoroastrian Faith

Zoroastrianism may have been the first monotheistic religion. It was the first religion not intended to be a privileged sphere for a mediating priesthood or hierarchy. On the contrary, it obviously came into being through Zarathushtra's opposition to ancient rites and guardians, the priest class of the magi. This religion, as represented by the original preaching of Zarathushtra, the *Gathas,* meant a broadening of the religious basis, expanding contact between the deity and people, and a universal inclusion of all people from every walk of life in the circle of the gods (www.religioustolerance.org).

In the Zoroastrian faith, people believe that the struggle between good and evil did not occur in the origin of life in the past, but it goes on in the universe as well as in the human soul. Furthermore, it will end in the ultimate triumph of light and goodness over darkness. Both the good and the evil have many attendant spirits or demons that have been degraded to a lower sphere. The features of good are the best justice, the sacred devotion, obedience, truth, and hope. The features of evil are unjustness, untruths, disobedience, and pessimism (Kahler, 1956: 58-59). The six major religious principles in the Zoroastrian faith are:

1. Light is the main source of truth.
2. Light is a source of life.
3. Life has been created by enlightenment of knowledge and wisdom.
4. Ahura Mazda is the source of light. Ahura is perceived as the creator of the cosmos, and Mazda is conceived as the source of (ultimate?) wisdom.
5. The animation of the spirit of goodness in human nature has been gifted by Ahura Mazda.

6. The duality of good and evil is the misconception of human pleasurable deviation into Ahriman. *"Spenta Mainyu"* as good and *"Angra Mainyu"* as evil (Ahriman) and an evil spirit of violence and death (Mehr, 1991).

The Six Pillars of Zoroastrian Faith

Zoroastrian faith inspires people to convert new societal features of goodness into their intentional behaviors through application of "Good Thoughts," "Good Words," and "Good Deeds." These features are personifications of abstract qualities and attitudes of goodness to the identical conception with the soundness, the wholesomeness, and the usefulness. These values are inspiring, and they manifest the evidence of goodness in a human deed. The following consequences will emerge:

1. Presentiment that human destiny as a whole is the progression of mankind's goodness.
2. There will be a day of final judgment (doomsday) when the world of good will prevail and the evil will disappear. That is, truthful life will continue according to the universal law of "asha," righteousness.
3. Ethics is a hygiene and a source of practical advice for people. Its main objectives are purification, perfection, and usefulness of a clean and sound natural life.
4. Goodness is not only contained in an individual character. It also includes societal congregations, such as the six five-day-long ceremonial thanksgiving celebrations during a year.
5. The cleanliness of the four vital essences of existence and enlightenment—water, air, earth, and fire (as symbols and sources of energy)—is a consequence of ethical environmental hygiene.
6. Zoroastrian temples keep the sacred fire lit as a permanent symbol of life and enlightenment for eternity.

Pragmatic Behavioral Life of Zoroastrians

In a pragmatic analysis, Zoroastrian religion shows three important features in human life:

1. A sober life, which is not to be attached solely to materialistic aspects of life.
2. A character, which is dynamic in nature
3. A tendency, which is a motive toward abstraction

In a conclusive statement, Zoroastrianism is a faith that directs people to make a distinction between good and evil. Also, it is a belief that is composed of a dual struggle between wisdom and ignorance, light and darkness, sound and silence, justness and unjustness, and pleasure and lustfulness.

Hinduism

In contrast to other religions, Hinduism has no founder. It is a cultural religion that dates back, perhaps, to prehistoric times. There is no standardized principle of faith among Hindus. Hinduism differs from region to region, from caste to caste, from class to class, and from rural illiterates to urban intelligentsia. Hinduism is a specific religious attitude of self, where intellect is subordinated to intuition, dogma to experience, and other experience to inward realization (Radhakrishnan, 1993).

To many, religion in India appears to be a confusing tangle of myths and many different gods and goddesses worshipped in countless forms (Sahay and Geoff, 1997: 419). Hindus recognize many gods and goddesses, such as Vishnu, the god of protection and preservation of the world. Shiva is the god of destruction and restoration. Brahma is the god of creation. The elephant is god of personality and good luck. Lakshmi is the goddess of wealth. Saraswati is the goddess of knowledge and learning. Indra is the god of the storm and fertility (Passion for India, 1999. "Spirit." http://Passionforindia.com/spirit.html.).

Hinduism is a tolerant and peaceful religion; minorities have nothing to fear (Baird, 1998). Hinduism is a very complex and synthesized religion which has been influenced by many generations of Aryan (Indo-European) and Persian (Iranian) civilizations with the indigenous Dravidian tradition of southern peninsular India. Eighty-two percent of India's population practices Hinduism. In addition, other long-resident Hindu populations are on the Indonesian island of Bali and northern Sri Lanka. During British colonial rule, Hindus immigrated into Africa, the Caribbean, and Southeast Asian countries, such as Malaysia and Fiji. Hindus have a sense of international adjustment and tolerance in difficult environments. According to the *1997 Encyclopedia Britannica,* there are over 746,797,000 Hindus around the world.

Hinduism started with *Mitraism, Gitaism,* and *Vedaism* around 2000 B.C.E. The early sacred literature of Hinduism has the retrospective title of *Vedas. Mitra* is the *Vedic* god of justice. *Gita* is the song of the *Vedic* gods. *Veda* means "knowledge" and the *Vedas* are written in Sanskrit. Some historians argue that the basic concept of Hindu religious text is based on the philosophy of reincarnation. Hindu religious philosophy is based on an extreme view that everything is temporary and all things that exist are associated with birth,

Hinduism Philosophy of Reincarnation

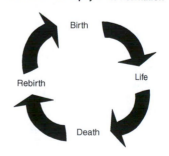

life, death, and rebirth, including gods. Hindus view that all five units of the existence of the cosmos (gods, humans, plants, animals, and inanimate substances) are composed of natural substances that are not only different, but are also inherently unequal. All five units in the domain of the cosmos (e.g. sun and stars, clouds, winds, thunder, and lightning) are ranked according to the power and purity of their substances. Accordingly, in a domain of living things (gods in a pantheon, castes of humans, and species of animals) higher forms in any domain are purer and more powerful than lower forms in that domain. There are four types of *Vedic* religious books:

1. *Samhitas: Rgveda Samhita (Veda of Chants) the Samaveda and Yajurveda Samhidas (Vedas of Melodies)* discuss multiple gods, the universe, and creation.
2. *Brahmanas: Brahmanas* are the elaboration of *Vedic* religion into the sacrificial religious systemization. *Brahmana* means a statement on *Brahma* that is on the cosmic importance or meaning of the *Vedic* sacrificial ritual, whether regarding each individual act *(karma)* and formula *(mantra)* or a combination of such acts and formulas that constitute a particular sacrifice. Brahmanas describe animal sacrificial formulas to gods. However, five male animals, including men, horses, bulls, rams, and goats, were among cosmic sacrifices.
3. *Epics* contain legendary stories about gods and humans. These texts are *Mahabharata* and the *Ramayana.*
4. *Upanishads* are commentaries on the *Vedic* texts. These texts speculate on the origin of the universe and the nature of deities, atman (the individual soul*),* and its relationship to *Brahman* (the universal soul). They introduce the doctrine of *karma* (one is born to a higher level of existence based on moral behavior in a previous phase of existence; life on earth is regarded as a burden) and recommend meditation and the practice of yoga.

Overall, Hinduism can be broken down into four periods characterized by an oscillation from disunity to unity, from unity to disunity, and disunity to unity. Fundamental to the self-definition of Hinduism is the distinction it takes between two classes of literature: *Sruti* and *Smrti. Sruti* is "what is heard," and refers to the whole corpus of *Vedic* literature (also called *Veda*) from the four *Vedas. Smrti* is "what is remembered," or tradition includes all that falls outside this literature. The most prospective corpus of *Smrti* literature is concerned with dharma (law or duty).

The Hierarchy of the Caste System

Hinduism can be interpreted as the most dynamic of religions because followers of this faith believe in reincarnation. Orthodox Hindu people are divided into four major heredity classes:

1. The *Brahmin* (priestly and learned class)
2. The *Kshatriya* (military, professional, ruling, and governing occupation)
3. The *Vaishya* (landowners, merchants, and business occupations)
4. The *Sudra* (artisans, laborers, and peasants)

Jainism

Jainism is an ancient religion whose community follows the religious path of Vardhamana Mahavira, a prophet known as Jina, or "Victor." He was born in Northern Bihar, India, in the sixth century B.C.E., the same time as Buddha Gautama.

The community of Jainism in 79 B.C.E. split into two main sects: (1) The Digambara, "sky or space-clad" (and thus naked), and (2) the Svetambara, "white-clad" (wearers of white cloth). In addition to the fifth commandment of Zoroastrianism, the animation of the spirit of goodness in human nature has been gifted by Ahura Mazda—that they were practicing in their religion, Jainism added two more principles: (1) confession and repentance and (2) nakedness. These two principles were recommended among those believers who took religious vows.

The earliest existing documents for Jainism's holy book are the canonical scriptures of the Svetambaras and the systematic teratism *(Prakarana)* of the Digambaras.

Jainism is based on pleading to many gods. Adherents believe that the cosmos is composed of three main parts: the lower, middle, and upper world. They believe in stellar gods (suns, moons, planets, constellations, and stars). Jains believe that these stellar gods overlook them at all times. They should not violate the nature of the principles of the faith.

Religious Practice of Jainism

Practicing Jainism is based on two elements: specific Jain convictions and the general Indian environment. Members of the fourfold congregation *(samgha)* composed of all Jainism believers include all monks and nuns, laymen, and laywomen. They share a common belief in the *Triratna* (three jewels): (1) The Right Faith, (2) The Right Knowledge, and (3) The Right Conduct.

The monks and nuns should take six more "great vows," as they are pleading to abstain from:

1. injuring life,
2. false speech,
3. taking what is not given,
4. unchastity,
5. appropriation, and
6. taking food at night and in darkness.

Monks should cultivate *samvara,* the spiritual path defined by the cessation of *karmic* influx, by means of established ethical and behavioral practices as follow:

1. The triple supervision of mental, verbal, and bodily activities.
2. The "fivefold care" not to hurt living beings when they are walking, acting, speaking, begging, or performing excretory functions.
3. The "tenfold righteousness" of patience, humility, uprightness, purity, truthfulness, restraint, austerity, renuciation, voluntary poverty, and spiritual obedience.
4. The twelve mental "reflections."
5. The twenty-two "traits" ranging from hunger to confusion (Eliade, 1987: 507-514).

Confucianism

The best known of all of China's ancient sages is Confucius. Confucius (K'ung Fu-tzu) was born in the northern state of Lu in China (551-479 B.C.E.). He is neither viewed as a prophet nor as a spiritual leader. Instead, he is considered a philosopher and moralist leader in the Oriental culture. The teachings of Confucius were compiled in a large volume simply called the *Analects,* which was to become the bible of the Chinese way until modern times. According to the 1998 statistical religious population of the world, there are 6,112,000 people in Chinese folk religions (*The Learning Network:* <http://www.infoplease.com/ipa/A0001484.html>).

Confucian Philosophy of Faith

The basis of faith for traditional China and East Asian countries is the principle that the universe is composed of and held together by two forces, the *yin* and the *yang,* or positive and negative. In this type of faith, there is a plus for every minus and it is the interaction of these *yin* and *yang* forces that creates life and gives the universe the form and the cycles that we see. Also, this belief is referred to as the principle of duality.

In Chinese faith, every aspect and facet of life must be in balance—in harmony—for things to be right with the world. In the modern scientific conception, scientists empirically accept that this philosophy of life from protons and electrons all the way up is based on the same principles, which originally were expressed by Chinese faith. The divined Chinese faith is the milestone of accepting the nature of universe (De Mente, 1989: 19).

Principles of Confucianism

1. Confucianism derives from the cult of ancestors, which places the spirits of dead relatives at the center of each household's praying.

2. Confucianism believes in maintenance and continuity of literal dialogues with ancestors through praying.
3. Confucianism believes the proper foundation for society is consideration of propriety based on respect for human dignity, which in turn is based on two principles: fairness and reversibility. Fairness means what is fair to all is fair to one. Reversibility means willingness to be the recipient of one's own manners and actions.
4. Confucianism is little concerned with metaphysical discussion of religion or with spiritual attainments. Instead, it emphasizes moral conduct and duty in relationship to the human sphere.
5. Confucianism is based on cultivation of virtue as a central tenet of humanity.
6. Confucianism provides a model for social relations, based on the doctrine of Tam Cuong, which prescribes how five important sets of interactions are to be considered. These five relations are between the king and/or ruler and subject, father and son, husband and wife, older and younger brothers, and friend and friend.

These relationships are reinforced by participating in ritual ceremonies such as ancestor worship. In the field of business, Chinese and Vietnamese employees expect their employers to be paternalistic, kind, and soft-spoken. At the same time, employees should be obedient to employers without question.

Taoism

Taoism is one of the major religions in China, Hong Kong, and Taiwan. It is a philosophical belief that originally was presented by Tao Te Ching's "Classic Book of Tao and Its Virtues." Traditionally, this book was thought to be the work of Lao-tze. The name of Lao Tzu (604-517 B.C.E.), the founder of the Taoism religion, is associated with philosophical paradoxes. He began by talking like a fool and ended by making his listeners wise. For example, Lao-tze himself spoke of it thus: "There is a thing which is all-containing, which was born before the existence of Heaven and Earth. How silent! How solitary! It stands alone and changes not. It revolves without danger to itself and is the mother of the universe. I don't know its name and so call it the Path," (Kakuzo 1956: 37). Lao Tzu as a philosopher himself, with his quaint humor, says: "If people of inferior intelligence hear of the Tao, they laugh immensely. It would not be the Tao's wisdom unless they laughed at it" (Kakuzo, 1956: 37).

Taoism is a matter of spiritual enlightenment through empirical observation that most, if not all, believers combine with group and individual enlightened elements. This dual reference may derive from the fact that each of the functions of Taoism is carried on most effectively within a religious belief. In Taoism, individuals need to use their maximum efforts to attain their religious objectives. Taoists refrain from disturbing the natural order of things.

By cultivating *wu-wei,* a type of inaction characterized by humility and prudence, a person can participate in the simplicity and spontaneity of Tao. Taking initiative is considered to be vain, the active life is disdained, and passivity is valued. These doctrines are summed up in the Taoist maxim: "Do nothing and everything will be accomplished spontaneously" (Furnham and Bochner, 1986: 99). Also, the groups need collectively to use their faith for inspiring and supporting their group member efforts. Tao, "The Path," is the ultimate reality of the universe. It is a creative process, and humans can live in harmony with it by clearing the self of obstacles. Confucianism paid scant heed to the question of individual salvation, for example; but this may account for the spread and the direction of development of Taoism and Buddhism, with which Confucianism learned to live in a somewhat uneasy coexistence.

Taoist Philosophy of Faith

The Tao literally means a "Path." It has been translated also as the Way, the Absolute, the Law, the Nature, the Supreme Reason, and the Mode. These renderings are not incorrect, for the use of the term by Taoists differs according to the subject matter of the inquiry. In addition, Taoist religion has emerged from the ancient philosophies of traditional shamanism; by the second century B.C.E., it constituted an organized religion.

Taoists believe that there is a thing which is all-containing, which was born before existence. With reluctance, it is called the Infinite. Infinity is the Fleeting, the Fleeting is Vanishing, the Vanishing is Reverting. Life is the Path because it passes by. Therefore, Taoism is believing in birth, passing through life, and reverting to the next growth cycle.

Taoism is believing that the spirit of Cosmic Change is the eternal growth which returns upon itself to produce new forms. It folds and unfolds, because subjectivity is the mood of the universe. Its absolute is the relative. Taoism cannot be understood without some knowledge of Confucianism and vice versa because it is related to ethics more than religious faith. Taoism is proknowledge because knowledge is power. Taoists do not believe in the nature of God as an absolute power because they believe "Absolute is the Relative." They believe in the laws and moral codes of society; to them, right and wrong are not different phenomena, they are relative in terms. "Absolute," "fixed," and "changeless" are terms meaning a stoppage of growth.

Taoists strongly believe in changing the truth, inventing a new path of values, and evolving in growth. Taoists accept the mundane as it is and, unlike the Confucians and the Buddhists, try to find beauty in our world. They believe that the comedy of human life could be made more interesting if everyone would preserve unity. To keep the proportion of things and give place to others without losing one's own position is the secret success in the mundane Path.

Practical Path of Taoism

Taoists strongly believe in mental concentration for longevity and immortality. They believe if followers of the faith harmonize body and mind energies through breathing exercises, meditation, use of medical plants, talismans, and magical formulas, they can discover the path of enlightenment. Since the beginning of Taoism, many sects have arisen within this faith. Some have emphasized the worshipping of immortals through meditation; others use alchemy for healing and exorcism.

Shintoism

Shintoism, the native religion of Japan, is primarily a system of nature and ancestor worship. The religious-cultural philosophy of Shintoism focuses on the worshipping of the *kami*. A *kami* is a host of supernatural and beautiful beings that could be known through forms. Shrines dedicated to particular *kami* are visited by parishioners for praying and traditional ceremonies, such as presenting a newborn child to the *kami*. These forms of *kami* could be perceived as objects of nature, such as a plant; extraordinary individuals, such as the emperor, spirits of ancestors; or abstract concepts, such as justice. Shintoism has been influenced by Taoism: *shin tao* means "way of the gods." Also, it has been influenced by Confucianism and by Buddhism. In the fifteenth century, Japanese people brought tea into Shintoism as a religious reflection of aestheticism—Teaism. Teaism is a cult founded on the adoration of a beautiful drinking ceremony among the sordid details of everyday existence. It inculcates purity and harmony in the romanticism of social order (Kakuzo, 1956: 4). Nevertheless, these mysterious and beautiful habits ultimately contain power for healing, inspiring, motivating, and energizing an individual's mental ability.

Shintoism has no principles of faith, such as believing in a holy writ. Through a political-cultural tradition, it is considered as the belief in brotherhood. However, Japanese culture, in supporting the morality of a nation and the emperor as preeminent in the hierarchy of values, departs markedly from the interpretation found in other religions such as Buddhism and Confucianism in China (Bobilin, 1968). Also, Holtom (1947: 54) indicates that according to the ideology of Shinto: "The sacred quality of the divine emperor attaches to a Japanese war. All the wars of Japan are holy wars since they are under the supreme command of an emperor who can do nothing wrong." Shinto made the Japanese state not merely a secular power, but a sacred place of worship as well.

It is a great mistake to think of the political nationalism ideology of Shintoism as a religious faith. Shintoism culturally believes in "war dances" as a religious ceremony. Religious-political ideology of Shintoism, like many other religions, is considered an effort to the degree of unity necessary for modern war by inspiration of the emperor of Japan (*The Learning Network:* <http://www.infoplease.com/ipa/A0001472.html>).

Buddhism

Buddhism is a major religious faith in Burma, Cambodia, Laos, Sri Lanka, and Thailand. It was founded in 563 B.C.E. in northern India by a son of a warrior prince known traditionally as Siddhartha ("he who has reached the goal") Gautama. According to *The World Almanac and Book of Facts* (1999), there are 353,141,000 Buddhists around the world, roughly 6 percent of the world population.

Buddha is not a name of the founder of Buddhism. It is a title signifying the Enlightened One. Prince Gautama spent his two decades in a life of ease and luxury. One day, he left his home, wife, and child to wander as an ascetic, seeking religious insight and a solution to the struggles of human existence. He was disturbed by human suffering and tried to release himself from such a condition through many trials and practical meditation to the extreme of self-denial. Gautama meditated for forty days under a sacred bodhi tree ("tree of perfect knowledge") and finally he discovered the enlightenment of the truth. His path of discovery to the truth was called the Middle Way, because he was avoiding the two extremes of self-indulgence and Hindu asceticism. Gautama taught his followers about his new spiritual discovery.

Despite the Hinduism that they believe—that the Brahmin caste (the class of people of great culture and intellect) alone can perform religious functions and attain the highest spiritual understanding—Buddhism is more egalitarian and accessible to all classes of people, regardless of their caste, who wish to be enlightened.

Elements of Buddhism

Like Hindus, Buddhists believe that existence consists of reincarnation, a continuous cycle of birth, life, death, and rebirth. Despite monotheistic religions (Judaism, Christianity, and Islam), Buddhists believe in *anatman* (that a person has no actual self) and the idea that existence is characterized by impermanence. Buddhism is highly tolerant of other religions.

Buddhism faith is considered as being a reformation of practical Hinduism. At the core of religious faith of Buddhism, there are four Noble Truths:

1. All existence begins with suffering.
2. The truth of this suffering is desire. Desires of all kinds are never fulfilled.
3. Desires can be overcome. Suffering ceases when desires cease.

4. There is a path that leads to avoid desires. This is the Noble Eightfold Path. There are eight conditions that a believer should consider:
   a. Right view is understanding and accepting the Four Noble Truths.
   b. Right thought is viewed as avoiding lust, ill will, cruelty, and untruthfulness.
   c. Right words is avoiding lying, talebearing, harsh language, and vain talk.
   d. Right conduct is abstaining from killing, stealing, and sexual misconduct.
   e. Right livelihood is avoidance of violence and freedom from luxury.
   f. Right effort is avoidance of badness and maintenance of what is good.
   g. Right concentration is contemplating the fact that the body is transitory and loathsome, and contemplating the feelings of oneness and of others, and contemplating the mind and other phenomena.
   h. Right meditation or ecstasy is complete devotion and concentration on a single object or phenomenon to achieve purity of thought: through freedom from all desires, hindrances, and distractions, and eventually, freedom from all sensation.

Sangha, the Buddhist monastic order is very well organized. Buddhist monks renounce the world. There is no attempt in Buddhism to regulate society, whereas in Islam, the law is detailed and full (Smith, 1965).

The Triple Factions in Buddhism

Buddhism, like other religions, has numerous sects. There are three major sects: (1) Theravada, (2) Mahayana, and (3) Vajrayana.

Theravada. Theravada is the oldest tradition, interested in the "Way of the Elders." By this faith, Buddha is considered a great sage but not a deity. This practice emphasizes meditation and ritual ceremonies that help individuals become *arhats* (enlightened beings). These believers depart from daily social life and dedicate themselves to the cause of meditation. Its followers believe in the earliest Buddhist scriptures. This sect is prevalent in Southeast Asia and Sri Lanka.

Mahayana. The second sect is based on the belief of the Mahayana (Greater Vehicle) tradition of Buddhism to concentrate more on humanity and social life. Members of this sect believe in Buddha as a supernatural eternal power, as the ideal of the *bodhisattva* (enlightened being). Followers of this sect pray to Buddha. This sect is prevalent in China, Korea, and Japan.

Vajrayana. The third sect believes in mentoring and guiding by a spiritual leader for enlightenment. These people believe in Zen. Zen is the name derived from the Sanscrit word Dhayana, which signifies meditation. It is a belief in contemplative actions. Zen is believing in nothing real except that which concerns the working of our own minds. Zen Buddhism encourages individuals to seek the Buddha in nature within their minds and practice their faith through continuous meditation to reach *satori* (spiritual enlightenment). This sect is prevalent in Japan, Tibet and Mongolia (*The Learning Network:* <http://www.infoplease.com/ipa/A0001470.html>).

Zen

Zen is actually a collaborative faith among Buddhism, Taoism, and Confucianism. Zen is a name derived from the Sanscrit word Dhayana, which signifies meditation. It claims that supreme self-realization may be attained through consecrated meditation. Meditation is one of the six ways through which Buddhahood may be reached, and the Zen sectarians affirm that Sakyamuni laid special stress on this method in his teachings, handing down the rules to his chief disciple Kashiapa. Kashiapa, the first Zen patriach, imparted the secret to Ananda, who in turn passed it on to successive patriachs until it reached Bodhi-Dharma, the twenty-eighth. Bodhi-Dharma came to North China in the early half of the sixth century and was the first patriarch of Chinese Zen (Kakuzo, 1956).

Zen seems to have affinity, on one hand, to the Indian Negativism of Nagarjuna and, on the other, to the Gnan philosophy formulated by Sanchracharya. Zen, like Taoism, is worshipping relativity. One master defines Zen as the art of feeling the polar star in the southern sky. It is a strong advocate of individualism. Nothing is real except that which concerns the working of our own minds.

Principles of the Zen Faith

Zen faith is based on spiritual adjustment to and harmony with nature. Followers of this faith believe that there is no absolute thing or phenomenon in the universe because everything is subject to the cycle of change. The followers of Zen aim at direct communion with the inner nature of things, regarding outward accessories only as impediments to a clear perception of truth. They believe that the present status of life is the moving identity toward the future. It is the legitimate sphere of the relativity in which everything is a function of other things. Relativity seeks adjustment; adjustment is art. They believe that the art of life lies in a constant readjustment to our surroundings.

Zen was often opposed to the percept of orthodox Buddhism even as Taoism was opposed to Confucianism. To the transcendental insight of the Zen, words were but an incumbrance to thought. Zen, with the Buddhist theory of evanescence and its demands for mastery of spirit over matter, recognized the house as only a temporary refuge for the body. The body itself is but a hut in the wilderness. Taoism furnished the basis for aesthetic ideals; Zen made them practical.

Judaism

Judaism is the first literate religious system. It also became the polity of the Jews. It is one of the oldest of the monotheistic faiths. There are around 14,890,000 Jews around the world; 5,836,000 in North America; 4,257,000 in Asia; 2,432,000 in Europe; and 1,084,000 in Latin America. Jewish population comprises of 0.26 percent of the world population (*The World Almanac and Book of Facts,* 1999).

The origin of Judaism faith goes back to the prophet Ibrahim. It was founded in Canaan, Mesopotamia. Mesopotamia was an ancient country in the Middle East between the Tigris and Euphrates Rivers in north Iraq. According to Scripture, Judaism affirms the existence of one God. Ibrahim's line descended through prophets Isaac and Jacob (also called Israel; his descendants came to be called Israelites).

According to Scripture, twelve Hebrew families migrated to Egypt where they were enslaved. Finally, they were led out of bondage by the prophet Moses. He united Israelites in line to worship Yehweh and called them Hebrews. The Hebrews returned from Egypt through the Nile River and Sinai desert after a forty-year sojourn, conquering from the local peoples the "promised land" that God had provided for them.

During the reigns of Saul and David (1200-1000 B.C.E.) the twelve Hebrew tribes lived in a covenant association, during the period of the judges. They were known as wise, knowledgeable, and heroic people. David's son, Solomon, unified the land of Israel and made Jerusalem its religious center. Hebrews were ordered to worship in that temple. Following Solomon's death, the kingdom was split into Israel in the north and Judah in the south.

Judaism's holy writings are known as the Torah, specifically, the five books of Moses (traditionally called the Old Testament by Christians, and the Sacred Books by Moslems) and the compilation of oral tradition known as the Talmud (which includes the Mishnah, or oral law).

Elements of Judaism

A glance at Judaism reveals that in early Hebraic religion, a combination of rules of ritual, prescribed beliefs, and moral requirements was initiated by Moses. In this tradition, Jews were ordered to follow a source of goodness and a sustainer of morality, such as the Ten Commandments.

As previously stated, Moses was a prophet of God. God had instructed Moses to climb Mount Sinai where he received the Ten Commandments. God spoke these commandments to Moses who then recited them to his followers. The Ten Commandments are:

1. I am the Lord your God who has taken you out of the land of Egypt.
2. You shall have no other gods but me.
3. You shall not take the name of the Lord your God in vain.

4. You shall remember the Sabbath and keep it holy.
5. Honor your mother and father.
6. You shall not murder.
7. You shall not commit adultery.
8. You shall not steal.
9. You shall not bear false witness.
10. You shall not covet anything that belongs to your neighbors.

Judaism Essenes and Zealots Split

In 721 B.C.E. political conflicts resulted in the conquest of Israel by Assyria; also Judah was defeated by Babylon in 586 B.C.E. Jerusalem and its temple were destroyed, and many Judeans were exiled to Babylon. During the era of the kings of Babylon and Persia, the Jewish prophets were active in Israel and Judah. Their sacred writings emphasized faith in Yahweh as the God of Israel and the entire universe, and they warn of the dangers of worshipping other gods. They also cried out for social justice. After Babylon was defeated by Persian rulers, all Judeans returned to Israel and resumed their faith and restored the temple of Jerusalem. Persian rule was ended by Alexander the Great and he conquered Israel in 332 B.C.E. The rule of Judea alternated between Egypt and Syria. Finally, the Romans conquered Jerusalem in 63 B.C.E.

During this period, the Sadducees (temple priests) and Pharisees (preachers of the law in the synagogues) offered different interpretations of Judaism as (1) Essenes and (2) the Zealots.

The Essenes, Pharisees, and Rabbinic Judaism

Essenes were smaller religious groups who believed in a religious order. Also, they were called Apocalyptists, who expected divine deliverance led by the Messiah. Rabbinic Judaism's philosophy was developed according to Pharisaic practice and centered on the Torah and synagogue as the primary expression of the Judean faith. The Scriptures became codified, and the Talmud (the Script of David) took shape. In the twelfth century, Maimonides formulated the influential thirteen Articles of Faith, including belief in God, God's oneness and lack of physical or other form, changelessness of the Torah, restoration of the monarchy under the Messiah, and resurrection of the dead.

The Zealots and Zionists

Zealots were majority groups of Jews who were prepared to fight for national independence. The Jews were scattered in the Diaspora (dispersion) and experienced much persecution. When the Zealots revolted in Jerusalem, this time the Roman armies destroyed Jerusalem and its temple (C.E. 70).

During the early twentieth century, the Zionist movement emerged from the European persecution of Jews. The full flowering of this movement occurred after the Holocaust of World War II, which took the lives of more than 6 million Jews. Finally, in 1948, the "promise of God" for the "Promised Land" became reality and the state of Israel was created (*The Learning Network:* <http://www. infoplease.com/ipa/A0001462.html>).

International Business and Judaism

Two expressions of present-day Judaism are: Orthodox and Reformed. Orthodox Jews' daily behavior is based on traditional faith and practice with great seriousness in all aspects of life, including social, political, and economical decisions and actions. They follow a strict kosher diet and keep the Sabbath with care.

Reform movements, resulting from the Haskala (Jewish Enlightenment), began in Western Europe but took root in North America.

Christianity

Christianity is a monotheistic religious faith founded by Jesus of Nazareth. He was born in about 7 B.C.E. Jesus proclaimed his prophecy in the kingdom of God to promote a loving life. The Christian holy book, the Bible, describes Jesus as a spiritual leader and a miracle prophet. The Roman Empire feared that Jesus' spiritual power and his faithful followers would destroy their political system. Consequently, the Roman Empire crucified Jesus in Jerusalem. Jesus' brutal death was viewed as the worst form of punishment for those who were considered a political threat to the Roman Empire and to the Jewish temples.

Followers of Jesus pursued his truthful legacy with faith in God. Christians believed him to be Christ, the Messiah. According to the *1999 World Almanac and Book of Facts* there are 1,929,987,000 believers in Christianity: Roman Catholics, 981,465,000; Protestants, including Anglicans, 755,414,000; and Eastern Orthodox Catholics, 218,350,000.

Trinity and Christianity

Christianity began to take shape as a distinctive doctrine, liturgy, and ministry in the first and second centuries. In 313 C.E., the first ecumenical councils defined the Trinity. Differences in the Christian doctrine and the threat to divide the church became a serious matter in an effort to standardize a creed and formulate it by bishops. The first of such ecumenical councils was held in 325 C.E. in Nicaea. In that congregation, the Christian creed as an important doctrine was defined concerning the substance of the Trinity. The creed defined clearly that there is one God in three persons: Father, Son, and Holy Spirit. Also, the nature of Christ is considered both divine and human. In other words, the concept of "substance," "person," and "nature," dominated the effect to express the doctrine of God as "Father, Son, and Holy Spirit." Christians believe Jesus to be "of one (not like) substance with the Father" (*The New Encyclopedia Britannica:* 271-289).

The Nature of Jesus

Christians believe that Jesus has two "natures," divine and human. He is simultaneously "one in being" with God and "one in being" with humanity, and therefore he is able to mediate between them. Christianity shows its continuing affinity for participating in the kingdom of God, as loyalty to the divine, based on the prior loyalty of the divine to the world and humanity.

Principle Faith in Christianity

Christianity is a system "of faith," "of hope," and "of love." It is a pattern of belief (thought), a community of worship (culture), and a way of life (society). Most Christians past and present have a shared body of beliefs about God, Christ, and the way of salvation. The Christian faith is viewed as:

- loyalty to the divine, based on the prior loyalty of the divine to the world and to humanity;
- confidence that God is trustworthy in truth and love;
- dependence on the Father of Jesus Christ, who is the source of all good in this life and in the life to come;
- given by divine revelation;
- the source of all good in this earthly life and in the life after in eternity;
- the source of commitment to inspire all thoughts and motivate good behavior in accordance with the divine word and will;
- a change of heart and repentance for sins; and
- love of God and concern for justice.

Split in Christian Faith

Like other religions, Christians of the East and the West broke their unity of faith, separating the church into three major groups. In 1054, the religious center for the Eastern Orthodox Church became Constantinople, and the Roman Catholic Church defined doctrine and practice of the Christian Faith for the West. In 1517, Christians of the West began the Reformation, which ultimately caused a schism in the Western Church. Reformers wished to correct certain practices within the Roman Church and also came to view the Christian Faith in a distinctively new way. The major Protestant denominations—Lutheran, Presbyterian, Reformed, and Anglican [Episcopalian]—

came into being. For further familiarity with differences of Roman Catholics, Protestants, and Eastern Orthodoxy, we will describe them in the following sections.

Roman Catholicism. Roman Catholics believe in the action of Jesus Christ himself. They trace and rest their faith as a mandate that Jesus Christ's action are the foundations of Christianity. Also they believe that Jesus Christ invested his power in Peter, and through Peter invested that in the Pope. Roman Catholics believe that Christ is the invisible head of his church, and, by his authority, the Pope is the visible head. This interpretation of the origin and authority of the church determines the attitude of Roman Catholicism.

Roman Catholics believe in the Trinity. There are three distinctive doctrines that have achieved definitive formulation during the nineteenth and twentieth centuries:

1. The infallibility of the Pope
2. The Immaculate Conception, and bodily assumption of the Virgin Mary
3. Centrality of the seven Sacraments: (1) Baptism, (2) Confirmation, (3) Eucharist, (4) Extreme unction, (5) Penance, (6) Matrimony, and (7) Holy orders—as channels of divine grace

The Church, the Sacraments, and the Mediators show that:

1. The Roman Catholic Church has traditionally emphasized the Church as not merely an organization, nor is it a school of doctrine, but the Church and the Sacraments are the principle elements of salvation.
2. The Church is the place where God and men (and women) meet, as God approaches humans through grace and humans approach God through worship. Hence, the focus of Roman piety is the Eucharist, which is both a Sacrament and a sacrifice.
3. The Church has a global hierarchy of holy offices. The Pope, cardinals, archbishops, bishops, and priests constitute a formal religious authority.
4. The Church is the place for confession. The priest can ask God to forgive people's sins because the priest as a mediator between God and humanity can forgive sins through truthful confession.
5. The Church and its priests are viewed as the intermediaries between God and people. People do not approach God directly, but rely on the Church and priests. There is a clear distinction between religious orders and the laity. Different requirements and standards of conduct apply to each. Roman Catholics believe that they cannot directly worship God. Catholics believe they need a mediator to speak to God. That mediator is clergy.

6. The church should baptize people. Roman Catholics believe that every human being faces the same choice between good and evil as Adam and Eve faced. Also, they believe that humanity since Adam and Eve has been under a curse: "original sin." Even a person without committing acts of sin is corrupted from birth. Therefore, each person needs to be baptized.

Protestantism. Historically, rejection of the authority of the Pope as the sole mediator between God and the Christians has caused the redefinition of the nature of authority and the church. Protestants stress less value on the role of Sacraments, mediating role of Mary, and the intermediary role of priests or ministers than Roman Catholics. Protestants believe that people can approach God directly through Jesus Christ. They believe that they do not need any mediators as priests or clergy between them and God other than Jesus himself. Protestantism is an individualistic faith that, in its understanding and practicing of worshiping God, calls upon followers to come together in a pluralistic praying behavior within the church. The church is defined as "the community of Christian worshipers." For such a principle of belief, there is great diversity among Protestants. The essence of Protestantism in two basic principles contains the one eternal truth and the one universal salvation. The divinity in Jesus' consciousness founded the divine spiritual mission that was inspired in Jesus by God through infusion of the Holy Spirit.

Eastern Orthodoxy. Neither belief in God as Trinity, nor the dogma of Christ as divine and human in nature, nor the doctrine of humanity as created in the image of God are the main issues in Eastern Orthodoxy. The principal difference, at least as seen both by the Protestant reformers and by the Roman Catholic adversaries, lay in the area of religious authority. Followers of Eastern Orthodoxy believe in the Bible alone. Their faith resides in the Scriptures, the ancient creeds, the decrees of the seven ecumenical councils, and the tradition of the church. The chief dogmatic difference between Roman Catholicism and Eastern Orthodoxy thought is the question of procession of the Holy Spirit from the Father and from the Son.

Eastern Orthodoxy has identified itself more intimately with national cultures and with national regimes than has Roman Catholicism. The church in Eastern Orthodoxy has sometimes tended toward the extreme of becoming a mere instrument of national policy.

Econopolitical Impacts of Christianity on Global Business

Since one-third of the worldwide population is Christian, the faith and doctrine of Christianity play an important role in international trade. Both Roman Catholicism and Protestantism periodically modify their religious practices in line with changing norms of social behavior in wider society. They influence decision-making processes in businesses. Third world countries are sometimes ambivalent toward Christians because Catholics and

Christian priests, monks, and missionaries provide education, medicine, and shelter for needy people.

Recently, some Christian denominations are more involved in activism. One example is the concerted effort by the Catholic bishops in the United States to oppose abortion in family clinics; another example is opposing nuclear armament. In addition, since the Christian faith has been promoted dynamically in developed nations, it is viewed as an influential factor in the international econopolitical policy. For example, the Christmas season is known to the Western countries as a high season for retailers and the annual peak in sales. Also, church properties and business affairs play important roles in international relations and transactions. Religious holidays affect the production and transactions of businesses. Religious leaders play an important role in confrontations between church and businesses. For example, on June 18, 1997, the Southern Baptist Convention led a boycott of Disney and its subsidiaries. Delegates at the convention voted overwhelmingly for a boycott, saying the entertainment conglomerate promotes homosexuality, inappropriate sexuality, and antifamily themes (*The Salt Lake Tribune,* 1997).

Islam

Islam means "submission to the will of God," the almighty, who determines the cosmic fate. Islam is one of the five major monotheistic faiths. It was founded in Arabia by Mohammed between 610-632 C.E. Mohammed was born in 570 C.E. at Mecca. Moslems believe that Mohammed, at the age of forty, with a strong image of believing in one God, was appointed by God as the Moslem Messenger or Prophet. God inspired him through the angel Gabriel. Mohammed was honored because he was going to be the final in the line of prophets. Islam believes in all previous prophets. The prophets in line are Abraham, Noah, Moses, and Jesus; Mohammad is the last one. Gabriel conveyed the eternal Words of God as the Koran (the Islamic holy book) to Mohammed. In the first phase of prophecy, Mohammed taught Islam in a secret way, gained only a small following, and suffered persecution. He eventually, in the year 622 C.E., made a *Hijra* (immigration) from Mecca to Medina, which marks the beginning of Moslem calendars. In most Moslem-dominated countries, there are two calender systems in addition to the usage of the Christian calendar: (1) Hijra lunar calendar and (2) Hijra solar calendar. Both Islamic calenders begin in 622 C.E. The year 2000 of the Christian calendar is the year 1378 of the Hijra solar calendar of the Iranian Shiites and the year 1420 Hijra lunar calendar, the Arab calendar. All Moslem countries use the Hijra lunar calendar, except Iranian Shiite Moslems, who use the Hijra solar calender for national events. For Iranians, the beginning of spring, which is March 21, is observed as the New Year *(Now Rooz)*. And for Sunnis, the beginning of the year and months are in rotation. In Islamic countries, consideration of these calenders is very important because there are many religious holidays that corporations should observe—from paying salaries and wages to the closing of businesses on these days. Also, Fridays are consecrated days for praying in Moslem countries and most government and business activities are closed. Therefore, in Moslem countries there are four international working days: Mondays through Thursdays, because Saturdays and Sundays are holy days in the West and Fridays are sacred days in the East.

Islam succeeded in uniting a worldwide belief that has included all nationalities, races, colors, and cultures into a unified agreement that Mohammed is God's last prophet, but disagreements concerning the succession of the prophet caused two major divisions, creating the Sunnis and Shiites. Moslems number an estimated 20 percent of the world's population. Sunnis comprise 83 percent; Shiites comprise 16 percent; others equal 1 percent (*The World Almanac and Book of Facts,* 1999). There are seventy-two sects in both Sunnis and Shiites, such as Wahhabi, Hanbali, Hanafi, Shafeii, Rafeii, Sufi, Ismaili, and others. Islam is more an ecclesia than a denomination. It is technically inclusive, but it exhibits a number of sectarian movements.

Sunnis-Shiites Split

All Moslems agree on the prophesy of Mohammed, but friction arose from succession of the prophet. As Christianity has Protestants and Catholics; Buddhism has Theravada and Mahayana; Judaism has Orthodox and Reformists divisions, so Islam is divided between Sunnis and Shiites. This division is based on the principle of heredity relations or cultural discipleship. The Sunnis (from the word *tradition*) accept the first three successors, Ossman, Abubakr, and Ommar, to Mohammed. Shiites claim that the fourth successor is Mohammed's son-in-law, Ali, who is the rightful leader and the other three are usurpers. The Shiites have more formal religious philosophy and have given stronger allegiance to religious leaders who are called "Saints or *Imams*." Through sociocultural and psychological views, each Moslem needs to accept the faith through four paths of perceptions: (1) wisdom, (2) Koran, (3) people, and (4) tradition: *Hadith.* These are considered the primary sources of Moslem theology, law, and practice. In the Sunni sect, there is no clergy *(Molla),* but Shiites are very dominated by a group of theologists called *Ulama* or *Mollayan.* Shiite Moslems need to be individual religious leaders if they believe that they are intellectually to guide themselves or to choose and "imitate" the views of one of these *Mollas* and exactly follow social-religious behavior with their *Fatvas.* A *Fatva* means the final religious order that followers of a high rank *Molla,* who is called Ayatollah or Imam, to be carried out. Slater (1968: 137), as a religious scholar, wrote that: "Islam is both belief and legislation which organizes all the relationships of man."

Elements of the Islamic Faith (Iman)

The word *Moslem* means one who is accepting and submitting to the will of God (in Arabic, *Insha Allah*—God willing). Moslems do not like to be called Mohammedans, a term they resent because it implies that they worship the prophet Mohammed, not God. They respect Mohammed but they do not worship him because he was a human being.

There are three philosophical shared pillars of the faith among all Moslems—both Sunni and Shiites: (1) *Towhid,* (2) *Nabov-vat,* and (3) *Ghiama.*

Towhid means the oneness of God. There is no other god but the one Great and Almighty God. This is epitomized in the statement: *La Ilaha Ella Allah* (There are no other gods, except one God—*Allah*).

Nabov-vat means to accept all the monotheistic Messengers of God whose names appeared in the Koran (such as Ibrahim, Noah, Moses, and Messiah) with the same respect, and to confirm that Mohammed is the last messenger for the whole world and all time to come.

Ghiamat means believing in resurrection after death in doomsday. This day is called the day of reckoning or the last day. God by His will shall restore all humans and will determine their deeds. Good deeds will be rewarded at the Last Judgment in paradise with eternal blessing; those condemned for their evil deeds will be punished and sent to Hell—the eternal abode of fire and torture.

In addition to the above philosophical beliefs, Shiites believe in two more principles: *Aaddl* and *Emmamat.*

Aaddl means justice. Shiites trust in God's judgment and justness for creating the universe with His excellent justified wisdom.

Emmamat means believing in heredity successorship of the prophet Mohammed immediately through twelve Imams—starting with Ali, his sons, grandsons, and ending with the twelfth Imam *Mehdi.* Shiiates, like Christians believe the Messiah will appeare before doomsday. However, Moslems believe that Mehdi will appear instead of the Messiah.

Principles of the Islamic Theological Mandates

1. *Aghl:* Wisdom
2. *Jamaat:* Society's opinion
3. *Koran:* The Sacred Islamic Book
4. *Sonnat:* The Islamic Traditions
5. *Ghias*: The Best Comparison
6. *Estehsan:* The Best Practices

Principles of Best Pragmatic Religious Mandates

Pragmatic religious behavior in the Islamic faith mandates every Moslem should observe five duties: (1) *Salat,* (2) *Sawm,* (3) *Zakat,* (4) *Hajj,* (5) *Jihad.*

Salat means the daily ritual of praying five times within twenty four hours: before sunrise, at noon, during the afternoon, after sunset, and in the evening. Moslems need to wash their hands, faces, and feet before each time of prayer.

Sawm (or *saum*) means fasting during the month of Ramadan in order to suppress an individual's desires and passions. During these thirty days, Moslems from sunrise to sundown should not eat, drink, smoke, or have sex.

Zakat means to pay financial dues to poor people. Every Moslem has to pay 2.5 percent of their annual cash balance and other liquid assets, such as gold, silver, and bonds, to those needy people regardless of their religious faith or political beliefs—supporting orphans, widows, impoverished, and unemployed people.

Hajj means an obligatory pilgrimage to Mecca—"The House of God." Originally, Mecca was built by the Prophet Ibrahim. Each Moslem who is financially capable needs to make such a trip once in his or her lifetime in order to repent sinful behaviors and to promise to pursue pure goodness in daily life.

Jihad means to defend the Islamic faith. It is essentially a test of sincerity as a believer to the faith. *Jihad* is not viewed as a forceful and offensive behavior. It is a peaceful and spiritual defensive action. However, through a combination of religious-political ideology, it is changing its meaning and direction toward aggression and acts of terror.

The five pillars of Islam define the practical identity of Moslems. These pillars are related to Moslem spiritual faiths, beliefs, and practices which can bind humanity into a fellowship of shared ethical and moral virtues and sociocultural values and concerns.

Islam and Politics

Historically, Islamic faith spread very rapidly during the first two centuries largely through religious-political forces. For fourteen centuries, moral and ethical Islamic faith has integrated people from diverse nationalities, races, languages, regions, and cultural value systems. However, Islamic belief, faith, and practices do not match with political images of monolithic and homogeneous international cultures. In fact, like Christianity, Islamic political universalism is not a reality because each of the seventy-two Islamic sects perceives the Islamic political philosophy differently. Islam promotes brotherhood through the absence of racial discrimination. In India, for example, many converts were from lower castes who saw a way to sidestep the restrictions of the Hindu caste system (Terpstra and David, 1991: 90). In Arabia, many slaves were converted to Islam and became free. The ideal of Moslem brotherhood is not trivial. Malcolm X, the chief lieutenant of the separatist Black Muslim movement, revised his vision of social change after making a pilgrimage to Mecca. In Mecca, he was highly impressed by the harmony among Moslems of many races and colors (Malcolm X, 1973). In the United States, there are 5,167,000 Moslems. Black Muslims in the United States are estimated to number 1,400,000 (*Encyclopedia Britannica,* 1998). Through contemporary political literature, some experts overwhelmingly perceive the Islamic faith as antimodernization, anticapitalism, and antidemocracy. Some writers even try to replace the Islamic faith by threatening worldwide political terrorism and antagonistic beliefs. Hadar (1993: 27) states: "America must prepare for a new global threat—radical Islam . . . —is described as a cancer spreading around the globe, undermining the legitimacy of Western values and threatening the national security of the United States." Such a perception is shared by some Western scholars, who also hold misconceptions concerning religious faith and religious-political ideology.

The negative image of the Islamic faith in the West, specifically in Europe, is due in part to the lack of adequate information about that "exotic" and "strange" religion, but the negative image is also rooted deeply in history. Of all the world's religions, Christianity is the closest faith to Islam. Hostility toward the Islamic faith is not a recent result of theological differences; it is a historical counterreflection of the political and ideological expansionism of the Arabs and the Ottoman Turkish Empires in Europe. The negative image of Islamic political power is due to the historical movements in medieval Europe when, for seven centuries, Arab and Turkish governments conquered parts of Europe and threatened the rest of it.

Max Weber (1952: 178) has brilliantly indicated how politics may enter into direct competition with religion, particularly in the human war for "an unconditionally devoted and sacrificial community among the combats,"— a community of united races, ethnicities, languages, and cultures that is internationally perceived as a brotherhood. The Arab and Turkish Ottoman armies culturally carried the Islamic faith to Spain, Sicily, and some other parts of Eastern Europe. They crossed the Pyrenees and raided France as far as Nimes. The Ottoman armies twice stood at the gates of Vienna and nearly occupied it. All this caused European politics to attack the Islamic faith rather to attack the Arab and Turkish governments, because European countries are in need of mineral resources.

International Business and Islam

The month of Ramadan, with its daylight fasting, is noted for its negative impact on both productivity and consumption. For thirty days, Moslem employees need to fast from sunrise to sunset. These employees observe very long days. At the end of the day, they lose their energy and are not capable of working productively. In addition, Moslem employees observe many religious holidays.

Most Moslem countries annually export mineral resources, such as oil, copper, uranium, magnesium, and phosphates, and import industrial goods and machinery from non-Moslem countries. For example, twelve member nations out of thirteen total members of the Organization of Petroleum Exporting Countries (OPEC) are Moslem.

Since in the Islamic faith receiving and/or paying interest on a loan is viewed as a big sin, some Islamic bankers pay and receive interest as a commission (*The Wall Street Journal*, 1975a: 21). In Moslem countries such as Iran, if a lender files a lawsuit against a delinquent debtor, the Moslem court will award only the principle. Since non-Moslem believers should not have access to the sacred place of Mecca, businesspersons cannot travel to Mecca. Every year, around 2 million financially qualified Moslems, in a special day called "Ai'id Al Azzha," need to make a pilgrimage to Mecca. For international business transactions, this trip for individuals from all over the world will provide an opportunity to earn $50 billion for Saudi Arabia and other MNCs. For such a reason, bankers, airlines, hotels, restaurants, retail stores, and medical and health industries are benefitting from such a congregation. Another example indicates that a Swedish firm had the engineering responsibility of building a traffic system in the city of Mecca, but they could not have access to that city as nonbelievers. The solution was for the Swedish company to use closed-circuit television to supervise Moslem workers and their project (*The Wall Street Journal*, 1975b: 13).

Sikhism

Sikhism is a faith which has emerged from a combination of Hinduism and Islamic beliefs. The word *Sikh* is derived from Sanskrit *sisya,* meaning disciple. The Sikhs are viewed as disciples of ten gurus beginning with Guru Nanak (1469 C.E.) and ending with Gobind Singh (1708 C.E.). A *Sikh* is defined as one who believes in the ten gurus and the *Granth Sahib* (also known as the *Adi Granth*), a scripture compiled by the fifth guru, Arjun Dev, in 1604. There are 19 million Sikhs, most of whom live in India (*The World Almanac,* 1999).

Guru Nanak, the founder of Sikhism, was born in April 1469. A mystical experience at age twenty-nine was the turning point in Nanak's life. While he was bathing in a nearby stream, he disappeared and was presumed drowned. Sikhs believe that he was summoned by God. He was missing for three days and nights but reappeared on the fourth day, and then proclaimed himself to be a savior. The opening pronouncement of his mission was: "There is no Hindu, and there is no Moslem," because Sikhs could not understand Hindu and Moslem scriptures for inspiration. Since Sanskrit was for understanding Hinduism and Arabic for Islam, Sikhs turned instead to their motherland language to read the guru's hymns, which were couched in a language that they could understand. Then, many Hindus and Moslems became his disciples.

Principles of the Sikh Faith

Nanak accepted the most traditional beliefs of Hinduism pertaining to the origin of creation and its dissolution. Nanak accepted the principle of *samsara,* reincarnation (the belief that the soul, upon the death of the body, moves to another body or form): the birth, life, death, and rebirth cycle. Also, he accepted Islam's principle of faith that there is only one God. However, he indicated that God changed his own nature and functions after creation of the world, and the nature of God himself is the authority of duality and delusion.

According to the Sikh faith, there are three main functions that Sikhs must consider: One is *Kirtan,* which is the singing of hymns from guru *Granth Sahib.* Second is *Katha,* which is reading the *Granth Sahib* and explanations. The third main function, carried out at every Gurdwara, is the *Langar,* meaning a free community kitchen for all visitors of all religions.

There are six physical articles of Sikh faith:

1. *Kesh,* long unshorn hair—a symbol of hygiene and discipline
2. *Dastar,* turban—a symbol of royalty and dignity
3. *Kjangha,* comb—a symbol of hygiene and discipline to the matted unkept hair of ascetics
4. *Kara,* steel bracelet—a symbol to remind the wearer of restraint in their actions and remembering God at all times
5. *Kachha,* soldier's shorts—a symbol of control and chastity
6. *Kirpan,* ceremonial sword—a symbol of dignity and the Sikhs struggle against injustice

The Sikh faith rejects idol worship, so the guru Granth Sahib is not sacred as an idol, but rather emphasis is placed on respect of the scripture for the writing which appears within. It establishes moral and ethical rules for development of the soul, spiritual salvation, and unity with God (http://www.sikhs.org/granth.htm).

Bábi Faith

On May 23, 1844, in Shiraz, Iran, a young man known as Siyyid (a title referring in Iran to a person who claimed that he was a descendant of Mohammed of Islam) Ali Mohammed—the Báb—announced the imminent appearance of the Messenger of God. The title Báb in Arabic means "the Gate." The Báb declared his purpose was to appear to mankind for his advent. Báb spent long periods in "meditation and prayer" and the main proclaimed purpose of his mission was to prepare for the coming of the "Universal Manifestation of God."

The principle belief of Bábi faith is based upon the creation of an entirely new society, one that retained a large measure of cultural and religious elements as events could arouse powerful new motivation. Bábis believe in an elaborate system of laws for the conduct of public affairs; for the maintenance of peace and public order; for the direction of economic activities; for such social institutions as marriage, divorce, and inheritance; and for the relationship between the Bábi state and other nations. Prayers, meditations, moral precepts, and prophetic guidance were revealed for individual behavior. Their aim is to affect a break with believers' Moslem frame of reference and mobilize them for a unique role in human history (Effendi, 1891: 24).

The Báb's claim was based on an ideology to change the whole system of Iranian sociocultural and econopolitical infrastructure. His desire was to seize political power from the Shah. For such an ideological motive, the Báb and his followers as Bábis were arrested and then all were executed in the public square of the northern city of Tabriz, Iran. Still, after more than a century and half, there are some believers in this path of faith. Thus, Bábi faith has been an introduction to the next religion as Baha'i.

Baha'i Faith

The founder of Baha'i faith is Bahaullah (1817-1892). Bahaullah was born in Mazandaran, the Northern State of Iran. Then he moved to Shiraz, a southern city in Iran. He meditated for many years in a mosque (Iil-e-Khani) in Shiraz and followed the path of Ali Mohammed Bob. After inspiration by God, Bahaullah proclaimed to be the prophet of God in Shiraz, Iran. There are 7,666,000 Baha'is living around the world (Famighetti, 1999: 687).

Baha'is believe in one God. For Baha'is, evolutionary process is an essential feature of all the phenomena of life, including the revelation of God. Since Bábi's ideology was based on changing the religious-political infrastructure of a country like Iran, the Baha'is' religious ideology is based on a message that humanity is one single race and that the day has come for its unification in one centralized global society. They believe in breaking down traditional barriers of race, class, creed, and nation, and that the world will, in time, give birth to a universal civilization. The principle challenge facing the people of the earth is to accept the fact of their oneness and to assist the processes of unification. Thus, the main cause of the Baha'i faith is to establish a global centralized government. In order to accomplish the mission of the New World Order, Baha'is should work to surround leaders in high positions and especially target the key advisory positions in order to inspire them for a universal council.

A worldwide community of some seven million Baha'is, representative of most of the nations, races, and cultures on the earth, is working to give Bahaullah's teaching practical effect. Their experience will be a source of encouragement to all who share their vision of humanity as one global family and the earth as one homeland. Finally, Baha'is believe that since all religions, such as Judaism, Christianity, and Islam, are divinely inspired, therefore, Baha'i faith incorporates all religions into a unified faith, because

Baha'is believe that such a unification is an integral divine plan (*The Baha'i World:* <http:// www.bahai.org/bworld/main.cfm>).

SUMMARY

The reality of today's global free market economy is that multinational corporations must recognize religious differences among home and host countries. Religious faiths, along with cultural norms, create differences across national boundaries that influence how people interact with one another. Cultural beliefs and religious faiths about similar circumstances also vary from country to country. Where individualized worship attitude is central to the North American Protestant value structure, the need to be obedient to the church system dominates the value structure of their Latin American counterpart. Religious symbols and daily interpretation play important roles in the field of international business. Consequently, multicultural organizations must establish appropriate policies and procedures for interaction between home and host countries. Sometimes, because of religious sensitivity to some business trademarks, brand names, logos, and advertising messages, corporations need to modify their policies and strategic plans in order to be able to market their products in host countries. Compatibility or fit between the home and host business value systems and religious beliefs must be considered in order to be able to operate dynamically in international marketplaces.

CHAPTER QUESTIONS FOR DISCUSSION

1. What is a difference between monotheistic and nonmonotheistic religions?
2. Why has religious faith influenced international business transactions?
3. What are some of the disagreements over religious values between Roman Catholics and Protestants?
4. What are some of the differences in values between Moslem Shiites and Sunnis?
5. What are differences between literate and nonliterate religions?
6. What is the difference between Sikhism, Islam, and Hinduism?
7. How does a religion becomes politicized?
8. How many religious holidays occur for Christians, Jews, Moslems, Baha'is, and Zoroastrians?
9. How do religious holidays affect international business transactions?

10. What is the difference between a solar calendar year and a lunar calendar year? Which one is used in Arab countries?
11. What are the major religious pilgrimage trips to sacred places in the world among Christians, Moslems, Hindus, and Shintos?

LEARNING ABOUT YOURSELF EXERCISE #11

How Do You Believe or Not Believe in a Religion?

Following are twelve items for rating how important each one is to you and to your organization on a scale of 0 (not important) to 100 (very important). Write the number 0-100 on the line to the left of each item.

Not important		Somewhat important		Very important
0	25	50	75	100

As a believer or nonbeliever in a religious faith, it would be very important for me to:

_____ 1. Believe in a divine God.

_____ 2. Perceive religion as a source of prosperity in my life.

_____ 3. Believe in worship places like churches, mosques, or temples, which have their own personality.

_____ 4. Believe the efforts to deal with the human situation by religious faith is a waste of time and resources.

_____ 5. Tolerate other religious faiths because I consider them to be valuable to humanity.

_____ 6. Read a few pages of my religious book every week.

_____ 7. View religion as a human-made invention.

_____ 8. Separate my religious faith from my daily life.

_____ 9. Believe that there is an order and pattern of superpower in life which someday we will come to understand and feel very well.

_____ 10. Believe that there is no sinful behavior by human beings.

_____ 11. Believe that I should not act according to my religious doctrine in my daily social life.

_____ 12. Believe that free sex is a natural inclination in human beings and it is not related to religious regulation.

Turn to next page for scoring directions and key.

SCORING DIRECTIONS AND KEY FOR EXERCISE #11

Transfer the numbers for each of the twelve items to the appropriate column, then add up the three numbers in each column.

Religionist	Psychosocialist	Atheist
1. _____	3. _____	4. _____
2. _____	5. _____	10. _____
7. _____	7. _____	11. _____
9. _____	8. _____	12. _____
Your Totals _____	_____	_____
Total Scores 400	400	400

The higher the total in any dimension, the higher the importance you place on that set.

Make up a categorical scale of your findings on the basis of more weight for the values of each category.

For example:

1.   400 religionist
2.   100 psychosocialist
3.   000 atheist

Your Totals   500
Total Scores   1,200

After you have tabulated your scores, compare them with others on your team or in your class. You will find different judgmental patterns among people with diverse scores and preferred modes of self-realization.

CASE STUDY:
THE GERMAN PRIVATE BUSINESSMAN IN IRAN:
WHEN BUSINESS INTERMINGLES WITH RELIGION

A fifty-seven-year-old German businessman, Mr. Helmut Hofer, was first arrested at Tehran Airport in September 1997 and was charged with having illicit sexual relations with a twenty-six-year-old Iranian female medical school student identified as Miss Vahideh Qassemi. Under the Islamic tradition and law of the Islamic Republic of Iran, that Mr. Hofer is a Christian and Miss Qassemi is a Moslem prohibits such a sexual relationship. Therefore, through a trial in the Islamic court, he was found guilty and sentenced to death. After the Islamic Revolution in 1979 and the taking of American hostages in Iran, the new Iranian government faced financial difficulties in international trade. Consequently, American government froze all Iranian government assets in America (around $15 billion). Then the Iranian government established a close commercial link with European countries, specifically with England and Germany. Germany exported goods worth about $1.2 billion to Iran in 1999.

In the Islamic faith, any sexual affairs between a man and a woman outside of legal and/or religious marriage is considered a sinful action. In addition, through the Persian cultural value system, no man or woman should have sexual relationships outside of marriage, because it can cause serious social and familial consequences for both parties.

In Moslem countries, marriages between a Moslem man and a non-Moslem woman is permitted. The woman needs not be converted to the Moslem faith. It is very common for a Moslem husband to attend his Mosque, and for a non-Moslem wife to attend her church, temple, or synagogue. However, it is Moslem tradition and law that children must be oriented to the father's religious faith. Conversely, marriage between a non-Moslem man and a Moslem woman is prohibited. The non-Moslem man needs to be converted to the Moslem faith before marriage. In addition, any sexual contact for both genders before marriage is viewed as unethical, immoral, and illegal within Islamic tradition and Islamic law.

In Iranian culture, females possess very high social and value statutes among family members. They are highly protected by males. Iranian male family members are very sensitive to the sexual relationships of their female family members with males before marriage. Caring and protection for female family members by family males is viewed as a religious, moral, and ethical duty. Iranian family members view female integrity and dignity as the most important and valuable spiritual family pride for their families. The female family members' social and cultural statutes are viewed as a pluralistic shared pride with males.

Source: Dinmore, G. (2000). "Hope of End to Boycott As Iran Frees German." *Financial Times,* January 21, p. 7.

Mr. Hofer appealed on the grounds that he had converted to Islam during an earlier marriage to a Turkish Moslem woman in Turkey and should receive a lesser sentence, but he was again sentenced to death in a retrial. Finally, on January 19, 2000, the case was dropped for lack of evidence, but Mr. Hofer was in and out of jail, facing new charges that resulted in retrial in the Islamic Revolutionary Court, where he was found guilty of insulting a prison warden. This time the charge became a political one.

Mr. Hofer had been a political pawn between the German and Iranian legal systems. Diplomats believed that the arrest was directly linked with the trial in Germany in 1997 of five men accused of assassinating four Iranian dissidents in a Berlin restaurant in 1992. Berlin judges found Kazem Darabi, an Iranian who worked as a grocer in Berlin, and Abbas Rhayel, a Lebanese man, guilty of murder and sentenced them to life in prison. Two of the other men were given prison sentences and one was acquitted (CNN, 1997).

On January 19, 2000, a Tehran court freed Mr. Hofer a day after the Berlin court handed down an eighteen-month suspended jail sentence to Hamid Khorsand, an Iranian, after finding him guilty of spying on exiled Iranian dissidents in Germany on behalf of Iranian secret services between 1995 and 1999.

The trial ended for Mr. Hofer with the payment of 20 million rials (Iranian currency), equivalent to $2,300, as a fine which was imposed for allegedly insulting a prison guard, although that charge was denied. Finally, Mr. Hofer flew back to Germany.

Chapter 12

Expatriate and Repatriate Employees: Multicultural Training Programs

The issue of multicultural training philosophy is pertinent to the real understanding of who grasps what the valuable cultural essence means, if not internalizes what orientation means.

CHAPTER OBJECTIVES

After studying this chapter, you should be able to:

- realize what the major conception of multicultural training programs are,
- understand the general means and ends to an expatriate training program,
- understand the various theoretical and practical foundations of international behavioral adaptability, adjustment, and integration in host countries,
- understand the psychosocial effect of religious cultural travelers,
- describe the nature of individual learning potential in multicultural training programs,
- analyze managerial styles on the basis of sociocultural, psychological, and behavioral orientation programs for an expatriate employee,
- discuss how managers should cope with the home and host countries' cultural values, beliefs, expectations, and traditions, and
- understand the efficacy of multicultural training theories.

INTRODUCTION

Today's global free market economy has created a competitive environment among multinational corporations (MNCs). Also, the intensive competitive trade transaction has caused the requirements for promoting socio-economic growth in all nations. Multicultural synergistic growth not only establishes new room for a concentric effort around multilateral understanding, but also results in more attentive emphasis on effective training programs. Any effective multicultural training program needs to enhance all dimensions of human life. It is clear that the function of preparing, training, and mentoring employees for foreign assignments is critical. Also, it is expected that the trainees should grasp the core concepts and the essence of multicultural value systems. Specifically, the importance of the training program is related to what a trainee does who really understands the multicultural value systems, and what a trainee does not do when he or she does not understand.

Within the international environments, expatriates can not only find that predeparture cross-cultural training programs are very effective, but also that they can successfully interact with people from various cultures and can effectively live and work in foreign countries. However, there are some international firms that do not believe in cross-cultural training programs in the home country. Much of the rationale for this lack of multicultural training orientation is an assumption that expatriates will gain practical experience in the host cultures during their assignments in foreign countries. In addition, some multinational corporate managers believe that managerial headquarter policies and procedures can guide expatriates in overseas assignments. Although multicultural awareness has proven to be an effective tool in the field of international business, less than one-third of expatriates are given such training orientations (Mendenhall and Oddou, 1986: 73-79). In U.S. firms, expatriate failure rates (i.e., managers who either request or are requested to return early) seem to range from 16 to 40 percent (Baker and Ivancevich, 1971; Copeland and Griggs, 1985) and cost $50,000 to $200,000 per early return (Copeland and Griggs, 1985; Harris, 1979; Misa and Fabricators, 1979). Even among those 60 to 84 percent of expatriates that do not return early, approximately half are considered ineffective by their firms (Seward, 1975). Because the costs of maintaining a manager in an overseas position averages $300,000 per year (O'Boyle, 1989), the costs for ineffective expatriates may well be higher than the costs of "failed" expatriates. Recent studies show that, in spite of the fact that MNCs devote a great deal of time and resources to orienting candidates to undertake foreign management assignments, 30 to 50 percent of all expatriate placements do not work out as anticipated (Fatehi, 1996: 312). In addition, recent studies show that MNCs underestimate the importance of multicultural training programs and evaluation of managers assigned abroad (Tung, 1984).

A vital issue for a multinational corporation's success in implementing its global strategy is linked to its expatriate multiticultural behavioral adjustment. One survey of 440 executives in European firms concluded that a shortage of very well-trained international managers was the most important constraint on expansion abroad ("Expansion Abroad," 1986).

The objective of this chapter is to describe and explain the psychosocial behavioral issues for exposure of expatriate employees, including managers, to novel and unfamiliar environments. It describes the theories that have been proposed to account for the effects of contacts with new cultures and lists actual consequences which have been revealed by systematic research experiences. In this section, the potentially stressful effects of exposure to unfamiliar cultures is discussed. The final section will describe some of the means of coping with cultural training theories. Furthermore, in the last section in this chapter, the techniques and procedures that have been employed to prepare expatriates and repatriates for their adjustment to the host countries and readjustment to their home country are explained.

CULTURE SHOCK

Culture shock is a psychosocial selective perception of an expatriate's reaction to an unpredictable, novel, odd, and unfamiliar situation in an environment. For example, many American and European expatriates do not eat dog and cat meat. Most restaurants in China serve dog and cat meat; in Korea dog and snake meat is served; in France, they serve frog legs; in North and South America, they serve pork; and in Saudi Arabia, camel meat is a regular staple. Expatriates who are not aware of these facts, when dining in the area for the first time, will find different tastes. If they ask and find out later what they actually ate, they then react to such a dietary habit. Such a reaction is called culture shock.

Much of the theoretical foundation for cross-cultural adjustment research is based on Oberg's work on culture shock. Essentially, researchers found that when people first enter a host culture, they are not sure what behavior is acceptable. They will discover that many behaviors which were acceptable in their home country are not acceptable in the host country and that behaviors which were offensive in their home culture are allowed in the host culture. Consequently, many symptoms of culture shock can be found, in part, due to the lack of a comprehensive predeparture training program. Therefore, factors that tend to reduce uncertainty of what to do and when to do it—or what not to do and when not to do it—in the host country generally facilitate adjustment (see Figure 12.1).

Today, it is becoming more and more frequent, particularly for MNCs, to assign employees to different geographical locations. Indeed, some service-oriented MNCs have an active program for regular movement and transferral jobs in the international markets. There are a number of dimensions and factors that should be considered during the transfer of employees from one location to another. Furnham and Bochner (1986: 150) identify these factors as distance, country, job, social support, time, returns, and volunteering. These factors are important for preparation, adjustment, adaptation, and repatriation of employees. These experiences in different countries vary. For instance, short-term assignments of employees for the first time to

FIGURE 12.1. The Expatriate and Repatriate Transitional Processes of Travelers

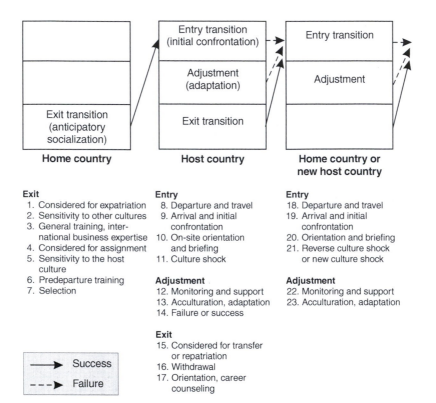

Source: Asheghian, P. and Ebrahimi, B. (1990). *International Business.* New York: HarperCollins, p. 470.

developing countries are likely to cause different culture shock than long-term assignments to developed countries. For all types of an international firm's employees, the first-time assignment is associated with dramatic culture shock.

As described by Oberg (1960), culture shock usually progresses through four stages:

1. *Honeymoon:* When positive attitude, expectations, excitement, and tourism feelings prevail (several weeks).
2. *Irritation and hostility:* When cultural differences result in problems at work, at home, and in daily life, expatriates and family members feel homesick and disoriented, lashing out at everyone (few months).

3. *Gradual adjustment:* A period of recovery in which an expatriate gradually becomes able to understand and predict patterns of behavior, use language, and deal with daily activities; family starts to accept their new lives (few years).
4. *Biculturalism:* The expatriate and family members grow to accept and appreciate local people and their cultural value systems and they will be able to function effectively in two cultures (lifetime).

The management of departure from the home country is largely related to the quality of preparation the expatriate has received. The entry transition of an employee to the host country depends largely on the company's orientation processes of logistics, monitoring, and supporting systems. The reentry of repatriates to their home or to another country in which the reverse culture shock happens depends on reacculturalization of expatriates and their family members (Feldman, 1981).

The management of expatriation and repatriation is as vital as the management of training. Unfortunately, many international companies minimize the potential effects of reverse culture shock. In fact, the evidence for supporting this crucial claim is based on a survey done by the American Society of Personnel Administration International (ASPAI). ASPAI revealed that only 31 percent had formal repatriation programs for executives and only 35 percent of those included spouses. In addition, only 22 percent of those had conducted the programs prior to the executive's departure for the assignment (Harvey, 1989).

MULTICULTURAL CONTACTS

In addition to the international business transactions and economic integrations among neighboring countries (e.g., NAFTA, EU, and ASEAN), there are a number of diplomatic interrelations and sociocultural exchange programs among nations. Given the magnitude of such global operations, the need for a multicultural effective training program for expatriates and repatriates is high. Asheghian and Ebrahimi (1990) identify the expatriate and repatriate transitional processes of travelers (see Table 12.1).

MULTICULTURAL UNDERSTANDING AND COMPREHENSION

Probably the first and foremost intellectual abilities and skills in the field of international business are those that involve understanding and comprehending the environmental cultural characteristics of both home and host countries. When expatriates are confronted with strangers, they are ex-

TABLE 12.1. Stages of Life Cycle of Expatriates

Stage	Perceptual Impression	Emotional Range	Rational Understanding	Behavioral End Results
Pre-Departure	Excitement and anxiety	Eagerness for experiencing novel things and meeting other people	Anxiousness for having good time	Experiential trial and error expectations
Contact	Feeling of alienation	Loneliness and homesickness	Judgmental analysis for reasoning of differences	Liking or disliking is manifesting
Adjustment	Familiarity with other cultural value systems	Stressful and eustressful pressures	Expressive behavior	Self-assertion Self-esteem
Assessment	Opportunities: Familiarity with the host country's culture	Continuing to stay and achieve objectives	Staying and challenging life	Attachment to the environment of the host country
	Threat: Disappointment from the host country	Anxious to leave the host country as soon as possible	Leaving and rebuilding life in the home country	Detachment from the host country, packing and leaving
Integration	Assimilated relaxation	Sensing the confidence	Linguistic and social familiarity	Assurance to survive and continue a normal life
Separation	Differences are recognized	Mixed feelings: happiness and sadness Anger and frustration	Assurance of controlling self-destiny	Taking good and bad memories to the home country
Repatriation	Readjustment: Differences and similarities are recognized	Full range of emotional and sensational adjustment is emerging	Renewal of creative job opportunities and appreciative novel values for a better lifestyle are promising	Sociopsychological and cultural differences are valued and reviewing sweet memories is enjoyable

pected to know what is being communicated, with whom they are communicating, and how to be able to make some use of psychometrical skills to grasp the real meanings and derivative objectives of the content of communication. In cross-cultural contacts, this task may be oriented toward the detection of the counterpart's business strategies and/or to persuade the other party to agree on certain principles for signing a contract, protocol, or agreement.

Although the terms *cross-cultural understanding* and *comprehension* have been frequently associated with behavioral contacts, here they are used in a somewhat broader manner, in that they are related to a greater variety of training skills in the forms of verbal, nonverbal, written, and symbolic observations and interpretation of communicated phenomena. The term *understanding* is an individual grasping clearly the cognitive meanings and attributes of a phenomenon or a concept and accepting them as facts. The term *comprehension* means the holistic sum of all those meanings and attributes (rational, sensible, emotional, ethical, and moral) which make up the directional content of a given general conception by all people. In another sense, the terms *understanding* and *comprehending* are somewhat more limited than usual because understanding is not made synonymous with holistic comprehension or even with the fullest grasp of symbolic observations and interpretation of meanings.

Since cross-cultural understanding is used to include those comparative observable objectives and manifested behavioral responses and reactions of home and host cultural value systems to certain phenomena or materials, comprehension is associated with the translation of symbols in coding, decoding, evaluating, analyzing, extrapolating, and interpolating the holistic philosophical and pragmatic meanings of observable, sensible, and imaginable causes, processes, and effects of cultural value systems. For instance, we "commonly" expect to understand the dynamic reasoning of actions, reactions, and frictions of material powers in physics or the harmonic rhythmic sounds of different instruments in a musical work played by an orchestra. Of course, we speak of understanding the above phenomena when they are presented in a verbal, pictorial, or symbolic form either on paper or in a pragmatic illustration. However, commonly we may not comprehend the natural power or inspirational causality of these phenomena. Reaching to such a comprehension, an individual needs to go through in-depth training. A cross-cultural training program is a plan that can facilitate understanding of the structural training guidelines for both home and host countries. In addition, a cross-cultural training program provides opportunities for home and host countries to establish a very in-depth comprehension of critical thinking for understanding the reasoning for the way in which cultural beliefs are valued.

Four types of cross-cultural understanding and comprehensive behavior are considered here: (1) translation, (2) interpretation, (3) extrapolation, and (4) interpolation.

Translation

Translation means that an individual can put coded symbolic cultural values and their attributed meanings into their mother language and then decode them into other languages, into other terms, or into another form of communication. There are two types of translations: (1) understanding translations, and (2) comprehensive translation. In the field of international business, comprehensive translations play very important roles for both home and host countries because agreements need to be comprehended equitably by all parties.

Understanding translation behavior occupies a dynamic transitional position between the intended classified behaviors under the category of culturally valuable meanings and the types of behavioral expected beliefs described under the headings of conversion of the exact objectives and coded meanings. Therefore, an understandable translator first needs to be very familiar with home cultural value systems in order to be able to translate those values into his or her mind and then to express them through his or her mother tongue. Second, an understandable translator needs to be familiar with equivalent meanings and usages of the host country's words, phrases, terms, and semantic familiarity with the relationship between the host country's language and culture.

Comprehension translation behavior is concerned with the conversion of either home or host cultural philosophical values, beliefs, and attitudes into another language and culture. It is necessary for a cross-cultural translator to possess the requisite or relevant knowledge in the domain of the subject matter. This indicates that the translator needs to know the general and even an aggregated form of transformed relevant ideas into concrete terms and symbols—either briefer or even more abstract—in order to facilitate communication.

Both understandable and comprehensive translations could be done through the following forms:

Technical Phraseology. To convert either home or host country value systems into concrete technical phraseology of another language.

Abstract Phraseology. To translate the lengthy part of a communication (either home or host) into briefer or more abstract terms of another language.

Illustrative Phraseology. To translate technical, abstract, and briefer pieces of communication into general principles by giving illustrative samples.

Symbolic Phraseology. To translate comparative relationships expressed into symbolic forms, including illustrations, tables, diagrams, graphs, directions, formulas, and ingredients of a product, into a written form or vice versa. Specifically, this type of translation is very crucial in labeling products for foreign markets.

Visual or Spatial Phraseology. To illustrate and convert the symbolic visual and spatial geometric shapes of an image into meaningful symbols of another popular culture. For example, in advertising the nude bodies of Adam and Eve, European cultural art follows realistic style and does not cover the sexual organs of Adam and Eve. But translation of the European art by a Middle Eastern illustrator uses an impressionistic style by covering the sexual organs of Adam and Eve with leaves; or, in the medical text books, the illustrator translates the sexual organs through another form by illustrating the internal organs, such as nerves, veins, and muscles, instead of the surface organs. Such an illustrative translation is based on the popular moral, ethical, and cultural value systems of either religious faiths of the home or host countries.

Metaphoric and Ironic Phraseology. To translate nonliteral statements (metaphor, irony, exaggeration) into another ordinary language. For example, "Kiss and Ride," or "Park and Ride" is a popular cultural sign around the metropolitan areas of major cities in America. Since in the Japanese culture, there is no word for kissing and it is assumed to be a filthy habit, the translation of such a message needs to be modified into Japanese culture by another type of phraseology for the purpose of advertising in Japan.

Interpretation

Cross-cultural interpretation involves dealing with the configuration of cultural value systems whose comprehension may require a reordering of the preferred modes of expected values into a new configuration in the minds of individuals. Evidence of interrelative behavior may be found in summarizations and generalizations produced by interpreter. Interpretation differs from analysis and evaluation. In the process of analysis, an analyst emphasizes the structural forms, the organization of parameters, the effectiveness of each segment over others, and the logic of the data. In the process of evaluation, an evaluator compares factual data with the explicit principles and criteria in order to find discrepancies or gaps. The interpreter should understand not only the meanings and applications of words and phrases, but also the various representational formulas. Interpreters must go beyond the part by part, point by pont, component by component, and finally the whole with a manner of comprehension beyond the formatted topic. The person in question needs to reorder, or to rearrange all parts and components in the mind to imagine and grasp the total views and applicable meanings of the object. They need to interrelate characteristics of the objects with ideas, beliefs, and faith. The essential behavior in interpretation is to facilitate abstract generalizations from specific meanings, reorganizing the essential and differential concepts from the lower priorities, and grasping a nice sense of meaning in judgment. Interpretation can be done through the following forms:

1. To interpret a cultural value system as a whole at any desired level of generalization of facts and ideas
2. To understand, comprehend, and interpret observable behavior with increasing depth and clarity of meanings and symbols

3. To distinguish any warranted or unwarranted contradictions, which drown the observable and hidden agendas. For example, when you hear these words: "Yes," "Oh yes," and "Oh Yes!?" you get three types of interpretations:

A. For "Yes," you are confirming the opinion or idea of the other party.

B. For "Oh yes," it means "Me too." You are agreeing with the opinion or idea of the other party.

C. For "Oh yes!?" with an exclamation and question, you are denying the opinion or idea of the other party.

For example, interpretation of the preferred valuable lifestyle between an Occidental religious leader and an Oriental monk in relation to attachment to material things is completely different. A Catholic priest, a Jewish rabbi, and a Moslem clergy (Ayatollah) put emphasis on possession of material things along with spiritual beliefs, while a Tibetan Buddhist monk lives in poverty and values detachment from possession of material things. By stating another example in the field of manufacturing, quality of products is perceived differently culture by culture. American industrialists follow total quality control (TQC), while Japanese manufacturers use total quality circle control (TQCC).

Extrapolation

Extrapolation means to make "estimates," or "predictions" based on the unbiased understanding of sociocultural and econopolitical tendencies of an individual concerning the future events of the host country. Accurate extrapolation requires the extension of trends or tendencies given beyond cultural reasoning. Extrapolation is a deductive task which can be used as an inference in judgment. It must have a degree of frequent probability with certain viable assurance of accuracy. It is related to past, present, and future conditions and situations. It may also involve making reference with respect to causal societal implications, consequences, and conditions of host country events. Extrapolation may involve judgments without application of given cultural criteria or procedural guidelines. Extrapolation can be deduced through the following forms:

1. An explicit statement drawn from the immediate inference of a cultural behavior

2. An accurate inference and tenable hypothesis for drawing an effective conclusion concerning a future behavioral prediction

3. An explicit judgment in predicting continuation of sociocultural and econopolitical trends

4. An ability to differentiate value judgments from prediction of consequences

Interpolation

Interpolation is regarded as a type of judgment with respect to the cultural intervals within a sequential classification and arrangement of procedures and criteria. Interpolation, as here defined, is to be distinguished from extrapolation. While extrapolation is concerned with estimation of external quantitative variables beyond their established ranges, interpolation is concerned with estimation of the internal forces and their values within the domain of assessment of an established range of variables.

Cross-cultural training programs need to orient trainees with the probability and certainty of possible predictions of cultural events in host countries. Expatriates need to understand and comprehend the cultural trends in order to accurately predict marketing decisions.

SOJOURNERS

A *sojourn* is defined as a temporary stay at a new place other than either the birthplace, workplace, and/or permanent residence. A *sojourner* is a person who lives in a new and unfamiliar environment. Sojourners are also persons who travel to different places for different purposes. Before explaining problems and issues of multicultural contacts, it is appropriate to identify different forms and types of sojourners who travel abroad for multiple purposes. It is necessary to group sojourners into twelve major categories, such as professional experts (medical doctors, professors, and researchers), businesspeople, diplomats, military advisors, students and scholars, expatriate managers, missionaries and voluntary workers, tourists, religious pilgrims, patients seeking treatment abroad, and seasonal workers and their family members. It is obviously important how these people can adjust their behavior to the host countries' cultures.

There are wide individual differences in how much and how quickly sojourners can adapt themselves to new environments, which may vary from country to country or culture to culture. There is very little research from this area. However, recently some research projects have been undertaken from a variety of academic perspectives, such as psychology, sociology, management, and international business. These research studies reveal that some problems and issues are related to language deficiency, dietary orientation, assimilation hardship, accommodation difficulties, racial discrimination, sexual orientation, career choice restrictions, financial stress, misunderstanding and mistrust, dependancy on alcohol, drugs, and gambling, loneliness, terrorism, robbery, fears of possible assassination or being shot, hostage taking, gun threat during carjacking, rape, and riots. In addition to these issues, there are other socioecological problems such as climate adjustment, dress codes, religious practices, family affairs, courtship and marriage, adequate housing and education for children, availability of adequate health and medical services, availability of alternative transportation systems, and rigidity in taxation systems which affect the behaviors of sojourners.

MULTINATIONAL CORPORATE EMPLOYEE PROFILES

An international firm that operates in several host countries has essentially three types of employees. These are parent company national employees (PCNEs: citizens or residents of the home countries in which the headquarters are located or they are working), host country national employees (HCNEs: citizens and residents of the host countries who are working for a foreign company), and third country national employees (TCNEs: citizens or residents of neither the home nor the host countries who are working for a foreign firm). The choice among these three types of employees is not entirely about the firm's preferences because most host countries regulate the number and the type of foreigners who are allowed to work locally.

Parent Company National Employees (PCNEs)

Multinational corporate employees who are working in a host country are commonly categorized as locals and expatriates. Multinational corporations, sometimes because of the lack of host countries' local experts and managers, must decide to send some of their employees as expatriates to host countries for different purposes. Expatriates are either home-country nationals (citizens of the home countries in which the firm's headquarters are located) or third-country nationals. There are seven major groups of employees who are identified as expatriates:

1. Managers
2. Technical experts
3. Surveyors and researchers
4. Negotiators and lawyers
5. Monitoring and auditing experts
6. Antiterrorism and security personnel
7. Translators

Selection of the above expatriates depends on attitudes of the headquarters' managers toward the importance of the firm's mission in the host countries.

Expatriate Managers

MNCs could be involved in four different international business activities such as joint venturing partnerships with the host countries, business alliances in research and development, operating through independent business subsidiaries in the host countries, and managerial and consulting contracts for the host countries. In all of these three international business activities, MNCs may choose their expatriate managers to fill managerial positions in foreign operations. A comparative study by Rochelle Kopp concerning incidence of international personnel problems among Japanese, European, and American firms, which was reported in 1994, found that Japanese firms seem to experience various behavioral problems, such as high turnover of local employees, more than European and American firms, as shown in Table 12.2.

This research project indicates that many expatriate managers have not been very well trained for working in the above countries.

Expatriate Technical Experts

For expatriate technical experts, such as engineers, technicians, craftspeople, designers, analysts, and programmers, who are assigned to a foreign country for the establishment of industrial facilities, basic sociocultural skills are crucial. Usually, expatriate technical experts are assigned to the "turnkey" projects. "Turnkey" projects involve construction of a facility such as military or commercial airport, factory, hospital, seaport, military base, underground metro, or dam in the host country. MNCs assign their technical experts to build such facilities and commence them for operations. MNCs that perform turnkey operations frequently deploy their heavy industrial equipment to the host countries, which need technical experts to operate them. *Size* is the project's magnitude as reflected in the volume of the engineering design and number of the project's tools, techniques, and operations to be used for transforming inputs into outputs. These technical experts need to be very well trained not only in their professional fields, but also they need to be oriented to the sociocultural and political conditions of the host country.

Expatriate Surveyors and Researchers

International investment and manufacturing operations need to be managed scientifically by international financial analysts, marketing researchers, tax assessors, and insurance adjusters. Surveys on consumer behavior in host countries should be conducted scientifically by experts in order to get the precise opinion results of customer profiles and consumer behavioral tastes. In addition, in most occasions, MNCs sign agreements for constructing large factories, plants, highways, and so on. Before and after signing the

TABLE 12.2. Incidence of International Personnel Problems

Type of Problems	Percentage of Japanese Firms Reporting Problems (n=34)	Percentage of European Firms Reporting Problems (n=23)	Percentage of U.S. Firms Reporting Problems (n=24)
Expatriate-related:			
Lack of home-country personnel who have sufficient international management skills	68%(60%)	39%	29%
Lack of home-country personnel who want to work abroad	26%(27%)	26%	13%
Expatriates experience reentry difficulties (e.g., career disruption) when returning to the home country	24%(20)	39%	42%
Average of expatriate-related problems	39%(36%)	35%	28%
Local national staff-related:			
Difficulty in attracting high-caliber local nationals to work for the firm	44%(53%)	26%	21%
High turnover of local employees	32%(20%)	9%	4%
Friction and poor communication between home-country expatriates and local employees	32%(47%)	9%	13%
Complaints by local employees that they are not able to advance in the company	21%(20%)	4%	8%
Local legal challenges to the company's personnel policies	0%(0%)	0%	8%
Average of local national staff-related problems	26%(28%)	10%	11%

Source: Kopp, R. (1994). "International Human Resource Policies and Practices in Japanese, European, and United States Multinationals." *Human Resource Management, 33*(4), Winter 1994, pp. 581-599.

contract they need to conduct feasibility studies in order to assess the bids and reassess the renewal of contracts. Bids include pricing for materials, component parts and machineries, construction costs, equipments, software and hardware, insurance, logistics, and overhead profit. Therefore, expatriate surveyors, analysts, adjustors, and researchers need to be very well trained to consider all phases of demographic, technical, economic, social, and ecological characteristics of the host country's projects.

Expatriate Negotiators and Lawyers

Increasingly, international business companies are faced with major issues to decide to initiate, carry on, or terminate their operations in host countries. Negotiations are implicit aspects of the managerial decision-making process in such instances. A company that is involved in direct investments, exporting goods and services, importing raw materials, or managing foreign corporations needs to negotiate carefully all terms of agreement with the host countries. The bargaining and concession power and process of negotiation, the range of provisions, and the terms of renegotiation are the major skills that expatriate negotiators and lawyers need (see Table 12.3).

In addition to the above transactions, sometimes MNCs must negotiate with their partners in terms of licensing, joint venturing, franchising, prices, quantities, payment terms, delivery times, maintenance, services beyond sale, and so on.

Cultural and legal orientation of negotiators often influences the smooth strategic negotiation processes. Negotiators need to know psychological profiles of partners and their strategies. *Negotiation* is a sociocultural process whereby two or more parties try to reach a mutually agreeable arrangement to make a deal. Globalization of the market economy has increased the frequency of multilateral negotiations, given that negotiations involve communicative exchanges between parties' desires and demands to reach a mutual agreement. All negotiations share six common elements:

1. The parties involved possess different strengths and weaknesses.
2. The parties involved desire to achieve their own objectives through a mutual concession.
3. The parties involved are in some way interrelated and interdependent on one another.
4. The parties involved are in conflict over their interests.
5. The parties involved are motivated and capable of influencing and persuading one another.
6. The parties involved believe they can reach an agreement to serve their personal objectives.

Graham (1981) suggests four stages in the negotiation process:

1. Non-task sounding
2. Task-related exchange of information
3. Persuasion
4. Concession and agreements

There are other aspects, such as the legal content and the formats of protocols, contracts, agreements, duration, sequence, termination, and renewal issues. These issues can differ from culture to culture and/or country to country. Expatriate negotiators need to be well trained before they depart

TABLE 12.3. Negotiation Training Styles from Multicultural Perspectives

Japanese	North American	Latin American
Emotional sensitivities are highly valued	Emotional sensitivities are not valued	Emotional sensitivities are valued
Hiding of emotions	Dealing straightforwardly or impersonally	Emotionally passionate
Subtle power plays; conciliation	Litigation; not as much conciliation; weakness	Great power plays; use of weaknesses
Loyalty to employer; employer takes care of employees	Lack of communication with employer; breaking ties by either employee or employer if necessary	Loyalty to employers (who are often family members)
Group decision making by consensus	Teamwork provides input to decision maker	Decisions come down from one individual
Face saving is crucial; decisions often are made on basis of saving someone from embarrassment	Decisions are made on a cost-benefit basis; face saving does not always matter	Face-saving is crucial in decision making to preserve honor and dignity
Decision makers are openly influenced	Decision makers are influenced by special interests but often this is not considered ethical	Execution of special interests of decision maker is expected and condoned
Not argumentative; quiet when right	Argumentative when right or wrong; impersonal	Argumentative when right or wrong; passionate
What is down in writing must be accurate and valid	Great importance given to documentation as evidential proof	Impatient with documentation, seen as obstacle to understand general principles
Step-by-step approach to decision making	Methodically organized decision making	Impulsive, spontaneous decision making
Good of group is the ultimate aim	Ultimate aim is profit motive or good of the individual	What is good for group is good for the individual
Cultivation of good emotion	Decision making is impersonal; avoidance	Personalism is necessary for good decision making
Social setting of decision making	Involvements, conflict of interest	Getting to know decision makers

Source: Adapted from Pierre Casse (1982). *Training for the Multicultural Managers: A Practical and Cross-Cultural Approach to the Management of People.* Washington, DC: Society for International Education, Training, and Research (SIETAR International).

from their home countries. Also, they need to be mentored and guided during their assignments in foreign countries.

Expatriate Monitoring, Inspecting, and Auditing Experts

Many multinational expatriates are working in foreign countries to monitor journals, technical conferences, distance learning, professional training programs, patent-office publications, databases, licensing, franchising, auditing, and consulting. In addition, there are some international projects funded by the United Nations. Subcontractors of MNCs assign experts to work on behalf of them in various countries. For example, in the 1990s, the UN hired some MNCs to forward their monitoring, inspecting, and auditing team experts to Iraq in order to review and to assess Iraq's atomic, biological, and biochemical mass destruction capabilities and weapons. These experts needed to be trained with the technological capabilities, legal systems, and sociopolitical values of home and host countries.

Expatriate Antiterrorism and Security Personnel

Dealing with terrorism is problematic for MNCs. The safety of expatriate employees and security of the property of an international firm depend on the degree of risk faced by the firm. These issues are related to home and host country characteristics, such as the types of governments, levels of economic development, stability of political systems, and religious sensitivities. Wars and revolutions and/or the prevalence of local and international terrorism increase personnel and property risks as well as business risks. In recent years, unexpected international acts of terrorism have been especially worrisome to both domestic and international firms. They may occur anywhere at home or in host countries, or on the ground, sea, or air at any time. For example, in the bombing of Pan Am flight 103 over Scotland by suspected Libyan terrorists, the passengers and crew lost their lives because of terrorist acts. In the summer of 1990, the Irish Republican Army targeted the heart of the British financial establishment by planting bombs in trash cans. On February 26, 1993, the World Trade Center in Manhattan, New York, was blasted by terrorists on the B2 level. It killed six civilians and injured 1,000 people.

MNCs annually spend a lot of money training their expatriate employees how to behave and cope with terrorist events and acts. In 1979, Ross Perot, the CEO of the Electronic Data System Corporation (EDS), organized a dramatic commando rescue of two EDS employees who were taken hostage in Iran after that country's revolution. He spent $2 million for such a rescue mission.

Although any act of terrorism increases the risk for some international companies, it is also true that some international companies benefit from them. For example, before the 1970s, security at international airports and on airplanes in the sky and on the ground was not a serious issue. In 1970, terrorists began hijacking commercial airplanes. Since the beginning of highjacking airplanes in the air, electronics companies have enjoyed a very booming businesses for installing metal detectors and electronic gates in airports around the world. Today, there are many antiterrorism companies that serve MNCs either as consulting firms, antiterrorism trainers, or providing MNCs with highly sophisticated computerized information systems to prevent and/or cope with terrorist actions.

Expatriate Translators

Translation plays a key role in all aspects of international transactions. Accuracy is of utmost importance in international business communication. An international corporation can be hurt by one inaccurate translation. A good translator can eliminate many of the communication problems between home and host countries. Translators need to be well trained in professional familiarity with the second language and to understand its nuances, colloquialism, slangs, and idioms. Expatriate translators need to be well trained in using appropriate words, sentences, phrases, and legal terms. Translators need to have access to home and host country libraries, experts in various appropriate fields of economics, law, medicine, and scientific languages.

Host-Country National Employees (HCNEs)

In-service training and staff development provided by international corporations for their HCNEs can result in more productivity. HCNEs need to be trained in how to perform their assigned tasks in the host countries. Specifically, HCNEs need to be oriented to the firm's policies and procedures. They need to have language proficiency in order to be able to read and implement the blueprint plans of the firms' strategies. The international firms need to elevate new-hire literacy and numeracy of their HCNEs. In most cases, international corporations need to furnish basic education in reading, mathematics, writing, and English as a second language (Wiggenhorn, 1990: 71-83). The aging of the workforce means that more training is necessary for HCNEs in order to better fit the needs of older workers (Sterns and Deverspike, 1989). The social interaction of expatriates with HCNEs will be positively related to both facet of adjustment and adaptability to the host culture. In addition, social support from HCNEs can reduce uncertainty among spouses and family members of expatriates. Building a network with HCNEs at work by expatriates is quite often popular for several reasons:

1. HCNEs understand their culture very well. They will be helpful in orienting expatriates with the host culture by providing appropriate information and explanations of the host culture.
2. HCNEs can provide feedback on appropriateness of expatriate behaviors in order to reduce tension and uncertainty within the firm's environment.

Third-Country National Employees (TCNEs)

The multicultural characteristics of a multinational corporation provide a truly global image to gain an impressive international experience. Due to the specific market locations and circumstances, many MNCs need to hire third-country nationals in order to deal with multiracial, multiethnic, and multireligious customers. TCNEs need to be highly trained in order to be assigned to all subsidiaries very easily. For example, a TCNE is a citizen of India working for IBM in South Africa. Many international tourist agencies and telecommunication companies operating in Israel and Saudi Arabia hire TCNEs in order to provide appropriate services for Christian, Moslem, and Jewish pilgrims during the Christmas season in Bethlehem and *Hajj* in Mecca. TCNEs need to be trilingual in order to deal with home, host, and fellow country people for the benefit of all.

Multicultural Training Processes

The most common type of multicultural orientation program takes the form of providing prospective expatriates with information about the new cultures. Expatriates can be provided with all sorts of information either in written form or in lectures or films, about the host country. Predeparture training programs are differentiated according to how long and vigorous they are. They range from very short on a quick foreign assignment for several days or for a long period of time such as several years. Black and Mendenhall have divided training programs into eight basic "scenarios." These categories are presented in the Table 12.4.

TABLE 12.4. Black and Mendenhall's Eight Training Scenarios

Scenario	Rigor	Duration	Techniques	Content
A	High	60-180 hours	Lecture, factual briefing, books, culture assimilator, role-plays, cases, field experiences, simulations	Equal emphasis on job and culture—job demands, constraints, choices, country economics, history, religion
B	Moderate	20-60 hours	Lecture, books, culture assimilator, cases	Equal emphasis on job and culture
C	Moderate	20-60 hours	Lecture, film, books, cases, role-plays, simulations	Emphasis on job demands, constraints, choices; less emphasis on culture
D	Low-Moderate	20-40 hours	Lecture, factual briefing, cases	Strong job emphasis with very little on culture
E	Moderate	40-80 hours	Lecture, film, books, cases, culture assimilator, role-plays, simulations	Little emphasis on job; much emphasis on culture, country economics, politics, history, religion
F	Low-Moderate	20-60 hours	Lecture, films, books, cases	Little emphasis on job; more on culture
G	Low-Moderate	30-60 hours	Lecture, films, books, cases, role-plays	Little emphasis on job; more on culture
H	Low	4-8 hours	Lecture, film, books	Little treatment of either culture or job

Source: Black, J. S. and Mendenhall, M. (1989). "A Practical but Theory-Based Framework for Selecting Cross-Cultural Training Methods." *Human Resources Management, 28*(4).

In the selection of the type of training programs, several factors should be considered. These are personalities, life experiences, cultural backgrounds, gender characteristics, assigned jobs, marriage/family lifestyles, friendships, standard of living, business strategy, language proficiency, novelty of the new job, novelty of the host country's culture, duration of job assignment, and frequent visits back to the home country (see Table 12.5).

TABLE 12.5. Nonverbal and Body-Style Communication

1. Expanding and shrinking facial gestures: smiles, frown, and lip movements; kissing (mouth, cheek, forehead, chest, hand, and foot)

2. Licking as greetings: the tip of the nose and cheeks

3. Eye contacts: gazing directly, blinking with one eye, closing and opening two eyes. Arabs look each other in the eye when they are talking with an intensity that makes some people uncomfortable

4. Horizontal and vertical head movements (head shaking and head nodding up and down for yes and no)

5. Hand and arm gestures: hand shaking with one or both hands, pressing the thumb in hand shaking (as a sign of brotherhood in Freemasonry belief), finger pointing, poking, putting hands in the pants pockets and playing with coins, crossing arms on the chest and bowing, clapping hands, pointing one or two thumbs up or down, pointing the reversed third finger up or down, making a circle with thumb and forefinger for either illustrating "zero" or "worthless" to French, "money" to Japanese, "male homosexual" in Malta and Iran, and a general sexual insult in Sardina and Greece

6. Postures: specific bending or contorting the body in various ways in public performance, exposing the chest hairs for males and breasts and thighs for females, putting hands together and bowing, putting one hand on the chest and bowing, gentle head and body maneuvering to attract attention of others, and swaying of the hips

7. Body contact (touching): patting (head, arms, shoulder, and low back); punching (face, shoulder, and chest); pinching (cheek and bottom); stroking (hair, face, upper body, knee); shaking (head and hands); embracing (shoulder, body); contacting with the whole body, or hands, arms, legs

8. Olfaction: scents or smells such as perfume

9. Hairstyles: hiding one eye and part of the face by hair, hair tied back, pony tail, parted, braided, curled, straightened, permed, spiked, shaved head, hair pieces, wigs, toupees

10. Facial hair: mustaches, beards, goatees, sideburns, plucked eyebrows, waxing facial hair, curling eyelashes, shaving facial hair

11. Cosmetics: lipsticks, blushes, foundations, powders, creams, eye shadows, eyeliners, lipliners, and *bindi* (Hindu's red sign between eyebrows)

12. Sitting postures: crossing legs, open legs, unzipped pants, very tight dressing

13. Silence: showing shyness by looking down, communicating with body language

14. Clothing: dressing codes and uniforms, hot pants, short shorts, daisy dukes shorts, tank tops, long and short sleeve shirts, halter tops, miniskirts, and long skirts and dresses

15. Head coverings: hats, caps, bandanas, handkerchiefs, scarfs, veils

16. Head to toes coverings: cloak (*Chador* for the Islamic female dressing code)

17. Artifacts: jewelry, lapel pins, fly wisks, etc.

The W-Shape Curve Processes of Training

International employees from the time of expatriation to the time of repatriation go through a series of phases in transferring from one location to another. This process has been described as a W-shape curve (Gullahorn and Gullahorn, 1963). In the initial phase, at the top of the curve, expatriates (PCNEs and TCNEs) are excited to go to the foreign assignments. Business expatriates, like other sojourners, often have a luxury lifestyle. Usually they fly in first class, live in very luxurious hotels, dine in very fancy restaurants, and ride in chauffeured vehicles. As shown in Figure 12.2, MNCs recruit potential expatriates either from the parent nationals or from third national countries. Then companies choose whether to select the candidates and the recruit chooses whether to accept the foreign assignment offers.

Generally, multicultural behavioral foreign assignment processes include eleven stages. Within the career U- or W-curve, companies can provide adequate information and training for expatriates in how to deal with the host country cultures. These stages are: (1) PCNEs and TCNEs recruitments, (2) home country professional training, (3) predeparture training, (4) foreign country assignment, (5) in-host country briefing and mentoring, (6) adjustment, (7) assessment, (8) adaptation, (9) integration or separation, (10) debriefing, and (11) repatriation training or returning.

Predeparture Training Programs

Multicultural training programs denote several broad areas such as ecological briefing, cultural sensitivity training, critical incidents and cases,

FIGURE 12.2. The Expatriate Behavioral Career U or W Curve

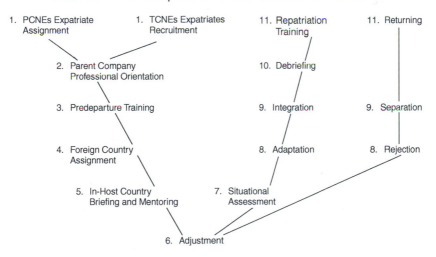

family adaptability, and hardship tolerance. In predeparture training programs, the first effort is to train expatriates with predeparture orientation. Some of the cross-cultural training models emphasize sociocultural issues and others concentrate on legal and economic orientations. These models can be scaled down for many objectives within a variety of targeting groups. Regardless of the expatriate's mission, there are three sets of informational profiles that trainees should be familiar with:

1. The home country's predeparture procedural information
2. Informational procedures for usage between the home and the host countries transitional period
3. The host country's arrival procedures

Trainees need to be provided with sufficient information in regard to where the host country is located geographically. In what part of the host country are the plants or subsidiaries operating? What are the company's market share and product positions in the host country? What are the home country rules and regulations in regard to which countries the expatriate can travel? In some occasions, because of political and safety problems, expatriates need to be informed how to get special permits to visit restricted countries from the state department and other agencies of their home country for foreign assignments. Expatriates need to be informed how to acquire a visa from the host country's embassy (in what city or country) for arriving into and working in that country. What types of visas and/or working permits are required to be acquired before departure? What types of medical tests are necessary and within what time frame before departure should the tests be done? Who will perform the tests? The appropriate certificate to be issued by what authorized medical examiner? Expatriates and their family members need to know about required types of clothing, health protection information, and hygiene. In regard to the health and vaccination processes, what types of vaccines are required to be administered before departure? For third-country national employees, what are the visa requirements for re-entry permits to both home and host countries? What are the ecological conditions of the host country? Which language/dialect is popular in the host country that expatriates need to learn? Which international business language is most popular in the host country? For example, beside the home countries language in Morocco, Tunisia, and Algeria (which is Arabic), their international business language is French. In Germany, France, and Spain, the international language is English.

Several principles should be applied in predeparture training programs, such as familiarity with the general vocabulary of the host country for meeting the daily objectives of life—for successful shopping, gaining alternative transportation, using medical and heath clinics, hospitals, nursing homes, nurseries, day care centers, and schools. In addition, expatriates need to be informed about the types of currencies, such as cash, coins (for emergency phone calls, vending machines, and transportation permits), credit cards, phone cards, traveler's checks, and bank drafts, as well as what amount of money should be carried or be ordered. They need to know how to transport their family cars, household goods, and furniture with home and host customs and procedures. Expatriates need to know how and when they should sell or rent their apartments or homes and how to arrange to pay mortgage install-ments, association fees, taxes, insurance premiums, or to be released from the present lease of their apartments or homes before or after their departures. Ex-patriates need to know how to deposit their precious belongings in safe de-posit boxes, considering the costs and insurance premiums both at home and host countries. Expatriate family members should be provide with sufficient information by the firm concerning the translated documents for the continu-ing education of their children in the host countries. The company needs to acquire information from expatriates before their departures as to which fam-ily member or friends in the home country should be contacted in the event of emergency situations, sickness, or death of the expatriates.

Language Efficiency

Language efficiency is a critical factor for expatriates. It is very complex and deals with deep-rooted behavior. Both content and skills that will im-prove interactions with host-country individuals will reduce misunder-standings and inappropriate lingual behaviors, including oral, written, body, sign, and symbolic languages. There is a close link between language and behavioral cultural orientation. It is impossible to understand a host's cul-ture without using its language. Equally, it is difficult to understand and learn a language outside of the context of a host culture. However, some ho-mogeneously cultural oriented host countries share the same culture and/or religion but speak different languages, and some host countries speak the same language but have different cultural value systems. Nevertheless, lan-guage influences cultures and cultures influence languages. For such a vari-ety of reasons, principles of multicultural training programs are the same, but their applications vary on the bases of both home and host countries lin-guistic and cultural characteristics.

Expatriates should know that the meaning of touch can vary from one culture to another. For example, a number of studies have suggested that Mediterranean cultures, Arabs, Jews, Hispanics, and Eastern Europeans are high-touch cultures, whereas the English, German, Northern European, Japanese, Chinese, and Korean cultures are low-touch cultures (Montagu, 1972; Sheflen, 1972; Mehrabian, 1981).

In-Host Country Briefing and Mentoring

Once an expatriate employee has arrived in the host country, there is usu-ally a short "honeymoon" phase before adjustment. The honeymoon phase usually occurs within the first few weeks to two months after arrival, and it is characterized by fascination with all the "new" and "interesting" aspects of the host culture and people (Adler, 1986). This fascination occurs because expatriates and family members have not yet had to cope seriously with the day-to-day life issues. MNCs need to provide on-site briefing and mentoring programs for expatriates. Mentoring is a behavioral relationship in which a person with greater knowledge and experience guides another to be familiar with personal and professional excellence.

A mentor is a wise and trusted teacher, counselor, and coach who provides instruction in direct judgment or conduct. Expatriates, during the early stage of in-country contacts, need to be coached. A mentor is a guide, a friend, a listener, a coach, and a truly responsive person. A mentor is not a savior or a therapist. International firms usually provide some training programs during the first few months of the expatriate's arrival in the host countries. A mentoring program will maximize adjustment of expatriates to the host country's cultural value systems through learning of the following seven guidelines:

1. Maximize similar value systems between home and host countries' value systems.
2. Provide much experience with the task being taught to the expatriates for the early orientation and adjustment.
3. Provide a variety of life behavioral skills for adaptation to the new environment.
4. Identify important features of the beliefs, values, expectations, and traditions in the host culture.
5. Make sure certain behavioral trends and ideas are rewarded or avoided.
6. Design training content so trainees can see applicability of these lessons in their day-to-day life.
7. Specifically, expatriate single women face greater barriers in their foreign assignments. Women must ask other expatriates to help them.

Adjustment to the Host Culture

The third phase of an expatriate's behavioral life in a host country is the phase of adjustment. In the predeparture orientation, trainees become familiar with certain procedural information concerning leaving the home country. In the second phase, expatriates become familiar with the early arrival in the host country. In the third phase, expatriates will be familiar with actual behavioral experiences. It is an adaptative phase to the host country's culture and climate. In this stage, expatriates will learn gradually what is important and crucial in order to survive in that country. They learn about the host country's behavioral pattern of serious promises. Expatriates learn about idiosyncratic or biased behaviors of their host people.

Usually expatriates find two general groups of cultures: homogeneous and heterogeneous. There are very few culturally homogeneous nations in the world today. North American countries (United States and Canada) and Western European countries (England, France, Germany, Italy, and Scandinavian countries), the Middle East (Saudi Arabia, Jordan, Iraq, Syria, and Oman), the Near Eastern cultures (Iran, Turkey, and Greece) and Asian countries (China, Vietnam, Japan, and Korea) are becoming culturally pluralistic, either through religious faith, customs, traditions, languages, or historically valuable similarities. Adaptability in homogeneous countries is easier than in heterogeneous ones. For example, expatriates may learn when "could be" means "maybe," when it means "possibly yes," and "could not be." The formal generic "Yes!", "Ok!", or "As you wish, I will do it!" sometimes means "No." In these situations, parties are involved in serious discussions that at the end can satisfy only one party. The other party says "Yes," but does not mean it and do it.

Expatriates experience their day-to-day lives through trial and error. For example, when shopping in a bargain market, if they cut the price into half, expatiates think that they got a very good deal. However, when they next find a similar product or sometimes one of higher quality cheaper, then they become very frustrated and blame the host nationals. The end result creates suspicion in their minds about the host people. This stage teaches them to get along with people through daily experiences not with trust but with careful consideration.

Another stressful symptom among expatriates' spouses and children starts with complaining about the new lifestyle. They feel that they have been left out by the host country. Then expatriates find themselves in between two different stressful environments, the family and the workplace. At home, they feel lonely and unhappy; at work, they feel that people treat them like strangers. The way to resolve this situation is simple: carefully assess the situation and find or create solutions one by one and step by step with patience, or rush to resign, pack, and go back home. They say that life should not be spent suffering, so finding a solution not to live that way is critical.

Host Country's Situational Assessment

Situational assessments begin with thinking about the conditional life fitness with psychosocial symptoms and economic gains of the workplace in host countries. Situational assessment does not occur quickly, nor is the result based on a single event. It is the result of many months (usually three to six months) of understanding the real situation. Successful expatriates recognize many problems and solutions. But unsuccessful expatriates face unresolved problems, and they do not want to have to make any concession. In so doing, frustration, disappointment, and fear on one hand and tolerance, patience, and prudence on the other hand confuse expatriates: stay or leave? In assessing the host country's situational factors, sometimes expatriates blame others for their frustrations—host nationals, company, or spouse (Adler, 1986: 196). In such situations, expatriates face three "Fs:" to "fight" with hardship and unpleasant conditions and to stay, to "flow" with both good and bad conditions and search for golden opportunities and then to leave, or to "flee" from the host country regardless of the employment consequences. Robert Kohls (1979: 65) fairly identified some of the challenging systems for expatriates as shown in Table 12.6.

Adaptation to the Host Culture

Although, there is undoubtedly a great deal of friction between the expatriates and the host country's cultural value systems, some expatriates prefer to stay and continue their mission. They rely on patience, creativity in finding solutions, and persistence to complete their assignments. Ricks (1983: 59) identifies that an effective expatriate must possess certain abilities and traits for adaption to foreign cultures. Among the most important characteristics are shown in Table 12.7.

Adaptation of expatriates to host cultures depends directly on multicultural sensitization training programs. Such a program does not only familiarize expatriates with information about the host cultural sensitivities, but at the same time expatriates will also be familiar with cultural awareness about biased, discrimination, prejudice, and stereotyping behaviors of both home and host countries. Expatriates learn how to accept the differences be-

TABLE 12.6. Expatriates' Challenging Kit

- Homesickness
- Boredom
- Withdrawal
- Need for excessive amount of sleep
- Compulsive eating
- Compulsive drinking
- Irritability
- Exaggerated cleanliness
- Marital stress
- Family tension and conflict
- Chauvinistic excesses
- Stereotyping of host nationals
- Hostility toward host nationals
- Loss of ability to work effectively
- Unexplainable fits of weeping
- Physical ailments (psychosomatic illness)

Source: Kohls, R. (1979). *Survival Kit for Overseas Living.* Chicago: Intercultural Press, p. 65.

TABLE 12.7. Adaptability of Expatriates to the Host Culture

1. An ability to get along well with people
2. An awareness of cultural differences
3. Openmindedness
4. Tolerance of foreign cultures
5. Adaptability to new cultures, ideas, and challenges
6. An ability to adjust quickly to new conditions
7. An interest in facts, not blind assumptions
8. Previous business experience
9. Previous experience with foreign cultures
10. An ability to learn foreign languages

Source: Ricks, D. A. (1983). *Big Business Blunders.* Homewood, IL: Dow Hones-Irwin, p. 59.

tween home and the host countries as fact. Cultural sensitization training adaptation is a comparative study looking at various values, beliefs, and behaviors from the perspective of each society. It develops a sensitivity to and awareness of cultural relativity in the sense that some cultural value systems are universal, and some values are individualized. This type of training program develops at two levels:

1. To achieve self-awareness and appreciation about the home country's value systems and to gain insight into one's own personal traits, attitudes, prejudices, biases, and interests
2. To realize similarities and shared values among home and host cultures regardless of prejudice, bias, and stereotyping behavior

Integration to the Host Culture

The basic idea of cultural integration is that behavioral changes may occur in an individual's personality. More precisely, the idea of integration is that individuals expose themselves to the host culture and transplant the host cultural value systems into their own daily behavior. Transplantation of the host cultural value system into an individual's personality can happen through two assimilative styles.

First, expatriates, particularly during long-term social contacts with another culture, can be absorbed to such an extent that they forget their original cultural value system and expected behaviors. Such a personality change occurs when expatriates find that the second culture has a higher status and is more meaningful to their own beliefs. Individuals then adapt themselves into the new culture. For example, in both European and American cultures, visits with relatives and friends are usually arranged in advance by appointment during regular day or evening hours. In Near, Middle, and Far Eastern countries, visiting relatives and friends without notice during the day, evening, and late night is a sign of affection and indicates a warm relationship. Punnett and Ricks (1992: 393) state that an expatriate manager from America was working in the South Pacific. He had hired local natives without regard to the traditional cultural status system of the islanders. He had inadvertantly hired too many of one group, which threatened to change the balance of economic power and social traditions of the islanders. The islanders discussed this unacceptable situation and independently came up with an alternative plan, but it had taken them until 3 a.m. to do so. Since time was not important in their culture, they saw no reason to wait until morning to make their suggestions known to the expatriate manager. They casually went to his place of residence; their arrival at such a late hour caused the expatriate manager to panic. Since he could not understand their language and traditions, and could not imagine that they would want to talk business at 3 a.m., he assumed that they were coming to riot—or worse, so he called the Marines! It was some time before the company was able to get back to "business as usual."

Second, some people possess the ability to synthesize both home and host cultural behaviors. These individuals adapt the second cultural value systems into their behavior as long as they are living in that culture. These individuals manifest two types of behaviors: the personal level, which is relevant to their original culture while they are in contact with their family and friends; and they acquire genuine bicultural or multicultural personalities while they are associated with the foreign culture. Many expatriates work in the host countries for very long periods of time and enjoy their lives. This system of integration could be called "Coca-Cola-ization" to American culture. For example, kissing is considered a universal affectionate and loving habit among Westerners and Easterners. However, some cultures, such as New Zealand (Maoris), the Australian aborigines, the Papuans, Tahitians, and other South Sea Islanders, as well as the Esquimau of the frozen north, were ignorant of kissing until they were taught the technique by the white man. The Chinese have been wont to consider kissing as vulgar and all too suggestive of cannibalism. To the Japanese, kissing is not at all natural; it is a deplorable habit, unnatural, and unhygienic. The Japanese have no word for kissing in their vocabulary (Pike, 1967: 11-12).

Separation from the Host Country or from the Company

Expatriates usually face two major types of life events in host countries: personal and organizational. Personal life events may be positive if they include better opportunities for employment in other international or domestic firms. These opportunities can cause expatriates to quit their jobs and return to their home country. Personal life events could be negative if they are threatened or have unpleasant experiences that motivate expatriates to leave their jobs. Also, negative life events in the host country can cause expatriates to leave earlier than planned. The more personal negative life events or organizational negative operations that exist in terms of intensity, the more likely expatriates appear to quit their jobs. The acts and decisions of expatriates often involve a number of important life events. The primary reason for the expatriates' failure are:

1. Unprofessional recruitment processes and selection of the wrong people for the job.
2. The lack of comprehensive predeparture training programs.
3. Inability to adjust properly to the new environment and new culture.
4. Sending people on foreign assignments who professionally are not suitable or ready to go to foreign countries.
5. The cultural toughness of the foreign environment; toughness is measured by the qualitative valuable distance and dissimilarity of the home and host cultures. The larger the cultural distance, the more difficult the adaptation process.

In Table 12.8, you will find two major categories of life events for expatriates who quit their jobs abroad and return to their home countries.

Repatriation to the Home Country

Repatriation is the transitional process of an expatriate who leaves the host country either to go to the location of the parent company headquarters or, return to the home country. It involves a mixed perception about the home culture and its changing characteristics. Return to the home country causes a readjustment. Most repatriates expect to restart their normal lives without experiencing culture shock. However, some repatriates find themselves in between home and host countries' cultures. They feel neither the home environment that they left is the same nor the host environment they were experiencing was wonderful. The fact is indicative that while repatriates experience changes in their behavior and perception, their companies, peers, and even laypeople at home experience changes too. Sometimes repatriates describe their reentry as being more difficult than the initial departure and entry into the host country. Sometimes they feel the same pattern of reentry culture shock in the home country. These repatriates need professional guidance for readjustment.

Although the starting point of the multicultural training program focuses on the cultural orientation of host countries, the ultimate point is to return to the home country and develop a general understanding of multiculturalism. When the expatriates return home, somehow they find themselves as strangers. This is particularly true when they have been away from their home

TABLE 12.8. Personal and Organizational Negative Life Events That Prompt Expatriates to Quit Their Jobs

Personal Negative Life Events*	Organizational Negative Life Events**
1. Death of spouse or children	1. Foreign government contracts may be terminated
2. Marital separation	
3. Foreign criminal convictions and jail terms	2. Foreign suppliers, creditors, and customers may be lost
4. Personal illnesses and injuries including natural causes or by host country member riots	3. Foreign contracts may be lost
	4. Foreign operations may be inefficient
5. Quit the job; resignation, to be fired, retired, and work injuries	5. Foreign employees may feel alienated (resulting in labor problems)
6. Pregnancy	6. The company's international reputation may be damaged
7. Self, spouse(s), and children's severe illnesses	7. The manager's self-esteem will be damaged; this can result in poor performance as well as stress-induced illnesses once back home
8. Change in social adjustment	
9. Ecological allergies such as climate, weather, health, cold, blood pressure, high altitude, humidity, and direct exposure to sunshine	8. Other potential expatriates and their families may be less willing to undertake foreign assignments
10. Nervousness and disturbance of sleeping patterns	9. Severe sociopolitical repression, frustration, and restrictions
11. Change in eating habits	10. War and revolution
12. Trouble with boss	11. Terrorism and political instability
13. Homesickness	
14. Boredom	
15. Feel unsafe and insecure	
16. Isolation	

Sources: *Adapted from Holmes, T. H. and Rahe, R. H. (1967). "The Social Readjustment Rating Scale." *Journal of Psychosomatic Research.* Vol. 11, p. 216. **Adapted from Punnett, B. J. and Ricks, D. A. (1992). *International Business.* Boston: PWS-Kent Publishing Company, p. 392.

countries for a very long period of time. Repatriation training and readjustment are as important as the expatriate training programs. Repatriation training programs include adaptability to and acceptance of those changes that have taken place during the expatriates' absence. The most important concern for repatriates are professional and socioeconomic readjustment to the home environment. They need to reestablish their lives with higher costs and inflationary rates of pricing systems. They will face the reality that there are no more incentives or fringe benefits. There are some economic hardships in reestablishing credit lines and procuring loans. Sometimes they need to restart their jobs from the entry level and go through extensive professional and technological training programs.

CROSS-CULTURAL TRAINING THEORIES

In cross-cultural training programs, some teaching and learning theories are similar from one culture to another; in other cases they are different. No one way exists to teach and learn things, no universal applicability of teaching and learning theories exists, and similarities and difference among teaching and learning theories exist around the world. Learning is a complex function in an individual's brain. Although several theories about learning endeavor to conceive of major functions of learning in different arrangements, the following principles appear to represent something of a hierarchical order of the different individual principles. These eight major principles are:

1. Knowledge
2. Understanding
3. Comprehension
4. Application
5. Analysis
6. Synthesis
7. Evaluation
8. Experience

Implicit in most strategic training approaches, establishing multicultural training programs can help MNCs operate successfully abroad. Surprisingly, the use of cross-cultural training (CCT) by MNCs is very limited (Harrison, 1992; Mendenhall, Dunbar, and Oddou, 1987; Mendenhall and Oddou, 1985; Ronen and Tung, 1981). Moreover, very little research on the effectiveness of cross-cultural and collaborative-teaching training theories has been conducted.

Ronen (1989) suggest specific techniques, including a field experience called the host-family surrogate, in which MNCs pay for placing an expatriate family with a host family as part of an immersion and familiarization program (see Table 12.9).

There is a classical debate in cross-cultural training program effectiveness: Which theory of teaching-learning is more effective—cognitivistic, pragmatistic, behavioristic, humanistic, or holistic? Although no study has attempted a multicomparative review of the above theories, two reviews have examined cultural cognitivistic assimilative type of training programs and their effectiveness (Fiedler, Mitchell, and Triandis, 1971; Mitchell et al., 1972). As Bennett (1986) indicates, cognitive assimilative approaches have dominated the field of cross-cultural training programs, with the most frequently used training methods (excluding language training) being area studies programs. The theoretical framework of this program is based on environmental briefing and acculturalization of trainees through presentation of information about a particular host country (McCaffery, 1986). On the

TABLE 12.9. Training Techniques

Methods	Techniques	Purposes
Didactic informational training	Lectures	Geographic area studies of the company
	Reading materials	Company operations
	Videotapes	Parent-country headquarters
	Movies	Host country's cultural behavior
Intercultural experiential workshops	Cultural assimilation	Culture general specific negotiation skills
	Simulations	Role-playing for reducing bias, discrimination, stereotype, and ethnocentrism
Sensitivity training	Communication workshops	Self-awareness, communication styles
	T group	Empathy and listening skills
	Outward bound trips	Nonjudgmentalism
Field experience	Meeting with repatriates	Customs, values, beliefs, host-family surrogates, nonverbal behavior, religion
Language skills	Classes	Interpersonal communication
	Cassettes	Job requirements, survival necessities

Source: Adapted from Ronen, S. (1989). "Training the International Assignee." In Goldstein, I. (Ed.), *Training and Career Development.* San Francisco: Jossey-Bass, p. 438.

other hand, as McCaffery (1986) indicates, experiential approaches, which are called pragmatistic, provided opportunities for trainees to engage in specific situational conditions, such as reviewing behaviors critically, abstracting some useful insight from the analysis, and applying the end results within a particular cross-cultural context. Pragmatistic cross-cultural training theories provide additional insight for trainees' enculturation within a specific host culture through application of different learning methods such as films, skill practices, field trip experiences, and role-playing simulations. Mendenhall, Dunbar, and Oddou (1987: 333) indicate: "Surprisingly, these two approaches are generally used separately rather than in combination." Albert (1983: 186) argues about the effectiveness of the above theories on the behavior of trainees, stating: "To function effectively in a new culture, however, individuals need both substantial knowledge and understanding of the other culture and the ability to demonstrate appropriate behaviors." Recently, Harrison (1992: 952) conducted comparative research on the combination of behavioral and cognitive cultural assimilative approaches; he concluded that neither approach examined other approaches, nor did they offer an evolutionary theoretical framework in a cross-cultural training program. Therefore, researchers and experts in the area of cross-cultural training programs advocated (1) combined cognitive assimilative and experiential, and (2) combined cognitive assimilative and behavioral training programs. Unfortunately, none of the above researchers made an effort to probe the effects of the fourth approach—humanistic.

In order to delineate the efficacy of multicultural training programs, another dimension of reviewing the issues, such as learning theories, was performed across a variety of disciplines in the social sciences and humanities—particularly cultural philosophy—through multiculturalization. These theories can provide insight into individuality, which can improve a better conceptual and practical understanding for trainees. Some known theories include:

1. *The Whole Brain Theories (WBTs).* The WBTs generally rest on a presumed preference for one of the two hemispheres of the brain. In most individuals, verbal thought is conducted primarily in the left hemisphere and spatial thought in the right. The right brain is considered the seat of creativity and emotion and the left brain is the seat of logic and reason. Regardless of cultural orientation, all human beings must use both modes of thinking, perceiving, judging, and applying—but most complex problems of any sort require input from both hemispheres (Sperry, 1986).

2. *The Neurolinguistic Programming Theories (NPTs).* The NPTs indicate that people have a variety of preferred modes of learning and communication. When they try to remember, they access the cultural values within their brains, which have been stored through visual, auditory, oratory, and kinesthetic cultural orientations in their lifetime. For example, people who are visually oriented tend to reveal themselves by using expressions like: "I see," "It looks good," and "I get the picture." Auditory learners may say: "I hear you," or "That doesn't ring a bell."

3. *The Seven Intelligences (SIs).* The SIs indicate individual conceptual abilities for a variety of preferred learning methods. This theory was brought up by Howard Gardner (1983). He frames the conceptual potential of the mind through application of the following abilities in learning and perceiving: sequential-linear, verbal, kinesthetic, visual-spatial, musical, interpersonal, and intrapersonal.

4. *Experiential Learning Theories (ELTs).* The ELTs identify four stages of learning which, in turn, require four learning abilities such as: concrete experience, reflective observation, abstract conceptualization, and active experimentation. Application of these experiential theories

is very popular in both industry and military training programs. There are three major experimental techniques: "training aids," "training devices," and "simulators." A training aid is a piece of equipment generally used by an instructor to illustrate the working relationships with some kind of hardware or device. For example, surveillance bugs are used in the secret detection of communication. Training devices are pieces of equipment that trainees use in similar situations in their home countries. Simulators are complex training devices that try to capture many significant features of the operational environment with as much fidelity as possible in order to minimize the degree of transfer from the training situation to the foreign job assignments (Branson, 1977: 372-373).

Cognivistic Theory

Contemporary cognitive teaching-learning theory generally views learning as a cognitive process. Cognition is used to include intellectual activities such as remembering and recalling knowledge, thinking critically, problem solving analytically, and creating synthetically. This theory assumes trainees are conscientious and actively participating in a teaching-learning environment. First, within the cognitive view, trainees draw on their past intellectual experiences as a basis for reassessment and reinforcement of their learning outcomes. This theory was developed by Fiedler, Mitchell, and Triandis (1971); Mitchell and colleagues (1972); Landis and colleagues (1976); Randolph, Landis, and Tzeng (1977); Worchel and Mitchell (1972); and Weldon and colleagues (1975) to test trainees' knowledge of cultural differences and their understanding of the effects of these differences on functioning in a foreign culture. This theory requires a joint venture, consisting of practitioners and academic instructors (sociologists, anthropologists, psychologists, economists, political scientists, and sophists), to prepare a series of short descriptions of interactions between the expatriates. It requires trainees to be grouped to study a series of those multicultural incidents collectively. Each incident is followed by the relevant multidimensional questions and few managerial presumable alternatives emphasizing different major disciplinary areas—ethical, legal, sociological, political, economical, anthropological, and psychological views. Trainees should respond by choosing the one alternative that they feel is most appropriate. Then the collaborative multidisciplinary professors provide their own assimilative alternatives through their own professional and specialized views. The collaborative trainers should respond with explanations as to why some trainees' responses were not correct, and then assign appropriate materials to be studied.

The cognitive collaborative teaching-learning theory must be tested in both laboratory and field settings (Barret and Bass, 1976). Then, through collaboration and cooperation of the host cultural experts, the accuracy of cross-cultural understanding could be tested by both the home and the host countries. The real measurement of the teaching-learning efficacy of this theory should be tested in terms of expatriates' actual experiences upon their return to their home countries. Harrison (1992: 953) indicates: "The cultural assimilation has been found to be more effective in terms of all four of Kilpatrick's (1967) training criteria than no training or training via essays on the host culture." No difference was found, however, between subjects receiving essays and those receiving no training (O'Brien and Plooij, 1977). Black and Mendenhall (1990: 115), in a computer-aided, interdisciplinary literature search, conducted a research to delineate the efficacy of cross-cultural training programs. They found twenty-nine studies to be included in their research. They concluded that: "Although no study has attempted a comprehensive review, two reviews have examined the cultural assimilation type of training and its effectiveness (Fiedler, Mitchell, and Triandis, 1971; Mitchell et al., 1972), but neither examined other approaches, nor did offer a theoretical framework." Also, Black and Mendenhall (1990: 116), through their studies, found that three lab studies were conducted but they found generally no significant relationships between cross-cultural training and performance (Chemers et al., 1966; Mitchell and Foa, 1969; Weldon et al., 1975). In their views of cultural assimilative training efficacy, they argued that, in general, lab studies do not allow time for the effects of cross-cultural training to be manifested in performance. Cognitivistic effectiveness is faster than other theories because it treats learners as adults, does not waste people's time, builds up a base foundation of information, concepts and rules, and provides the rationale upon which action is based (Kramlinger, 1990).

Pragmatic Theory

The laboratory experiment gives the collaborative researchers the most viable controlled research outcomes. By creating an artificial environmental setting similar to a real cultural situation, researchers can control almost every possible factor in that setting. They can manipulate certain variables in the study and examine their effects on other variables. People's lives, beliefs, expectations, and ethical and moral principles are constantly shaped by participating in and watching events. The conclusions that could be drawn from these experiences can either reinforce trainees' existing ethical and moral standards or change them. For instance, an airline corporate code of ethics may instill respect for the ethical, moral, health, safety, and legal decisions concerning crews, passengers, and cargoes. In the airline industry, money laundering and drug smuggling can be used for increasing the corporate profit. Therefore, all airline employees including ground and air crews would be involved in such unethical, immoral, and illegal purposes and operations. It is wrong for any airline or its crews to be involved in any money laundering or drug smuggling rings. However, by some personal or business objectives, motivated parties become involved in these types of businesses. If an airline corporation or its crews find that other competitors are doing well and are involved in drug smuggling and making a very good profit, then other airlines or their employees may be tempted to do so. On the other hand, if those airlines or crews who are smuggling drugs or laundering money get caught and sent to jail, then they will think that such behavior is wrong. Then if airlines and crews find out that one of their airplanes crashed because of sabotage and the airline lost money and lives, then their experiences may lead them to believe that the safety and security of their crews, passengers, and people on the ground is the highest business objectives for their corporation.

Experience is never free from a conative element—from some kind of desire or aversion. The very fact of having a sustained, keen interest in perceiving a cross-cultural experience is a kind of desire or willingness to see or hear more facts. There is no basic desire or aspiration toward pure cultural values, distinct from the rest of other cross-cultural values. Cross-cultural experiences are not necessarily satisfactory or pleasant for experiencers. In most cases, experiential thinking about another's cultural beliefs and expectations can be disagreeable when the difficulties of modality of behaviors or perceptions are excessive and the practicality of failure inevitable.

Experiential testing in laboratories prevents some of the problems of other types of research. Advantages include a high degree of control over and precise measurement of variables. Specifically, in an experiential teaching-learning laboratory, trainees hear and watch the perceptions and behaviors of the cultural models demonstrating effective learning points and relevant behaviors in a problem situation. Then, they become the role-players and demonstrate the interactive processes. Next, they reveal cause-effect relations and, finally, express the criteria of reactions and unknown motivations and perceptions about other cultures. Providing the trainees with a satisfactory understanding of a host cultural value system will help them be well trained and adjust themselves to the new environment. Nevertheless, some cultural value systems of a host country may not be to trainees' tastes. They may be ugly, shocking, disgusting, repellent, or they may drive the trainees to anger and resentment. These experiences may be deeply satisfying, if they are in a state of mind to welcome and understanding them.

In a collaborative cross-cultural experiential training program, five component processes should be applied. They are (1) *attention*, (2) *selection*, (3) *detachment*, (4) *emphasis* and *intensity*, and (5) *variety* and *contrast*.

First, *attention* means to attract and hold a close concentration on selective events. Thus, attention is always selective in an experiential training setting. It means noticing some things and ignoring others. Attention processes determine what type of selectivity is observed or deduced from the abundance of a busy world of multicultural valuable objectives. If experiential training processes have much chance of attracting and holding attention of trainees, there are several things that trainees must learn. These should be noticed in a heterogeneous cultural setting within a cultural environment similar to that of the host country. Some cultural values do not demand close attention, because they are similar to the trainees' cultural values. Second, *selection* means to pick up certain sets of cultural values, beliefs, and patterns of behavior to be analyzed and learned. Third, *detachment* means to choose those cultural values, beliefs, and patterns of behavior which are different from trainees' own cultural setting or contextual values in their cultural environment. Merely taking a thing out of its normal context will help, as in taking a seashell from the beach and placing it on a table. Then, the detachment is further underlined by surrounding the chosen materials with some kind of boundaries or limits, which tend to restrict attention from wandering. Such a cultural detachment from the trainees' cultural setting would suggest and stimulate the assumption of a different attitude toward what is within another culture. Fourth, *emphasis* means concentrating and holding attention on what has been selected—to make it somehow more conspicuous and active than what lies. Within a set of selected cultural values, certain parts may be emphasized more than others. Emphasis is not necessarily to be made on a matter of strength in rationality; it may depend on emotional associations. Different people in different cultures possess different emotive power of images. The emotive power of images varies considerably according to the individuals' own perceptual values—but there is also much agreement within a given culture. Fifth, *variety* and *contrast* are essential, if the cultural environment is intense and conspicuous in the same way, the learning task of trainees will not stand out emphatically. It must be seen or heard from surroundings which are different from it and if possible less conspicuous. Aside from differences of emphasis, variety and contrast tend to hold attention; monotony and uniformity tend to lose it. When trainees find that all details of other cultural values, beliefs, and behaviors are similarly rooted or traced within a cultural philosophy, then they tend to lose their interests in those values. This tendency is deeply embedded in instinct and practical experience of human beings.

Behavioristic Theory

In recent years, considerable attention has been devoted to a specific type of vicarious learning called social learning. Social learning theory suggests that behavior is determined by a person's cognitive and social environmental condition (Bandura, 1969; Sims, Jr., and Gioia, 1986). Also, learning is a processes which is affected by both observation and experience (Bandura, 1977). Behavioral learning is based on the specific modality of societal learned values. A behavioristic cross-cultural collaborative teaching-learning theory is similar to a laboratory experiment, except that it is conducted in a real cultural environment—similar to having trainees take a field trip to another country to observe cultural patterns directly. Every culture has a purposeful group behavior. What differs significantly is the qualitative modes of perceptions, interactions, and behaviors within social groups, as well as between groups. Some societies have an individualistic orientation, while others have a more collectivistic orientation. Some cultures temper competitive interaction with strong ideals of cooperative behavior within and between groups. Some societies are comfortable with more participated interactions, and cooperative psychological mentality, while others favor more rigidity and psychodogmatic ranked interactions. In a cross-cultural field trip, learners attempt, through their observational processes, to detect and control certain variables and manipulate others to assess the effects of manipulated variables on outcome variables. The eight components of cross-cultural collaborative behavioristic training theory are (a) observation, (b) attention, (c) perception, (d) apperception, (e) retention, (f) innovation, (g) adaptation, and (i) behavioral modification.

Humanistic Theory

Modern humanistic cultural training theory is concerned with two main types of teaching-learning phenomena. One consists of cultural philosophy: ethics, morality, literature, poems, religion, and other distinguished fields of inquiry such as metaphysics (cosmology, ontology, and causality), epistemology, and axiology. The second consists of related human ritual activities, modes of collective cultural perceptions and experiences in creativity, productivity, or performing arts and those involved in perceiving, appreciating, using, enjoying, evaluating, managing, teaching, and preaching values dealing with it. Norms appear in all these phenomena: transitory and recurrent configurations in physical objectivity and events, in overt behavior and covert experiences, and in perceptual mechanistic universality. Norms in the broad sense of a mode of arrangement include structural cultural values, beliefs, and expectations—they contain various kinds of forms in terms of cultural elements, parts, materials, images, ideas, and beliefs, and of the ways in which these are interrelated and combined—as a whole culture. It draws upon wisdom and experience of people within a culture.

A humanistic cross-cultural training theory challenges trainees to stimulate new thinking, perceiving, and behaving through cultural philosophy and free ways of understanding. It is founded on the theory that learning occurs primarily through reflection on personal tastes and orientations. The work of a collaborative group of trainers—multicultural trainers—is not to put anything in the minds or repertoires of the trainees, but to extract views from the trainees' own sensational and rational insights and experiences. It is a deductive and dialectic teaching-learning approach. On the basis of trainees experiences, trainers explain stimulated statements, then trainees make new connections in a composite formation. It is a Socratic and Platonic method of belief that all knowledge exists within the minds of people. Both teaching and learning processes are inductive in terms of reasoning, assertion, visualization, reflection, and generalization of the facts. A humanistic approach is manipulated neither by trainers nor trainees. It is the natural flow of approaching and experiencing with highly motivated techniques. It is an integrated task between audience and mentors. It is highly integrated and sophisticated in terms of initiation, creativity, innovation, intuition, novelty, and independent thinking.

Holistic Theory

Holistic cultural learning is defined as a mode of perceptual and expository understanding that arranges a comprehensive integrative detailed learning so as to explain or interpret cultural phenomena in terms of general characteristics, causal principles, interrelations, tendencies, and both rational and sensational values. It includes some reference to concrete understanding, but as a means of explaining or supporting a general conception, rather than for purely sensuous or imaginative ends. Its appeal is usually somewhat intellectual, to satisfy a desire to know and understand the forces for causation and processes for specific consequences within the realm of cultural intellect.

By combining the four collaborative theories, trainees can develop an in-depth knowledge based on holistic ability, transcendentally—going beyond ordinary limits, surpassing extraordinary modes of infinite beliefs, supramental abstract, and beyond the contingent and accidental reasoning—but not beyond all human knowledge. This theory is a breakthrough of designing a mental model of a projected value system which could exist within the cultural minds of human beings. It is sketching and drafting of interrelatedness and extrarelatedness of mental synergy—it is virtual reality within virtual beauty in all human cultures.

Using holistic theory can orient people transindividually (across people's mental and physical entities). An individual can think, perceive, and act without doing anything from what they would learn in the real sense of objectivity as opposed to a virtual one. That means a trainee will be able to do things with the ability of their own hands and mind. The mind of a person, despite the person's hands, is multifunctionally oriented internally. This means that there are three areas in which the human mind is more capable to function than any computer algorithm yet designed. These are: (1) pattern recognition—whether visual or aural; (2) valuative orientation—whether haptical and/or sensational. Haptic apperception involves understanding the body's internals, that is the sense of proprioception which informs about the state and position of the body's limbs in relation to one another, and sensationally by lumping together the category of touch to understand our position within the contextual cultural and physical space around us; (3) the overall sensing of the context that enables us to recall, at appropriate moments, locations and situations.

The human haptic system is a means for understanding the virtual cultural reality of all cultures with all values within it. That is where intellectual amplification can happen in a synergistic pattern for the understanding of a novice toward the insight of cultural image. Human psychological holistic and haptic systems can be extremely capable at decoding both the national cultural and international values—what it needs is learning.

From a psychological view, learning is a relatively permanent change in behavior or potential behavior based on direct or indirect experience. Also, from a sociological point of view, learning is a social adaptive conceptual permanent change in behavior based on direct or indirect investment of new concepts into one's repertoire of both rational and emotional meanings. Thus, learning involves: first, processing meaning investments in human perception; second, changing human judgments; third, adapting long lasting meanings of concepts; fourth, changing behavior or potential behavior; and finally, change brought about learned results from direct or indirect experience (Moorhead and Griffin, 1992). It is through holistic collaborative theory that a trainee can achieve their cross-cultural learning objectives.

SUMMARY

Coping with difficulties in cross-cultural understanding are attributed to a lack of appropriated training skills rather than to some deficiency in personality. Expatriates are expected to adjust their behavior to the cultural value systems of the host countries. They should be familiar with selected parts of the host cultural traditions. This does not mean an expatriate can go under a basic shift in his or her behavioral values and conform to a new set of norms. Cultural training programs identify a distinction between orientation skills and values in the host countries. The notion of cross-cultural training programs does not end with predeparture orientations; it is a continuous effort based on counseling, mentoring, and coaching expatriates during their foreign assignments. It is also related to repatriation training orientations.

Assessment of the effectiveness of application of cross-cultural training programs can lead to an overall debate on conceptualization of collaborative teaching-learning strategies that resolves one question of the debate: Which theory is the best for creating an understanding between home and host countries cultures? The first purpose of this chapter was to review pertinent literature to verify the empirical validity of applied efficacy of five training theories—cognitivistic, pragmatistic, behavioristic, humanistic, and holistic. This review proves that application of cross-cultural training theories, in general, has a positive impact on the acculturation of an individual's perception and adjustment to other cultural situations. It is obvious that the effectiveness of the application of each theory depends upon understanding the mainstream of training objectives to be achieved. Major factors must be considered in collaborative cross-cultural acculturalization:

1. Manifestation of the truthful interest of both home and host collaborative instructional teams
2. The evidence of showing interest and tendency toward collaborative understanding by both instructors and learners
3. The abilities and expectations of trainees in cross-cultural socialization
4. The openness of the collaborative cultures

However, compared to training theories in general, the cross-cultural collaborative training theories have received no attention in empirical research.

CHAPTER QUESTIONS FOR DISCUSSION

1. Define sojourners, expatriates, and repatriates.
2. What do we mean by cross-cultural contacts, assimilation, integration, and adaption to the host culture?
3. List the situations in which expatriates are challenged in remaining in host countries.
4. List the major negative factors which cause expatriates to quit their jobs and return to the home country.
5. Describe characteristics of MNCs' employee profiles.
6. Describe different types of expatriate groups who could be assigned to foreign jobs.
7. Describe the stages of predeparture training programs.
8. Describe five theories of cross-cultural training theories.
9. Describe repatriates' readjustment difficulties.
10. Assess the effectiveness of different training techniques.

LEARNING ABOUT YOURSELF EXERCISE #12

How Do You Believe or Not Believe in Teaching and Learning?

Following are twelve items for rating how important each one is to you and to your organization on a scale of 0 (not important) to 100 (very important). Write the number 0-100 on the line to the left of each item.

Not important		Somewhat important		Very important
0	25	50	75	100

Learning is viewed as an effective domain of experiencing the new knowledge. I believe learning is:

_____ 1. An acquisition in responding to factual pragmatic experiences.
_____ 2. An awareness of scientific facts.
_____ 3. The willingness to receive information.
_____ 4. The selected attention of my cognitive judgment.
_____ 5. The willingness to respond to the necessity of curiosity.
_____ 6. The acceptance of cultural value systems.
_____ 7. The preference between priority of valuable intellectual thoughts.
_____ 8. A commitment or conviction to humanity.
_____ 9. A satisfactory responsive mode of understanding concerning comprehension of causes, processes, and effects.
_____ 10. Characterization of the meanings of real things.
_____ 11. A discussion concerning the technical terms of the thing learned.
_____ 12. Perceiving my understanding on the basis of the modes of creativity, innovation, and discovery of the truth.

Turn to the next page for scoring directions and key.

SCORING DIRECTIONS AND KEY FOR EXERCISE #12

Transfer the numbers for each of the twelve items to the appropriate column, then add up the three numbers in each column.

Pragmatic	Behavioristic	Cognivistic
2. _____	1. _____	6. _____
3. _____	5. _____	7. _____
4. _____	9. _____	8. _____
11. _____	12. _____	10. _____
Your Totals _____	_____	_____
Total Scores 400	400	400

The higher the total in any dimension, the higher the importance you place on that set.

Make up a categorical scale of your findings on the basis of more weight for the values of each category.

For example:

1. 400 behavioristic
2. 100 cognivistic
3. 100 pragmatistic

Your Totals   600
Total Scores   1,200

After you have tabulated your scores, compare them with others on your team or in your class. You will find different judgmental patterns among people with diverse scores and preferred modes of self-realization.

CASE STUDY:
AN AMERICAN AIRLINES' MANAGER
REPATRIATES TO THE U.S.A.

American Airlines is the only U.S. airline that flies directly to Colombia, South America. Currently, American Airlines asserts that its fleet has several advantages over its competitors. It is young and efficient. It has a frequent flyer program, AAdvantage, which is the largest program in the industry. It provides great customer support at all times. In 1997, American Airlines reported revenues of $15.86 billion and a net income of $780 million.

On January 25, 1930, a company by the name of American Airways, Inc., a subsidiary of the Aviation Corp., was founded to engage in the operation of an air transport system. However, on February 19, 1934, the air mail contracts held by American Airways were annulled by the postmaster general of the United States because they did not comply with the air mail laws of 1934. Consequently, the Aviation Corp. was forced to organize a new company to make bids on these air mail contracts so that they would not be forfeited. The birth of American Airlines, Inc. occurred in the month of May 1934. Since then, American Airlines, Inc., better known as "American," has been providing passengers from all over the world air transportation, as well as freight and mail services.

American Airlines spends $15 million a year to employ and train personnel. On August 25, 1999, a total of fifty-eight people were indicted for smuggling heroin, cocaine, marijuana, guns, and hand grenades into Miami from Colombia by using American Airlines as their means of transportation. From these fifty-eight individuals, fifty-three were American Airlines employees and five others were relatives of American Airlines employees.

In recent years, American Airlines has been involved in several embarrassing incidents involving the smuggling of illegal drugs. Officials have stated that the incident on August 25, 1999, the end of a two-and-a-half year undercover operation, occurred because federal agents caught employees stashing cocaine and marijuana in backpacks, packages, and luggage, which they would put on luggage ramps, taking advantage of their security clearance. Arrests made in Miami and Fort Lauderdale areas and in New York were carried out by the Drug Enforcement Administration, U.S. Customs Service, Bureau of Alcohol, Tobacco, and Firearms, and the Miami-Dade Police Department. American Airlines cooperated with undercover federal agents in the investigation dubbed: "Operation Ramp Rats." Law enforcement resources told CNN that American Airlines ramp agents unloaded what they thought was cocaine from American Airlines flights arriving from Colombia, Chile, Ecuador, and Bolivia.

Sources: CNN (1999). Web site. <http://cgi.cnn.com/US/9908/25airline.drug.sting.04/>; Moody's Industrial Manual (1999). Zottoli Jr., D. A., Publisher, New York: Moody's Investors Service, Inc., pp. 6626-6631.

Repatriation can be a very hard experience for international corporate employees. Take the case of American Airlines director in Colombia, Mr. Robbins. Mr. Robbins and his family members returned from a five-year mission in the American Airlines office in Colombia. Before their initial departure to Colombia, his son was twelve years old and his daughter was fifteen years old, and they were very reluctant to leave their classmates, activities, and friends behind when Robbins was transferred to Colombia. His wife, Jane, had to sell her 50 percent interest in a coffee shop that grossed nearly an annual income of $80,000 in Newport Beach, California. They sold their new home for $800,000 in the subdivision of Concordia Complex, Irvine, California and resided in Colombia.

After five years away from the United States, Robbins family was facing readjustment problems. Since five years had passed, the children were much older and not even returning to their old schools but starting new ones. The reception Robbins received from the American Airlines office in the John Wayne Airport essentially conveyed this message: "Welcome home. Here is your desk, and in a few months maybe we can fit you into the assistant vice president of special training program position here at American Airline's headquarters."

References

Chapter 1

Allen, W. R. (1967). *International Trade Theory: Hume to Ohlin*. New York: Random House.

Arenson, K. W. (1986). "How Wall Street Bred Ivan Boesky." *The New York Times*. November 26, p. 8F.

Bass, B. M., Burger, P. C., Doctor, R., and Barrett, G. V. (1979). *Assessment of Managers: An International Comparison*. New York: The Free Press.

Beer, M., Eisenstat, R. A., and Spector, B., (1990). "Why Change Programs Don't Produce Change." *Harvard Business Review, 68*(6), pp. 158-166.

Bruzonsky, M. A. (Ed.) (1977). *The Middle East U.S. Policy, Israel, Oil and the Arabs*, Third Edition. Washington DC: Congressional Quarterly Inc.

Copeland, L. (1988). "Valuing Diversity, Part 1: Making the Most of Cultural Differences at the Workplace." *Personnel, 65*(6), p. 52.

Cox Jr., T. (1993). *Cultural Diversity in Organizations: Theory, Research, and Practice*. San Francisco: Berrett-Koehler Publishers.

Daniels, J. D. and Radebaugh, L. H. (1994). *International Business: Environments and Operations,* Seventh Edition. Reading, MA: Addison-Wesley Publishing Company.

De George, R. T. (1995). *Business Ethics,* Fourth Edition. Englewood Cliffs, NJ: Prentice-Hall.

de Vries, S. (1992). *Working in Multi-Ethnic Groups: The Performance and Well-Being of Minority and Majority Workers*. Amsterdam: Gouda Quint bu— Arnhem.

Donaldson, T. and Werhane, P. H. (1988). *Ethical Issues in Business: A Philosophical Approach.* Englewood Cliffs, NJ: Prentice-Hall.

Drucker, P. (1980). *Managing in Turbulent Times.* New York: Harper and Row.

Eccles, R. G. (1991). "The Performance Measurement Manifesto." *Harvard Business Review, 69*(1), pp. 131-137.

Eitman, D. K. and Stonehill, A. I. (1979). *Multinational Business Finance,* Second Edition. Reading, MA: Addison-Wesley.

Fabrikant, G. (1995). "Battling for Hearts and Minds at Time Warner." *The New York Times.* February 26, p. 9.

Fernandez, J. P. (1991). *Managing a Diverse Work Force: Regaining the Competitive Edge*. Lexington, MA: Lexington Books.

Foster, L. G. (1983). The Johnson & Johnson Credo and the Tylenol Crisis. *New Jersey Bell Journal, 6*(1, Spring), 2.

Friedman, M. (1970). "The Social Responsibility of Business Is to Increase Profit." *The New York Times Magazine.* September 13, pp. 32-33, 122-126.

Fullerton, H. N. (1987). "Labor Force Projections: 1986-2000." *Monthly Labor Review, 110*(9), pp. 19-29.

Gordon, M. W. (1993). *Doing Business in Mexico.* New York: Transnational Juri Publications, Inc., Part II, Chapter 3, p. 6.

Harrison, J. R. and Carroll, G. R. (1991). "Keeping the Faith: A Model of Cultural Transmission in Formal Organizations." *Administrative Science Quarterly 36,* pp. 552-582.

Harvey, C. and Mallard, M. J. (1995). *Understanding Diversity: Readings, Cases, and Exercises.* New York: Harper Collins College Publishers.

Hill, J. and Dulek, R. (1993). "A Miss Manners Guide to Doing Business in Europe." *Business Horizon, 36*(4) July/August, pp. 51-52.

Hofstede, G. (1980a). *Culture's Consequences: International Differences in Work Related Values.* Beverly Hills: Sage Publications.

Hofstede, G. (1980b). "Motivation, Leadership, and Organizations: Do American Theories Apply Abroad?" *Organizational Dynamics* (summer), pp. 42-63.

Hofstede, G. (1993). "Cultural Constraints in Management Theories." *Academy of Management Executives, 7*(1), pp. 81-94.

Horwitz, T. and Foreman, C. (1990). "Clashing Cultures." *The Wall Street Journal.* October 2, p. A1.

International Financial Statistics. International Monetary Fund (1998). LI(2), February. Washington, DC.

Jackson, J. H., Miller, R. L., and Miller, S. G. (1997). *Business and Society Today: Managing Social Issues.* New York: West Publishing Company.

Jackson G. C. and O'Dell, C. (1988). *American Business: A Two-Minute Warning.* New York: The Free Press.

Johnson & Johnson Web site <http://www.jni.com/who_is_jnj/cr_usa.html>.

Johnson, R. B. and O'Mara, J. (1992). "Shedding Light on Diversity Training." *Training and Diversity,* (May), pp. 45-52.

Johnston, W. (1991). "Global Work Force 2000: The New World Labor Market." *Harvard Business Review 69,* (March/April), pp. 115-127.

Kirrane, D. E. (1990). "Managing Values: A Systematic Approach to Business Ethics." *Training and Development Journal 44*(11), pp. 53-60.

Kolberg, W. H. and Smith, F. C. (1992). *Rebuilding America's Work-Force: Business Strategies to Close the Competitive Gap.* Homewood, IL: Irwin.

Laurent, A. (1983). "The Cultural Diversity of Western Corporations of Management." *International Studies of Management and Organization 13*(1-2, Spring-Summer), pp. 75-96.

Magaziner, I. and Patinkin, M. (1990). *The Silent War: Inside Global Business Battles Shaping America's Future.* New York: Vintage Books.

Marquardt, M. J. and Engel, D. W. (1993). "HRD Competencies for a Shrinking World." *Training and Development,* (May) 47(5), p. 59.

Mohrman, S. A. and Mitroff, I. I. (1987). "Business Not As Usual." *Training and Development Journal, 41*(6), pp. 37-34.

Newsweek (1983). The Tylenol Scare. October 11, pp. 32-36.

The New York Times (1997). "10 in Argentina Indicted Over I.B.M. Contract." May 21, Section D. Business/Finance Desk, News, p. 12.

O'Reilly, C. A., III, Caldwell, D. F., and Barnett, W. P. (1989). "Work Group Demography, Social Integration and Turnover." *Administrative Science Quarterly* 34(March), pp. 21-37.

Parhizgar, K. D. (1994). "Affordability and Solvency Implications of Privatization of Government-Owned Industries in the Third World Countries (TWCs)." *Journal of Business and Society, 1*(1), p. 109.

Parhizgar, K. D. (1995). "Creating Cultural Paradigm Structures for Globalized Corporate Management Ethics." In Evans, J. R., Berman, B., and Barak, B. (Eds.). *Proceedings: 1995 Research Conference on Ethics and Social Responsibility in Marketing.* Homestead, NY: Frank G. Zarb School of Business, Hofstra University Press, pp. 137-150.

Parhizgar, K. D. (1999). "Globalization of Multicultural Management." *Journal of Transnational Management Development, 4*(3/4), pp. 1-25.

Parhizgar, K. D. and Jesswein, K. R. (1995). "Socio-Ethical and Economic Fairness—Affordability of Developing Nations' Repayment of International Debt." In Fatemi, K. and Nichols, S. E. W. (Eds.) (1995). *International Business in the 21st Century.* Volume II, pp. 463-473.

Parhizgar, K. D. and Landeck, M. (1997). "Characteristics and Perceptions of Female Workers Regarding Their Work Environment in Mexican Maquiladoras." In Lemaster, J. (Ed.), *Southwest Review of International Business Research: Proceedings of the 1997 Academy of International Business Conference,* p. 427. Edinberg, TX: University of Texas—Pan American.

Pascal, R. T. (1985). "The Paradox of Corporate Culture." *California Management Review, 27*(2), pp. 26-41.

Porter, M. E. (1990). *The Competitive Advantage of Nations.* New York: The Free Press.

Rhinesmith, S. H. (1991). "An Agenda for Globalization." *Trading and Development Journal, 45*(2), pp. 24-27, 131-137.

Riche, M. F. (1991). "We're All Minorities Now." *American Demographics, 13*(10), p. 34.

Schein, E. H. (1968). "Organizational Socialization and the Profession of Management." *Industrial Management Review, 9*(16), pp. 1-15.

Smith. A. (1776). *An Inquiry into the Nature and Causes of the Wealth of the Nations.* Houston, TX: Institute for Advanced Interdisciplinary Research.

Smith, C. G. and Cooper, A.C. (1988). "Established Companies Diversifying into Young Industries: A Comparison of Firms with Different Levels of Performance." *Strategic Management Journal, 9*(March-April), pp. 111-121.

Solomon, C. M. (1993). "Managing Today's Immigrants." *Personnel Journal, 72*(2), p. 58.

Stewart, J. B. (1991). "Scenes from a Scandal: The Secret World of Michael Milken and Ivan Boesky." *The Wall Street Journal.* October 2, p. B1.

Swierczek, F. (1988). "Cultural and Training: How Do They Play Away from Home?" *Training and Development Journal, 42*(11), p. 76.

U.S. Department of Commerce/Patent and Trademark Office (1989). *Annual Report: Fiscal Year 1989.* Washington, DC.

Weir, D. (1987). *The Bhopal Syndrome.* San Francisco: Sierra Club Books.

Wheelen, T. L. and Hunger, J. D. (1995). *Strategic Management and Business Policy.* Reading, MA: Addison-Wesley Publishing Company.

Williams, C. J. (1995). "9 Years Later, Chernobyl Disaster Looks Worse." *The Los Angeles Times.* April 27, p. A4.

World Bank (1991). *World Development Report.* Washington, DC: The World Bank Publication, 1, p. 25.

World Investment Report: An Executive Summary (1993). United Nations Conference on Trade and Development Program on Transnational Corporations. New York: United Nations Publications, pp. 1-4.

Wormser, M. D. (1981). *The Middle East: Congressional Quarterly Inc.* Fifth Edition. Washington, DC: Congressional Quarterly Inc., p. 82.

Yankelovich, D. (1982). "The Work Ethic Is Underemployed." *Psychology Today.* May, pp. 5-8.

Chapter 2

Adler, N. (1986). *International Dimensions of Organizational Behavior.* Boston, MA: Kent Publishing Company.

Ayer, A. J. (1950). *Language: Truth and Logic.* New York: Dover Publications.

Barrett, M. (1991). *The Politics of Truth: From Marx to Foucault.* Stanford, CA: Stanford University Press.

Berelson, B. and Steiner, G. A. (1964). *Human Behavior.* New York: Harcourt, Brace and World.

Dupuios, A. M. (1985). *Philosophy of Education in Historical Perspective.* Landham, MD: Rand McNally and Company.

Elstrom, P. (1998). "The Internet Space Race." *Business Week.* June 1, p. 48.

Fatehi, K. (1996). *International Management: A Cross-Cultural and Functional Perspective.* Upper Saddle River, NJ: Prentice-Hall.

Ferraro, G. P. (1994). *The Cultural Dimension of International Business,* Second Edition. Englewood Cliffs, NJ: Prentice-Hall.

Finkel, I. (1994). "Needed—A Curriculum That Promotes a New World View." In Rudiger, C. W. (Ed.), *Proceedings of the Educational Studies and Research Group, the Association of Management 12th Annual International Conference, 12*(1), pp. 79-80.

Gardener, H. (1993). *Frames of Mind: The Theory of Multiple Intelligence.* New York: Basic Books.

Geertz, C. (1970). "The Impact of the Concept of Culture on the Concept of Man." In Hammel, E. A. and Simmonson, W. S. (Eds.), *Man Makes Sense* (pp. 47-65). Boston: Little Brown.

Glazer, N. and Moyniham, D. P. (1975). *Beyond the Melting Pot,* Second Edition. Cambridge, MA: MIT Press.

Harpaz, I. (1990). "The Importance of Work Goals: An International Perspective." *Journal of International Business Studies, 21*(2), pp. 75-93.

Heenan, D. A. and Perlmutter, H. V. (1979). *Multinational Organizational Development.* Reading, MA: Addison-Wesley Publishing Company.

Hosmer, L. T. (1987). *The Ethics of Management.* Homewood, IL: Irwin.

Hosmer, L. T. (1991). *The Ethics of Management.* Homewood, IL: Irwin.

Kluckhohn, F. R. and Strodtbeck, F. L. (1961). *Variation Value Orientations.* Evanston, IL: Row, Peterson and Company.

Lane, R. E. (1962). *Political Ideology: Why the American Common Man Believes What He Does.* New York: Free Press.

Luthans, F. (1985). *Organizational Behavior,* Fourth Edition. New York: McGraw-Hill.

Marger, M. N. (1985). *Race and Ethnic Relations: American and Global Perspectives.* Belmont, CA: Wadsworth Publishing Company.

Maslow, A. H. (1965). *Management.* Homewood, IL: Dorsey-Irwin.

Moody's Industrial Manual (1998). Zottoli Jr., D. A., Publisher. New York: Moody's Investors Service, Inc., pp. 6095-6098.

Moran, R. T. and Harris, P. R. (1982). *Managing Cultural Synergy.* Volume 2. Houston: Gulf Publishing Company.

Mullins, W.A. (1972). "On the Concept of Ideologies in Political Science." *American Political Science Review, 66*(2), pp. 498-511.

Myers, I. B. and McCaulley, M. H. (1990). *Manual: A Guide to the Development and Use of the Myers-Briggs Type Indicator.* Palo Alto, CA: Consulting Psychologists Press.

Nelson, D. L. and Quick, J. C. (1994). *Organizational Behavior: Foundations, Realities, and Challenges.* Minneapolis/St. Paul, MN: West Publishing Company.

Parhizgar, K. D. (1993). "Evolutionary Visions of the Nature of the 21st Century Businessman and the Emergence of Strategic Business Education Toward Polycentric, Regiocentric and Geocentric Designs." In Moncarez, R. (Ed.), *The World Order and Trade and Finance,* Volume V (pp. 1197-1222). Miami, FL: Florida International University.

Parhizgar, K. D. (1994). Conceptual and Perceptual Paths of Cultural Power-Gender Philosophies Towards Entrepreneurial Management. In Yin, W. S., Kao, R., and Liang, T. W. (Eds.), *The Main Proceedings of the ENDEC World Conference on Entrepreneurship: The Pursuit of Opportunity.* July 7-9, Marina Manderin Singapore: NTU-Entrepreneurship Development Center, Nanyang Technological University: 524-534.

Sanford, F. H. and Wrightsman, Jr., L. S. (1970). *Psychology,* Third Edition. Belmont, CA: Brooks Cole.

Smith, E. D. and Pham, C. (1998). "Doing Business in Vietnam: A Cultural Guide." In Maidment, F. (Ed.). *International Business 98/99,* Seventh Edition. Guilford, CT: Dushkin/McGraw-Hill, p. 174.

Sproul, L. S. (1981). "Beliefs in Organizations" in Nystrom, P. C. and Starbuck, W. H. (Eds). *Handbook of Organizational Design* (pp. 204-205). New York: Oxford University Press.

Terpstra, V. and David, K. (1991). *The Cultural Environment of International Business.* Cincinnati, OH: South-Western Publishing Company, p. 106.

Chapter 3

Bellah, R. N. (1957). *Tokugawa Religion.* New York: The Free Press, p. 35.
Bellah, R. N. (1964). "Religious Evolution." *American Sociological Review, 29*(June), pp. 358-374.
Bleek, J. and Ernest, D. (1995). Is Your Strategic Alliance Really a Sale? *Harvard Business Review 73*(January-February), pp. 97-105.
Brown, M. A. (1976). "Values—A Necessary But Neglected Ingredient of Motivation on the Job." *Academy of Management Review 21*(1), pp. 15-23.
Downs, J. F. (1971). *Cultures in Crisis.* Beverly Hills, CA: Gelenco Press.
Drucker, P. (1995). The Network Society. *The Wall Street Journal.* March 29, p. 12.
Durkheim, E. (1938). *The Rules of Sociological Methods.* New York: Free Press.
Evans-Pritchard, E. E. (1954). *Social Anthropology.* New York: Cohn and West.
Ferraro, G. (1994). *The Cultural Dimension of International Business,* Second Edition. Englewood Cliffs, NJ: Prentice-Hall.
Finkel, I. (1994). "Needed—A Curriculum That Promotes a New World View." In Rudiger, C. W. (Ed.), *Proceedings of the Educational Studies and Research Group, the Association of Management 12th Annual International Conference 12*(1), pp. 79-80.
Geertz, C. (1966). In Michael Banton (Ed.), *Anthropological Approaches to the Study of Religion* (pp. 1-6). New York: Frederick A. Praeger, Inc.
Gilford, J. C. (1960). "The Type-Variety Method of an Indicator of Cultural Phenomena." *American Antiquity 25*(2), pp. 341-347.
Goody, J. (1961). "Religion and Ritual: The Definitional Problem." *British Journal of Sociology, 12,* 142-164.
Gordon, M. M. (1964). *Assimilation in American Society.* New York: Oxford University Press.
Harvey, C. and Allard, M. J. (1995). *Understanding Diversity: Readings, Cases, and Exercises.* HarperCollins College Publishers.
Hatch, E. (1985). "Culture." In Kuper, A. and Kuper, J. (Eds.), *The Social Science Encyclopedia* (p. 178). London: Routledge and Kegan Paul.
Hofstede, G. (1980). "Motivation, Leadership, and Organization: Do American Theories Apply Abroad?" *Organizational Dynamics 50*(Summer), pp. 25-63.
Hofstede, G. (1994). "Management Scientists Are Human." *Management Science 40*(1) January, p. 4.
Horton, R. (1960). "A Definition of Religion and Its Uses." *Journal of the Royal Anthropological Institute, 90,* Part 2, 201-226.
Kodama, F. (1992). "Technology Fusion and the New R and D." *Ministry of International Trade and Industry, 70*(July/August), pp. 70-78.
Kroeber, A. L. and Kluckhohn, C. (1952). "Culture: A Critical Review of Concepts and Definitions." *Papers of the Peabody Museum 47*(1). Cambridge, MA: Harvard University, p. 181.

Magaziner, I. and Patinkin, M. (1990). *The Silent War: Inside the Global Business Battles Shaping America's Future.* New York: Vintage Books.

Marger, M. N. (1985). *Race and Ethnic Relations: American and Global Perspectives.* Belmont, CA: Wadsworth Publishing Company.

McAteer, P. F. (1994). "Harnessing the Power of Technology." *Training and Development 48*(August), pp. 61-68.

McCollum, K. (1998). "Founder of Utilitarianism Is Present in Spirit at 250th-Birthday Teleconference." *The Chronicle of Higher Education.* February 27, p. A28.

Moody's International Manual (1998). Zottoli Jr., D. A., Publisher, New York: Moody's Investors Service, Inc., Volume 4, pp. 10777-10779.

Moran, R. T. and Harris, P. R. (1982). *Managing Cultural Synergy,* Volume 2. Houston: Gulf Publishing Company.

Mussen, P. H. (1963). *The Psychological Development of the Child.* Englewood Cliffs, NJ: Prentice-Hall.

Petracca, M. F. and Sorapure, M. (1995). *Common Culture: Reading and Writing About American Popular Culture.* Englewood Cliffs, NJ: Prentice-Hall.

Shani, A. B. and Sena, J. A. (1994). "Information Technology and the Integration of Change: Sociotechnical System Approach." *Journal of Applied Behavioral Science, 30*(June), pp. 247-270.

Smiley, D. H. (1995). "Can Labor-Capital Models Predict the Responses of Agrarian Societies to Development?" *The American Journal of Economics and Sociology 54*(21), October, p. 290.

Snow, C. P. (1959). *The Culture and Scientific Revolution.* Cambridge, England: Cambridge University Press.

Spradley, J. P. (1979). *The Ethnographic Interview.* New York: Holt, Rinehart, and Winston.

Steiner, G. A. and Steiner, J. F. (1997). *Business, Government and Society: A Managerial Perspective, Text and Cases,* Eighth Edition. New York: The McGraw-Hill Companies, Inc.

Symington, J. W. (1983). "Learn Latin America's Culture." *The New York Times.* September 23, p. 1.

Terpstra, V. and David, K. (1991). *The Cultural Environment of International Business.* Cincinnati, OH: South-Western Publishing Company.

Thernstrom, S. (1982). "Ethnic Groups in American History." *Ethnic Relations in America.* Englewood Cliffs, NJ: Prentice-Hall.

Trice, H., and Beyer, J. (1993). *The Cultures of Work Organizations.* Englewood Cliffs, NJ: Prentice-Hall.

Tylor, E. B. (1924). *Primitive Culture,* Seventh Edition. New York: Brentano's, Inc.

Van Fleet, D. D. (1991). *Behavior in Organizations.* Boston: Houghton Mifflin Company.

The Wall Street Journal (1998). "U.S. Judge Says Whistle-Blowers to Get $42.3 Million." April 10, p. 1.

Webber, R. A. (1969). *Culture and Management.* Homewood, IL: Irwin.

Weber, C. O. (1960). *Basic Philosophies of Education.* New York: Rinehart and Winston.

Wheelen, T. L. and Hunger, J. D. (1986). *Strategic Management and Business Policy,* Second Edition. Reading, MA: Addison-Wesley Publishing Company.

Yinger, J. M. (1970). *The Scientific Study of Religion.* London: Macmillan.

Chapter 4

Abramson, H. (1980). Assimilation and Pluralism. In Thenstrom, S. (Ed.), *Harvard Encyclopedia of American Ethnic Groups.* Cambridge, MA: Harvard University Press, 150-160.

Adler, N. J. (1986). *International Dimensions of Organizational Behavior.* Boston, MA: Kent Publishing Company.

Babiker, I. E., Cox, J. L., and Miller, P. M. C. (1980). "The Measurement of Culture Distance and Its Relationship to Medical Consultation, Symphomatology and Examination Performance of Overseas Students at Edinburgh University." *Social Psychiatry 15*(3), pp. 109-116.

Ball, D. A. and McCulloch Jr., W. H. (1988). *International Business: Introduction and Essentials,* Third Edition. Homewood, IL: Irwin.

Beals, R. L. and Hijer, H. (1959). *An Introduction to Anthropology.* New York: Macmillan.

Berelson, B. and Steiner, G. A. (1964). *Human Behavior.* New York: Harcourt, Brace, and World.

Cohen, D. (1995). *Legal Issues in Marketing Decision Making.* Cincinnati, OH: South-Western College Publishing.

Cohn, E. (1979). Rethinking the Sociology of Tourism. *Annals of Tourism Research 2*(6), pp. 18-35.

De George, R. T. (1995). *Business Ethics,* Fourth Edition. Englewood Cliffs, NJ: Prentice-Hall.

Demott, J. S. (1985). "Fiddling with the Real Thing." *Time* (May 6, 1985), p. 55.

Elstrom, P. and Kerwin, K. (1998). "New Boss, New Plan: CEO Armstrong Is Moving Fast to Cut Costs and Position the Giant to the Digital Age. Will His Strategy Work?" *Business Week,* February 2, 122: 126, 128, 132.

Englehart, R. and Carnally, M. (1997). Does Latin America Exist? (And Is There a Confucian Culture?): A Global Analysis of Cross-Cultural Differences." *Psychology 30*(1), p. 37.

Fatehi, K. (1996). *International Management: A Cross-Cultural and Functional Perspective.* Upper Saddle River, NJ: Prentice-Hall.

Ferraro, G. P. (1994). *The Cultural Dimension of International Business,* Second Edition. Englewood Cliffs, NJ: Prentice-Hall.

Fowles, J. (1995). "Advertising's Fifteen Basic Appeals." In Petracca, M. F. and Sorapure, M. (Eds.), *Common Culture: Reading and Writing About American Popular Culture* (pp. 58-76). Englewood Cliffs, NJ: Prentice-Hall.

Furnham, A. and Bochner, S. (1982). "Social Difficulty in Foreign Culture: An Empirical Analysis of Culture Shock." In Bochner, S. (Ed.), *Culture in Contact: Studies in Cross-Cultural Interaction* (pp. 21-25). Oxford: Pergamon.

Furnham, A. and Bochner, S. (1986). *Culture Shock: Psychological Reactions to Unfamilar Environments.* London and New York: Methuen.

Greenwald, J. (1997). AT&T's Second-Chance CEO: Hughes Electronics Boss C. Michael Armstrong Takes the Top Job a Year After Turning It Down. *Time.* October 27, p. 103.

Hartley, R. F. (1998). *Marketing Mistakes and Successes,* Seventh Edition. New York: John Wiley and Sons, Inc.

Harvey, C . and Allard, M. J. (1995). *Understanding Diversity: Readings, Cases, and Exercises.* New York: HarperCollins College Publishers.

Luthans, F. (1985) *Organizational Behavior.* New York: McGraw-Hill.

Meyes, B. T. and Allen, R. W. (1977). Toward a Definition of Organizational Politics. *Academy of Management Review 2*(4), pp. 672-678.

Moody's Industrial Manual (1998). Zottoli Jr., D. A., Publisher. New York: Moody's Investors Service, Inc., pp. 2673-2678.

Moran, R. T. and Harris, P. R. (1982). *Managing Cultural Synergy.* Houston: Gulf Publishing Company.

Morgan, C. and King, R. (1966). *Introduction to Psychology,* Third Edition. New York: McGraw-Hill.

Oxford English Dictionary (1963). Second Edition. Prepared by Simpson, J. A. and Weiner, E. S. C. Oxford, UK: Clarendon Press.

Parhizgar, K. D. (1994). "Affordability and Solvency Implications of Privatization of Government-Owned Industries in the Third World Countries." *Journal of Business and Society 7*(1), p. 110.

Parhizgar, K. D. (1996). "Cross-Cultural Implications of the Popular Cultural Damping in the International Movie Market." In Lemaster, J. and Islam, M.M. (Eds.), *Southwest Review of International Business Research, Proceedings of the 1996 Academy of International Business, Southwest Regional Meeting,* pp. 308-316.

Pegrum, D. F. (1959). *Public Regulation of Business.* Homewood, IL: Richard D. Irwin.

Robbins, S. P. (1998). *Organizational Behavior: Concepts, Controversies, and Applications.* Upper Saddle River, NJ: Prentice-Hall.

Selznick, P. (1948). "Foundations of the Theory of Organizations." *American Sociological Review 13*(February), p. 25.

Terpstra, V. and David, K. (1991). *The Cultural Environment of International Business.* Cincinnati, OH: Southwestern Publishing Co.

Therstrom, S. (1982). "Ethnic Groups in American History." In Lance Liebman (Ed.), *Ethnic Relations in America.* Englewood Cliffs, NJ: Prentice-Hall.

Torbiorn, I. (1982). *Living Abroad: Personal Adjustment and Personnel Policy in the Overseas Setting.* Chichester, UK: Wiley.

Trice, H. M. and Beyer, J. M. (1993). *The Culture of World Organizations.* Englewood Cliffs, NJ: Prentice-Hall.

Van Fleet, D. D. (1991). *Behavior in Organizations.* Boston: Houghton Mifflin Company.

Weber, C. O. (1960). *Basic Philosophies of Education.* New York: Holt, Rinehart, and Winston.

Wundt, W. (1879). Mehadalab (Structuralism). In Luthans, F. (1988) (Ed.), *Organizational Behavior.* New York: McGraw-Hill, p. 36.

Yoder, S. K. (1992). "How IBM's Heirs Plan to Expand Empires in Computer Industry." *The Wall Street Journal* (December 21, 1992), pp. A1 and A4.

Zangwill, I. (1909). *The Melting Pot.* New York: Prompt Book, p. 198.

Zimbardo, P. G. (1992). *Psychology and Life,* Thirteenth Edition. New York: Harper-Collins Publisher, pp. 17-267.

Chapter 5

Adams, J. S. (1963). "Toward an Understanding of Inequity." *Journal of Abnormal and Social Psychology 67*(November) pp. 422-436.

Adams, J. S. (1965). "Inequity in Social Exchange." In Berkowitz, L. (Ed.), *Advances in Experimental Social Psychology,* Volume 2 (pp. 267-299). New York: Academic Press.

Afnan, S. (1968). *A Philosophical Lexicon in Persian and Arabic.* Beirut, Lebanon: Dar El-Mashregh.

Alderfer, C. P. (1969). "An Empirical Test of a New Theory of Human Needs." *Organizational Behavior and Human Performance 4*(May), pp. 142-175.

Alderfer, C. P. (1972). *Existence, Relatedness, and Growth: Human Needs in Organizational Settings.* New York: Free Press.

Aristotle (348-322 B.C./1980). "Moral Character." In Albert, E. M., Denise, T. C., and Peterfreund, S. P. (Eds.), *Great Traditions in Ethics,* Fifth Edition, (p. 36). Belmont, CA: Wadsworth Publishing Company.

Atkinson, J. W. (1964). *An Introduction to Motivation.* Princeton, NJ: Van Nostrand.

Awadudi, A. A. (1989). *Towards Understanding Islam.* Jamaica, NY: The Message Publications.

Berelson, B. and Steiner, G. A. (1964). *Human Behavior.* New York: Harcourt, Brace & World.

Coser, R. L. (1975). "Stay Home Little Shiba: On Placement, Displacement, and Social Change." *Social Problems 22,* pp. 470-480.

Covey, S. R. (1993). "Transforming a Swamp." *Training and Development 47*(5), 42.

Dollins, M. (1988). "Settlement Reached in Suit Over Radioactive Oatmeal Experiment." *The New York Times,* Late Edition, January 1, p. 19.

Epstein, C. F. (1991). "Ways Men and Women Lead." *Harvard Business Review 69* (1), pp. 150-160.

Filley, A. C., House, R. J., and Kerr, S. (1976). *Managerial Process and Organizational Behavior,* Second Edition. Glenview, IL: Scott, Foresman.

Goodman, P. S. (1977). "Social Comparison Processes in Organizations." In Staw, B. M. and Salanci, G. R. (Eds.), *New Directions in Organizational Behavior.* Chicago: St. Clair, pp. 97-131.

Greenburg, J. (1988). "Equity and Workplace Status: A Field Experiment." *Journal of Applied Psychology 73*(4), pp. 606-613.

Herzberg, F. (1968). "One More Time: How Do You Motive Employees?" *Harvard Business Review.* September-October, pp. 53-62.

Hunt, J. G. and Hill, J. W. (1969). "The New Look in Motivation Theory for Organizational Research." *Human Organization.* Summer, p. 104.

Jackson, D. (1984). "Murray's Manifest Needs." *Personality Research Form Manual.* Port Huron, MI: Research Psychologist's Press, Inc.

Labich, K. (1991). "Can Your Career Hurt Your Kids?" *Fortune,* May 20, pp. 38-56.

Lewin, K. (1938). *The Conceptual Representation and the Measurement of Psychological Forces.* Durham, NC: Duke University Press.

Maslow, A. H. (1943). "A Theory of Human Motivation." *Psychosocial Review 50,* pp. 374-396.

McClelland, D. (1961a). *The Achieving Society.* Princeton, NJ: Van Nostrand.

McClelland, D. C. (1961b). "Business Drive and National Achievement." *Harvard Business Review,* (July-August), pp. 99-112.

McGregor, D. (1960). *The Human Side of Enterprise.* New York: McGraw-Hill.

Moody's Industrial Manual (1998). Zottoli Jr., D. A., Publisher, New York: Moody's Investors Service, Inc., pp. 4173-4174.

Moorhead, G. and Griffin, R. W. (1992). *Organizational Behavior: Managing People and Organizations,* Third Edition. Boston: Houghton Mifflin Company.

Murray, H. A. (1938). *Explorations in Personality.* New York: Oxford University Press.

The New York Times. "Settlement Reached in Suit Over Radioactive Oatmeal Experiment." Late Edition (East Coast), January 1, 1998, Section A, p. 19.

Parhizgar, K. D. (2000). "Ethical Analysis of the Kinetic and Quiddity Existence Need Theory (KQUENT) in Mutinational Organizations." *Journal of Transnational Management Development 5*(3): 1-25.

Pinder, C. (1984). *Work Motivation.* Glenview, IL: Scott, Foresman.

Steers, R. M. and Porter, L. W. (1991). *Motivation and Work Behavior,* Fifth Edition. New York: McGraw-Hill.

The Random House Dictionary of the English Language (1966). Stein, J. and Urdang, L. (Eds.). New York: Random House.

Tolman, E. C. (1932). *Purposive Behavior in Animals.* New York: Appleton-Century-Crafts.

Van Fleet, D. (1991). *Behavior in Organizations.* Boston: Houghton-Mifflin Company.

Vroom, V. (1964). *Work and Motivation.* New York: Wiley.

Weber, M. (1969). "The Protestant Ethics and the Spirit of Capitalism." In Webber, R. A. (Ed.), *Culture and Management* (pp. 91-112). Homewood, IL: Richard D. Irwin.

Chapter 6

Allport, G. W. (1935). "Attitudes." In C. Murchison (Ed.), *Handbook of Social Psychology.* Worcester, MA: Clark University Press, pp. 798-844.

Allport, G. W. (1958). *The Nature of Prejudice.* Garden City, New York: Doubleday.

Berelson, B. and Steiner, G. A. (1964). *Humanor.* New York: Harcourt, Brace and World.

Berry, B. and Tischler, N. M. (1978). *Race and Ethnic Relations,* Fourth Edition. Boston: Houghton Mifflin.

Campbell, N.A. (1993). *Biology.* Redwood City, CA: The Benjamin/Cummings Publishing Company, Inc.

Cattail, R. B. (1963). "Theory of Fluid and Crystallized Intelligence: A Critical Experiment." *Journal of Educational Psychology 54*(1), pp. 1-32.

Colvin, G. (2001). "Changing of the Guard." *Fortune,* January 8.

Cookson, C. (1999). Scientists Close to Secret of Vital Human Genetic Code." *Financial Times.* September 23, p. 16.

D'Andrade, R. G. (1984). "Cultural Meaning Systems." In R. A. Shweder and R. A. LeVine (Eds.), *Culture Theory.* Cambridge, MA: Cambridge University Press.

de Bettignies, H. C. and Evans, L. (1977). "The Cultural Dimensions of Top Executives' Careers." In T. O. Weinshall (Ed.), *Culture and Management.* Middlesex, England: Penguin Books, Ltd.

Ehrlich, H. J. (1973). *The Social Psychology of Prejudice.* New York: Wiley.

Erickson, E. (1963). *Childhood and Society,* Second Edition. New York: Norton.

Festinger, L. (1957). *A Theory of Cognitive Dissonance.* New York: Harper and Row.

Fillol, T. R. (1961). *Social Factors in Economic Development: The Argentine Case.* Westport, CT: Greenwood Press.

Gardner, H. (1983). *Frame of Mind: Theory of Multiple Intelligence.* New York: Basic Books.

The GE Fact Sheet (2001). <http://www.ge.com/factsheet.html>.

Gerhart, B. (1987). How Important Are Dispositional Factors As Determinants of Job Satisfaction? Implications for Job Design and Other Personnel Programs. *Journal of Applied Psychology 72*(3), pp. 366-373.

Griffin, R. W. (1987). "Toward an Integrated Theory of Task Design." In Larry L. Cummings and M. Staw (Eds.), *Research in Organizational Behavior 9,* (pp. 79-120). Greenwich, CT: JAI Press.

Horovitz, J. (1979). "The Frontiers of Management European Style." *Vision.* January Edition.

Jackson, J. H., Miller, R. L., and Miller, S. G. (1997). *Business and Society Today: Managing Social Issues.* Cincinnati, OH: West Publishing Company.

James, W. (1963). *Psychology,* Abridged Edition. New York: Fawcett.

Kelley, H. H. (1967). "Attribution Theory in Social Psychology." In D. Levine (Ed.), *Nebraska Symposium on Motivation,* Volume 15. Lincoln, NE: University of Nebraska Press, p. 193.

Kelley, H. H. (1973). "The Process of Causal Attribution." *American Psychologist,* February, pp. 107-128.

Kelley, H. H. and Michela, J. L. (1980). "Attribution Theory and Research." *Annual Review of Psychology 31,* 457-501.

Kuczmarski, T. D. (1995). *Innovation: Leadership, Strategies for the Competitive Edge.* Lincolnwood, IL: NTC Business Books.

Lane, H. W. and DiStefano, J. J. (1992). *International Management Behavior,* Second Edition. Boston: P. S. Kent.

Lippmann, W. (1922). *Public Opinion.* New York: Macmillan.

Luthans, F. (1985). *Organizational Behavior,* Fourth Edition. New York: McGraw-Hill.

Mailer, N. (1977). Is quoted in B. Lowe, *The Beauty of Sport: A Cross-Disciplinary Inquiry.* Englewood Cliffs, NJ: Prentice-Hall, p. 255.

Marger, M. N. (1985). *Race and Ethnicity Relations: American and Global Perspectives.* Belmont, CA: Wadsworth Publishing Company, pp. 10, 25-27, 49.

Mervis, C. B. and Rosch, E. (1981). "Categorization of Natural Objects." *Annual Review of Psychology.* Vol. 32, pp. 89-115.

Miller, D. J. and Ross, M. (1975). "Self Serving Bias in Attribution of Causality: Fact or Fiction." *Psychology Bulletin.* Vol. 82 (2, March), pp. 213-225.

Moorhead, G. and Griffin, R. W. (1992). *Organizational Behavior.* Boston: Houghton Mifflin Company.

Moran, R. T. and Harris, P. R. (1982). *Managing Cultural Synergy,* Volume 2. Houston, TX: Gulf Publishing Company, p. 18.

Morgan, C. T. and King, R. A. (1966). *Introduction to Psychology,* Third Edition. New York: McGraw-Hill.

Nahavandi, A. and Malekzadeh, A. R. (1999). *Organizational Behavior: The Person-Organization Fit.* Upper Saddle River, NJ: Prentice-Hall.

Newsweek (1983). "What Does the World Think of America?" July 11, p. 50.

Omni, M. and Winant, H. (1986). *Racial Formation in the United States from the 1960s to the 1980s.* New York: Routledge and Kegan Paul.

Parhizgar, K. D. (1998a). "International Cross-Cultural Collaborative Teaching and Training Theories (ICCCTTT)." *Journal of Teaching in International Business* *9*(3), p. 35.

Parhizgar, K. D. (1998b). "An Intelligent Paradigm for Quality Education in Cross-Cultural Teaching and Learning Environments." In Y. Cano, F. H. Wood, and J. C. Simons (Eds.), *Creating High Functioning Schools* (pp. 65-85). Springfield, IL: Charles C. Thomas Publisher, Ltd.

Parhizgar, R. R. and Parhizgar, S. S. (2000). "Analysis of Three Types of Personhood: Geotype, Phenotype, and Phylontype in Biotech Enterprise." In Maniam, B. and Mehta, S. A. (Eds.), *Proceedings of the 31st Annual Conference of the Decision Sciences Institute Southwest Region.* San Antonio, Texas, pp. 185-187.

Psychology Today (1989). "Re-Examining Freud." September, pp. 48-52.

Rosen, B. and Jerdee, T. H. (1976). "The Influence of Age Stereotypes on Managerial Decisions." *Journal of Applied Psychology* *61*(4), pp. 428-432.

Salancik, G. and Pfeffer, J. (1977). "An Examination of Need Satisfaction Models of Job Attitudes." *Administrative Science* *22*(3), pp. 427-456.

Salancik, G. and Pfeffer, J. (1978). "Social Information Processing Approach to Job Attitudes and Task Design." *Administrative Science Quarterly.* Volume 23(2), pp. 224-253.

Smith, A. (1909). *An Inquiry into the Nature and Causes of the Wealth of Nations.* Volume 10 of *The Harvard Classics,* G. J. Bullock (Ed.). New York: P. F. Collier and Son.

Sperry, R. (1973). Is Quoted in E. Ewarts, "Brain Mechanisms in Movements." *Scientific American 229*(1), p. 103.

Stewart, T. A. (1999). "First: The Contest for Welch's Throne Begins: Who Will Run GE?" *Fortune.* January 11, pp. 26-27.

Tandon, K., Ansari, M. A., and Kapor, A. (1991). "Attributing Upward Influence Attempts in Organizations." *Journal of Psychology 125*(1), pp. 59-63.

Trice, H. M. and Beyer, J. M. (1993). *The Cultures of Work Organizations.* Englewood Cliffs, NJ: Prentice-Hall.

Zimbardo, P. G. (1992). *Psychology and Life,* Thirteenth Edition. New York: Harper Collins Publishers.

Zin, M. B. and Eitzen, D. S. (1993). *Diversity in Families,* Third Edition. New York: Harper Collins College Publishers.

Chapter 7

Abrahams, P. (1999). "Debt Collector Told Client to Sell a Kidney." *Financial Times.* November 1, p. 1.

Adorno, T. W., Frenkel-Brusnswick, E., Levinson, D., and Sanford, R. N. (1950). *The Authoritarian Personality.* New York: Harper and Row.

Allport, G. (1937). *Personality: A Psychological Interpretation.* New York: Holt, Rinehart and Winston.

Allport, G. (1961). *Pattern and Growth in Personality.* New York: Holt.

Allport, G. (1966). "Traits Revisited." *American Psychologist 2*(1), pp. 1-10.

Argyris, C. (1957). *Personality and Organization.* New York: Harper and Row, Publishers, Inc.

Barrick, M. R. and Mount, M. K. (1991). "The Five Big Personality Dimensions and Job Performance: A Meta-Analysis." *Personnel Psychology 44*(1), Spring, pp. 1-76.

Brislin, R. W. (1981). *Cross-Cultural Encounters: Face-to-Face Encounters.* New York: Pergamon.

Buda, R. and Elsayed-Elkhouly, S. M. (1998). "Cross-Cultural Differences Between Arabs and Americans." *Journal of Cross-Cultural Psychology 29*(3), pp. 487-492.

Bull, G. (1961). (Trans.) N. Machiavelli. *The Prince.* Middlesex, England: Penguin Books.

Cattell, R. B. (1963). *The Scientific Analysis of Personality.* Chicago: Aldine.

Cattell, R. B. (1973). *Personality and Mood by Questionnaire.* San Francisco: Jossey-Bass.

Coser, R. L. (1975). "Stay Home, Little Sheba: On Placement, Displacement, and Social Change." *Social Problems 22,* pp. 470-480.

Costa, Jr., P. T. and McCrae, R. R. (1985). *The NEO Personality Inventory Manual.* Odessa, FL: Psychological Assessment Resources.

Covey, S. R. (1993). "Transforming a Swamp." *Training and Development 47*(5), pp. 42-46.

Daws, G. (1968). *Shoal of Time: A History of the Hawaiian Islands*. Honolulu, HI: University Press of Hawaii.

Digman, J. A. (1990). "Personality Structure: Emergence of the Five-Factor Model." *Annual Review of Psychology 41*(1), pp. 417-440.

Fallding, H. (1965). "A Proposal for the Empirical Study of Values." *American Sociological Review 30*(April), pp. 223-233.

Farely, F. (1990). "The Type Personality, with Some Implications for Practice." *The California Psychologist 23*(2), p. 29.

Freeman, L. C. and Winch, R. F. (1957). "Social Complexity: An Empirical Test of a Typology of Societies." *American Journal of Sociology 62,* pp. 461-466.

Friedman, M. and Rosenman, R. H. (1974). *Type A Behavior and Your Health.* New York: Knopf.

Furnham, A. and Bochner, S. (1986). *Culture Shock: Psychological Reactions to Unfamiliar Environments.* London: Methuen.

Hofstede, G. (1980a). *Cultures' Consequences: International Differences in Work-Related Values.* Thousand Oaks, CA: Sage Publications.

Hofstede, G. (1980b). "Motivation, Leadership, and Organization: Do American Theories Apply Abroad?" *Organizational Dynamics, 9*(Summer), pp. 42-63.

Hofstede, Geert (1993). "Cultural Constraints in Management Theories." *Academy of Management Executive 7*(1), pp. 81-94.

Johnson, P. (1976). "Women and Power: Toward a Theory of Effectiveness." *Journal of Social Issues 32*(3), pp. 99-110.

Jung, C. G. (1971). *Psychological Types* [Bollingen Series XX]. *The Collected Works of C. G. Jung,* Volume 6. Princeton, NJ: Princeton University Press. (Original work published 1923.)

Keene, J. (1967). "Religious Behavior and Neuroticism, Spontaneity, and World-mindedness." *Sociometry 30*(2), pp. 137-157.

Kets de Vries, M. F. R. and Miller, D. (1984). *The Neurotic Organization.* San Francisco: Jossey-Bass Publishers.

Kluckohn, C. and Strodtbeck, F. L. (1961). *Variations in Value Orientations.* Westport, CT: Greenwood Press.

Kroeger, O. and Thuesen, J. (1981). Typewatching Training Workshop. Fairfax, VA: Otto Kroeger Association. In Nelson, D. L. and Quick, J. C. (1999). *Organizational Behavior: Foundations, Realities, and Challenges.* Minneapolis-St. Paul, MN: West Publishing Company, p. 86.

Luthans, F. (1985). *Organizational Behavior,* Fourth Edition. New York: McGraw-Hill Book Company.

Marger, M. N. (1985). *Race and Ethnic Relations: American and Global Perspectives.* Belmont, CA: Wadsworth Publishing Company.

McFarland, A. S. (1991). "Interest Groups and Political Time: Cycles in America." *British Journal of Political Science IV*(21), pp. 257-284.

Moody's Industrial Manual (1997). Zottoli Jr., D. A., Publisher. New York: Moody's Investors Service, Inc., pp. 6626-6631.

Myers, I. B. (1962). *The Myers-Briggs Type Indicator.* Palo Alto, CA: Consulting Psychologists Press.

Myers, I. B. (1976). *Introduction to Type,* Second Edition. Gainsville, FL: Center for Applications of Psychological Type.

Myers, I. B. (1985). *Gifts Differing.* Palo Alto, CA: Consulting Psychologist Press.

Norman, W. T. (1963). "Toward an Adequate Taxonomy of Personality Attributes: Replicated Factor Structure in Peer Nomination Personality Ratings." *Journal of Abnormal and Social Psychology 66*(1), pp. 547-583.

Parhizgar, K. D. (1984). "Affordability and Solvency Implications of Privatization of Government-Owned Industries in the Third World Countries." *Journal of Business and Society 7*(1), pp. 109-119.

Parhizgar, K. D. (1994). "Conceptual and Perceptual Paths of Cultural Power-Gender Philosophies Towards Entrepreneurial Management." Proceedings: Fifth ENDEC World Conference on Entrepreneurship. July 7-9, Marina Mandarin Singapore, pp. 524-534.

Parhizgar, K. D. (1995). "Cross-Cultural Collaborative Teaching and Training Theories (CCCTTT)." In Rudiger, C. (Ed.), *Proceedings: The Thirteenth Annual International Conference of Association of Management 13*(1). Vancouver, British Columbia, Canada, pp. 104-117.

Parsons, T. and Shils, E. D. (1951). *Toward a General Theory of Action.* Cambridge, MA: Harvard University Press.

Psychology Today, (1989). "Who Becomes an Authoritarian?" March, pp. 66-70.

Rigby, J. M. (1985). "Multinational Team Development." *Proceedings of the O.D. Network National Conference,* San Francisco, CA.

Rogers, C. (1959). "A Theory of Therapy, Personality, and Interpersonal Relationships, as Developed in the Client-Centered Framework." In S. Kock (Ed.), *Psychology: A Study of a Science.* New York: McGraw Hill.

Rosenman, R. And Friedman, M. (1971). "The Central Nervous System and Coronary Heart Disease." *Hospital Practice 6,* pp. 87-97.

Ruch, F. L. (1963). *Psychology and Life,* Sixth Edition. Chicago: Scott, Foresman.

Salgado, J. F. (1997). "The Five Factor Model of Personality and Job Performance in the European Community." *Journal of Applied Psychology 82,* pp. 30-43.

Schoderbek, P. P., Cosier, R. A., and Aplin, J. C. (1991). *Management.* San Diego, CA: Harcourt Brace Jovanovich, Publishers.

Schwartz, F. N. (1989). "Management Women and the New Facts of Life." *Harvard Business Review 67*(1), pp. 65-67.

Sheldon, W. (1942). *The Varieties of Temperament: A Psychology of Constitutional Differences.* New York: Harper.

Smith T. W. and Rhodewalt, F. (1986). "On States, Traits, and Processes: A Transactional Alternative to the Individual Difference Assumption in Type A Behavior and Psychological Reactivity." *Journal of Research in Personality 20*(3), pp. 229-251.

Stevenson, R. W. (1999). "Texaco Is Said to Set Payment Over Sex Bias." *The New York Times,* January 6, section C, p. 1, column 5.

Sturbe, M. J. and Werner, C. (1985). "Relinquishment of Control and the Type A Behavior Pattern." *Journal of Personality and Social Psychology 48*(3), pp. 688-701.

Triandis, H. (1990). "Cross-Cultural Studies of Individualism and Collectivism." In Berman, J. (Ed.), *Nebraska Symposium on Motivation, 1989.* Lincoln. NE: University of Nebraska Press, pp. 42-133.

Weber, Max (1969). "The Protestant Ethic and the Spirit of Capitalism," and Kember Fullerton, "Calvinism and Capitalism," in R. A. Webber (Ed.), *Culture and Management.* Homewood, IL: Richard D. Irwin, pp. 91-112.

Weiss, R.S. (1987). "Reflection on the Present State of Loneliness Research." *Journal of Behavior and Personality 2*(2), 1-16.

Zimbardo, P. G., (1992). *Psychology and Life,* Thirteenth Edition. New York: Harper Collins Publisher.

Chapter 8

Albert, E. M., Denise, T. C., and Peterfreund, S. P. (1984). *Great Traditions in Ethics.* Belmont, CA: Wadsworth Publishing Company.

Bentham, J. (1838). In Bovering, J. (Ed.), *The Works of Jeremy Bentham.* London: Simpkin, Marshall, Vol. 1, p. 16.

De George, R. T. (1995). *Business Ethics.* Englewood Cliffs, NJ: Prentice-Hall, pp. 5, 19, 87, and 256.

De Mente, B. L. (1989). *Chinese Etiquette and Ethics in Business: A Penetrating Analysis of the Morals and Values that Shape the Chinese Business Personality.* Chicago, IL: NTC Publishing Group, pp. 27-28.

Ember, N. and Hogan, (1991). "Moral Psychology and Public Policy." In Kurtines, W. and Gewirtz, J. (Eds.). *Handbook of Moral Behavior and Development,* Volume 3. Hillsdale, NJ: Lawrence Erlbaum Associates.

French, W. A. and Granrose, J. (1995). *Practical Business Ethics.* Englewood Cliffs, NJ: Prentice-Hall.

Friedman, M. (1983). "The Social Responsibility of Business Is to Increase Profits." In Beauchamp, T. L. and Bowie, N. E. (Eds.). *Ethical Theory in Business,* Second Edition, pp. 81-83.

Hardman, W. and Heidelberg, J. (1998). "Sexual Harassment in the Global Arena: When Sexual Harassment Is a Foreign Affair." In Maidment, F. (Ed.). *International Business 98/99* (pp. 202-206). Seventh Edition: Sluice Dock, Guilford, CT: Dashkin/McGraw-Hill.

Hobbes, T. (1839). *Leviathan and Philosophical Rudiments,* from the *English Works of Thomas Hobbes.* In Sir William Molesworth (Ed.). London: John Bohn, Volume XIII, 110-112.

Jackson, J. H., Miller, R. L., and Miller, S.G. (1997). *Business and Society Today: Managing Social Issues.* New York: West Publishing Company.

Madinal-Monawarah, Al (1970). "Meanings and Commentary (Translation), The Kingdom of Saudi Arabia: The Auspices of the Ministry of Haj and Endowments. Sourah Ahzzab, Ayah, pp. 70-71, 1268.

Newton, L. H. and Schmidt, D. P. (1996). *Wake-Up Calls: Classic Cases in Business Ethics.* Belmont, CA: Wadsworth Publishing Company.

Oesterle, J. A. (1957). *Ethics: The Introduction to Moral Science.* Englewood Cliffs, NJ: Prentice-Hall, Inc.

The Oxford English Dictionary (1963). Oxford, U.K.: Clarendon Press.

Parhizgar, K. D. and Jesswein, K. R. (1998). "Ethical and Economical Affordability of Developing Nations' Repayment of International Debt." In Baker, J. C. (Ed.). *Series in International Business and Economics: Selected International Investment Portfolios* (pp. 141-152). Great Britain: Pergamon.

Parhizgar, K. D. and Lunce, S. E. (1996). "Implications of Employees' Informational Integrated Discovery Systems." In Beardwell, I. (Ed.), *Contemporary Developments in Human Resource Management* (pp. 393-404). An International Publication of the Scientific Committee of the Montpelier Graduate Business School, Editions ESKA.

Rand, B. (1901). *The Classical Moralists.* New York: Houghton-Mifflin, p. 539. Reprinted from *The Philosophy of Kant* (J. Watson, Trans.). Glasgow, 1901.

Shaw, W. H. (1996). *Business Ethics.* Second Edition, Belmont, CA: Wadsworth Publishing Company.

Sklare, M. and Greenblum, J. (1967). *Jewish Identity on the Suburban Frontier: A Study of Group Survival in the Open Society.* New York: Basic.

Stewart, J. B. (1992). "Scenes from a Scandal: The Secret World of Michael Milken and Ivan Boesky." *The Wall Street Journal.* October 2, 1992, p. B1.

Van Der Werf, M. (1999). "Police Rule Death at Hillsdale College a Suicide." *The Chronicle of Higher Education, XLVI*(16), December 10, p. A42.

Walton, C. C. (1977). "Overview." In Walton, C. C., (Ed.), *The Ethics of Corporate Conduct* (p. 6). Englewood Cliffs, NJ: Prentice-Hall, Inc.

Watson, T. J. Jr. (1963). *A Business and Its Beliefs: The Ideas That Helped Build IBM.* New York: McGraw-Hill Book Company, Inc.

Weber, C. O. (1960). *Basic Philosophies of Education.* New York: Holt, Reinhart, and Winston.

Wolfe, A. (1999). "The Hillsdale Tragedy Holds Lessons for Colleges Everywhere." *The Chronicle of Higher Educaiton, XLVI*(15), December 3, p. A72.

Yinger, J. M. (1970). *The Scientific Study of Religion.* London: The Macmillan Company.

Chapter 9

Abramson, H. (1980). "Assimilation and Pluralism." In Thernstrom, S. (Ed.), *Harvard Encyclopedia of American Ethnic Groups* (pp. 150-160). Cambridge, MA: Harvard University Press.

Alpin, J. and Cosier, R. (1980). "Managing Creative and Maintenance Organizations." *Business Quarterly,* Spring, p. 59.

Bennett, M. (1986). "A Developmental Approach to Training for Intercultural Sensitivity." *International Journal of Intercultural Relations 10*(2), pp. 179-196.

Carnival, A. P. and Stone, S. C. (1995). *The American Mosaic.* New York: McGraw-Hill, Inc.

Cox Jr., T. (1993). *Cultural Diversity in Organizations: Theory, Research, and Practice.* San Francisco: Berrett-Koehler Publishers.

Cox, T. H. and Blake, S. (1991). "Managing Cultural Diversity: Implications for Organizational Competitiveness." *Academy of Management Executives 5*(3).

De Vos, G. A. (1980). "Ethnic Adaptation and Minority Status." *Journal of Cross-Cultural Psychology 11,* p. 101.

Feltes, P. R., Robinson, K., and Fink, R. L. (1992). "Employee Responsibilities of Multinational Corporations." *Business Forum,* Summer Edition, pp. 18-21.

Fuchs, L. (1990). *The American Kaleidoscope: Race, Ethnicity, and the Civic Culture.* Hanover and London: Wesleyan University Press.

Gates, Jr., H. L. (1992). *Loose Canons: Notes on the Culture Wars.* New York/Oxford: Oxford University Press.

Gorry, G. A. (1971). "The Development of Managerial Models." *Sloan Management Review 12*(2), Winter, pp. 1-15.

Grant, J. (1996). "Learning from Experience: A Cycle of Growth and Empowerment." In Cross, E. Y. (Ed.), *The Diversity Factor: Capturing the Competitive Advantage of a Changing Workforce.* Chicago: Irwin.

Hanebury, J. M., Smith, P. C., and Gratchev, M. (1996). "HR Lessons for Competition: Knowing the Practices and Politics." *Journal of Global Competitiveness 5*(1), p. 54.

Harvey, C . and Allard, M. J. (1995). *Understanding Diversity: Readings, Cases, and Exercises.* New York: Harper Collins College Publishers.

Heskin, A. D. and Heffner, R. A. (1987). "Learning About Bilingual, Multicultural Organizing." *Journal of Applied Behavioral Science 23*(4), p. 525.

Higgins, J. M. (1994). *The Management Challenge.* New York: Macmillan Publishing Company.

Hofstede, G. (1993). "Cultural Constraints in Management Theories." *Academy of Management Executives 7*(1) February Edition, p. 81.

Hunter, J. D. (1991). *Culture Wars: The Struggle to Define America.* New York: Basic Books/Harper Collins.

Jamieson, D. and O'Mara, J. (1991). *Managing Workforce 2000: Gaining the Diversity Advantage.* San Francisco: Jossey-Bass Publishers.

Johnson, R. B. and O'Mara, J. (1992). "Shedding Light on Diversity Training." *Training and Diversity.* May-June, pp. 45-52.

Kallen, H. (1915/1979). "Cultural Pluralism." In Mann, A. (Ed.), *The One and the Many: Reflections on the American Identity* (pp. 136-148). Chicago: University of Chicago Press.

Locke, D. (1993). *Increasing Multicultural Understanding: A Comprehensive Model.* Newbury Park, CA: Sage.

Loden, M. and Rosener, J. B. (1991). *Workforce America! Managing Employee Diversity As a Vital Resource.* Homewood, IL: Irwin.

Mann, A. (Ed.) (1979). *The One and the Many: Reflections on the American Identity.* Chicago: University of Chicago Press.

Maremont, M. (1995). "Blind Ambition: How the Pursuit of Results Got Out of Hand at Bausch and Lomb." *Business Week,* October 23, pp. 78-92.

Marger, M. N. (1985). *Race and Ethnic Relations: American and Global Perspectives.* Belmont, CA: Wadsworth Publishing Company.

Mills, D. Q. (1989). *Labor-Management Relations.* New York: McGraw-Hill Publishing Company.

Palmer, J. D. (1989). "Three Paradigms for Diversity Challenge Leaders." *OD Practitioner.* Volume 21, pp. 15-18.

Parhizgar, K. D. (1999). "Comparative Analysis of Multicultural Paradigm Management System and Cultural Diversity Models in Multicultural Corporations." *Journal of Global Business 10*(18) Spring, pp. 43-54.

Rivera, M. (1991). *The Minority Career Book.* Holbrook, MA: Bob Adams, Inc. Publishers.

Rohlen, T. P. (1973). "Spiritual Education in a Japanese Bank." *American Anthropologist 75*(October), pp. 1542-1562.

Schlesinger Jr., A. M. (1992). *The Disunity of America: Reflections on a Multicultural Society.* New York: W. W. Norton.

Schoderbeck, P. P., Cosier, R. A., and Alpin, J. C. (1991). *Management.* New York: Harcourt Brace Jovanovich Publishers.

Szapocznik, J. and Kurtines, W. (1993). "Family Psychology and Cultural Diversity Opportunities for Theory, Research and Applications." *American Psychologist 48,* pp. 400-407.

Terpstra, V. and David, K. (1991). *The Cultural Environment of International Business.* Cincinnati: South-Western Publishing Company.

Tichy, N. M. (1983). *Managing Strategic Change: Technical, Political, and Cultural Dynamics.* New York: John Wiley and Sons.

Toak, G. M. and Beeman, D. R. (1991). *International Business: Environments, Institutions, and Operations.* New York: HarperCollins.

Zangwill, I. (1909). *The Melting Pot.* New York: Macmillan Company.

Chapter 10

Avicenna, A. A. (1380/1960). Madkur, I. (Ed.), *Ketab-e-Shafa: Al Elahyiat (The Book of Healing: Metaphysical)* (pp. 435-455). Cairo: Al-Haya al-Amma li-Shuun al-Matabi al Amiriya.

Barney, J. (1991). "Firm Resources and Sustained Competitive Advantage." *Journal of Management 17*(1), pp. 99-120.

Beard, C. (1913). *An Economic Interpretation of the Constitution of the United States.* New York: Macmillan.

Cavanagh, G. F. (1990). *American Business Values,* Third Edition. Englewood Cliffs, NJ: Prentice-Hall.

Converse, P. E. (1963). "The Nature of Belief Systems in Mass Public." In Apter, D. (Ed.), *In Ideology and Discontent.* New York: The Free Press.

Covey, S. R. (1993). "Transforming a Swamp." *Training and Development 47*(5), pp. 42-46.

Darwin, C. R. (1842). *The Autobiography of Charles Darwin 1809-1882 with Original Omissions Restored (1958)*. London: Collins.

De George, R. T. (1990). *Business Ethics,* Fourth Edition. Englewood Cliffs, NJ: Prentice-Hall, Inc.

Deutsche, K. W. (1967). *Nationalism and Social Communication*. Cambridge, MA: MIT Press.

Duncan, W. J. (1989). "Organizational Culture: 'Getting a Fix' on an Elusive Concept." *Academy of Management Executives 3*(3), August, pp. 229-236.

Epicures (1926). In Bailey, C. (Trans.), *Epicures: The Extant Remains*. Oxford: Clarendon Press.

Ferraro, G. (1995). *Cultural Anthropology: An Applied Perspective,* Second Edition. Minneapolis/St. Paul: West Publishing Company, p. 233.

Fiol, C. M. (1991). "Managing Culture as a Competitive Resource." *Journal of Management 17*(1), pp. 191-211.

Friedman, M. (1962). *Capitalism and Freedom*. Chicago: University of Chicago Press.

Geertz, C. (1963). "The Integrative Revolution: Primordial Sentiments and Civil Politics in the New States." In Geertz, C. (Ed.), *Old Societies and New States: The Quest for Modernity in Asia and Africa*. New York: The Free Press.

Goldberg, H. (1993). "The New Male-Female Relationship." *The Sunday Denver Post,* May 29, pp. 10E-12E.

Grant, R. M. (1991). "The Resource-Based Theory of Competitive Advantage: Implications for Strategy Formulation." *California Management Review 33*(3), pp. 114-135.

Gregory, K. L. (1983). "Native-View Paradigms Multiple Cultures and Culture Conflicts in Organizations." *Administrative Science Quarterly 28*(3, September), pp. 359-367.

Hall, R. (1993). "The Strategic Analysis of Intangible Resources." *Strategic Management Journal 13,* pp. 135-144.

Higgins, J. M. (1994). *The Management Challenge*. New York: Macmillan Publishing Company.

Hill Jr., A. C. and Scott, J. (1992). "Ten Strategies for Managers in Multicultural Work Force." *HR Focus 69*(8, August), p. 6.

Hillman, J., Sonnenberg, S. M., Miller, A., Szazz, T., and Singer, J. L. (1989). Re-examining Freud. *Psychology Today 23*(9), 48-52.

Hirschheim, R. A. (1985). "Information Systems Epistemology: An Historical Perspective." In Mumford, E., Hirschheim, R. A., Fitzgerald, G. and Wood-Harper, A. T. (Eds.), *Research Methods in Information Systems*. North-Holland, Amsterdam.

Hoeble, A. (1960). *Man, Culture and Society*. New York: Oxford University Press.

Hofstadter, R. (1970). "The Pervasive Influence of Social Darwinism." In Brewer, T. B. (Ed.), *The Robber Barons: Saints or Sinners?* New York: Holt, Rinehart, and Winston, p. 37.

Hosmer, LaRue T. (1987). *The Ethics of Management*. Homewood, IL: Irwin.

Inglehart, R. and Carballo, M. (1997). "Does Latin America Exist? (And Is There a Confucian Culture?): A Global Analysis of Cross-Cultural Differences." *Psychology 30*(1), p. 34.

Itami, H. (1987). *Mobilizing Invisible Assets*. Cambridge, MA: Harvard University Press.

Jordan, L. (1996). "Strategic Control in Reengineering the Complex Organization." *Human System Management 9,* pp. 1-7.

Kaufman, W. and Hollingdale, R. J. (Trans.) (1967). Nietzsche, F. W., *On Genealogy of Morals*. New York: Vintage.

Kelley, L., Whatley, A., and Worthley, R. (1987). "Assessing the Effects of Culture on Managerial Attitudes: Three-Culture Test." *Journal of International Business Studies 18*(2, Summer), pp. 17-31.

Kelley, L. and Worthley, R. (1981). "The Role of Culture in Comparative Management: A Cross-Cultural Perspective." *Academy of Management Journal 24,* pp. 164-173.

Kreitner, R. (1998). *Management,* Seventh Edition. Boston: Houghton-Mifflin Company.

Kroeber, A. L. and Kluckhohn, C. (1952). "Culture: A Critical Review of Concepts and Definitions." Papers of the Peabody Museum of American Archaeology and Ethnology, *47*(1), p. 1.

Lado, A. A. and Wilson, M. C. (1994). "Human Resources Systems and Sustained Competitive Advantage: A Competency-Based Perspective." *Academy of Management Review 19*(4), pp. 699-727.

Lippman, S. A. and Rumelt, R. (1982). "Uncertain Immutability: An Analysis of Interfirm Differences in Efficiency Under Competition." *Bell Journal of Economics 13*(2), pp. 418-438.

Luthans, F. (1988). *Organizational Behavior.* New York: McGraw-Hill Book Company.

Mannheim, K. (1946). *Ideology and Utopia: An Introduction to the Sociology of Knowledge*. London: Kegan Paul, Trench, Trubner and Company.

Mason, J. W. T. (1967). *The Meaning of Shinto*. Port Washington, New York: Kennikat Press, Inc.

Miles, R. E. and Snow, C. C. (1978). *Organizational Strategy, Structure, and Process*. New York: McGraw-Hill.

Miller, D. and Shamsie, J. (1996). "The Resource of the Firm in Two Environments: The Hollywood Film Studios from 1936 to 1965." *Academy of Management Journal 39*(3), pp. 519-543.

Mischel, W. (1971). *Introduction to Personality*. New York: Holt.

Parhizgar, K. D. (1988). "Objective and Subjective Assessments of Strategic Decision-Making in Non-Profit Organizations (Colleges and Universities)." In Copur, H. (Ed.), *1988 HRMBO Annual Conference Proceedings* (pp. 132-136). Long Beach, CA.

Parhizgar, K. D. (1993). "Evolutionary Visions of the Nature of the 21st Century Businessman and the Emergence of Strategic Business Education Toward Polycentric, Regiocentric and Geocentric Curriculum Designs," *The New World Order and Trade and Finance*, Volume V, pp. 1197-1222.

Parhizgar, K. D. (1994). "Conceptual and Perceptual Paths of Cultural Power-Gender Philosophies Toward Entrepreneurial Management." In Yin, W. S., Kao, R., and Liang, T. W. (Eds.), *Main Proceedings of the ENDEC World Conference on Entrepreneurship: The Pursuit of Opportunity.* Singapore: NTU-Entrepreneurship Center, Nanyang Technological University Press, pp. 524-534.

Parhizgar, K. D. and Lunce, S. E. (1994). "Genealogical Approaches to Ethical Implications of Informational Assimilative Integrated Discovery Systems (AIDS) in Business." In Beardwell, I. (Ed.), *Contemporary Developments in Human Resource Management* (pp. 55-60). Montpellier, France: An International Publication of the Scientific Committee of the Montpellier Graduate Business School, Editions ESKA.

Parhizgar, K. D. (1996). "Comparative Utopian Leadership Philosophies of Men and Women in Strategic Decision-Making Process." In Fleming, M. J. and Shooshtari, N.H. (Eds.), *Proceedings of the 1996 Conference of the Association for Global Business: Selected Papers and Abstracts* (pp. 287-293). Montana-Missoula: School of Business Administration, The University of Montana-Missoula.

Rahmatian, S. (1996). "Global Infopreneurship: The Virtual Value Chain and the World Wide Web." In Shahrokhi, M. (Ed.), *The Third Annual Global Conference Proceeding.* April 4-6, Honolulu, Hawaii. Fresno, CA: Craig School of Business, California State University, Fresno Press, p. 147.

Schwartz, F. N. (1989). "Management Women and the New Facts of Life." *Harvard Business Review 67*(1), pp. 65-67.

Shaw, W. H. and Barry, V. (1998). *Moral Issues in Business,* Seventh Edition. Belmont, CA: Wadsworth Publishing Company.

Spencer, H. (1888). *Education, Intellectual, Moral, and Physical.* New York: D. Appleton.

Spinosa, B. (1898). "On the Improvement of the Understanding and the Ethics." In Elwes, R. H. M. (Trans.), *The Chief Works of Benedict Spinosa.* Volume II, London: George Bell.

Steiner, G. and Steiner, J. (1997). *Business, Government and Society: A Managerial Perspective, Text and Cases,* Eighth Edition. New York: The McGraw-Hill Companies, Inc.

Suhrewardi, Shahab Al Dean Yahya (1186). "The Philosophy of Illumination" *(Hikmat-e-Ishragh).* In Corbin, H. (Ed.), *Oeuvres Philosophiques et Mystiques.* Volume 3, Bibliotheque Iranienne, n.s. Tehran: Academie Imperiale Iranienne de Philosophie, 1976-77.

Taylor, E. B. (1871). *Origins of Culture.* New York: Harper and Row.

Triandis, H. C., Bontempo, R., Bond, M., Leug, K., Brenes, A., Georgas, J., Hui, C. H., Marin, G., Setiati, B., Sinha, J., Verma, J., Spangenburg, J., Touzard, H., and de Montmollin, G. (1986). "The Measurement of the Ethic Aspect of Individualism and Collectivism Across Cultures." *Australian Journal of Psychology 38*(3), pp. 257-267.

Vazsony, A. (1980). *Introduction to Data Processing.* Homewood, IL: Richard D. Irwin, Inc.

Ver Steeg, C. L. (1957). "The American Revolution Considered As an Economic Movement." *Huntington Library Quarterly.* August.

Vlachos, E. (1978). "The Future in the Past: Toward a Utopian Syntax." In Mayuyama, M. and Harkins, A. (Eds.), *Culture of the Future* (pp. 293-311). Paris: Mouton Publisher.

Weber, C. O. (1960). *Basic Philosophies of Education.* New York: Holt, Rinehart and Winston.

Wheelen, T. L. and Hunger, J. D. (1995). *Strategic Management and Business Policy.* Reading, MA: Addison-Wesley Publishing Company.

Zinn, M. B. and Eitzen, D. S. (1993). *Diversity in Families,* Third Edition. United States: Harper Collins College Publishers.

Chapter 11

The Baha'i World: The Baha'i World. <http://www.bahai.org/bworld/main.cfm>.

Baird, R. D. (1998). "Traditional Values, Governmental Values, and Religious Conflict in Contemporary India." *Brigham Young University Law Review, 2,* pp. 337-356.

Barry, D. D. and Barner-Barry, C. (1987). *Contemporary Soviet Politics: An Introduction,* Third Edition. Englewood Cliffs, NJ: Prentice-Hall, Inc.

Bobilin, R. (1968). "Religion." In Cutler, D. R. (Ed.), *The Religious Situation.* Boston, MA: Beacon Press.

Bokhari, F. (1999). "Court Orders Islamabad to Ban Interest." *Financial Times.* Friday, December 24/Saturday December 25, p. 4.

CNN (1997). "German Court Rules Iranian Leaders Ordered Berlin Slayings." CNN World News, April 10 <http://www.cnn.com/WORLD/9704/10/germany. iran.pm/>.

Comstock, W. R. (1972). *The Study of Religion and Primitive Religions.* New York: Harper and Row, Publishers.

De Mente, B. (1989). *Chinese Etiquette and Ethics in Business: A Penetrating Analysis of the Morals and Values that Shape the Chinese Business Personality.* Lincolnwood, IL: NTC Business Books.

Dinmore, G. (2000). "Hope of End to Boycott As Iran Frees German." *Financial Times,* January 21, p. 7.

Effendi, S. (1891). *God Passes By.*

Eliade, M. (Ed.), (1987). *The Encyclopedia of Religion.* New York: Macmillan Publishing Company, Volume 7.

Encyclopedia Britannica (1998).

Famighetti, R. (Ed. Dir.), (1999). *World Almanac and Book of Facts.* A Primedia Company.

Furnham, A. and Bochner, S. (1986). *Culture Shock: Psychological Reactions to Unfamiliar Environments.* London: Methuen.

Geertz, C. (1966). "Religion as a Cultural System." In Banton, M. (Ed.), *Anthropological Approaches to the Study of Religion.* London: Tavistock Publications.

Hadar, L.T. (1993). "What Green Peril?" *Foreign Affairs* 72(2), pp. 27-28.

Holtom, D. C. (1947). *Modern Japan and Shinto Nationalism*. Chicago, Illinois: University of Chicago Press.

Horgan, J. (1999). "In Studying the Stubborn Mind, What Is the Upside?" *The Chronicle of Higher Education*. October 8, p. A72.

<http://Passionforindia.com/spirit.html>.

<http://www.infoplease.com/ipa/A0001462.html>.

<http://www.sikhs.org/granth.htm>.

Jaspers, K. (1953). *The Origin and Goal of History*. London: Routledge.

Johnson, G. (1998). "Essay on Science and Religion: Bridging the Great Divide: A New Push Is on to Find a Grand Unified Theory for 20 Very Different Ways of Viewing the World." *The New York Times*. Tuesday, June 30, p. B12.

Kahler, E. (1956). *Man the Measure: A New Approach to History*. New York: George Braziller, Inc.

Kakuzo, O. (1956). *The Book of Tea*. Rutland, Vermont/Tokyo, Japan: Charles E. Tuttle Company.

Krauss, L. M. (1999). "An Article of Faith: Science and Religion Don't Mix." *The Chronicle of Higher Education*. October 8, p. A88.

The Learning Network: <http://www.infoplease.com/ipa/ A0001462.html>.

The Learning Network: <http://www.infoplease.com/ipa/ A0001470.html>.

The Learning Network: <http://www.infoplease.com/ipa/ A0001484.html>.

Luckmann, T. (1967). *The Invisible Religion*. New York: The Macmillan Company.

Malcolm X (1973). *The Autobiography of Malcolm X, as told to Alex Haley*. New York: Ballantine.

March, R. R. (1909). *The Threshold of Religion*. London: Methuem.

Meat Industry Insights, Internet News Service (1998). "Zealots Vandalize McDonald's in Israel, June 10." Available online: <http://www.lighq.net/spc/mii/980639.htm>.

Mehr, F. (1991). *Zoroastrian Tradition: An Introduction to the Ancient Wisdom of Zarathustra*. United Kingdom: Harper Collines.

The New Encyclopedia Britannica (1985). Volume 16, pp. 271-289. Chicago: The University of Chicago Press.

Niebuhr, R. (1968). *In the Religious Situation*. In Cutler, D. R. (Ed.). Boston, MA: Beacon Press, 1.

Otto, R. (1965). Quoted in Evans-Pritchard, E. E. *Theories of Primitive Religion* (pp. 38-39). London: Oxford University Press.

Parsons, T. (1951). *The Social System*. New York: The Free Press.

Radhakrishnan, S. (1993). *The Hindu View of Life*. New Delhi: India.

Sahay, S. and Geoff, W. (1997). "Social Structure and Managerial Agency in India." *Organization Studies 18*(3), pp. 415-444.

The Salt Lake Tribune (1997). "Conservative Groups Join Disney Boycott." Thursday, July 24, p. 1.

Slater, R. (1968). *World Religions and World Community*. New York: Columbia University Press.

Smith, D. E. (1965). *Religion and Politics in Burma*. Princeton, NJ: Princeton University Press.

Terpstra, V. and David, K. (1991). *The Cultural Environment of International Business*. Cincinnati, OH: South-Western Publishing Co.

Toynbee, A. J. (1954). *A Study of History, Volume 7. United States and Universal Churches*. London: Oxford University Press.

The Wall Street Journal (1975a). January 20, p. 21.

The Wall Street Journal (1975b), January 30, p. 13.

Wallace, A. F. C. (1966). *Religion: An Anthropological View*. New York: Random House, Inc.

Weber, M. (1952). *Ancient Judaism*. (Trans. and Ed.) Gerth, H. H. and Martindale, D. New York: The Free Press.

The World Almanac and Book of Facts, 1999 p. 687.

<www.religious tolerance.org>.

Yinger, J. M. (1970). *The Scientific Study of Religion*. London: The Macmillan Company.

Chapter 12

Adler, N. (1986). *International Dimensions of Organizational Behavior*. Boston: PSW-Kent.

Albert, R. D. (1983). "The Intercultural Sensitizer or Culture Assimilation: A Cognitive Approach. In Landis, D. and Brislin, R. N. (Eds.), *Handbook of Intercultural Training,* Volume 2 (pp. 186-217). New York: Pregamon Press.

Asheghian, P. and Ebrahimi, B. (1990). *International Business*. New York: HarperCollins.

Baker, J. C. and Ivancevich, J. M. (1971). "The Assignment of American Executives Abroad: Systematic, Haphazard, or Choice?" *California Management Review 13,* pp. 39-44.

Bandura, A. (1969). *Principles of Behavior Modification*. New York: Holt.

Bandura, A. (1977). *Social Learning Theory*. Englewood Cliffs, NJ: Prentice-Hall.

Barret, G. V. and Bass, B. M. (1976). "Cross-Cultural Issues in Industrial and Organizational Psychology." In Dunnette, M. D. (Ed.), *Handbook of Industrial and Organizational Psychology* (pp. 1671-1673). Chicago: Rand McNally.

Bennett, J. M. (1986). "Modes of Cross-Cultural Training: Conceptualizing Cross-Cultural Training as Education." *International Journal of Intercultural Relations.* Volume 10, pp. 117-134.

Black, J. S. and Mendenhall, M. (1989). "A Practical but Theory-Based Framework for Selecting Cross-Cultural Training Methods." *Human Resources Management.*

Black, J. S. and Mendenhall, M. (1990). "Cross-Cultural Training Effectiveness: A Review and a Theoretical Framework for Future Research." *Academy of Management Review 15*(1), pp. 113-136.

Branson, R. K. (1977). "Military and Industrial Training." In Briggs, L. J. (Ed.), *Instructional Design: Principles and Applications* (pp. 372-373). Englewood Cliffs, NJ: Educational Technology Publications, Inc.

Casse, P. (1982). *Training for the Multicultural Managers: A Practical and Cross-Cultural Approach to the Management of People.* Washington, DC: Society for International Education, Training, and Research (SIETAR International).

Chemers, M. M., Lekhyananda, D., Fiedler, F. E., and Stolurow, L. (1966). "Some Effects of Cultural Training on Leadership in Heterocultural Task Groups." *International Journal of Psychology 1,* pp. 301-314.

Copeland, L. and Griggs, L. (1985). *Going International.* New York: Random House.

"Expansion Abroad: The New Direction for European Firms," (1986). *International Management 41*(1, November), p. 22.

Fatehi, K. (1996). *International Management: A Cross-Cultural and Functional Perspective.* Upper Saddle River, NJ: Prentice-Hall.

Feldman, D. C. (1981). "The Multinational Socialization of Organization Members." *Academy of Management Review 6*(2, April), pp. 309-318.

Fiedler, F., Mitchell, T., and Triandis, H. (1971). "The Cultural Assimilation: An Approach to Cross-Cultural Training." *Journal of Applied Psychology 55*(2, April), pp. 95-102.

Furnham, A. and Bochner, S. (1986). *Culture Shock.* London: Methuen.

Gardner, H. (1983). *Frames of Mind: The Theory of Multiple Intelligences.* New York: Basic Books.

Graham, J. L. (1981). "A Hidden Cause of America's Trade Deficit with Japan." *Columbia Journal of World Business 6*(3, Fall), pp. 5-15.

Gullahorn, J. T. and Gullahorn, J. E. (1963). "An Extension of the U-Curve Hypothesis." *Journal of Social Sciences 19*(3), pp. 33-47.

Harris, P. H. (1979). "The Unhappy World of Expatriate." *International Management 34*(7, July), pp. 49-50.

Harrison, J. K. (1992). "Individual and Combined Effects of Behavior Modeling and the Cultural Assimilation in Cross-Cultural Management Training." *Journal of Applied Psychology 77*(6), pp. 952-962.

Harvey, M. G. (1989). "Repatriation of Corporate Executives: An Empirical Study." *Journal of International Business Studies 20*(Spring), pp. 131-144.

Holmes, T. H. and Rahe, R. H. (1967). "The Social Readjustment Rating Scale." *Journal of Psychosomatic Research 11*(2), p. 216.

Kohls, R. (1979). *Survival Kit for Overseas Living.* Chicago: Intercultural Press.

Kopp, R. (1994). "International Human Resource Policies and Practices in Japanese, European, and United States Multinationals." *Human Resource Management 33*(4, Winter), pp. 581-599.

Kramlinger, H. (1990). "Behaviorism Versus Humanism." *Training and Development Journal 44*(12), pp. 41-45.

Landis, D., Day, H. R., McGrew, P. L., Thomas, J. A., and Miller, A. B. (1976). "Can a Black Culture Assimilation Increase Racial Understanding?" *Journal of Social issues 32*(2), pp. 169-183.

McCaffery, J. A. (1986). "Independent Effectiveness: A Reconsideration of Cross-Cultural Orientation and Training." *International Journal of Intercultural Relations 10,* pp. 159-178.

Mehrabian, A. (1981). *Silent Messages,* Second Edition. Belmont, CA: Wadsworth.

Mendenhall, M., Dunbar, E., and Oddou, G. R. (1987). "Expatriate Selection Training and Career-Pathing: A Review and Critique." *Human Resource Management 26*(3), pp. 331-345.

Mendenhall, M. and Oddou, G. (1986). "Acculturation Profiles of Expatriate Managers: Implication for Cross-Cultural Training Programs." *Columbia Journal of World Business 21*(4), pp. 73-79.

Mendenhall, M. and Oddou, G. R. (1985). "The Dimensions of Expatriate Acculturation: A Review." *Academy of Management Review 10*(1), pp. 39-47.

Misa, K. F. and Fabricators, J. (1979). "Return on Investment of Overseas Personnel." *Financial Executives 47*(4), pp. 42-46.

Mitchell, T. R., Dossett, D., Fiedler, F., and Triandis, H. (1972). "Cultural Training: Validation Evidence for the Cultural Assimilation." *International Journal of Psychology 7*(2), pp. 97-104.

Mitchell, T. R. and Foa, U. G. (1969). "Diffusion of the Effect of Cultural Training of the Leader in the Structure of Hetero-Cultural Task Groups." *Australian Journal of Psychology 21*(1), pp. 31-43.

Montagu, A. (1972). *Touching: The Human Significance of the Skin.* New York: Harper and Row.

Moorhead, G. and Griffin, R. W. (1992). *Organizational Behavior: Managing People and Organizations.* Boston: Houghton-Mifflin Co.

Oberg, K. (1960). "Culture Shock: Adjustments to New Cultural Environments." *Practical Anthropology.* July-August, pp. 177-182.

O'Boyle, T. (1989). "Grappling with the Expatriate Issue." *The Wall Street Journal.* December 11, p. B1.

O'Brien, G. E. and Plooij, D. (1977). "Comparison of Programmed and Pose Culture Training Upon Attitude and Knowledge." *Journal of Applied Psychology 62*(4), pp. 499-505.

Pike, E. R. (1967). *The Strange Ways of Man.* New York: Hart Publishing Co.

Punnett, B. J. and Ricks, D. A. (1992). *International Business.* Boston: PWS-Kent Publishing Company.

Randolph, G., Landis, D., and Tzeng, O. C. (1977). "The Effects of Time and Practice Upon Culture Assimilation Training." *International Journal of Intercultural Relations 4*(1), pp.105-119.

Ricks, D. A. (1983). *Big Business Blunders.* Homewood, IL: Dow Jones-Irwin.

Ronen, S. (1989). "Training the International Assignee." In Goldstein, I. (Ed.), *Training and Career Development.* San Francisco, CA: Jossey-Bass. p. 438.

Ronen, S. and Tung, R. (1981). "Selection and Training of Personnel for Overseas Assignments." *Columbia Journal of World Business,* Spring, pp. 68-78.

Seward, J.(1975). "Speaking the Japanese Business Language." *European Business.* Winter, pp. 40-47.

Sheflen, A. E. (1972). *Body Language and the Social Order.* Englewood Cliffs, NJ: Prentice-Hall.

Sims Jr., P. and Gioia, D. (1986). *The Thinking Organization.* San Francisco: Jossey-Bass.

Sperry, R. W. (1986). "Consciousness, Personal Identity, and the Divided Brain." *American Antiquarian Society.* 96, Part 1, April, pp. 26-37.

Sterns, H. L. and Deverspike, D. (1989). "Aging and the Training and Learning Process." In Goldstein, I . L. and associates, (Eds.), *Training and Development in Organizations* (pp. 299-332). San Francisco: Jossey-Bass.

Tung, R. L. (1984). "Strategic Management of Human Resources in Multinational Enterprise." *Human Resources Management.* New York: John Wiley and Sons.

Weldon, D. E., Carlson, D. E., Rissman, A. K., Slobodin, L., and Triandis, H. C. (1975). "A Laboratory Test of Effects of Culture Assimilation Training." *Journal of Personality and Social Psychology 32*(2), pp. 300-310.

Wiggenhorn, W. (1990). "Motorola U: When Training Becomes an Education." *Harvard Business Review 68*(4), pp. 71-83.

Worchel, S. and Mitchell, T. R. (1972). "An Evaluation of Effectiveness of the Culture Assimilation in Thailand and Greece." *Journal of Applied Psychology 56*(6), pp. 472-479.

Person Index

Subject Index